COUNTY GOVERNING BODIES
IN NEW JERSEY

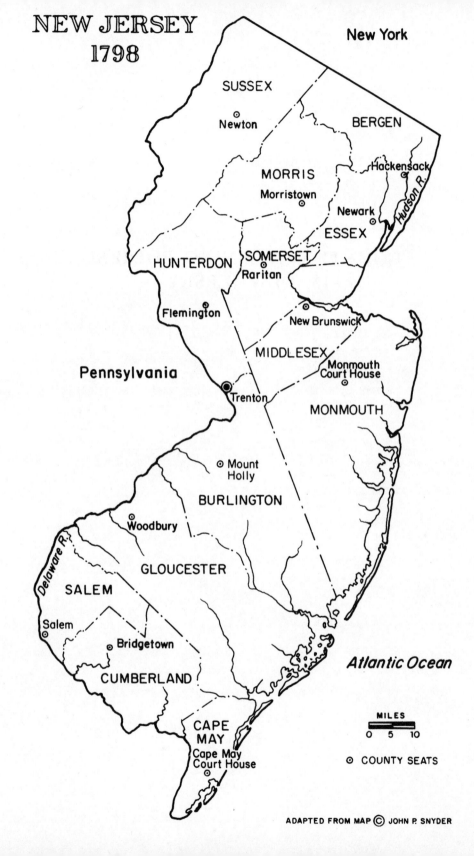

NEW JERSEY
1798

New York

SUSSEX

Newton

BERGEN

Hackensack

MORRIS

Morristown

Newark

ESSEX

Hudson R.

HUNTERDON

SOMERSET

Raritan

Flemington

New Brunswick

MIDDLESEX

Monmouth
Court House

Pennsylvania

Trenton

MONMOUTH

Mount
Holly

BURLINGTON

Woodbury

Delaware R.

GLOUCESTER

SALEM

Salem

Bridgetown

Atlantic Ocean

CUMBERLAND

CAPE
MAY

Cape May
Court House

MILES

0   5   10

⊙ COUNTY SEATS

ADAPTED FROM MAP © JOHN P. SNYDER

HARRIS I. EFFROSS

COUNTY GOVERNING BODIES IN NEW JERSEY

Reorganization and Reform of Boards of Chosen Freeholders, 1798 - 1974

RUTGERS UNIVERSITY PRESS

New Brunswick, New Jersey

The publication of this book was made possible through the encouragement and support of the New Jersey Association of Chosen Freeholders and the Rutgers University Bureau of Government Research

First Printing

Library of Congress Cataloging in Publication Data

Effross, Harris Ira.
  County governing bodies in New Jersey.

  Bibliography:
  1. County government—New Jersey.   I.   Title.
JS451.N55E43   352'.0073'09749   75-17836
ISBN 0-8135-0765-0

To the memory of
my mother, Dorothy Brody Effross,
and to
my wife, Susi Hillburn Effross,
both teachers, by training, by inclination,
and by example

CONTENTS

ILLUSTRATIONS

PREFACE

If the county has remained "the dark continent of American politics," this is especially true in New Jersey where the county governing bodies bear the unique designation "boards of chosen freeholders." Lacking until now was detailed information on the evolution of the county's functions, of the freeholder board's structure since 1798, and of pertinent theories of local representation. Even learning the apportionment of freeholders for a given county during certain years could prove difficult for a trained researcher.

Previous studies concerned with New Jersey county government have emphasized administrative rather than electoral problems and have treated the system of representation either in general terms or selectively by counties. But because the scheme of allotting board membership was almost without exception based on municipal units or subunits, exploration of New Jersey's urban history has been absolutely essential.

By showing how the changing role of the county, the rivalries between municipalities, and the partisan politics in the legislature affected the assignment of seats on all boards of freeholders, this volume deals with the same choices offered by the Optional County Charter Law of 1972: size of freeholder board, term of office, type of constituency, and need for executive leadership. Such legislation must be considered as the culmination of more than a century of debate.

HARRIS I. EFFROSS

New Brunswick, New Jersey
May 1975

ACKNOWLEDGMENTS

Increasingly, the author has come to agree with Arnold Toynbee's comment: "I think if a writer is wise, he gets all the help he can from other people. The responsibility is on him, it must pass through his mind, but he takes help where he can get it." Not only have many contributed to this study, mostly by locating and making available primary source materials, but they have provided counsel and concern. Individual freeholders, board clerks, and county clerks offered splendid cooperation, as did newspaper editors throughout the state. To single out some for mention would be an injustice to the rest. But if enumerating all such persons is not possible, acknowledging their assistance is a pleasure.

Librarians lead those who have shared their time and expertise. At the Alexander Library of Rutgers University I am particularly indebted to University Librarian Virginia P. Whitney; Donald A. Sinclair, Curator of Special Collections, and Clark L. Beck, Jr., and Ronald L. Becker of his staff, and to Anthony Nicolosi and Irene K. Lionikis, formerly on that staff; Francis X. Grondin, head of the Government Documents (now retired) and his assistants Mary Fetzer and Leslie Ota; Oliver K. Westling, head of the photo-duplication department (now retired) and his then assistant, Denes Suhayda; Robert J. Mulligan, reference librarian, and Warren Sledd, reference librarian (now retired).

At the New Jersey State Library my gratitude goes to Roger H. McDonough, State Librarian; Kenneth Richards, head, Archives and History Bureau; Herta Prager, head of the Law, Legislative and General Reference Services Bureau (now retired); her successor, Susan Roumfort, together with members of her staff: Stephen Breedlove, Marjorie Garwig, Joseph McQuade, Joseph Pizzullo, and Janet Tuerff; former law librarians Rebecca S. Lutto and Charlotte Kitler; and Bernard Bush, executive director of the New Jersey Historical Commission, and his staff members, William C. Wright and Paul Stellhorn.

Miriam Studley, of the Reference Division (now retired), Newark Public Library; librarians of the New Jersey Historical Society; and municipal librarians throughout the state have searched their files to provide local data.

Many thanks are due to the New Jersey Association of Chosen Freeholders. Without commenting on editorial content or exercising any control whatsoever, it provided assistance toward publication of this manuscript. Jack Lamping, the Association's executive vice-president, supplied information on request and has been unfailingly helpful in arranging for the examination of source materials.

To Dr. Ernest C. Reock, Jr., director of the Bureau of Government Research, Rutgers University, which sponsored my research project, I am particularly grateful. His criticism of preliminary drafts was most helpful, because of his wide knowledge of local government in New Jersey.

Others whose valuable assistance should not remain unrecognized are Leonard Etz and Robert J. Del Tufo, who served at one time as Associate Counsel and Assistant Counsel, respectively, to the New Jersey County and Municipal Law Revision Commission; Frank W. Haines, Jr., executive director, New Jersey Taxpayers Association; Robert P. Belmonte, former Bergen County purchasing agent; and Frederick P. Wertheimer, advertising director of the magazine, *New Jersey County Government.*

To Claire Freeman Luma, secretary at the Bureau of Government Research, I am indebted for her careful and conscientious typing of the manuscript of this book.

My family's forbearance during the time of this work's preparation was surely a major contribution toward its completion. In addition, my wife, Susi, read the text and suggested changes in the interest of clarity. With our sons, Walter and David, she provided encouragement and understanding.

H.I.E.

COUNTY GOVERNING BODIES
IN NEW JERSEY

1

TOWNSHIPS AND COUNTIES: FROM PURE DEMOCRACY TO REPRESENTATIVE GOVERNMENT

Today the governing bodies of a growing and influential level of government, the boards of chosen freeholders in New Jersey counties began as lightly regarded agencies with limited functions. They have progressed beyond the large, costly bodies of unsavory reputation that they became in the late nineteenth century, but their constantly changing organization and the procedures used for selecting their membership can be properly understood only in light of the historical development of the state's townships and other forms of municipal government. In the process of change, complications arose from attempts to have the members represent equal numbers of people, rather than municipalities; from efforts to achieve economy and efficiency of operation; and from experiments with executive leadership, an increasingly important consideration as the counties assumed new obligations.

Electing representatives from districts always presents problems of equity; but these are minimal, if the districts are approximately equal in population. Such was largely the case in 1798, when each of New Jersey's 104 townships was incorporated by state law and required to elect two freeholders (property-owners) to a county governing body, one of the then thirteen boards of chosen freeholders.[1] Even as late as 1834, a gazetteer of the state could still characterize its local subdivisions as "examples of a pure democracy [townships] and simple representative government [counties]." According to the description of the first: "The people in their township meetings (and the word township comprehends precincts and wards), discuss their common wants, propose the remedies, and appoint the agents to give them effect."[2] After all, when these words were published the number of townships had increased to only 125, 40 percent of them with fewer than 2,500 inhabitants; 87 percent with not even 4,000.[3] It was still possible for the township voters themselves to "make and ordain" the "regulations and by-laws" (ordinances).[4]

But if it could be said in 1834 that "the [dual] system works well,"[5] that very year saw the beginning of the end of the original scheme of direct citizen participation. The legislature authorized the voters of any town meeting to resolve to vote by ballot, instead of by voice,[6] for the numerous township officers and for the chosen freeholders (who were commonly regarded as township officials).[7] "Those gatherings, the purest Democracies in our system of government, died, to all intents and purposes, with the introduction of the ballot into them," it was to be observed almost a half-century later.[8] In 1838, the first statute was passed making a vote by ballot *mandatory* for all appropriations of money, as well as for the election of local officials in certain townships (Manchester, Paterson, and Aquackanonk in Passaic County).[9] Such a system was made optional in 1860 for voters in the townships in Salem, Cumberland, Sussex, Warren, and Camden (repealed for this county in 1861), and was made optional for all of the State's townships in 1862.[10]

The old system was further eroded by new legislation regulating the general elections in November. Township officials were required (1866) and then simply authorized (1867) to designate the boundaries of 800-voter election districts in which paper ballots were to be used. Establishment of such districts in townships was made mandatory again in 1868.[11] When the voter maximum in a district was lowered to 600 by one act in 1876, another provided that all township officers in townships with a population of less than 6,000 were to be chosen by ballot in elections "held and conducted in the same manner that the general elections are held and conducted."[12] By 1880 there was "no such thing as a township meeting in New Jersey anymore."[13]

In that year, broad powers were vested in the township committee,[14] which previously had been empowered only to "examine, inspect and report" to the town meeting "the accounts and vouchers of the township officers, and to superintend the expenditures of any monies raised by tax for the use of the township. . . ."[15] Population growth prompted passage of a revision act of 1899,[16] giving virtually complete power of municipal government to the township committee, and repealing 195 township laws and forty-two parts of general laws. But even then, the direct appropriation of money by the people was retained.[17]

The township meeting type of government, abandoned reluctantly during the nineteenth century, was recognized as clearly unsuitable for use at the county level:

In the larger districts, where legislation in their proper persons would prove inconvenient, as well as by the distance of the people from each other, as from their number when collected, the citizens have developed the necessary legislative power upon agents, endowed also with an adequate executive capacity.[18]

Obviously, the author was correct. After Cape May's 4,945 inhabitants, county populations ranged from 14,091 (Cumberland) to 41,928 (Essex).[19] Moreover, Monmouth and Gloucester each included more than 1,000 square miles and extended sixty-five and fifty-five miles, respectively. The length of all but three counties (Sussex, Essex, Somerset) exceeded thirty miles, a formidable journey in those days.[20] Second, not the people, but the townships as basic taxing units, were to be represented in the county governing body. Specially chartered by the legislature, cities, boroughs, and towns were not yet entitled, as such, to levy taxes for the general municipal government or to elect their own chosen freeholders. For these purposes, their residents had to participate in the township meeting held in the townships whose area included the special municipalities.

In significant ways the board of chosen freeholders differed from a township committee. In 1798, the freeholders had been formally separated from the judges of the county court, with whom they had formerly "constituted the county legislative authority,"[21] and were authorized to "put into execution such by-laws, ordinances and regulations as shall seem necessary and convenient for the government of their respective corporations, provided the same are not contrary to the constitution and the laws of this State." Such bodies could "vote, grant and raise" money for

the building, purchasing or repairing of poorhouses, gaols, courthouses and bridges, the surveying and ascertaining the lines, the prosecuting and defending the rights, defraying the public and other necessary charges, and doing, fulfilling and executing all the legal purposes, objects, business and affairs of such county as they or the major part of them shall deem adequate or proper. . . .[22]

Unlike a township committee, whose members were originally unpaid for their meetings,[23] a freeholder board could approve the financial claims submitted by any member (a major cause of corruption). And rather than only three or five members, as on a township committee, the governing body of a county could include as many as thirty or forty persons elected by subdivisions (townships). At any rate, it was difficult to fix reponsibility in a body whose membership was usually greater than that of the legislature's upper chamber, where there was one member for each county.

Moreover, a freeholder board differed from its counterparts in adjacent states. Pennsylvania elected its three-man county commissions in each county at large, and members of New York's boards of county supervisors served concurrently as township executives. New Jersey's system of county government, then, lay between these two forms developed in the Middle Atlantic colonies, themselves a compromise between New England's type, in which the town unit included almost all functions, and the South's, where the county undertook a broad range of activities.[24] Even the title "Board of Chosen Freeholders" was unique.

2

COUNTY RESPONSIBILITIES
CHANGE AND GROW, 1798–1802

Until the close of the Civil War, counties were generally reluctant to assume more significant responsibilities, and the people and the legislature were not eager to entrust them to the freeholder boards. In some cases, increased authority was circumscribed by joint participation with the voters and the judiciary. It was generally recognized that along with new opportunities for service to the freeholders' constituencies came additional chances for patronage and graft—all reasons for fighting over the systems of apportioning board members. An examination of five of their more important functions will illustrate some of the changes.

BRIDGES

Maintenance of bridges, one of the most important duties of the freeholder boards throughout most of the nineteenth century, was not originally a concern of New Jersey counties. Although English common law had charged the county residents with such responsibility, "when this colony began to be settled, almost the first thing they did was to relieve the inhabitants of counties from the obligation to repair, by putting it on the townships."[1] Consequently, "the liability remained here for an hundred years until the Revolution."[2] Not until 1760 did "the first attempt on the part of this colony to assimilate our legislation to that of England" occur.[3] A statute of that year provided for repair of bridges in two groups of counties. Where there was a bridge in any of the "Towns, Divisions, and Precincts" (townships) of Burlington, Somerset, Salem, Cumberland, and Sussex "which cannot well be repaired by Day Labourers," the township highway overseers were to assemble two justices of the peace of the county and the two chosen freeholders of that township to contract with tradesmen to have the bridge built. The money was to be collected from the affected municipality.[4] But another section of the statute noted and complied with requests from Middlesex, Monmouth, Essex, Bergen, Hunterdon, and Morris. In those counties "all bridges requiring Handicraft Work, may be built, rebuilt, repaired and amended at the sole Charges and Expences of the whole County, wherein such Bridge and Bridges do lie." The highway overseers of such localities were to call together three of the county's justices of the peace and *every* chosen freeholder and surveyor of highways in the county to contract for the work and assess the county's residents.[5] These provisions of the 1760 act were very nearly copied in the 1774 statute that repealed it; only two counties (Sussex, Somerset) were added to those paying for bridge repair.[6] According to the first Constitution of the State of New Jersey (1776), so much of the colonial statute law and the common law of England as had been used here should *continue* in force until altered by the legislature.[7] But no English common law could contravene the colonial statute law charging the townships with responsibility for bridge maintenance.[8]

Two laws of 1798 instituted county control of bridges. Financing their construction, purchase, and repair was authorized by the statute incorporating freeholder boards; and "An Act respecting Bridges" passed nine months later, detailed the procedure for freeholder participation. Should the expense of any bridge in a township (or between any two townships in the same county) exceed $150, the *entire* freeholder board was to be convened to consider the matter. If the cost were between $30 and $150, the two freeholders from the affected township and also the pairs of freeholders from each of the next two adjoining townships would consult. For expenses less than $30 only the two freeholders from a single township and the municipal highway overseers would decide what to do. A majority vote was necessary for affirmative action in each of the above situations.[9] In 1845 the categories were changed to (1) expenses exceeding $500; (2) those between $50 and $500; and (3) those less than $50.[10] With several exceptions,[11] these groupings continued until passage of an 1898 act limiting a freeholder committee to an expenditure of $200.[12] But the several methods of making appropriations for bridges continued until 1918, despite other miscellaneous bridge acts.

PENAL INSTITUTIONS

The first new activity, the *operation*, as well as the financing of penal institutions, was authorized for the freeholder boards within one year of their incorporation in 1798, and was to be shared with their respective sheriffs. Serving in colonial times as almshouses for the relief and employment of the poor,[13] workhouses were authorized and entrusted to the custody of the county governing bodies by a 1799 act. Criminals could be confined at hard labor for a period not exceeding six months, as could all disorderly persons and others who should be ordered by law to be sent there. Two or more counties could unite in building or purchasing such an institution, which would be managed by some fit person to be appointed by the freeholders.[14] A 1796 statute had provided that "the sheriff in each county in this state shall have the custody, rule, keeping and charge of the gaol or gaols within such county and of the prisoners in such gaol or gaols."[15] County jails (not involving hard labor) and workhouses were "entirely distinct in their origin, object, and government, and in all our state legislation they are treated as entirely different institutions," the state Supreme Court was to observe.[16]

But if the freeholders were slow in gaining authority in the correctional field, they were slower still to use their existing powers. On March 2, 1847, the boards in Essex, Passaic, and Burlington were authorized to convert parts of their jails into workhouses, and two days later a similar act applying to all counties in the State was passed.[17] It did "not appear that the boards of chosen freeholders have acted under these powers," the New Jersey Prison Reform Association complained after almost three years had elapsed. Only one county (Middlesex) had contemplated the employment of criminals by providing workshops, the Association's report noted. "With this exception, no county of the thirteen from which reports were received, has ever established a workhouse within its limits, or a workshop in connection with the county jail." Therefore, it was "fair to presume that this is the case throughout the state."[18]

"Not until Hudson county erected its noted workhouse or penitentiary at Snake Hill in 1869 was there any thoroughgoing attempt on the part of any county in the state to avail itself of the provisions of the law of 1799," observed one study of correctional institutions.[19] The 1796 act had been impliedly repealed in 1857, so far as it related to the two largest counties by "An act to transfer the charge and keeping of the jails, and custody of the prisoners in the counties of Essex and Hudson, from the sheriffs to the boards of chosen freeholders . . . ." In each of the two counties, the board-appointed jailer was also to be the master of the workhouse; "and the workhouse therein, or so much of it as shall be so declared by the board of freeholders," would be "part of the common jail of said county. . . ." With the consent of the board, and under such conditions as it might impose, the courts of other counties could send prisoners to such a jail.[20] An 1874 supplement to the 1857 act provided that the Essex County penitentiary then being erected in Caldwell, and the workhouse "which may be established in connection therewith, or as a part thereof, or so much thereof as shall be so declared by said board of chosen freeholders, shall be deemed to be a part of the common jail of said county of Essex." Both were to be in the custody of the freeholder board.[21] (With the construction in 1892 of a workhouse in Mercer, the number of such institutions remained fixed at three well into the twentieth century.)[22]

In the other counties the 1796 act for control of the jails by the sheriffs remained in full force for almost a century. An 1887 law allowed *any* freeholder board to assume custody of the county jail and prisoners, whenever two-thirds of the board's membership should so vote and file a certificate to that effect in the office of the secretary of state. Then the board could appoint a jailer, keeper, or warden.[23]

Local political considerations insured that the sheriffs' loss of power to the freeholder boards did not remain unchallenged. Over the veto of Assembly Bill No. 224 by Democratic Governor George T. Werts, the 1894 legislature (Republican by 2 to 1) repealed on May 16 the 1857 statute for freeholder control of the jails in Essex and Hudson. "The reason for the change is purely partisan and is found in the fact that in both counties the present jailers belong to one political party and the Sheriffs to another," Werts objected.[24] On the same day, he submitted his veto of a companion bill (Assembly Bill No. 225), subsequently overridden, restoring to the sheriffs the custody of the common jails, but containing the proviso that it should not apply to counties of the second or third classes,[25] where the freeholder boards had previously or might thereafter appoint a warden or keeper of the jail. There was a further proviso that the sheriff of any county might voluntarily transfer custody to the freeholder board, which should thereupon appoint a warden or jailer. In the Governor's view, this measure had been "necessitated because it was apprehended that one of the parties for whose benefit Assembly 224 was passed might refuse to avail himself thereof." The second proviso, Werts maintained, "virtually continues in one of the two first-class counties the system which Assembly No. 224 purports to abolish."[26] On May 25 he signed a third act explictly providing that a sheriff in a *first-class* county should have custody of the jails and could surrender it to a freeholder board which could then appoint a jailer or warden. (In 1900 these provisions were extended to all counties with a population of less than 125,000.) But this act would "not apply to any jail or penitentiary [workhouse] upon any county farm in any county of the first class [Hudson]." Presumably, the Essex County penitentiary, but not Hudson's, was to remain under the control of the freeholder board.[27]

Finally, the matter of jail and workhouse control came full circle. After the sheriff of Essex took charge of the jail for a few days in 1894, he surrendered its custody to the freeholder board, who remained in control until November 1899, when they were ousted by the prosecutor. The New Jersey Supreme Court held in 1901 that the state constitution vested the custodianship of the counties' common jails in the sheriffs (by virtue of their office), and that it could not be transferred by the legislature to other officers to be selected by that branch of government. But the Court declared that a workhouse (Essex penitentiary), as distinct from a jail, was within the authority of the legislature, and that existing statutes vesting control of the workhouse in a freeholder board were valid.[28]

LUNATIC ASYLUMS

Another major change concerned care for the insane. According to the 1847 statute establishing the New Jersey State Lunatic Asylum at Trenton, the counties and townships were to share costs with the State.[29] The local share was limited to two dollars per week per patient in 1849,[30] and another act the following year made the county, rather than the municipality, responsible for the support of the poor and indigent insane.[31] By the latter act, "a motive has been given to the officers of the townships to extend the benefits of the institution to many cases long deemed incurable, and therefore retained at home."[32] But the freeholder boards came to have reasons of their own in seeking to establish county asylums: new jobs and contracts for local politicians, in addition to cheaper maintenance costs. "In the 1870's and for decades thereafter, county asylums were identified with the spoils system whereas the state asylums were identified with nonpolitical and medically directed care," notes an authority on charity and correction in New Jersey.[33]

Crowded conditions of the institution at Trenton *forced* the counties to erect asylums. In 1869, for example, the Hudson freeholder board adopted a resolution that a suitable building to care for the mentally ill be erected locally.[34] When this proposal was found to involve too great an expense, the board adopted another resolution to "donate to the State of New Jersey so much of the County Farm as may be necessary" for the location of a lunatic asylum.[35] The offer of this site of the county almshouse and county prison, noted the legislature's Joint Committee on Asylum, was based upon the desire of the Hudson officials to have the structure located where it would be accessible to persons in that part of the State. "Aside from this reason, your Committee do not find, on examination, that the proposed locality has any special merits for the purpose," the report continued; it was "inexpedient" for the State to accept the land.[36] One year after the original resolution, the freeholder committee on the lunatic asylum reported the inadequacy of the almshouse to accept any more patients; in addition, members of the county governing body were told that the State Asylum was "filled to its utmost capacity, and that we are liable at any time to have some of our lunatics returned to us, as has already been done to some other counties of this State." The Committee on County Farm was directed to make proper accommodations available.[37]

Only two counties responded immediately when a circular letter to several of them was sent in May 1872 by the State Asylum's Board of Managers "requesting the removal of so many of the supposed incurable and harmless cases as would enable the institution to continue to receive such new cases of a necessitous character as might apply."[38] The first county asylum was built in that year by Essex, which had no almshouses of its own and therefore was relying on municipal institutions. Really a poorhouse that simply maintained the insane without medical care, the new building on the outskirts of Newark was originally regarded as temporary.[39] Hudson's new asylum on Snake Hill admitted its first patients on March 8, 1873.[40] Because work began about then on the erection of a new State Asylum near Morristown, a joint legislative committee expected it to be available for occupancy by July 1874. "During the comparatively short interval that is to occur," the counties were asked again to provide locally for their surplus number of patients.[41] Soon afterward the press could report that "the various counties have made temporary provision for their insane by erecting asylums or securing their confinement in their local almshouses."[42]

Financial assistance was extended to the counties in order to relieve the pressure on the institution at Trenton. In 1873 the legislation recognized these "temporary asylums" by authorizing the state treasurer to pay one dollar per week for each county patient confined in a lunatic asylum established by a freeholder board.[43] Two counties received funds for that year: Essex, $1,328.85; and Hudson, $1,993.00. Before the new state institution at Morristown was opened in mid-1876, Middlesex, Burlington, and Mercer had been added (raising the State's payments to $18,691.86).[44] Governor Joseph D. Bedle advised the next legislature: "It now being the policy of the State to take care of its insane in the two Aylums, I respectfully recommend the repeal of that act [of 1873]."[45] But his advice was ignored, and by 1880 there were 581 state-supported mental patients in the five county institutions (Burlington, Camden, Essex, Hudson, Passaic), more than the number of patients in either of the state asylums in Trenton (502) or Morristown (549).[46] Within four years Essex erected a permanent asylum.[47] In 1888 the state increased its payment to two dollars for each county patient;[48] and that same amount was still being paid in 1902 to nine counties, Atlantic, Cumberland, Gloucester, and Salem having been added to the list. Although most of them had special structures, the latter two counties had "no separate buildings that can in any way be regarded as suitable for the care and treatment of the insane"; and Passaic maintained an almshouse which generally accommodated "mild cases of insanity which can be suitably cared for in an institution as has been provided."[49]

HIGHWAYS

1. Early Roads

Even though it was not until after the Civil War that maintenance of county roads in the State of New Jersey was assigned to the boards of chosen freeholders, their pre-Revolutionary forerunners did share in this responsibility, but not in the expense. Proprietary East Jersey's Assembly provided in 1683 that there should be a sort of road board for each county "to View and lay out the respective High-ways, Bridges, Passages, Landings, and Ferries. . . ." In 1686 the inhabitants of each town were authorized to choose four or five men who should have Power to make such Rates and Taxes, as well for making and maintaining all Highways, Bridges, Landings, and Ferry's which are or hereafter shall be laid out, by the Commissioners for that end appointed, as also for defraying all other public Charges within their respective Limits.

These rates would have to be approved by the Justices of the Peace at their Quarter Sessions.[50] West Jersey's "tenths" along the Delaware River were empowered in 1684 to have highway Commissioners with similar functions. When East and West Jersey were united in 1702 as the royal colony of New Jersey, general road legislation remained substantially the same. But beginning in 1716, inhabitants of each township could choose four persons for surveyors of the highways, of whom the justices of the peace selected two.[51] If the inhabitants made proper application, six of these surveyors were permitted to lay out roads "from one Town or Division to another, or to any public Landing Place, or Market, or Mill, or from any Town to the King's High-way." The justices in each county also selected two overseers in every town to make and keep in good repair all roads in their respective towns.[52] Both the surveyors and the overseers became elected officials in 1760.[53]

After the Revolution, participation by chosen freeholders in road maintenance was largely limited to confirming the performance of others. An 1807 statute provided that any person holding that the surveyors had committed an illegality or irregularity in laying out a public road could apply for the appointment of six chosen freeholders to view the road. They would be selected by the county's Court of Common Pleas or by the state Supreme Court, if more than one county were involved. A positive finding could not be appealed, and a negative one would be binding for one year.[54] Starting in 1811, anyone aggrieved by the impassability of a by-road previously used, but not legally laid out, could apply in writing to three of the chosen freeholders nearest the road for them to lay it out as a private road, until it could be vacated or altered.[55] Just before the outbreak of the Civil War, any township committee, any applicant for a private road, or any owner of land or real estate who was dissatisfied with the surveyors' road assessment could file a notice of appeal with the court that had appointed the surveyors. Three "disinterested" chosen freeholders of the county or counties involved would be appointed to review the assessment; and the majority report would be conclusive.[56] The only significant road function of the freeholders that required their initiative resulted from an 1818 statute authorizing the erection of milestones and also allowing the boards to determine at which intersections there should be directional posts or stones. Such guides were to be set up and repaired by the freeholders or by their appointees "at the expense of the counties respectively."[57] Not until the close of the nineteenth century were roads to become a major concern of the freeholder boards.

2. Essex County

Special legislation for the two most populous counties followed the Civil War. In 1868 the Governor signed "an Act constituting a Public Road Board for the laying out, constructing, appropriating, improving and maintaining public carriage roads in the county of Essex." The text named three persons to be the first members and provided that their successors should be elected annually by the freeholder board.[58] But only one year later, a statute with the identical title repealed it and named five persons to serve as temporary commissioners at an annual salary of $1,000. They were to be succeeded by one person annually appointed by the freeholder board, and the other four to be elected by the county's voters for two pairs of staggered two-year terms.[59]

Established without a referendum, New Jersey's only county road board (Essex) was divested of popularly elected members by the 1881 legislature without prior approval of the voters. Such boards "which now exist or may hereafter exist in any of the counties of this state, under the laws thereof" were to consist of members of the freeholder boards of those counties, respectively, and were to be appointed in the same manner as were standing committees. The new road commissioners were to continue in office only during their terms as freeholders and were to be subject to removal at the pleasure of the freeholder board which fixed their compensation. But it was provided that "no more than a major part of the commissioners of any public road board shall be of the same political party."[60] The statute's constitutionality was upheld by the Court of Errors and Appeals, New Jersey's highest tribunal.[61]

3. Hudson County

Dealing with the other populous county proved more difficult for the legislature. "An Act to provide for the appointment of Commissioners to devise plans and make estimates for the opening, construction, and maintenance of one or more prominent avenues or highways in the county of Hudson" was passed in 1868, the preamble declared, because it had been "represented that said desired improvements cannot be properly or suitably made without further legislation." The Hudson freeholder board was allowed to request the circuit court to appoint seven "judicious" commissioners who were to submit a detailed report on their activities.[62] When that document concerning a road through nine municipalities was transmitted by the freeholder board to the legislature, a supplement to the original statute was enacted in 1869 conferring on the Hudson commissioners "power to construct the works thereby proposed."[63] But instead of confining themselves to one central route, the commissioners proposed to make three boulevards at a total cost of about $12,000,000, and the people's "overwhelming opposition" was aroused. Consequently, an 1870 law was passed requiring a referendum on whether the boulevard should be built, and the proposition was defeated by a large majority.[64]

But "public sentiment, nevertheless, still favored the construction of a boulevard at a cost within reasonable bounds . . . ."[65] In 1873 Jersey City's *Evening Journal*, heartily endorsing Assembly Bill No. 382 for the laying out of a county road, maintained that the "only" difficulty in the way of getting at it is the question of who shall supervise the great work?" The newspaper's management had "never been able to see how such a work can be rightly done by any such body as the Board of Freeholders." After all, "The conflicting interests represented in that Board, its large numbers, its constantly changing composition are all against the practicableness of the proposition that they shall control the work." Appointment of a commission of able and honest men with ample powers was the only efficient method of operation.[66] Yet enactment of the bill naming nine persons as the Hudson County Avenue Commissioners (to be succeeded by the freeholder board after three years)[67] led to litigation because of disagreement about the course of the proposed road. Soon afterward, the New Jersey Supreme Court held that the act was invalid, because the legislature could not allow a board of commissioners to determine in what proportion the expense should be imposed on the townships or city wards. That power could not be delegated.[68]

Even after special legislation for counties was constitutionally prohibited in 1875, it was continued the next year in "An act concerning public road boards," ostensibly a general law. Whenever a county without a road board should have more than 75,000 inhabitants according to the latest official federal or state census (Hudson), twenty-five taxpayers could make a written request for such a body to the freeholders. They, in turn, could submit the question to the voters at a special election after at least six weeks' notice in two of the county's newspapers. If there were approval at the polls, the freeholder board was to appoint five persons for terms of one, two, three, four, and five years, respectively; their successors would be appointed for staggered five-year terms. Whenever one hundred taxpayers in the county should present a written petition to the road board declaring their desire to have a free public road constructed or improved and stating their willingness to be assessed for such purposes, that board could proceed to perform the work.[69] But, as the *Evening Journal* pointed out in defending the new law, there was ample provision against any actual building of the county road in case of objection by the property owners who were to be assessed.[70]

Low regard for the freeholder board was evident in the pre-referendum discussion and in the ballot returns on the proposition in January 1877. Jersey City's mayor, Charles Siedler, wrote a letter to the *Evening Journal*'s editor noting the "danger that the power to appoint Road Commissioners will be given to the Board of Freeholders, through ignorance of the law, on the part of the citizens and taxpayers." He emphatically stated that this power should be denied the county governing body because of "their late action in relation to the purchase of a Court House site."[71] Despite its apparent support of this means to have a county boulevard built, the *Evening Journal* observed that the freeholder board's extraordinary action in voting $225,000 for a new courthouse site had "created a general and deep feeling of distrust, in the minds of the people, of the wisdom, if not the honesty, of the Freeholders." Had they been "wise enough" to announce proposed road board appointees to whom no one could object, such apprehension might have been allayed. Moreover, "If some member of the legislature had introduced and put through a bill taking away the appointing power from the Freeholders, that would have helped the chances of the 'road' amazingly." The proposition's defeat might mean a long wait before that boulevard project would be revised, readers were warned; and they were reminded again that the property owners involved could arrest any proceedings under the act.[72] Apparently unconvinced, the electorate voted 4,198 for the proposal to 6,141 against.[73]

Additional legislation affecting Hudson was subsequently declared unconstitutional by the judiciary. The Court of Errors and Appeals struck down as special legislation applicable only to that county an act passed in 1883 ". . . to make certain roads, . . . county roads, and to provide for the payment of the expenses of constructing by the county. . . ."[74] Because it excepted from its operation "such counties as have a county road board [Essex]," an 1886 act ". . . to authorize the board of chosen freeholders in the respective counties in the state to lay out, open, and improve a public road in each of the respective counties . . . ." was also held by the State Supreme Court to be invalid.[75] It had been approved 3 to l in the required November referendum, after an endorsement by the *Evening Journal.*[76] In addition, "An Act to provide for the payment of certificates of indebtedness, issued for the purpose of constructing or improving a road or roads in counties of this state" (1887) could not be upheld because it concerned certificates which had "heretofore" been lawfully issued.[77]

But Hudson's voters were soon given another opportunity to decide whether a county boulevard should be constructed. An 1888 act was "drawn with a special view of overcoming not only the legal objections to the former acts, but those having reference to the manner in which the road shall be built."[78] Any freeholder board in the state (including Essex this time) could by resolution submit to the electorate the question of constructing and maintaining a public road extending through the county. Approval would require affirmative votes not by a majority of all persons eligible to vote at the general election, as in 1886, but simply agreement by a majority of those who should participate in the referendum.[79] Because it was "not probable, judging from the past, that an act can be procured from the Legislature transferring the power to build the road to any commission," the *Evening Journal* supported the new statute. It "restrains the Freeholders so far as it is possible to curb them, and yet leave them reasonably unfettered," readers were advised. For example, the chief engineer of the proposed road, who was to be appointed by the Court of Common Pleas, would have to approve all payments for work, unless overruled by a two-thirds vote of the freeholder board.[80]

With negative votes cast mostly in the West Hudson municipalities of Harrison and Kearny, the county road was approved, 14,570 to 1,871.[81] The freeholder board immediately provided for the issuance of bonds, and in order to insure their legal sale, authorized the special committee on the county road and the board counsel to have the statute's validity determined without delay.[82] It was upheld in 1889 by the state Supreme Court, and the decision was affirmed in 1890 by the Court of Errors and Appeals. According to New Jersey's highest tribunal, the act was not an unconstitutional delegation of legislative power; nor was it local and special legislation, either as to the laying out of highways or in the regulation of internal affairs. "The law confers a discretionary power

upon localities, which may occasion diversities by being exercised
in one locality and not exercised in another," the opinion stated.
Such differences arose "if at all, solely from the execution or non-
execution of it, but the law prevails everywhere."[83]

4. *General Road Legislation*

Not until 1889 was the freeholder board of *every* county authorized to "acquire, improve, maintain and assume full and exclu-
sive control of *any* public road or roads or parts thereof in their
county [italics added]" without a referendum. Each board was empowered to levy a tax of no more than one-quarter of 1 percent on the
assessed value of the taxable property in the county, or, if necessary,
to issue bonds with the permission of the circuit court. One-third of
the cost was to be paid by the municipalities through which the roads
passed. In addition, a competent engineer could be employed at an
annual salary to inspect the roads and to order repairs on them.[84] As
one Middlexex County newspaper observed, "The roads have
heretofore been left to the tender mercies of township supervisors,
who probably did the best they knew, but who met all criticism with
the one monotonous cry of 'no money to do more.' "[85]

Union's jealousy of the excellent Essex roads provided the impetus for such legislation, although there had been petitions circulating for some time in Somerset, Morris, and other counties.[86]
Elizabeth's city attorney had complained to the press about the "vast
and complicated mass of statute and judicial law which has become
both impracticable and intolerable." With "only particular griev-
ances or points in mind," the legislature had annually passed "a
half dozen or so of fragments of statutes" to remedy the bad township
road situation. "As the matter now stands every township and road
district is at liberty to patch and repair general public highways in as
many different ways as there are districts," he noted. Only Essex
with its road board was not controlled by "the law of the middle
ages."[87] In the vanguard of the reform movement, the *Elizabeth
Daily Journal* was just as explicit: "The people of Union county
know full well the advantages of Essex county roads, and they
respect and admire the enterprise, sound judgment and well
founded public policy which Essex has manifested in building such
roads."[88] Even before Union's grand jury handed down a presentment against the bad condition of the county's roads,[89] the *New York
Times* could correctly predict that James L. Miller (R-Union) would
sponsor the type of corrective measure that did result.[90]

Miller's Senate Bill No. 61 was drafted by two meetings of

Union's community leaders and endorsed by the Elizabeth Board of Trade and unanimously by the County Board of Agriculture.[91] Although the measure was "perhaps a little too broad to suit every phase of opinion in Union County," the *Elizabeth Daily Journal* noted, it was not too liberal "when it is considered that the law must cover all the various conditions in the twenty other counties in the state. . . ." Enactment of the Miller bill should "give all the counties in the state a chance to make good roads if they want to, or to leave them alone if they do not want them improved."[92]

Arguments against passage were offered by the press. The Sussex *Herald* insisted that the farmers were already unable to pay their heavy taxes and that there was really no longer any need for such good roads, because the distances to markets had become shorter. Better roads were being demanded chiefly by those who drove for pleasure. The Plainfield *Times* protested that Plainfield had done its duty in the matter of good roads, and every other municipality could do the same.[93] Although proponents of the Miller bill were maintaining that it would not affect Hudson, Jersey City's *Evening Journal* could find a specific exemption only for Essex, which still had a public road board. "Any bill which is open even to the suspicion of giving the Freeholders more power, is to that extent a bad bill," readers were warned. Hudson needed roads, "but not badly enough to allow Freeholders to make a pretence of providing them," and the county's members of the legislature were advised to secure "such amendment as would save the County from the impending evil."[94]

If bipartisanship in the legislature allowed the measure to become law,[95] a carefully drawn text permitted it to survive judicial challenge as well. Just before its passage, Foster M. Voorhees (R-Union) maintained that it was better to entrust the care of the roads to freeholders than to any new officials.[96] Because it provided that previous laws concerning the Essex Public Road Board should be unaffected, the Miller Act could "be made inoperative at any time [as special legislation]," the *Evening Journal* announced. [97] But the newspaper was wrong. The constitutionality of the act was upheld by the state Supreme Court in 1890 on the ground that the Essex Public Road Board was "simply a committee of the board of chosen freeholders of the county, and absolutely under and within the control of the latter board." The Essex freeholders "may, in their discretion, elect to exercise all the powers conferred by the general act, as fully as may the freeholders of any other county in the state," the opinion continued.[98] In 1894 the legislature abolished all public road boards in the counties (Essex) and transferred their powers, rights, and properties to the freeholder boards. By 1902 only Cumberland and Hunterdon had made no expenditures for roads.[99]

5. *Changing Farmers' Interests and County Finance of Roads*

The farmers had misgivings over freeholder control of the roads. A committee report early in 1890 to the state Board of Agriculture predicted: "The present road law is severely criticised, and from the action of several [county agriculture] Boards, this body will undoubtedly be petitioned (if not already), to use its influence for changes that will enure to our benefit."[100] Just before adoption of a resolution endorsing a three-member county commission to replace each freeholder board, the delegates approved a resolution for the repeal of "The Union County Law" of 1889. It was the wrong time to increase taxes "when everything is at such a low figure the farmer has to sell," one speaker insisted, and it was "feared the freeholders will take charge of the roads." Such sentiment was "particularly the case" in Mercer, where the city (Trenton) elected a majority of the county governing body.[101]

But "the tendency of legislation [toward standardized control by larger governmental units] is now in the opposite direction from what has been the rule for the last forty years," noted one commentator.[102] "From 1850 [actually 1853] to 1875, when our Constitution was amended, there were a host of acts [81][103] passed by the legislature, special in their nature, applying to particular townships and containing provisions not at all in harmony with one another." Under some of these statutes there were roads maintained by school districts or by township committees, instead of overseers. Under other laws a township could be divided into permanent districts, each electing its own overseer, or special overseers were elected for special districts at the annual town meeting, "even where no special law or general law authorized such elections." After 1875, laws were passed providing that township committees might, where they had not already done so, establish road districts, each with an elective overseer.[104] But in 1888 the legal voters of a township were allowed to abolish the election of road overseers and to place all control of the roads and streets in the township committee.[105] Full supervision by the township committee was made *mandatory* in 1891.[106]

A more centralized highway administration was becoming acceptable, even to the farmers. In 1891 the state Board of Agriculture adopted a resolution calling for dividing the road expenses in these proportions: 33 percent to the State; 33 percent to the *county;* 24

percent to the township; and 10 percent to the adjoining property owners.[107] The law that was enacted three months later appropriated $20,000 for good roads and provided that whenever two-thirds of the property owners on a section of road not less than a mile should agree to pay 10 percent of the cost of a macadamized road, the *county* must pay 56⅔ percent, and the State, 33⅓ percent.[108] Unanimously, in 1892 the farmers' organization endorsed the first such state aid law for highways in the United States.[109] Inoperative for a year, it was amended to assign enforcement duties to the president of the state Board of Agriculture and to raise the appropriation to $75,000.[110] In 1894 an act creating the office of State Commissioner of Public Roads was approved.[111]

6. *Hudson County Boulevard Commission*

But county road boards did not disappear entirely. Because Hudson County's Boulevard had reached an extraordinary state of disrepair in 1898, "the people were stirred to such a pitch that both parties saw that nothing short of the abolition of the Board of Freeholders would satisfy public demands."[112] The legislature "should provide a Commission of Charities and Corrections to manage the county institutions" and "also provide that the county roads and bridges should be cared for by a Commission," the *Evening Journal* advised.[113] Although Hudson's Republican candidates for the Assembly, subsequently defeated, had promised to secure the passage of such measures, two of the elected Democrats from the county introduced them. There was "no hope" of passing Allan Benny's Assembly Bill No. 7, which allowed the freeholder board in any county to authorize a referendum to reduce its membership to nine. Consequently, Hudson's Democrats supported James J. Murphy's Assembly Bill No. 64, providing for a Boulevard Commission to be elected at large. "A commission created in that manner would be of the same character as the present Board of Freeholders," the Jersey City newspaper complained; and it heartily endorsed the proposal to amend the measure by giving the judiciary power to *appoint* three commissioners (one of them to be from the minority political party). As a supplement to the 1888 Boulevard Act, the text would not apply to any other county.[114]

A "compromise" was effected. Murphy's bill was amended to provide for the *election* of three Commissioners, only two of whom could belong to the same political party. This was done because it did not appear that the state Supreme Court would approve a law that would delegate to itself the authority to select administrative officials, nor would Acting Governor Foster M. Voorhees approve a bill giving him power to appoint such officials.[115] "In its present form" the bill would "take the great county road away from the gang which has brought it to almost irreparable ruin," the press observed. And the Boulevard would be "saved," if it were "placed in the hands of a Commission of three men as quickly as possible." After all, "It would not be wise to endanger the whole scheme of saving the Boulevard because there is one bad feature in the bill."[116]

The amended version became law[117] and produced what a foremost critic of county government has cited as an example of "democracy via complication." With "powers comparable to those of a separate municipality," the *new* commission could fix its own appropriations and make them mandatory upon the freeholder board.[118] When the act's constitutionality came into question in 1901 (because a similar method of election was struck down by the Court of Errors and Appeals)[119] the *Evening Journal* remarked, "Any change was welcome because it could not be worse, therefore no one felt interested in attacking the Boulevard Commission act."[120] It was not legally (and successfully) challenged until 1966.[121]

Contrary to popular belief, counties in post-Revolutionary New Jersey performed no really significant road functions until late in the nineteenth century. In fact, when the two most populous counties undertook to do so, their freeholder boards were not immediately considered sufficiently trustworthy to be put in charge. Originally named by the legislature, the Essex road board afterwards consisted mostly of popularly elected members, with only one of them designated by the freeholders; not until 1881 was the entire road board changed to consist entirely of freeholders, and even then almost half of them were required to come from the minority political party. In Hudson, the judiciary appointed the first road commissioners; subsequently, they were selected by the legislature; and, finally, the voters defeated a proposal to allow the freeholders to appoint members of a road board. General road legislation of 1889 authorized the freeholder board of every county to assume full control of any public road within its borders. But Hudson's residents were permitted to have an elective boulevard commission with minority party representation, rather than allow freeholder control of the county's most important road project.

PARKS

It was late in the nineteenth century before the two most populous counties began efforts to establish county park systems. No efforts in behalf of a system of county parks were made in Hudson County until 1888, when the legislature passed Senate Bill No. 130, enabling any county in the State to acquire and improve lands for public parks and to maintain and regulate them. Application to the Circuit Court for the appointment of five unsalaried commissioners could be made by two hundred or more resident owners of real property in the county and by any incorporated company of New Jersey owning land in the county, when the aggregate assessed value of the land was at least $2,000,000. The commissioners were to serve initial terms of one, two, three, four, and five years, respectively, and thereafter, five-year terms. In accordance with the act, Judge Manning M. Knapp designated the members on May 19, 1888, but the freeholder board was not so willing to comply. Immediately refusing to approve the commissioners' application for $2,000 in preliminary expenses, it agreed with the county collector who called the law "a most dangerous measure, which to say the least, should have been submitted to the people for their approval." After selecting three sites for parks, the Commission made an application for an issue of bonds to provide money for the purchases. This time the board refused on the ground that the act was unconstitutional.[122] Years later, the local press noted that "on a test" (in 1891) the statute had been "declared unsound by the Supreme Court," adding that "no opinion was filed with this decision, however, and none has since been filed in the case."[123] At any rate, the park law of 1888 and its supplements were repealed in 1893.[124]

But in 1894 Essex County began official action toward the first county park system in the nation.[125] The passage of Senate Bill No. 205, sponsored by George W. Ketcham (R-Essex), authorized the justice of the Supreme Court presiding over the courts of any county with more than 200,000 population (Essex, Hudson) to appoint a commission of five persons for two-year terms "to consider the advisability of laying out ample open spaces for the use of the public in such county." The members were to have "authority to make maps and plans of such spaces and to collect such other information in relation thereto as the said board may deem expedient" and "as soon as conveniently may be" to "make a report in writing of a comprehensive plan for laying out, acquiring and maintaining such open spaces." Serving without compensation, the commissioners were to be reimbursed for expenses incurred "in the discharge of their duties" and were authorized to employ assistants. These expenditures, not to exceed $10,000, were to be certified to the Supreme Court justice, who would order the freeholder board to direct payment by the county collector from highway or bridge appropriations.[126]

In February 1895 the temporary commission submitted its report to Justice David A. Depue, and a copy was also sent to Senator Ketcham together with the draft of a measure that he promptly introduced as Senate Bill No. 114.[127] It authorized the Justice of the state Supreme Court presiding in any county having a population of more than 200,000, on the application of ten or more property owners and residents of the county, to appoint five park commissioners to serve for terms of one, two, three, four, and five years, respectively; and, subsequently, full five-year terms. On the commission's requisition, the freeholder board was to issue bonds to an amount not exceeding $2,500,000.[128] But before the bill passed the Senate, two of the temporary commissioners "incidentally, and almost accidentally" learned that the previous park legislation used by Hudson had been declared unconstitutional. In order to avoid that same fate for the proposed law, the Essex commissioners "decided that they would 'trust the people on the issue.'" An amendment was prepared to provide that the act was not to take effect until after its approval in a referendum at the *next* election in which the people of the entire county could vote for local officers (April 9 in Essex).[129] With this amendment, the bill was passed 13 to 0 in the upper chamber, and 50 to 0 in the Assembly. The approval of Governor George T. Werts was followed by the favorable vote of the Essex electorate: 19,335 to 11,015.[130]

"Framed almost entirely after the Essex Park bill of 1895" in order to insure its constitutionality, according to its sponsor, Assembly Bill No. 141 of 1901 enabled Hudson to try again to establish a county park system. Nevertheless, when he introduced the measure, George G. Tennant (D-Hudson) observed that "some of the provisions of that [Essex] bill have been entirely changed, others modified, some entirely omitted." After approval by a referendum in any county, the presiding Supreme Court justice could appoint an unsalaried five-member commission for initial terms ranging from one to five years, with full five-year terms for their successors. No specific appropriation was authorized, but bonds not exceeding 1 percent of the total county ratables could be issued by the freeholder board.[131] Before long a "curious and startling" rumor had developed that Tennant's Democratic colleagues were unanimously opposed to the *appointment* of the commission "because it would deprive a Democratic Board of the opportunity of spending nearly $2,000,000 of the public money."[132] Consequently, the Assembly committee substitute that was adopted provided for a bipartisan commission of four members *elected* in the county at large for concurrent two-year terms. Passed 50 to 0 in the Assembly and 13 to 0 in the Senate, the substitute was signed by Governor Foster M. Voorhees.[133]

But the constitutionality of this park act was called into question about three months later by a decision[134] of the Court of Errors and Appeals which invalidated an act to establish an excise department in cities of the first-class. Also passed in 1901, in order to "insure the Republicans in Jersey City an equal share in the responsibility of granting liquor licenses,"[135] that law provided for an elected bipartisan board of four excise commissioners. At the first election held under the excise law, each major political party would nominate two candidates, one to serve two years; the other, only one year. Then a citizen would vote for two nominees; thereafter, for one candidate to be elected for a full two-year term.[136] In the unanimous (12 to 0) opinion of the Court, that system violated Article II, paragraph 1 of the New Jersey Constitution which provided that every voter "shall be entitled to vote for all officers that now are or hereafter may be elective by the people."[137] The park act was different, the press had pointed out, in that all four candidates for the park commission would be elected for two-year concurrent terms, rather than staggered terms. Moreover, the park act contained a referendum clause.[138]

On the day after the decision, even before the text of the opinion was made public, it was correctly predicted that there would be no park commission elected in the fall. "Even if one were elected, it would be unable to float bonds in order to buy park property because nobody would buy the bonds," announced County Collector and Democratic leader, Robert Davis.[139] In an editorial, the *Evening Journal* agreed:

. . . it is doubtful if any one will consent to become a candidate under its [the park act's] provisions. Any one who does will be elected to the losing side of a law suit. It is probable that the law will be allowed to lapse, and a new bill will be prepared next winter to remedy the defects of the existing law. . . .[140]

Accordingly, the legislature passed Tennant's Assembly Bill No. 244, introduced the following year (1902). It provided that after approval in a referendum authorized by the freeholder board in any county, the judge of the court of common pleas sitting in that county should *appoint* four park commissioners for terms of one, two, three, and four years, respectively, and thereafter, for four-year terms. Each commissioner was to receive $1,500 a year. Upon requisition of the commission, the freeholder board was to issue bonds "to a sum, in the aggregate, not exceeding one percentum of the assessed value of all property, real and personal in the county, liable to taxation for county purposes."[141] In November the people approved, 13,854 to 5,116.[142]

Just before the referendum, the New Jersey Supreme Court handed down a decision[143] that caused Judge John A. Blair to refuse to appoint members of the park commission. He feared that the marketability of the bonds would be seriously hampered by the Court's ruling that the power to appoint to office, being an administrative duty, was a constitutional function of the executive department of government and therefore could not be conferred upon the judiciary. A taxpayer then applied to the Supreme Court for a peremptory writ of mandamus requiring the judge to make the appointments, and the case[144] was argued at the February term, 1903. But at the March term of the Court of Errors and Appeals, another case[145] arising from the appointment of county park commissioners in Essex by a justice of the Supreme Court was argued, and the decision in effect overruled the first case by sustaining the power of the judiciary to make appointments to office in pursuance of a law that granted such authority. As a result,[146] the Supreme Court directed the peremptory writ of mandamus to be issued, and Judge Blair appointed the four Hudson County commissioners.[147]

The slow and halting evolution of New Jersey county government during the nineteenth century was achieved despite widespread public reluctance and in the face of hostility toward the boards of chosen freeholders. Even by 1902, not a single new function had been accepted and was being performed in every one of the twenty-one counties; in some cases, only two or three counties were involved. In Hudson, the freeholder board had gained the authority to contract for the construction and maintenance of bridges "in such manner as the said board may elect"; but the old statutory procedures remained in every other county. From 1799 to 1869, not one freeholder board used its authority to erect a workhouse or penitentiary; decades later such institutions existed in just three counties. Only after the State in 1869 refused to accept an offer of part of the county farm to use as a state lunatic asylum, did Hudson follow the lead of Essex and establish its own institution. More than twenty years elapsed between the establishment of the first county road board in Essex and the 1889 legislation permitting every county to construct and maintain roads; thirteen years later, Cumberland and Hunterdon still had not made use of the law. In that same year of 1902, only two counties had been authorized to establish parks.

Mistrust of freeholder boards was common. Even where new county functions were recognized as necessary, attempts were made to assign the responsibility to other agencies, such as road boards or park commissions, with the selection of members coming through appointment by the judiciary or with guaranteed minority representation.

And yet, change had taken place, and the role of county government had grown. Led by the two most urbanized, Essex and Hudson, counties had at least been authorized to undertake new tasks. The construction and operation of penal institutions was now an accepted function of the boards of chosen freeholders, and was not limited to sheriff-operated "gaols." Mental institutions, still called "lunatic asylums," were operated by nine counties, with the State government's assisting through weekly payments for patients. By 1902, most of the counties were in the road building and maintenance business, and control of the activity had been recaptured by the freeholder boards from separate and special road boards. And an entirely new service, unheard of in 1798, the development and maintenance of county parks, was now an accepted county function, though control would still elude most boards of chosen freeholders for many years. Chosen freeholders by the end of the nineteenth century were no longer simply bridge-builders. The growth in their responsibilities undoubtedly formed the backdrop, and, to a considerable extent, the cause for the bitter struggles during the latter part of the century over the methods to be used for their election.

3

THE PUBLIC IMAGE: CRITICISM
OF FREEHOLDERS' PERFORMANCE

Reluctance of New Jersey citizens to entrust new responsibilities to boards of chosen freeholders was grounded in a tradition of criticism. The freeholder system had "largely outlived its usefulness," according to a series of lengthy letters in a New Brunswick newspaper of 1874. Although "nominally somewhat extensive" like those in other counties, the duties of the Middlesex County board were "in reality, limited to the overseeing of the construction and repairs of bridges in the county." The freeholders were supposed to fix the amount of tax to be levied upon the county's taxpayers, and they went through the formality of distributing to the townships the school monies which by a "legal fiction" were supposed to be controlled by them. But the apportionment of the school fund and of the county tax was generally the duty of the county collector, who arranged the board's reports, together with the specially-paid clerk. "Very little knowledge or assistance" was contributed by the freeholders; the funds did "seldom come within touching distance of their office." In fact, the county collector did almost seven-eighths of the work for which the freeholders were credited. Moreover, the care of the jail and the examination of the sheriff's accounts were done by a committee, specially, but "not niggardly paid" for the service. Fixed by law or ordered by the judges, court expenses could not be increased or diminished by the freeholders and were only nominally audited by them.[1]

Despite its limited scope of responsibilities, there had not been a board of freeholders in Middlesex County for the nine years prior

to 1871 that did not have at least one member indictable under the
law dealing with misappropriation of funds, charged the same critic.
Even the recent statute forbidding a board from contracting with any
of its own members to perform work for the county was already being
"systematically disregarded." Yet he could not recall a grand jury
during all that time which had not been composed largely of
freeholders, or ex-freeholders and their friends. "How," he wondered, "is an economical administration of the county finances possible, if the only body that can sit in judgment upon official pecula-
tions is made up in great measure of the very men whom it was
intended to act as a check upon?"[2]

The large membership of freeholder boards (as many as forty in
Essex) had become more than ever the target of reform efforts. In
most cases the prompt decisions required by official business were
"impossible," ran the argument; for all large deliberative bodies
move slowly. The more members on a committee, the more time
would be wasted deliberating, and the greater would be the uncertainty of its action. Three or four men could be made to agree with
"tolerable precision," but every additional person would be "one
more to object, and consequently one more to convince."[3]

Fee System

The system of per diem payments of $1.00, provided in the 1798
statute, encouraged corruption of the freeholders. In arguing for a
daily rate of $5.00, a leading mid-nineteenth century critic of county
government in New Jersey wrote:

In regard to increasing the pay of the chosen freeholders, there is hardly
a taxpayer in the State fully conversant with the facts who will not concede
that the present per diem allowance, is a disgrace to all parties. We elect men
to offices of trust, we place in their hands the credit of counties, we require (if
we don't get it) a strict account at their hands of the moneys raised and
disbursed by them, amounting sometimes to hundreds of thousands of
dollars in a year, and we pay them ONE DOLLAR! for each day's service.
We say to them, "Ye shall not steal," and *take* (if they live up to the law) their
time and travelling expenses, just when and where we please to want them,
for One Dollar per day; and we grumble at the dishonesty and rapacity of
those whom we have ourselves taught to steal. We need a thorough over-
hauling of this matter of salaries throughout the State. The time is gone by
when men will work or pay for office just for the sake of the honor it
confers.—And if we would have better men, we must pay better prices in
the future. No man takes office in these times unless he has an axe to

grind—he can't afford it. He *can't* live on his pay, and he *must* live some-how, and therefore bribery and corruption are rampant from our legislative halls down to our Township Committees. . . .[4]

In that year (1867), the legislature raised the compensation to $2.00 for all freeholders.[5]

The arguments for greater compensation for freeholders per-sisted, because getting good men to serve as freeholders was the "chief difficulty," magazine readers were told. The board was "composed generally—not always—of the most ignorant business man in each Township, and the one who has the most axes to grind in the way of performing, and getting personal friends to perform work for the County." In the "parsimonious pay" lay the secret; for a man of good business qualifications could not afford to serve for $2.00 a day. It was "almost an insult to ask it of him." Would it not be better, asked the editorial, to pay a "premium" of $5.00 a day on first-class businessmen and *"feel secure"* about public expenditures than to pay five or ten times that amount "in extravagant outgoes—the result of stupidity and corruption?"[6]

It was "nonsense" to believe that a freeholder "must be a mason by trade or carpenter, and understand exactly the construction of bridges." This was the "same as saying that a man who deals in wagons must be a blacksmith, wheelright [*sic*], and carriage trim-mer." In fact, experience had taught both Somerset and Hunterdon that the fewer masons and carpenters who became freeholders the better. After all, "A good common-sense business man can sell a bridge, and bind the constructor to build it in a strong and durable manner as well as a mason." Moreover, he would be "far less likely to put his finger into the pie of work and pay, and thus do pre-cisely what the law says he shall not do."[7]

Abuse of the per diem system of payments was pervasive. Ac-cording to a Somerset County grand jury presentment of 1872, for example, "special meetings of the Board and of the committees (erroneously so-called) were greatly more numerous than the public interests required."[8] Subsequent scrutiny by the press revealed that Somerset paid for 1950 days in 1875; the number had been just over 200 in 1862.[9] Committee meetings of more than one freeholder for such purposes as viewing bridges cost almost $2,093 in 1878, more than half of the total expense bills.[10] Presenting financial statistics, the local newspaper noted "how, with scarcely an exception, each Freeholder increases his expenses *after the first year*."[11] "By no means uncommon," according to a Salem County weekly newspaper, was the practice of charging the county several times for service on the same day. If he had six bridges to inspect, an unscrupulous freeholder would ask for $12.00 instead of the $2.00 allowed by law.[12] The system's inherent opportunities for promoting graft for the freeholder boards did not escape judicial notice, the state Supreme Court observed:

... The proper work of these corporate bodies is commonly delegated to subordinate committees of their own members; so that in the construction and repairs of county buildings and structures, and in furnishing supplies to county institutions, these committees, often consisting of a single freeholder, have power to expend and to incur public obligation to pay large sums of county money. The committee's own report of labor performed and expenditures made is often the only accessible evidence of the correctness of their claims against the county, and, on their authority, warrants upon the collector for payment are drawn. . . .[13]

It was the cost of the board's supervision of bridges, particularly, that was regarded as "outrageous."[14] During the ten-year period ending in 1874, Middlesex County's expenditures for building and repairing bridges varied from $11,000 to about $30,000, "the greatest amount not exceeding the business of an ordinary retail merchant but requiring for its proper administration considerable practical knowledge and some executive capacity." In mileage and other expenses, each of the twenty-eight freeholders cost $5.00 for every day of actual service, the board's total bills amounting to $5,000 to $7,000 per year.[15] This represented a commission of 25 percent to 60 percent of the cost of the work, "enormous at the lowest figures and terrific at the higher ones."[16] "Would any of the business men of New Brunswick . . . pay any such price for that amount of work, to say nothing whatever of its quality?" inquired the correspondent. "Or would any man in Middlesex County contract to pay a similar percentage on work done for himself, knowing the manner and form of the supervision?"[17]

According to state statute, the number of freeholders required for supervising the building or repairing of bridges depended on the cost of the contract. For a bridge costing less than $50, "a mere culvert," the attention of two freeholders at a public expenditure of $30 was necessary. The two would have to meet at least three times at an actual cost of $5.00 per day for each official: first, to consider the necessity for the bridge; second, to let the job; and third, to accept it when completed. If the job cost from $50 to $500, six freeholders were required. At a minimum of three meetings, the extra charge would be $90. For a job of more than $500 the legally required supervision of the entire board (28 members in Middlesex) would mean an exorbitant expense to the taxpayers.[18]

The type of financial arrangement that was prevalent is apparent from the arguments in the 1879 case of the director of the Middlesex freeholder board tried in that county's Court of Quarter Sessions. He was charged (1) with taking $3.20 from the county as a freeholder and officer of the county, instead of the legal compensation of $2.00, and (2) with collecting from the county $809.80 for 1878–79, whereas the sum of $579.40 was the amount that was alleged to be justly due him. Defense counsel argued that the indictment was based upon a charge of extortion, as specified in the bills by the Grand Jury, and that the state had utterly failed to show anything of the kind. A corrupt mind had not been shown. "The prevalence of a custom of taking certain fees may not make it legal, but it tends to show that there was no guilty intent in taking it," the defense maintained. The Middlesex director's attorney read the 1878 law (Chapter 163) relating to county expenditures and noted that one section provided for "the compensation and lawful expenses of chosen freeholders and committees, and for the salaries of their offices." The words "lawful expenses" were put into the law in view of the fact that it had been the custom "from time immemorial" to receive mileage. "How can the Freeholders be charged with receiving money corruptly, and with intent to defraud, when they are only following in the steps of their predecessors for fifty years?" the jury was asked. Where but in the freeholder board was the authority to say what these lawful expenses were to be?[19]

On the count of unlawfully obtaining the sum of $809.80, the jurisdiction of the Court of Quarter Sessions was challenged. The legislature had authorized the board of freeholders to approve this bill, and from it the only appeal was to the Supreme Court, the defense counsel insisted. In his view, the point at issue was whether the board of freeholders had the power judicially to determine what the correct amount was. "When the party who pays the bill admits it to be just and true how could there be any corruption on the part of the person presenting the bill?" In citing an 1870 act giving the justices of the Supreme Court a salary of $5,000, defense counsel asked how the justices could also accept $3.00 per day fees (under an earlier act) as judges of the Court of Common Pleas. He wondered "if a poor Freeholder can't get mileage without being dragged into court as a criminal, why are not the judges of the Supreme Court served in the same way?"[20]

The jurors were briefly charged concerning the law in the case. Members were instructed that the defendant should be acquitted on the first count (accepting the $3.20), because the state had failed to make a case. On the second count (accepting the $809.80), he should have to be acquitted also unless the services charged had not been justly and lawfully rendered. It took only five minutes for the jury to return a "not guilty" verdict; and the prosecutor, by direction of the Court, entered a *nolle prosequi* in the cases of all the other indicted freeholders.[21]

The following year (1880) a statute prohibited a freeholder not paid an annual salary from accepting any allowance or emolument in addition to the "two dollars for each day he shall be actually and necessarily employed in discharging the duties enjoined on him as such officer. . . ." In addition, he was to file an itemized bill for such service, verified by affidavit.[22] Reimbursement of three cents for every mile of necessary travel in going to and from sessions of the board was provided for by the 1882 legislature. But two classes of counties were excepted: those with at least 100,000 inhabitants (Essex, 189,929; Hudson, 187,994); and those where the freeholders received annual salaries. The statute was enacted without the Governor's signature.[23]

By this time there were three counties in which per diem payments had been abolished and in which a freeholder's acceptance of extra emoluments, formerly just forbidden, had been made a misdemeanor punishable by a fine of not more than $250. No longer could a freeholder receive additional payment by virtue of his position as chairman of any regular committee of the board.[24] An 1858 statute had allowed each Camden freeholder $25 a year "as full compensation for all his services as such officer," except in the case of one selected as a trustee for the county poorhouse, who was to receive an additional $25 annually. "No mileage or other fees" was permitted.[25] An 1874 act had set the salary of a Passaic freeholder at $150 a year in lieu of all other emoluments, with $25 additional compensation for the chairman of every regular committee.[26] According to the 1875 act organizing the Hudson freeholder board, each member was to receive $500 a year; and the director, $1,000. The salary was to be

in lieu of any per diem heretofore allowed, and in lieu of all other fees for committees or otherwise, perquisites, carriage hire, or traveling expenses or personal entertainment whatever, and no other compensation shall be allowed, given or paid to any of said members or the director for any services or expenses whatever. . . .[27]

Annual salaries for freeholders were subsequently instituted in Mercer (1892)[28] and Essex (1894).[29]

During the 1870's blatant public misbehavior by freeholders exacerbated the criticism of their financial irresponsibility. There was "a growing sentiment that the Board of Freeholders is an expensive luxury, and that another form of county government might be substituted with advantage to the public interests."[30] A Middlesex County freeholder's complaint that it would not be dignified for the board to limit the number of bottles to be disposed of at its dinner led one critic to comment that "the mention of 'dignity' in connection with these gentlemen is such a new phase of their extremely various manifestations, that I am almost inclined to hope a reform is likely to begin in their most unlikely quarter." He noted that " 'dignity' implies self-respect, and self-respect is quite incompatible with stealing." Was it "dignified," he asked, for the freeholders, whose allowances were legally fixed at $2.00 a day to "eke out this very scanty allowance by dinners and mileage, and unknown to the law, and unpracticed by similar officers in several of the counties in this State?" Was it "dignified" for the board "dining without law, at the County's expense, to invite twenty or thirty dead-beats to keep them in countenance and increase the bill?" Was it "dignified" for the board to "wash down" the dinner with "from ninety to a hundred dollars worth of wine and whiskey at a single sitting also at the County's expense?" Was it "dignified" to "get so very much elated or elevated or refreshed" as to order their tavern bill paid without knowing or caring what it amounts to? Was it "dignified" to get so drunk at these dinners that participation in further business afterward became impossible? Was it "dignified" to "persist in 'laying on the table' and sneering at resolutions to amend its manners in these particulars," that had been "inspired by the decided vote of a majority of the inhabitants of North Brunswick and the whole of the voters of the South-Brunswick expressed at their last Town Meetings?" Finally, was it "dignified" for the board to persist in its "disgraceful" actions, "because *their constituents have not seen fit 'to express their dissatisfaction with it at the polls?'* "[31]

No taxpayer would find fault with the cost of about fifteen board meetings per year at $7.00 dinner expense per meeting, remarked a Somerset County newspaper in 1879. "He would be a mean man who would strain a point to deny these gentlemen dinners to the extent of $105 a year, even if illegal." But in 1868 hotel accommodations for the Somerset freeholders "actually began to assume the proportion of Belshazzar's feats [*sic*]. "By the following year their cost was $1,802.96. As analyzed by the press, that sum would represent 2,404 dinners at the ordinary price of 75¢ per meal. With nine freeholders plus a clerk, this would amount to 240 dinners for each, or dinners for everyone of them every day, exclusive of Sundays, for more than nine months of the year. "Of course," readers were told, "there was not so much dining as that, but a good deal of *wining* instead and some feeding of horses." Another reason for hotel bills of $20 to $50, rather than $7.00, was that every freeholder's meal, whether he dined with the board or with his committee was "paid for *at a rate from 33⅓ to 50 per cent above that paid for by any ordinary man or men.*" If all board meetings had been held in the county seat as the law required, and not in "out-of-the-way places in the County," Somerville's hotel keepers would have profited even at established rates.[32] Yet more than half of all the board's meetings from 1867 through most of 1879 had been "illegal" by reason of location. "What if, when some taxes were ordered to be raised at some meeting along a creek, taxpayers had refused to pay, and taken their case to the Supreme Court!" exclaimed *The Somerset Gazette.*[33]

LACK OF EFFECTIVE PUBLIC ACCOUNTABILITY

Lack of publicity had been responsible for the freeholders' squandering of public moneys, declared a New Brunswick newspaper in 1865.[34] By a general act of 1846 dealing with freeholders, each board was required to cause to be made out and published in one or more newspapers circulated in the county "a full and complete account of all their expenditures for the preceding year" within sixty days of the mandatory annual meeting every May.[35] But if this provision had not compelled a clear showing of the county's financial affairs, the local press[36] expected that there would be a "strict accountability" supplied by an 1865 statute. Section 1 defined the required financial account as

. . . a detailed statement of all the expenditures of said boards, for the preceeding year, including every description of expenditure by items, the amount claimed, and the amount allowed in each instance, for what purpose, by whom ordered, and to whom paid; also, a full statement of all moneys paid on account of matters incident to the war, for bounties to volunteers, substitutes, or drafted men, and whom paid, including discounts or commissions allowed to any person or corporation for negotiating sale of bonds, notes, or other obligations issued by said boards.

Section 2 made it the duty of the clerk of the board to make out and cause the annual statement to be published in the newspapers printed in the county (number of newspapers not specified) within thirty days of the board's annual meeting. Every neglect by the clerk to do so would be a misdemeanor to be punished by a fine not exceeding $50.[37] By the terms of an 1872 statute, that same fine was to apply to every freeholder in the state who did not file with his township committee a detailed statement of all moneys that had been expended during the previous year "for the construction or repair of bridges or other county purposes." The township committee was to read such a statement at the annual town meeting and then file the document with the cleik.[38]

For the most part, these laws were ineffective. One could still complain in 1879 that bookkeepers in Middlesex County had "never learned the use of bookkeeping by double entry, and only write out and publish a Day Book without arrangement or order." It was "difficult to trace the details of any particular transaction."[39] According to a Sussex newspaperman in 1880, "In almost every instance where the counties in this State have been made the scene of gross abuses and frauds, the thieves have endeavored to cover up their crimes by curtailing and even neglecting to publish a full account [*sic*] of their transactions as public officers." Nevertheless, the wisdom of a detailed publication of the proceedings of governing boards had been "fully demonstrated by the late investigation in Somerset County." With the records of the freeholder board stolen, the chief evidence against the officials had been obtained through the partial publication of its minutes in the local press.[40]

But constantly changing legislation regulating the annual reports was becoming more stringent. An 1879 statute required a freeholder board to select for their publication at least two newspapers of the largest circulation printed in the county, and not more than half the number designated for this purpose could be adherents of one political party. Instead of the clerk of the board, the county collector was made responsible for the financial statement.[41] In 1882 the act was amended to cause the annual reports to be published by the county collector in (1) such newspapers in the county as would be designated by the Governor and the comptroller to publish the laws generally; and (2) in such other newspapers as the freeholder board should select. There was to be as nearly as possible an equal division of the journals representing the two political parties.[42] Each of the two statutes included a proviso that it should not apply to counties where the annual statement was published in pamphlet form according to law.

Certain counties had been excepted from the requirement for newspaper publication of the annual report. At least 1,000 copies of the Camden pamphlet had to be published for circulation, and one of them filed in the office of the county clerk, according to an 1874 statute.[43] Another act of that year provided that Hudson's 1,000 copies had to be deposited for free distribution with the county collector, as well as with the county clerk; and that shortly thereafter the clerk of the freeholder board was to advertise such deposits in two Hudson County newspapers for two weeks.[44] By 1875 the less populous Middlesex was required to publish 3,000 pamphlet copies for distribution by the township collectors and to file five pamphlets in the offiice of the county collector.[45] Two additional counties were exempted from other provisions of the 1865 act. In 1870, the legislature repealed Section 2 (a thirty-day limit on publication) so far as it related to Union,[46] and in 1874 another statute provided that publication of the less detailed financial account required before 1865 should be sufficient in Gloucester.[47]

"The manner of publishing our county finances is a farce and an outrage upon the citizens generally," maintained a daily newspaper in a county using the pamphlet form. Although the law required that the financial statement be published within thirty days after the annual meeting of the freeholder board, the *New Brunswick Daily Fredonian* noted that in recent years such accounts had not been published within from three to four months thereafter. Even then, "only a few copies" had reached the taxpayers. In the three counties that were using the pamphlet form, argued the newspaper, the people "are sick of that system as it does not accomplish the purpose intended—that of informing the taxpayers of what becomes of their money." The editorial writer suspected that this was the very reason why some officials were clinging so tenaciously to the "absurd pamphlets." Declining an invitation to bid for the contract to print the pamphlets, since it had twice lost money on the job, the *Fredonian* nevertheless argued that the "only proper way" to publish county finances was in the newspaper. Then the work could be done within a reasonable time and reach twenty times as many readers.[48] A Union County newspaper agreed: "Perhaps if old Middlesex had published the Collector's reports in the newspapers there would have been fewer defaulting collectors in that unfortunate County."[49]

After another decade of regulating the printing of financial statements in the newspapers, publication by pamphlet was all but

ended. In those counties using the public press, the power to designate the newspapers on a bipartisan basis was returned to the
freeholder boards in 1886.[50] But three years later this power of
selection was made optional on the part of the boards and was
continued as an addition to the duty of the county collector to publish the statement in all the county newspapers that were selected by
the Governor and Comptroller to print the laws. Any county using
the pamphlet form could change to publication in at least one newspaper in each of that county's Assembly districts.[51] In 1893, each of
the freeholder boards in second-class counties (Passaic, Camden,
Mercer, Union, Monmouth, Middlesex, Burlington, Morris) were
required to publish *monthly* financial statements in a newspaper
that it had selected for the coming year.[52] As a first-class county, only
Hudson was not required to revert to newspaper publication of its
financial accounts.

More than any other official, the freeholder earned a bad reputation in the nineteenth century; but it was the existing legislation that
tolerated and even promoted dishonesty and inefficiency. Although
he was not the only one paid on a fee basis, the freeholder was really
accountable for his financial transactions to his colleagues from the
various constituencies. Any indiscretion or fraud was committed at
the expense of the county treasury, possibly even to the advantage of
the people in the freeholder's locality. In any case, his renomination
was not likely to attract much attention during an election for municipal officers, who performed the more vital services of local government. The only effective challenge that could result was a criminal
indictment, but the grand jury was probably on excellent terms with
the politicians. Legislative efforts to control the freeholders through
exposure of their fiscal activities were ineffective. For it was really
the system of representation on the governing board that was responsible for most malfunctions of county government. There were
just too many freeholders, inequitably apportioned.

4

A UNIFORM REPRESENTATIVE SYSTEM UNDER STRESS, 1798–1852

EQUAL MEMBERSHIP FOR MUNICIPALITIES, 1798

As early as 1798 demands for changing the system of equal municipal representation were heard. During that year's debate in the General Assembly on the statute incorporating the freeholder boards in each of New Jersey's then thirteen counties, William S. Pennington (Essex) argued that the proposed election of two freeholders from each township was improper, because representation and taxation ought to go hand in hand. But if a township with 1600 taxable inhabitants were to have the same voting strength on the board as a township that had only two hundred, the will of the comparatively greater number of small municipalities would prevail. Creation of an additional county governing body to be elected at large was also proposed. Included in Pennington's motion for varying the size of the municipal delegations to the freeholder boards was a proposal that "two [persons] may be chosen from each county to sit at the same time with the board, but in another room, and that no business should be valid without the joint consent—this being a kind of county legislature." Another Essex member of the Assembly, Jonas Wade, urged such a check by a five-man body and observed that the function hitherto performed in each county by three justices who served the county at-large "tho' feeble was efficacious." He pointed out to his colleagues that the Legislative Council was a check on their own legislative chamber. Against the motion were arguments that under such a system "the large townships would have good bridges, &c. over every little rivulet, while the small would have none at all or very poor ones." Pennington's motion was lost.

Another motion was made for the election of a five-man body in each county to check the freeholders. It was opposed by Artis Seagrave (Salem) as an unnecessary expense, and also because this "directory" could dominate the board. (Nevertheless, he urged the appointment of a magistrate from each township as a check, because "the heart of man was very prone to take advantage where opportunity offered.") In the view of Samuel R. Stewart (Hunterdon), the second elected body would operate as a "clog" rather than as a check. Some populous townships could elect a majority of the five members; and if a bridge were needed in a remote part of the county, no attention would be paid to the matter. While sarcastically suggesting that the establishment of *three* governing bodies in each county would make for a more effectual check, he insisted that the real need was for a spur. Aaron Kitchell (Morris) approved of a second elective unit, because its membership would most likely be chosen from different parts of the county and would be an improvement on a hitherto very "aristocratical" check. The proposed system would form "a kind of political school, wherein men raised themselves by degrees to more usefulness," according to Pennington, who likened the check to that performed by the United States Senate. "Gentlemen may as well find fault with the constitution as with the proposed section," the assemblymen were told. But they were unpersuaded, and the motion was defeated.[1]

Apportionment of chosen freeholders was not mentioned in the incorporation statute that was passed. It dealt with the board's powers, procedures, and the compensation for each member ("one dollar for each day he shall be necessarily employed in discharging the duties enjoined on him by this act").[2] But the basis of representation was established eight days later by "An Act Incorporating the Inhabitants of Townships, designating their Powers and Regulating their Meetings." In Section 12, the list of officers to be elected annually by each township's voters included "two freeholders commonly called chosen freeholders."[3] More than a half-century was to elapse before this rigid system of allotting members of the county governing body began to change.

PROLIFERATION OF MUNICIPALITIES:
A RESULT OF THE 1844 CONSTITUTIONAL CONVENTION

Until the early 1840's, the number of freeholders was kept down by the creation of new counties formed largely by the transferrence of existing townships. The establishment of Warren from Sussex in 1824 reduced the parent county's original (1798) allotment of freeholders from thirty to twenty-two, despite its simultaneous gain of two newly incorporated townships. When Atlantic was formed in 1837, Gloucester lost its distinction as the county with the greatest area (1,114 square miles) and the then largest governing body (twenty-eight). Reduced to twenty members, that board's membership was scheduled to reach twenty-four, just before the establishment of Camden from Gloucester in 1844. Only ten freeholders remained in the older county then;[4] but that number was to triple, in dramatic contrast to events in other counties.

The minutes of the New Jersey State Constitutional Convention of 1844 show no general dissatisfaction with the statutory provisions for freeholder boards. The majority report of the Committee on Appointing Power and Tenure of Office provided in its draft article on civil officers only one provision concerning county governing bodies: "Constables and freeholders shall be elected every year, at the annual town-meetings of the townships in the several counties of the state." In the Committee of the Whole this section was struck out as "unnecessary," and the Convention in plenary session agreed.[5]

The 1844 Constitution had much to do with the proliferation of townships, and, therefore, of freeholders. During the Convention some delegates urged that the current practice of holding general elections on *two* days, each in a different location within a township, be continued in order to lessen congestion at the polls and to inconvenience fewer voters. But the majority held that expenses would be reduced and opportunities for fraud eliminated by holding the elections in the township election districts on only one day. By a strict party vote, the Democrats determined that it was to be the second Tuesday in October, unless the legislature should alter the date.[6] The following year the single-date provision became established, when a Whig-controlled legislature made the date of the general election coincide with the federal election (Tuesday after the first Monday in November),[7] and the 1846 legislature enacted a comprehensive election statute providing for a single election day and eliminating the authorization for holding elections at more than one place within a township.[8]

"The new constitution, by providing that our elections should hereafter be held on but one day, made this division of townships absolutely necessary," retorted a Whig newspaper to Locofoco (Democrat) protests on the numerous municipal incorporation bills that were before the 1845 legislature. "It was perfectly understood in the constitutional convention, that the constitution could not be properly put in operation in this particular, until the large townships should have been divided," the newspaper continued, noting that the document "directed that the elections should not be held on one day, until after the meeting of this legislature in order that those very bills might be passed."[9] Although the "duty of dividing the large townships" afforded the legislators "an excellent opportunity of increasing the number of Whig townships, and thereby increasing the township *spoils* for their party," the ten townships incorporated in 1845 were "supposed to be" five Whig and five Locofoco. In any case, "perhaps more, perhaps less than half" would not be Whig. "Again, in a great number of cases, the lines were agreed upon by both parties, and the bills were compromise measures, and supported and voted for on both sides," readers were told.[10]

After adoption of the new Constitution, there were sizeable increases in the rate of growth of municipal incorporations, as well as significant changes in the kinds of local units that were established. From 1798 until 1840 the number of townships had risen from 104 to 144; between 1840 and the end of 1843, only six townships and one borough were created; and in 1844, six more townships. But during the rest of the decade there were thirty-one municipal incorporations, not all of them townships, followed by thirty-seven in the 1850's; fifty-eight in the 1860's; and thirty-nine from 1870 through 1875. In the latter year, the census enumerated 260 *townships*, almost 81 percent more than had been included in the statistics for 1840. Other forms of local government were unreported in the census, although their numbers were rising.[11]

Because not all municipalities in New Jersey were created equal, not all of them—only the *townships* or those that had earlier been incorporated as townships—were originally entitled to elect freeholders. Actually, almost one-quarter (24 percent) of the municipalities organized between 1850 and 1875, as compared with only two (4½ percent) during the 1840's, were thus originally deprived of separate representation on a county governing body. In this category were two cities, four boroughs, and three towns set up in the 1850's; two cities, ten towns, and one village, in the 1860's; and four boroughs, five towns, and one village, from 1870 through 1875.[12] Nevertheless, the charters granted to other cities, boroughs, and towns during the same period did include authorization for the election of their own freeholders.[13] As the state Supreme Court subsequently noted (1871), such differentiation was legally permissible:

Acts of the legislature have been passed incorporating towns and villages within townships, for special and limited purposes. In such cases the inhabitants of the township within which the town is situate, for all purposes except those within the objects of the municipal government, and the jurisdiction of the township officers continues over them in so far as is not inconsistent with the provisions of the incorporating act. . . .[14]

But the following year Governor Theodore F. Randolph could remark to the legislature:

The larger proportion of town charters would obviously be improved under a system of clear, explicit, and well-defined authorities. As a whole, these charters are now the source of vexation and wrong to our people, cumbersome in detail, framed frequently for sinister purposes, and almost inviting the corrupt among town and municipal officers to frauds and oppressions with which the times are fraught.[15]

Within such a context of special legislation the freeholder system was to develop until 1875.

The rise in municipal incorporations reflected New Jersey's population growth and increasing urbanization. In the half-century between 1790 and 1840, one scholar has noted, the number of inhabitants doubled, growing at a "slow and steady rate" with "no pronounced internal shifts in the distribution of the population."[16] During those five decades the rates of increase had been 14.6; 16.3; 13.0; 15.6; and 16.4, respectively; and from 1840 to 1850 it was 31.1. Readers of a leading newspaper were told:

It will be seen that the State increased in a greater ratio during the 10 years preceding 1850. Between 1790 and 1800 the ratio of increase in Pennsylvania was more than twice as great, and in N. Y. nearly five times as great; while between 1840 and 1850 the ratio of increase in N. J. was greater than that of N. Y. and nearly as large as that of Pennsylvania.[17]

But the 1840 total was to double within twenty-five years and almost triple by 1875.[18] Moreover, during that time the number of municipalities with more than 5,000 residents rose from twelve (the City of Newark and eleven townships) to twenty-nine (sixteen cities, twelve townships, one town); and they included almost 53 percent of the State's population. Besides the two cities (Newark, Jersey City) that exceeded the 100,000 figure in 1875, four others (Paterson, Camden, Elizabeth, Trenton) could each claim more than 25,000. Significantly, all six cities were county seats: three of them in counties created between 1840 and 1875; and two in counties established just prior to that period (1837; 1838).[19]

Unsuccessful Efforts to Reduce Membership, 1840's

At least as early as 1844, which began with 42 percent more freeholders in New Jersey than the total in 1798, there was some sentiment for reducing the membership of county governing boards.[20] It was expressed in two petitions presented on the same day to that year's legislature by Hunterdon's Democratic representatives. State Senator William Wilson offered one from "sundry citizens" of his county for an act to divide each county in the state into three districts for the election of one freeholder each and to reduce the number of persons on the township committee from five to three. After being read, it was ordered to lie on the table.[21] A petition from Hunterdon residents "praying the passage of a law to reduce the number of Freeholders, necessary for said county and other purposes" was submitted by Assemblyman Jonathan Pickel and referred, without reading, to the Committee on the Judiciary.[22] No further action on the subject was taken during the session.

In 1845 there were numerous efforts in Hunterdon to halve the number of freeholders. Noting that the people of Kingwood Township had determined to petition the legislature to decrease the number of freeholders and also of surveyors of highways to *one* in each township, *The Hunterdon Gazette* declared it "an excellent movement" and went on to "suggest the propriety of other townships doing likewise." Readers were advised: "The present number [18] only entail upon us unnecessary *taxation*."[23] Sixteen petitions from Hunterdon residents demanding fewer freeholders were presented during February by that county's new Democratic senator, Alexander Wurts.[24]

As chairman of the Committee on the Judiciary to which the first two Hunterdon petitions had been referred, Wurts reported a bill entitled, "An act respecting Chosen Freeholders." It provided for the election in every county of only one freeholder from each township and ward. But when the bill was called up on a second reading for the second time, the first section concerning the allotment of freeholders was defeated on a bipartisan vote, and the bill was returned to committee.[25]

Because the membership of its freeholder board was increasing the most rapidly, Monmouth was to lead the fight to end the rigid system of two freeholders per township. Since Dover Township's incorporation in 1767, only one additional township (Howell, 1801) had been created; yet from 1844 through 1849 the number of townships more than doubled. During that time, Monmouth's fourteen-member county governing body was augmented by four freeholders in 1844 (Millstone, Jackson); by two in 1845 (Plumsted); by two in 1847 (Atlantic); by four in 1848 (Marlboro, Raritan); and by four in 1849 (Manalapan, Ocean). Just before Ocean County was created from it in 1850, Monmouth would have a thirty-two-member board, then the largest in New Jersey. Despite the transferral of townships to the new county, Monmouth's increase in freeholders from fourteen to twenty-two during the previous decade was at the highest growth rate (57 percent) in the state, excluding Hudson's. In that recently established county (1840), doubling its initial membership would still bring the number to only twelve at mid-century.[26]

By 1848 even Monmouth's freeholder board joined residents in the movement for legislation to change its composition. That county's Democratic Assemblyman William W. Bennett presented the board's petition for a law reducing the number of freeholders to just one from each township. Eight days later, another Monmouth Democrat, Joel Parker, of the Judiciary Committee, reported such a bill applying only to his county.[27] On three separate occasions during the next several weeks, the Assembly received additional petitions from citizen groups. Parker presented one from 161 Monmouth residents asking for passage of the bill to reduce the number of freeholders, which had been reported from committee, and he submitted another from his constitutents simply calling for a statute providing for a single freeholder from each township.[28] A petition similar to this was offered by Bennett while the measure awaited final passage.[29]

On the bill's third reading, Francis B. Chetwood (Whig-Essex) argued that it would change without any good reason a fundamental law that had been uniform and universal since the formation of New Jersey's state government. Furthermore, the change would be made "partially and for a local purpose only." In his view, the election of two freeholders from each township contemplated that more than one interest in a township be represented in the board; and the reduction to a single freeholder, calculated to represent the interest of only one section in a township, would produce a sectional contest.[30]

Parker supported the bill, replying that the great argument in opposition to it was that there should be no departure from settled usage; and that Chetwood dreaded changing the state's law and custom forever. If such a principle were to be adopted, Parker continued, then New Jersey would stop its advance and would be unable to compete with its sister states in wholesome reforms. Only a few years earlier, New Jersey had no public school system and was governed by a constitution grown venerable by age, he noted. If Chetwood's principle had been adhered to, there would have been no new state constitution, which was a monument to those who framed it. The legislature's duty was to judge each case on its own merits. "The sole object of the bill is to lessen the expense, and have the business done better and more speedily then the present large number can do it," he insisted.[31]

Voting in both houses showed the Democrats solidly supporting the measure. By 35 to 14 it passed the Assembly with the majority split almost evenly: eighteen Whigs and seventeen Democrats. All the nays were cast by Whigs, and five other Whigs abstained. But the balloting was not sectional: each side included Whigs from both East Jersey and West Jersey.[32] In the Senate, the bill was reported from committee without amendment and considered by sections on second reading. The first section allocating one freeholder per township was narrowly approved, 6 to 5 (five Democrats and one Whig to four Whigs and one Democrat). At least six other Whigs abstained.[33] There were no abstentions when the bill was defeated, 8 to 11, on final reading. Only the affirmative ballot of Senate President John C. Smallwood (Whig-Gloucester) marred his party colleagues' complete opposton. To a man, the Democrats supported the change for Monmouth County.[34]

During 1849 there were more than fourteen petitions for change in the freeholder system in particular counties, and the legislature acted on another bill for reducing the membership of the governing bodies. Besides the *unanimous* resolution of the Monmouth board, presented by Assembly Speaker Edward W. Whelpley (Whig-Morris),[35] Assemblyman Alfred Walling (D-Monmouth) submitted five petitions, and Senator John A. Morford (D-Monmouth) offered another.[36] Hunterdon's Democratic Assemblymen produced even more: Andrew Banghart, one; John Lambert, six; and David Van Fleet, an undisclosed number.[37] After considering several of these petitions from the two counties, a committee reported Assembly Bill No. 78, limiting Monmouth County townships to one freeholder each. On second reading, the bill was amended to apply also to Hunterdon's freeholders. As in the previous year, the measure passed the Assembly by a bipartisan vote, but this time there was a greater majority: 39 to 7. Twenty-five Whigs were joined by fourteen Democrats in overriding seven negative Whig votes. As in 1848, the bill was defeated in the Senate with all the nays cast by Whigs, and only one of their colleagues joining the Democratic minority. The vote was 8 to 10, with one Whig abstention.[38]

FIRST SIGNIFICANT CHANGES IN REPRESENTATION, 1851–1852

In 1851 a public notice in the press invited the people of Hunterdon "of all parties" to meet at the Court House in Flemington on February 12 "for the purpose of considering the propriety and expendiency of amending the present law relating to the Board of Chosen Freeholders."[39] The "large and enthusiastic" attendance discussed and adopted the following resolution:

BELIEVING that the election by the people of a board of 3 or 5 Commissioners for each County in the State, in the place of the present organization of the Board of Chosen Freeholders; and also, the like election of the County Collector, would be more in accordance with the wishes of the people, and would better comport with economy, convenience and efficiency; therefore,

Resolved, that the Legislature be urged during the present session to pass a law giving the people the right to choose said Commissioners and Collector at their annual State Election; and that the law be so framed that one of said Commissioners' terms of office expire each and every year.[40]

A committee was appointed to draft an address to the county residents on the subject and also a petition that those in agreement with the resolution could sign. The meeting also resolved that a copy of the proceedings be forwarded to each member of the legislature from Hunterdon as well as published in the county's newspapers.[41]

For the most part, *The Hunterdon County Democrat* approved of the resolution. The idea that twenty-six men should be paid $2.00 per day (actually $1.00 per day, not including expenses) each to build a small bridge costing perhaps $20 or $30 was "regarded among other useless things connected with this body, as having had an existence long enough—and the people are impatiently expecting and exacting a Reform." The newspaper's editorial agreed with the allegation that three commissioners could do the county business just as well. But there were other statutory duties, it noted, which it was "doubtful whether three Commissioners could as well and satisfactorily perform." These included the raising and assessing of money for county purposes, the election of a county collector, and bringing suits at law or in equity for the benefit of the county. *The Democrat* did not doubt that a law could be so framed as to embrace all that would be necessary and proper for the public safety and convenience, leaving to the people the authority to elect the county collector. Readers were advised that the bill reducing the number of freeholders in Monmouth and Hunterdon, already passed in the Assembly, "would do to begin with"; for the newspaper expressed the "hope to see the Reform continue until the number is reduced to three, and a new law passed creating Commissioners."[42]

After a review of the freeholders' duties, a report "To the Citizens of Hunterdon County" stated the drafting committee's unanimous endorsement of a smaller board: "All history testifies and experience has proved that in all questions of financial importance . . . the chances of success increase or diminish as the number of agents employed is less or greater. . . ." With a few exceptions, the committee observed, the freeholders' duties were "entirely executive, requiring skill and experience in management of business, and wisdom in determining the proper methods of executing the several designs in view." Their principal responsibility concerned bridges, and it was "absolutely essential that the members of the Board should not only possess a knowledge of the most known and general principles of bridge architecture," but should be "conversant with the forms and methods of building best suited to give strength, durability and convenience, and be prepared to estimate with fairness and impartiality and expense attending the erection, rebuilding and repair of a specified structure." In the committee's view, there were many instances of well-founded accusations that freeholders had put the county to unnecessary expense by ordering the erection of poorly constructed bridges and by charging more to view a bridge than the entire cost of building it.[43]

"The fault is, however, in the system, and not in the officers employed," Hunterdon residents were assured. For it could not be "expected that men selected chiefly from walks in life which are themselves entirely different from the range of duties required to be performed by the Board of Chosen Freeholders should possess the practical knowledge requisite to enable them to discharge efficiently and faithfully their several trusts." Commissioners elected at large by the county for a term of years "would represent and be chosen from the most intelligent portion of her citizens." These individuals would be "conversant with the different modes of mechanism and architecture, and the management of business."[44]

There could be "no question but that the expense of supporting the proposed board would fall essentially below that required to sustain the present system," because "extraneous services" of from twenty-one to twenty-three officers would be eliminated. The report denied that the commissioners' fees would have to be raised in proportion to the increase of service performed; it also denied that the "extended range" of the commissioners' duties would prevent timely and proper action on the contingencies that might arise in different parts of the county at the same time. To retrench county expenses even further, the committee suggested a law authorizing the overseers of the highways to build and repair all *bridges* within their respective divisions, if the expense would not exceed $30. The amount of fees paid to commissioners for this service would thereby be reduced. "With respect to the election of the County Collector by the county at-large," the report to the people added in conclusion, "nothing need be said in favor of a proposition so manifestly in accordance with the spirit of our civil and political traditions." It would obviate the difficulties sometimes experienced in choosing that officer, allow no basis for charges of partiality in his selection, and permit a fair contest for all candidates.[45]

Doubtless Pennsylvania supplied a convenient model for the *county-wide* election of a small board at this time and subsequently. In 1711 that state's Assembly had appointed three commissioners in each county to remain in office until the next session, and for the next eleven years they were always authorized by statute on a temporary basis (with Philadelphia County sometimes assigned five members). A law of 1722 and its replacement in 1725 established the commissioners permanently as elective, with three-year staggered terms.[46] At-large election within the county for terms longer than a New Jersey freeholder's one year is perhaps explained by the observation that "in Pennsylvania the towns were of little importance, and the machinery and functions of town government were vague and indefinite," whereas towns in New York and New Jersey "had important powers of local government and were recognized in the county organization."[47] Nevertheless, when the office of county commissioner finally achieved full constitutional status in 1874 (after simply being mentioned in the Pennsylvania Constitution of 1776),[48] some New Jersey legislators were even to be attracted by the neighbor state's new scheme to insure minority representation: selection by the voter of only two members of a three-member board serving concurrent terms.

The first significant changes in the freeholder system of representation occurred after a year of almost total legislative inactivity on the matter. Monmouth County Democrat Alfred Walling notified the Assembly in 1850 of his intention to ask leave to introduce a bill limiting his county (then with sixteen townships) to one freeholder for each township.[49] But there is no record that he subsequently did this, nor was any similar measure introduced, probably because the creation of Ocean County during that year reduced Monmouth's freeholders from thirty-two to twenty-two. In 1851 Bernard Connolly (D-Monmouth) sponsored Assembly Bill No. 57, practically identical with Bennett's 1848 bill. Besides prescribing a single freeholder for each Monmouth township, it reduced the membership of every township committee in the county to three. The Assembly amended the text to include Hunterdon in the freeholder provision and voted for final passage, 40 to 13. In the majority were twenty-eight Democrats, eleven Whigs, and an Independent; the minority was entirely Whig.[50] Instead of a solitary Whig ballot cast for passage in the Senate, as in 1848 and 1849, this time seven Whigs joined nine Democrats in a display of bipartisanship. The only nay came from a Whig, and two of his colleagues abstained.[51] With the signature of Democratic Governor Daniel Haines, the bill became law.[52]

Several weeks later in 1851, Jersey City became the first municipality in the state to vary from the system of equal representation within a county (and to elect *more* than two freeholders). When the city's 6,856 residents were united with Van Vorst Township's 4,617 to form a single municipality, they accounted for a greater population than the total of Hudson County's four remaining townships (10,349).[53] According to the revised charter enacted by the legislature, the expanded city was to elect two freeholders from each of its four newly created wards, which would then account for half the freeholder board's membership.[54] In the same year, Paterson Township, with more than half of Passaic County's inhabitants, became a city.[55] But not until two years later was each of its three wards assigned two freeholders;[56] and even then the city's representation on the governing body was outnumbered by the members from the county's five other municipalities. No legislative action was taken to change the representation of Newark, the only other municipality in New Jersey with more than half its county's population.[57]

On the second day of the 1852 legislative session, Senator Silas D. Canfield (D-Passaic) presented a resolution from the President and Council of Paterson for permission to elect two chosen freeholders from each ward in that city or to reduce the number of his county's freeholders (twelve) to one from each ward and township.[58] The latter scheme was embodied in Senate Bill No. 1 that Canfield introduced on the following day. When the bill had been amended on second reading, Stephen Congar (Whig-Essex) presented a petition from Newark inhabitants for a law granting the several wards (seven) of that city an equal representation with the townships (seven) in the county.[59] After additional amendments on another second

reading, the final Senate version provided for one freeholder in each
township and ward in Passaic, Somerset, Essex, and Warren.[60] Those
provisions in acts of 1851 and 1836,[61] which provided two freeholders from Paterson and two from Newark, respectively, were to be
repealed. Thirteen Democrats and four Whigs approved the measure; two Whigs opposed.[62]

Readers of *The New Jersey Journal* (Elizabeth) were warned
that the bill would "become a law unless *immediately* and energeti-
cally opposed."[63] Pursuant to a public notice, a meeting of
Elizabethtown's residents was held at the courthouse. After adopting one resolution in favor of separating the southern townships of
Essex and establishing them as a new county, and another resolution
to continue efforts to achieve this, the group turned its attention to
the freeholder system. The meeting resolved, according to the press:

> that the law now before the Legislature reducing the representation of each
> township in the Board of Chosen Freeholders to one, and giving seven to the
> City of Newark, with the probability of another within the coming year, was
> unjust and improper, that it had been brought before the Legislature without
> the knowledge or consent of the people of the county at large and that its
> enactment would be disapproved by the meeting.[64]

The *Journal* could "see no good reason" for such a measure "except
the rapacity of our Newark neighbors." The editorial argued:

> The Chosen Freeholders do not represent population, but the
> sovereignty of independent townships, and the only argument which has
> been advanced in favor of the project would apply with equal force to the
> representation of counties in the State Senate or of States in the Senate of the
> United States.[65]

A committee was appointed to circulate a remonstrance against the
proposed law, and the meeting was adjourned until two days later,
when additional committeemen were added.[66]

Accepting the amendments reported by the Committee on
Municipal Corporations, the Assembly amended Senate Bill No. 1
further on second reading. In the version that appeared for third
reading, Essex and Passaic had been "stricken out partly on account
of the petitions therefore; and partly because many members were
jealous of allowing power to the cities. . . ."[67] On the motion of
Thomas McKirgan (D-Essex), the bill was recommitted to a different
committee (Judiciary).[68]

Meanwhile, before Senate Bill No. 1 had been reported from

Assembly committee, Burlington Democrat John W. Fennimore had introduced a bill regarding freeholders into the lower house. In the next two weeks he and Burlington Democrat Charles Haines presented petitions for the election of only one freeholder in each township in their county.[69] As reported from committee, the Fennimore bill (no numbered designation) provided for one freeholder for each township in Burlington and Somerset.[70] A motion by Burlington Whig Allen Jones to strike out the enacting clause was defeated, 10 to 41, on a partisan vote. Only one Democrat favored the motion; only four Whigs opposed it. Thereupon, the Assembly amended the text to apply also to Warren County's freeholders.[71] After defeating a move by Jones to postpone further consideration of the bill on the following day, the Democratic Assembly passed it, 38 to 14. Two Whigs (from Essex) were in the majority; four Democrats, in the minority. The bill passed the Democratic Senate, twelve Democrats and one Whig opposed by six Whigs, and was signed into law by Democratic Governor George F. Fort.[72]

Change even extended to the eligibility for the office of chosen freeholder. On the same day that the Monmouth-Hunterdon bill was approved in 1851, Governor Daniel Haines also signed "An act to abolish the freehold qualification." It would "not be necessary, hereafter, for any person to possess a freehold, in order to qualify him to be elected to, and hold, occupy, possess, and enjoy any public office whatever in any county or township in this state" (or "to serve on any grand, petit, or other jury or inquest. . . .").[73] The act was passed in response to complaints about a system that was "most inconsistent, most contradictory, most topsy-turvy." As a Trenton newspaper had pointed out: "We require no freehold qualification of the men who make laws for the Union or for the State; but we will not trust any man but a freeholder to manage the affairs of a county." Executives such as the President, Governor, or U.S. Marshall were not required to be freeholders, nor were members of the federal or state judiciary. Yet sheriffs and jurors had to own real property.[74]

Bills to eliminate the property requirement for holding county and township offices had been considered in previous years. Such a measure had been passed by the Assembly in 1849, after approval of a motion to retain that prerequisite for members of freeholder boards. But the Senate postponed consideration of the measure to the following session.[75] In 1850 the vote on a bill abolishing property qualification for all jurors, township and county officers was 26 to 21, less than the affirmative majority required for passage.[76] Finally, in 1851 the bill was passed in the Assembly, after a legislator was persuaded to withdraw his amendment to continue the property requirement for chosen freeholders, offered because he "merely wished to see no clashing in the name of the officers and the qualifications for office."[77] But before the bill could be passed in the Senate, there were defeats for a similar amendment as well as a proposal to change the name of each freeholder board to the "Board of County Commissioners."[78]

For the first half of the nineteenth century, the system of aportioning freeholders remained absolutely rigid: two freeholders for each township, town (Belvidere in Warren), or city that was formerly a township. But when the number of townships in a county began to grow at an appreciable rate, the board membership became unwieldy. Its size was reduced significantly through timely creation of new counties (Atlantic, Camden, Ocean). Even the constant large size (thirty) of the Sussex board had been decreased by the incorporation of Warren, New Jersey's first postcolonial county. Although not so intended,[79] the establishment of these four counties (and to a lesser extent, Passaic, Mercer, and Hudson) served as a "safety valve" in the matter of limiting the size of freeholder boards.

Dramatic increase in the membership of freeholder boards caused by the proliferation of municipalities in the late 1840's sparked more insistent demands for smaller boards. The first major changes in the system of representation occurred (1851) when the number of freeholders in Monmouth and Hunterdon were halved to one from each township, and the same adjustment followed the next year in Burlington, Warren, and Somerset. Five of the then twenty counties had broken the pattern of uniformity, and in a sixth county Jersey City had become the first municipality in the state to elect ward representatives to the county governing body. In almost every case, Democratic legislators supported attempts at change, but successful action became possible only when some Whigs could be persuaded to break from their party's usual opposition and vote with the Democrats or when the Democrats gained control of the legislature. The way was opened for constant modifications in the system.

5

THE SYSTEM FRAGMENTS:
PRE-1876 SPECIAL LEGISLATION

Once the uniform system of equal township representation had been breached in 1851 and 1852, increasing urbanization and the rapid growth in number of municipalities in the state caused constant pressure for changing the method of apportioning members of freeholder boards. Until the constitutional amendment of 1875 prohibited special laws regulating the internal affairs of towns and counties, such statutes were enacted to change the assignment of freeholders in most of the counties. In some of them the membership was simply halved to one freeholder from each township: Ocean (1855); Bergen (1871); or to one from each township and city: Salem (1871); or to one from each township, town, and city: Atlantic (1873).[1] This type of change was accompanied in some counties by the replacement of ward-elected freeholders with different numbers of board members elected *at large:* In Mercer (1868), Trenton was assigned five instead of six; in Union (1868), Elizabeth was allotted four, rather than three; and Rahway's three at-large freeholders were reduced to two.[2] Legislation effecting the 50 percent reduction for the townships also inaugurated separate representation for city wards in Camden County (1858) and confirmed that system in Hudson (1857) and Passaic County (1869).[3] In almost every instance there was not even one nay recorded on final passage of the pertinent legislation. By 1875 the system of electing two freeholders from each township had been completely abandoned in fourteen counties. Even in three other counties retaining the old plan, there were additional board members assigned to certain cities: in Essex, five

freeholders at large (1857), one freeholder per ward (1862) to
Newark; in Middlesex, three freeholders at large (1861), one
freeholder per ward (1871) to New Brunswick; and in Cumberland,
two freeholders per ward to Bridgeton (1864) and Millville (1866).[4]
The only counties to remain unaffected by changes in the scheme of
representation were Cape May, Gloucester, Morris, and Sussex,
none of which had a city of any size.

In eleven counties the system had been altered by ward representation. By 1860 this had been legislated for four of New Jersey's
six largest cities: Jersey City (1851); Paterson (1853); Camden
(1858); and Elizabeth (1860).[5] Moreover, there were freeholders
elected from wards in Hoboken (1855) and the Town of Orange
(1860).[6] In order followed Newark (1862); Hudson City (1864);
Bridgeton (1864); Town of Bergen (1865); Trenton (1866); Millville
(1866); Salem (1867); New Brunswick (1871); Town of Phillipsburg
(1872); Lambertville (1872); and Passaic (1873).[7] By 1875 nine
municipalities[8] with populations greater than 10,000 and three[9] of
the twenty municipalities in the 5,000–10,000 range were electing
members of the county governing bodies by wards or aldermanic
districts (Jersey City). But only two municipalities[10] with fewer than
5,000 inhabitants were not electing their freeholders at large.

The more significant developments in the several counties follow:

HUDSON COUNTY

1. Pre-1870 Legislation

Both special legislation and the multiplication of municipalities
in Hudson County caused its original board membership of six in
1840 to quintuple by 1872.[11] In the same year (1851) that the legislature made Monmouth and Hunterdon the first counties to be exceptions to the general law concerning the distribution of freeholders,
Jersey City became the first municipality to be assigned more than
two of them. The new charter extending the city's boundaries to
include Van Vorst Township gave two freeholders to each of Jersey
City's newly created wards (then four). Instead of electing two of the
twelve-member board, Jersey Cityites were now permitted to
choose half of Hudson's sixteen freeholders.[12] In 1855 when the
township of Hoboken became a city, it was assigned two freeholders
for each of its three wards.[13] At that time board membership for the
county's six municipalities reached twenty-two, including eight

from Jersey City's four wards. These figures were halved by an 1857 statute limiting each township and ward in Hudson County to a single freeholder.[14] But the number increased again with the incorporation of new muncipalities and the creation of new wards in Jersey City (1861, 1867); Hudson City (1864); Bergen (1865, 1866); and Hoboken (1869).[15] The total rose to twenty-nine with an act of 1870 consolidating the cities of Jersey City (seven wards), Hudson City (four wards), and Bergen (four wards), and dividing the enlarged Jersey City into sixteen wards with a freeholder for each.[16]

2. Election by Assembly Districts as Aldermanic Districts

A new system of electing members of New Jersey's county governing bodies which would ignore township and ward boundaries and still provide for representation of areas within the county was proposed in Hudson as early as 1867. In May of that year, Mayor James Gopsill, of Jersey City, recommended the "reconstruction" of the county board of assessors and the freeholder board as a "proper remedy" for their "highly oppressive" acts in making the valuation of real estate in his city proportionately greater than in other parts of the county. He called for a law requiring that members of both boards be chosen by the Assembly districts established by the legislature, "thus securing, on the true principles of democracy, the fair ratio of representation for population."[17]

Since 1852, each county had been divided into districts, each of which elected one member to the General Assembly. The districts, revised in 1861 and in 1867 following new censuses, did not vary greatly in population at this time, although hints of gerrymandering, which was later to become extreme, were already apparent. Mayor Gopsill's concern for fair representation of population may not have been quite so "fair" as it first appeared, for the three Jersey City Assembly districts in 1867 averaged 12,457 population (according to the census of 1865), while one South Hudson district had 23,207.[18]

A few years later the local press campaigned for such a reform. "The business [of electing Hudson's freeholder board] has got into a most singular and unexpected shape," declared Jersey City's *Evening Journal* in reviewing legislative developments of 1871. It complained that 45,000 residents of the ten muncipalities outside Jersey City had elected nearly as many members (thirteen) as had that city's 85,000 population with sixteen ward-elected freeholders and more than two-thirds of the county's tax burden. Discussion by assemblymen and prominent citizens of both major parties had prompted a decision to have a law passed reducing the number of freeholders, basing their election on population instead of on geographical and township divisions, and "giving to the several tax paying portions of the county a just representation."[19]

Accordingly, Assembly Bill No. 519 was introduced into the Republican-dominated legislature by Josiah Hornblower (R-Hudson, Sixth District) reducing the number of freeholders from twenty-nine to sixteen, two from each of the county's new total of eight Assembly districts. In addition, there was an "obviously correct" provision changing the election of freeholders from the spring to the fall on the ground that they "should be chosen at the same time as other county officials." The current board was to be continued in office until after the forthcoming fall election. "Up to this point we favored the bill; after that we had nothing to do with its passage," announced the *Evening Journal.*[20] Hudson's entire delegation of four Republicans and two Democrats was included in the majority of twenty-one Republicans and thirteen Democrats who voted to pass the bill in the Assembly. Only one Hunterdon Democrat was opposed to it.[21]

Amendments were made in the Senate on the following day (April 6) "in consequence of the earnest protest" of nonresidents of Jersey City, including Assemblyman Michael Coogan (D-Hudson, Fifth District) whose constituency included all North Hudson municipalities except Hoboken and Weehawken.[22] The revised bill provided for *three* freeholders from each of Jersey City's six newly created (March 31)[23] aldermanic districts (coterminous with the Assembly districts that had been reluctantly approved by the Governor on March 22)[24] and one from each ward and township in the remaining two new Assembly districts (including Hoboken alone and the seven other North Hudson municipalities).[25] An allotment of three freeholders to a single constituency of any kind was unprecedented in New Jersey.

Bipartisanship prevailed again. In the upper house, eight Republicans and six Democrats favored the bill; and no Senator oppposed it.[26] When the amended version was returned for Assembly action on the last day of the legislative session, it won an even greater majority than on the initial passage: twenty-four Republicans and eighteen Democrats, opposed only by a Sussex Democrat. But this time, half of each political party's delegation from Hudson abstained: two Jersey City Republicans and a Hoboken Democrat.[27]

Considerable confusion ensued because of differences in terminology and in election dates between the Hudson freeholder bill and a new charter for Jersey City enacted over Governor Theodore

F. Randolph's veto on March 31. At one time, two different groups claimed to be the legitimate Hudson County Board of Chosen Freeholders, and the county was faced with the possibility of having a fifty-two-member board. Eventually, the New Jersey Supreme Court ruled, in two separate decisions, in favor of the election of three freeholders from each of the city's six aldermanic districts.[28]

The clash between Jersey City and the rest of Hudson County is clear in the lower house's action the following year (1872) on Assembly Bill No. 485. Introduced by Jersey City's Republican George S. Plympton, the bill provided for a board of twenty-four members, three to be elected from each Assembly district in Hudson at the annual charter and township elections in the spring. Representation by municipalities and wards outside Jersey City, continued in the 1871 act, would thereby be eliminated. Such a measure, commented the *Evening Journal*, was "right and just and should pass, for in that case our county legislature would really represent the people fairly, each section having its just share of members. . . ."[29] Reported from committee without amendment on the day after its introduction, the measure was passed two weeks later by a 38 to 8 bipartisan vote (twenty-two Republicans and sixteen Democrats against five Republicans and three Democrats). In the opposition were the members from both North Hudson districts who "fervently begged the House to reconsider" the bill's passage. Anthony H. Ryder, the Republican from the county's Eighth Assembly District, composed of seven municipalities, protested that his constituency would lose four freeholders. The Democrat from the Seventh District (Hoboken), John A. O'Neil, also "did his best to get the work undone" (doubtless because his municipality would lose one of its four ward-elected freeholders). To these objections George H. Farrier, a Jersey City Republican, retorted that the bill fixed representation fairly with respect to both population and taxation; and Dennis Reardon, a Jersey City Democrat, rose to speak in its favor. A motion to reconsider failed narrowly, and the bill was sent to the upper chamber.[30]

Partisanship was more in evidence in the Senate. After repeated efforts at amendment, the bill was finally brought to a vote, but only mustered seven of the eleven votes required for passage. Senator MacPherson, of Jersey City, had the support of five fellow Democrats and Charles Hewitt, a Mercer Republican from Trenton, who had voted previously to increase his own city's freeholder representation. The six nays were all Republican.[31] Hudson's board continued to be composed of three freeholders from each of Jersey City's six aldermanic districts, one freeholder from each of Hobo-

ken's four wards, and one freeholder from each of the other eight
municipalities (plus one freeholder from Greenville, until it was consolidated with Jersey City in 1873).

3. *Municipal Representation Ended*

During a January 1875 meeting of the Hudson County board,
some freeholders from Jersey City attempted to gain endorsement
for a new variation of the system of representation. One of their
number introduced resolutions requesting the Hudson delegation
in the legislature to press for passage of an act requiring Hudson to
elect a director at large and only one freeholder from each of the
(eight) Assembly districts in the county. According to the preamble,
"the business of the county could be more expeditiously performed"
and Hudson's economy and good government would be greatly
subserved." In moving that these resolutions be adopted, another
Jersey City freeholder expressed a desire for a seven-member board.
However, a motion to lay the resolutions on the table was adopted by
a 16 to 9 vote, with all but one of the nays cast by Jersey Cityites. The
majority included at least two members from that municipality who
favored reduction of membership from the current total of thirty to
two freeholders from each of the eight Assembly districts. Also
announcing himself in favor of decreasing board membership, but
not according to the resolution, was a freeholder from the Town of
Union.[32]

At the next board meeting two weeks later, a freeholder from the
Township of Union, in Hudson's multimunicipality Eighth Assembly District, offered a resolution urging the county's legislators in
Trenton to promote passage of a different law. It would create a
seventeen-member board of freeholders in Hudson: *two* persons
from each of its first seven Assembly districts and *three* from the
Eighth District "which in territory is about as large as the balance of
the County together, and is otherwise the largest District by way of
taxation and the number of votes." Such a scheme, the resolution
read, would prevent "the large list of clerks and other subordinate
officers of the board that would result from enactment of a law
requiring a director at-large and only one freeholder from each
Assembly district."[33]

A Jersey City member's motion to lay the resolution on the table
was lost, 11 to 13. All the affirmative votes were from Jersey Cityites,
except one from a Hoboken freeholder. After a motion for indefinite
postponement of the resolution lost on a tie vote, that member
offered a substitute:

Resolved, That the Counsel to the Board of Chosen Freeholders be directed to draft a bill recommending that the Board of Freeholders consist of two members from each Assembly District, to be elected in the fall of the year, the compensation of the members to be $____ per annum, except the Director, who shall receive $____ per annum.

After considerable maneuvering, the resolution was approved, and the board voted to recommend salaries of $1,000 for each freeholder and $1,500 for the Director.[34]

The demand by county officials for organizational change persisted. In its presentment of February 15 concerning the Hudson County freeholder board's Joint Committee on Snake Hill (composed of the Committee on the Penitentiary, Lunatic Asylum, and Alms House), the grand jury was satisfied that the Committee was "one of the great wrongs existing in the Board of Chosen Freeholders . . . and the Board itself, consisting of thirty members is too numerous and should be reduced by the Legislature."[35] Three days later the Joint Committee's report included a resolution

That the last Grand Jury, with the exception of two or three of its number, were not competent to decide that the present Board of Freeholders is too large—they being nearly all men unused to public affairs, and not caring to make proper inquiry into the matter while holding the power of Grand Jurors.

Nevertheless, another resolution provided

. . . that the Legislative Committee be instructed to consider and act upon the matter of reducing the number of the Board, if necessary, of granting powers that are needed from the great increase of the County, burdens and business, and for the enactment of proper restraints against acts of wrong, neglect or malversation on the part of the Chosen Freeholders.

After some parliamentary maneuvering, the set of resolutions was adopted. Moreover, the previous meeting's resolution was amended to recommend two-year terms for freeholders.[36]

On the first day of the 1875 legislative session, the *Evening Journal's* political reporter predicted that Thomas Carey, Democratic assemblyman from Hudson's Sixth District would, as soon as the opportunity offered, present a bill for the reduction of freeholders in the county.[37] That very day he introduced Assembly Bill No. 1 with the provisions that had been outlined in the newspaper. The bill provided for a board of *nine* freeholders, each Assembly district to elect one member, except Carey's own Sixth District which would elect two in separate subdistricts. Bayonne would vote for one of these freeholders, and the remaining portion of the Sixth District in Jersey City would vote for the other. The salary was to be fixed at $240 per annum with $100 additional for the director; and the only perquisite allowed board members was to be ten cents per mile traveled by the most direct route in the discharge of their duties.

A different bill for the reduction of Hudson's board size was introduced in the upper chamber on February 10 by another local Democrat, Leon Abbett (D-Hudson). Senate Bill No. 108 provided for the election of one freeholder at large who was to be director of the board at $1,500 per annum for a two-year term, and one freeholder elected annually in each of the eight Assembly districts, to be paid $1,000 per annum. Acceptance of fees, perquisites, and traveling expenses was to be prohibited. In addition, each of the nine members would have to give a bond for the faithful performance of his duty in the sum of $25,000 with two good and sufficient sureties to be approved by a justice of the state Supreme Court. The *Evening Journal* erroneously reported at this time that the bill gave the director veto power.[38]

Abbett's bill received prompt action in the Republican Senate. Within five days it was reported from committee without amendment, subsequently read a second time, laid over, and amended. The text was changed to lower the director's proposed salary from $1,500 to $1,000; and the salary of each of the other freeholders, from $1,000 to $500. Instead of a $25,000 bond, a freeholder would be required to give a bond of only $10,000; in the case of the director, $20,000. The director was to be given a power of veto over the board's resolutions, which could be overridden by a two-thirds vote of all the members. By a 12 to 0 vote (eight Republicans, four Democrats), the Senate passed the bill on February 24.[39]

Although Carey's bill was the first one introduced into the Democratic Assembly, it had still not been called up on second reading after an amended version had been reported from committee. Fearful that Abbett's bill would be read in the Assembly first, Carey had attempted unsuccessfully to have his own bill read on February 24. He claimed to have forty votes in its favor. If that measure were to pass, warned the *Evening Journal*'s reporter, "the reform so much needed in the management of our county affairs may not be secured." He observed that when Hudson's Assemblymen had met to consider Carey's bill, four of them demanded the increase in the number of freeholders from nine to sixteen—two from each

Assembly district. "Anxious to have their support," Carey complied with their wishes and so cut out of the bill "the only good feature it possessed." Local readers were told: "In its present shape it may be authoritatively said, that the people of Hudson County don't want his bill at all, and Abbett's bill is the one which should be adopted."[40]

When Carey's bill was called up on second reading, John D. Carscallen, Jersey City Republican, submitted an amendment providing that "no moneys shall be paid out of the treasury of the county for any liquors, segars or refreshments for the use of any members of said Board of Chosen Freeholders." Violation would be a misdemeanor punishable by a fine not exceeing $500, imprisonment in the county jail for a period of not less than ten days or both.[41] Such an amendment was an insult to the Hudson freeholders, Carey protested, since it held them up to public view as a party of drunkards.[42] After the amendment carried, he moved a reconsideration of the vote by which the bill was ordered to third reading. The motion won, thrity-two Democrats to sixteen Republicans and three Democrats; and Assembly Bill No. 1 was sent back into the committee room.[43] "This virtually kills it and ensures the passage of Senator Abbett's bill," predicted the *Evening Journal*'s State House correspondent.[44]

Another "sharp encounter" followed in which Carscallen "led the van of the forlorn hope." The committee met immediately, embodied his amendment in a little different shape, and reported Assembly Bill No. 1 again just as the afternoon session opened. Unsuccessfully supporting the change punishing by fine or imprisonment *any* violation of a freeholder's official duties, Carscallen contended that the lack of such a law allowed the grand jury's actions to result only in a presentment; it did not permit the indictment of any guilty board member. Carscallen also offered an amendment to reduce the number of freeholders from sixteen to nine, one of which would be elected at large as director of the board. Because the Senate had already committed itself to Abbett's nine-freeholder bill, he argued that the Assembly's passage of the sixteen-freeholder bill might defeat all efforts at reform. Moreover, Carscallen insisted that the at-large election of a director, as in the Senate bill, would allow that official to be unhampered in his official actions by obligations to other freeholders; for he would not have to court their votes to secure a position of leadership. A Jersey City Democrat, Alexander T. McGill, supported Carscallen, insisting that public sentiment in Hudson County favored the election of only one freeholder from each district. Carey's assistance came from Rudolph F. Rabe, a Hoboken Democrat, who assured the legislators that the people of

his city wanted two freeholders; from Edward S. McDonald, a
Democrat of Hudson's Eighth Assembly District, composed of
seven municipalities, who agreed that each district should have two
freeholders; and from Patrick Sheeran, the Democrat elected by
Jersey City's "Horseshoe District."[45] A solid Democratic vote of
thirty-one members rejected Carscallen's proposed amendment;
while sixteen Republicans and only two Democrats approved.[46]

Hudson's freeholders journeyed to Trenton and were "in strong
force" in the State House lobby, urging passage of Carey's bill
during the Assembly debate on final passage. They heard Jersey
City's McGill and Carscallen argue that a nine-member board would
be better than one with sixteen freeholders, because in bodies with
many members it was difficult to fix responsibility for official action.
Besides, McGill claimed, the Hudson voters demanded almost to a
man that there be only one freeholder per district. Carey's certainty
that his Bayonne-Jersey City district wished to have two freeholders
was challenged by McGill, who said that he had visited this constituency to determine voter sentiment. Bayonne's mayor and all the
other officials, he assured the Assembly, had asked that there be only
one freeholder rather than two representing Hudson's Sixth Assembly District. From a personal enemy of Abbett's, Carey had borrowed his charge that the Senate bill included "a boulevard
scheme," the Republican press asserted. But it pointed out that the
Abbett bill gave the board the power to condemn lands only for such
uses as the legislature by special act might direct. McDonald, the
assemblyman from North Hudson's multimunicipality district,
"viewed the matter wholly from the standpoint of the politician." If
the Abbett bill were to pass, he wondered, what man seeking the
position of director of the board at $1,000 per year could afford to
campaign throughout the county, or what person seeking election as
a member would campaign throughout an entire Assembly district
for a $500 salary?[47] If any assemblyman pointed out that members of
the New Jersey legislature were paid only $500, the newspaper did
not record the fact.

In the course of his remarks, Carey charged that Abbett had
asked for a compromise and would allow the sixteen-freeholder
provision to be inserted into his bill, if the Assembly would pass the
rest of it. Senator Abbett, on the Assembly floor at the time, heard this
statement and authorized McGill to deny it. That member was "very
eloquent" and delivered his "best speech" ever in the chamber, but
he was "unfortunate enough" to say that a certain Jersey City ward
was full of Irishmen who, it was well known, were eager for official

positions and wanted places on the board of chosen freeholders. Two Jersey City Democrats, Sheeran and McDonald, rallied to the defense of their "countrymen," and the debate "might have continued indefinitely" if a vote had not been demanded.[48] With only one vote to spare, Carey's bill passed the Assembly along almost strict party lines. The thirty-two affirmative votes were all Democratic, except for one from Essex; the seventeen opponents included only one Democrat besides McGill.[49] In committing the Assembly to the Carey bill, declared one newspaper account, the Hudson freeholders had "achieved a partial triumph over public sentiment."[50]

In his annual report to the Hudson board, the director commented during a March 4 meeting that "in order to remedy many of the evils in the mangement of County affairs, many changes are needed in the law under which the County Freeholders are at present elected, and perform their duties." Stating (erroneously) that the existing law had not been revised since 1846, he called the Hudson board "too large," and "like all cumbersome bodies," it was moving "with friction." Either the bill for one freeholder per Assembly district or the bill for two freeholders would be welcome "as a change for the better", but he preferred the latter. The director's report recommended that "the Legislative Committee of the Board upon consultation with our attorney take under careful consideration the subject of revision of the present law."[51]

At the same meeting the Democratic member from the Town of Union offerred a resolution that the director appoint a committee of three to wait upon the Hudson members of the legislature in reference to the proposed acts affecting the board's organization. Since "neither [sic] of said members have as yet been officially notified," the appointees would present the board's views according to the resolution that it had previously adopted. The county was not to pay any committee expenses, except for one trip to Trenton. A Jersey City Democrat argued that it was time for the baord to stop this business of meddling about bills to reduce its membership and that the matter should be left entirely with the legislature to carry out the wishes of the people. After the resolution was adopted and the special committee named, all acts and papers of the regular legislative committee were referred to it. A motion to limit reimbursible expenses to $25 was tabled.[52]

The following week, "numberless" Hudson freeholders appeared in Trenton to fight against the probable passage of the Abbett bill. Even the director of the board that had been presented twice for

fraud by the grand jury was vigorously supporting the Carey bill.
Still, he was "keeping shady" by not showing himself in the lobbies,
but only in the assemblymen's rooms after the lower chamber adjourned for the day. The Hudson freeholders "have made Carey the
lion of the hour, and they cluster around his desk like sea-weed
around the rock that succors it," observed an *Evening Journal*
reporter. Although they "pretend to have the highest idea of the
beauties of the sixteen freeholders bill," they "like it but little, if any,
better than they like Abbett's bill," he continued. "Their whole
game is to block legislation and so secure another short term of
office," Jersey City readers were advised.[53]

A compromise was effected. Abbett agreed to increase the
number of freeholders that would be elected annually by Assembly
districts from nine to sixteen, but Carey had to accept the provision
for a director with veto powers who would be elected *at large* for two
years beginning November 1875. More than once the Hudson assemblyman had protested vehemently that he would never consent
to such a plan. The new agreement on Abbett's bill would give the
director no vote in the board, except in case of a tie, but he would
have to approve every board resolution regarding county interests
before it could be in force. After ten days of his failure or refusal to do
so, a two-thirds vote of the entire membership could override his
veto. Where the salaries for the freeholders and the director had
been set at $240 and $340, respectively, in Carey's Assembly bill,
and $1,000 and $1,500 in Abbett's original Senate bill, compensation
was fixed at $750 and $1,000 by the two legislative leaders. The
salaries were to be in lieu of all pay or perquisites whatever, and
bonds of $10,000 were to be required of each freeholder, except for a
$20,000 surety from the director. In Hudson's Sixth Assembly Dis-
trict one of the two freeholders was to be a resident of Bayonne and
the other from the Jersey City portion; in the Eighth District one of
the freeholders was to be a resident of that portion lying between the
Hackensack and Passaic Rivers (i.e. Town of Harrison and Township
of Kearny); and the other, from the remaining territory. Unlike
Carey's original proposal for the Sixth District, there would be no
freeholders elected from areas smaller than Assembly districts. In all
cases a freeholder from either the Sixth or the Eighth Assembly
Districts would be elected at large from his Assembly district; but
each freeholder would have to have been a resident of his portion for
one year prior to his election.[54]

Not all Hudson assemblymen approved the compromise version of Senate Bill No. 108 on second reading. When Carscallen

objected to the increase in the number of freeholders, Carey pointed out that Abbett had consented to it. McGill, of Hudson's First District, declared that he had voted for nine freeholders as a matter of principle and that he did not believe in compromising a principle. Even though he had been told by politicians that sixteen freeholders would be a better number, the right number was really nine, according to the County Central Democratic Committee, the taxpayers of his district, and his own conscience and judgment. Sheeran and McDonald made little speeches in favor of the compromise. Hoboken's Rabe warned that it was dangerous to place control of the county's affairs in the hands of only nine freeholders, because five bad men could constitute a majority. To this an Essex assemblyman replied that the people had no right to elect bad men. Carscallen's motion to lower the freeholder's salary to $500 and the director's to $1,000 elicited a lively discussion and was finally adopted.[55]

Thereafter the bill encountered no difficulty. Without any recorded opposition it passed both houses on March 17. In the Democratic Assembly, twenty-seven Democrats were joined by seventeen Republicans; in the Republican Senate, ten Republicans voted with five Democrats. Only McDonald's abstention upset the Hudson delegation's complete support of the bill. Two days later Governor Randolph signed it into law.[56] Just as the text was about to be read at a Hudson County freeholders' meeting that week, a motion to adjourn barely lost by one vote. Scarcely had the clerk's reading begun before the remainder was postponed and the board adjourned until the following week.[57] Doubtless the members were aware of the provisions in the statute that required the election of sixteen freeholders on April 13 and a director at large on November 2. "While it is not, in all of its provisions, such an act as commends my unqualified support, it is a vast improvement over the acts under which we have performed our labors, and will be of advantage to the county," the director's final report assured the outgoing board, after the new smaller one had been elected.[58] Before long, the freeholders and the voters alike would not be so certain.

ESSEX COUNTY

One of the four counties into which the province of East Jersey was divided in 1682, and subdivided into three townships in 1693,[59] Essex was electing two freeholders from each of twelve townships by 1830.[60] When Newark township was incorporated six years later as a city with four wards, its representation was not increased.[61] With almost 39 percent of the county's population in 1840, Newark was still choosing less than 8 percent of the freeholder board. The number of city wards increased to five in 1848; seven in 1851; eight in 1853; and nine in 1854.[62] By the time the Tenth and Eleventh Wards were established in 1856,[63] Newark's population had risen to more than 54 percent of the Essex total; yet the city was still entitled to only two of twenty-eight freeholders.

Newarkers hoped to remedy the situation through amendment of the city charter, whose various supplements had "rendered the whole confused and in some respects incongruous."[64] A Committee of Revision, appointed in 1854, reported the following year to the Common Council a revision bill that in turn was presented to the legislature with a recommendation for passage. When protest meetings were held and charges made that the Committee had exceeded its duty to put the existing system in order, the bill was not pressed before the legislature. A new committee of two residents from each Newark ward was appointed to confer with a similar committee of the Council. The joint sessions were so protracted that their work was not ready for the 1856 legislature, but was completed for presentation to the following one. Included in the draft bill was a provision for a single freeholder elected from each ward, instead of two elected at large in the city.[65]

The charter revision bill (Assembly Bill No. 1½) embodying this scheme was introduced in 1857 by the American Party's William K. McDonald, representing the district coterminous with Newark's Fourth Ward. Among the legislators, Newark interests seemed to be the principal topics of conversation, observed one newspaper correspondent. "Objection is made to the clause in the new charter relating to Freeholders, as conflicting with the interests of the county," he noted. Many thought that the time had come when "Newark should, with its suburbs, be erected into a county by itself."[66] On the bill's second reading, Democrat John C. Denman of the Elizabeth-Rahway Assembly District (then still in Essex) proposed to strike out the new allotment of freeholders. Bipartisan support for rejecting the proposed change to ward-elected freeholders came from all of the Essex assemblymen from districts outside Newark, while three legislators elected from within the city supported the change and helped defeat the amendment by 20 to 28.[67]

But neither the opponents nor the supporters of the plan to give Newark increased representation surrendered. When the amendment to strike out the freeholder provision in Assembly Bill No. 1½ was again proposed the following day by Samuel Keys, a Burlington

Democrat, it was narrowly accepted, 22 to 21. Included in the majority of eighteen Democrats and four Opposition men were the same Essex legislators who had previously voted for the amendment, while the three Newark Assemblymen continued to vote in favor of preserving the original text of the bill.[68] As predicted by a Newark newspaper correspondent during the subsequent period when the bill was under postponement, the charter revision measure passed the Assembly (41 to 2). But the correspondent was also correct in his understanding that the city and county legislators from Essex would compromise and assign to Newark five freeholders elected at large in order that the bill so amended could pass the Senate.[69] After its 16-to-0 success there, the amended Assembly Bill No. 1½ won approval in the lower house, 50 to 0, and was signed into law.[70]

Newark gained strength on the board in two ways: (1) from an increase in membership from two to five, granted in the new city charter; and (2) by the creation of Union County (1857) from seven municipalities in Essex, which reduced that county's freeholders from twenty-eight to nineteen (five from Newark and two from each of the remaining seven townships).[71] But the smaller size of the governing body was only temporary. From 26 percent of the total membership then, Newark's share dropped again to less than 21 percent of a twenty-four-man board in 1862. For although its newly established Twelfth (1860) and Thirteenth (1861) Wards did not alter the number of freeholders, Newark's power was diminished by the reincorporation of Orange Township as a town (1860) with three ward-elected freeholders and by the creation of the townships of South Orange (1861) and Fairmount (1862), each with two.[72]

Subsequent authorization of ward representation did not end Newark's complaints. In 1862 Newark Democrat Thomas McGrath introduced Assembly Bill No. 163, providing for one freeholder from each of Newark's thirteen wards. It passed the lower house with bipartisan support, 39 to 3. Three Democrats and three Republicans from Essex, whose districts included Newark wards, voted for the measure; and the Republican from a four-township Assembly district voted nay. In the Senate, too, the measure received bipartisan support, 14 to 0.[73] The following October, Newark elected thirteen freeholders.

But both population growth and the incorporation of new municipalities were proceeding at a rapid pace in Essex county. After the April 1863 elections in the other Essex municipalities, the board consisted of thirty-four members.[74] Now Newark with more than 70 percent of the county's population was electing 38 percent of

the board membership.[75] Even with the creation of the Fourteenth
and Fifteenth Wards in 1871,[76] the county seat could not achieve a
share of freeholder representation that would be commensurate
with its portion of the Essex population.

In January 1874 a citizens' committee, appointed by Newark's
Common Council to explore consolidation of Essex County townships with the city, unanimously reported that it was "impracticable
and uncalled for." But setting off Newark into a county by itself
would "promote the peace and the welfare of both sections of the
present county of Essex." The report noted that for a long time it had
been apparent that "the conflicting objects and interests of the city
and the townships cannot be reconciled on any terms that will be
satisfactory to both . . . ." In the committee's view, "The dispropor-
tion of the representation in the Board of Freeholders, and of the
relative contributions toward the county expenses, are increasing
causes of complaint on the part of Newark, while they seem to be
equally unsatisfactory to the townships." With its population of
about three-fourths (73 percent) of the whole county, Newark
elected only "one third" [fifteen of thirty-eight] of the freeholders.
"An extreme instance of this inequity" was the city's Thirteenth
Ward with one representative for 15,000 residents, while the township of Livingston with 1,122 people elected two freeholders. In
fact, not one of the townships have even half the population of that
ward. "Yet with all this advantage," the committee observed, "the
townships constantly manifest a sense of injustice." Moreover, "a
large portion of their people" had "no interest in common with those
of the city of Newark."[77]

The nature of the report was "entirely unexpected to the parties
who proposed the committee and was simply astounding to the
townships," remarked a newspaper editorial. They had been in the
habit of assuming "in all debate and argument, that municipal virtue
can never be found until one gets off the sidewalk and mires in the
mud as he crawls along the corner of a railfence." When the Common
Council unanimously approved the report, "the townships began to
wonder." Why should there be any trouble whatever? They were
unconscious of any quarrel. If there were a wrong in the freeholder
board's system of representation, "as assuredly there was," the
townships were ready to rectify it by giving only one freeholder to
each town and ward. Newark would thereby gain full control of the
county finances. But that proposition had been "promptly killed by
the vote of the city members in the legislature," ran the townships'
argument. "It seems to be settled that the intention of divorce has

been deliberately adopted by the stronger party," they charged.[78] But the facts prove that it was the assemblymen from township districts who opposed increased board representation for Newark.

Six days after the submission of the citizens' committee report, Republican Samuel Morrow, representing Newark's populous Thirteenth District as well as Clinton and South Orange, had introduced Assembly Bill No. 188 to allow each ward (in Newark and Orange) and township in Essex only one freeholdler. This would give Newark fifteen of twenty-eight freeholders, or almost 54 percent of the board's membership. Naturally, it was opposed by assemblymen from the districts outside Newark. When Republican Elias O. Doremus (Orange, East Orange, West Orange) moved to postpone consideration of the bill indefinitely, the Assembly agreed, 30 to 25, in bipartisan balloting. Doremus and his Republican colleague, Moses E. Halsey (Bloomfield, Montclair, Caldwell, Livingston, Millburn), were the only ones of the Essex delegation to support postponement. The others—four Republicans and three Democrats —all represented at least some Newark constituents and voted negatively. Doremus and Halsey were the only Essex assemblymen voting with the majority who opposed a subsequent motion to reconsider the postponement. More than a month later—on the day before adjournment—the Assembly voted to reconsider the postponement, but no further action was taken.[79]

As soon as Morrow's bill for single freeholder representation was postponed, Democrat Julius C. Fitzgerald, elected by two Newark wards, introduced Assembly Bill No. 411 to allot two freeholders to each ward as well as to each township in Essex. Because the bill incorporating Franklin Township (thereby increasing the Essex board to forty members) had been approved by the Governor on the previous day,[80] the Fitzgerald plan would increase Newark's representation to thirty of fifty-eight freeholders. But the bill received only twenty-six affirmative votes (five less than the number required for passage) to twenty-four negative votes. The three Newark Democrats and three Newark Republicans recorded in favor of the measure received no support from those assemblymen (Doremus, Halsey, Morrow) whose districts included more than one township.[81]

The following year (1875) Fitzgerald introduced Assembly Bill No. 398, allotting one freeholder to each ward and township in Essex County. David Dodd, a Democrat representing Orange, East Orange, and West Orange, attacked the bill on third reading, arguing that its effect would be to place the townships at the mercy of the cities. In defending the measure as necessary to secure equality of representation, Fitzgerald pointed out that his two-ward constituency in Newark had a combined population of 25,000, with but one freeholder for each ward; while even the smallest township had two freeholders. With a total population of about 35,000, the townships had more members on the board than did Newark with 130,000 or 140,000, Fitzgerald noted. His city was paying 80 percent of all the county taxes, he continued, yet all the county matters were under the control of the townships paying only 20 percent.[82]

When the bill lost, 11 to 30, both Essex assemblymen whose districts lay wholly outside Newark voted negatively.[83] A motion to reconsider prompted Fitzgerald to remark that he did not understand why the Assembly opposed the bill, because there was no valid reason against it. Dodd explained his own opposition and that of Republican Andrew Teed from the Essex County five-township district by noting that if New Jersey's (old) First Congressional District had included five state senators, as many as the (old) Fifth Congressional District, then the townships were likewise entitled to their current allotment of two freeholders each. After Fitzgerald ridiculed the plan whereby the smaller municipalities had only twenty-five freeholders to Newark's fifteen, Dodd took issue with him in regard to the population statistics for the townships. The motion to reconsider lost; none of the Essex delegation representing Newarkers voted against it.[84]

After the Assembly had considered only one other bill, Democrat Patrick Doyle, elected by three Newark wards, introduced Assembly Bill No. 539, providing that each ward and township in Essex should elect *two* freeholders. Dodd's motion to refer the bill to the proper committee, thereby probably delaying or ending consideration of it at that late date (April 1), lost, 12 to 19. Teed was the only other supporter in Essex.[85] By 22 to 20, a motion was passed to suspend the rules in order to allow the bill to be printed without reference. Here the only Essex votes in opposition were cast by the township-elected legislators, Dodd and Teed. The Assembly agreed to make the Doyle bill a special order for April 5, at which time it was ordered to a second reading.[86] On its third reading two days later, Dodd contended that fifty-eight freeholders would be too many and that some other arrangement could be agreed upon during 1876, after the new census had been taken. Teed argued that the current number (forty) was about right. Republican William H. Kirk from Newark objected to the proposed number as too large, although he said that he would be glad to see a more equitable apportionment between Newark and the townships. Samuel Morrow, Jr., representing Newark's Thirteenth Ward, Clinton, and South Orange, urged passage of the measure "as it would bundle a large number of freeholders together and so complicate matters as to at last draw the attention of the people so that some remedy might be had." He was the sole Republican in the Assembly to vote for passage of the Doyle bill when it lost, 17 to 33. Kirk was the only Essex member to join the bipartisan team of Dodd and Teed in opposition.[87]

Almost immediately, Morrow introduced Assembly Bill No. 552, providing for two freeholders to be elected from each Assembly district in Essex. Because five of the nine legislative districts were wholly in Newark and each of two others included a Newark ward, that city could thereby be expected to gain overwhelming control of the freeholder board. Placed on the calendar without reference, the Morrow bill still had received no further action when the legislature's session ended two days later.[88]

UNION COUNTY

First organized in 1857, with two members elected from each of seven municipalities,[89] Union County's freeholder board was soon involved in adjustments to give greater representation to the cities. In 1860 a freeholder was assigned to each of the three wards of Elizabeth,[90] thereby giving 20 percent of the governing body's membership to almost 42 percent of the county's population. Three freeholders were to be elected at large in Rahway, according to a statute of 1865.[91] At that time, consequently, both cities had equal representation, although Elizabeth's population was 17,373; and Rahway's, only 5,128. By bipartisan votes (48 to 0; 14 to 0) in a Democratic legislature,[92] the system was changed in 1868 to provide for four freeholders to be elected at large in Elizabeth; two in Rahway; and one from each township.[93] But if Rahway was equitably represented (14 percent of the freeholders elected by 15 percent of the county's 1865 population), Elizabeth was not so fortunate. With mroe than 49 percent of Union's residents, the county seat was allotted only 30 percent of the thirteen board members. The 1870 census statistics show that the situation had not changed: Elizabeth, with almost 50 percent of the county inhabitants, was entitled to choose less than 29 percent of the freeholder board, now increased to fourteen members with the incoporation of Summit Township.[94]

In Union County, as in Hudson, the press of the most populous municipality was supporting a bill in 1871 for "fairer representation" in the hopes of lightening the burden of taxation. Presumably because Union County's entire delegation to Trenton was Democratic, a Morris County Republican, Nathaniel Niles, was chosen to introduce into the Republican legislature a bill to remedy this inequity.[95] Assembly Bill No. 374, amending and revising Elizabeth's charter, included a provision requiring each of the city's wards (then eight) to elect one freeholder. After one week the bill was reported favorably without amendment from Assembly committee and was awaiting further action.[96] Another two weeks passed, and the Township of Cranford was incorporated,[97] thereby adding a fifteenth freeholder in the spring to dilute Elizabeth's strength on the board to less than 27 percent. The efforts by the county seat's newspaper to have the charter revision bill passed were met by opposition from the freeholder board, which had instructed its committee "to use every honorable means in their power" to defeat the freeholder provision and had requested Union County's senator and assemblymen to cooperate with the committee in defeating the bill.[98] Assembly Bill No. 374 remained completely inactive. Nevertheless, just before the general elections in the fall, the newspaper's editors could still "trust that another session of the Legislature will not be held without securing a change in the law for electing freeholders."[99]

Six days before the introduction of the Plympton bill of 1872 for the election of three freeholders from each Assembly district in Hudson County, Republican John H. Lufberry of Union sponsored Assembly Bill No. 396 to establish in his own county a nine-member board consisting of three freeholders from each Assembly district. Elected for staggered *three-year* terms, members would take an oath and give bonds to the State in the sum of $10,000 to perform their duties faithfully. The annual meeting would be held on the first Wednesday in January of each year. It would be a misdemeanor for any freeholder or any other official, employee, or contractor hired by the county willfully to violate or permit the violation of any law, ordinance, or resolution applicable to the county. In addition to the usual penalties imposed by law, such a person found guilty would forfeit his office and be excluded thereafter from holding any county office. A citizen claiming to have suffered damage by any dishonest act prohibited by law could bring suit for recovery of damages against the wrongdoer and all persons knowingly and willfully profiting by the wrong.[100]

"A step forward made in accordance with the spirit of the times" was the *Elizabeth Daily Journal*'s judgment of the Lufberry bill. Its passage "would save the county in the matter of salaries and 'feed' alone at least half of what the present board cost it." Moreover, the proposed system would correct "another glaring injustice" by giving a fair representation to each district. Although Elizabeth included half the county's population and paid more than half the county tax, the newspaper editorial complained, the city elected only four of Union's sixteen freeholders.[101] Even though the actual number of board members was only fifteen at the time,[102] the newspaper's example of unequal constituencies was correct: "Little Clark township with a score or two of votes, has as large a representation as any two wards of Elizabeth."[103]

"The only arguments we have seen advanced for the retention of the Board of Freeholders are utterly contemptible," declared the *Elizabeth Daily Journal,* as it cited some of them. Because the board's meeting room had been expensively furnished for fifteen members, it would not be suitable for nine, the *Rahway Democrat* had argued. This newspaper had advanced the "Tammanyish consideration" that a candidate for the new freeholder board would have to spend as much time and cash to campaign in an Assembly district as if he were a candidate for the Assembly. Moreover, the *Democrat* had dismissed charges of extravagance and dishonesty with the comment that thanks to the detailed financial statements published in the county newspapers, the freeholders did "not have much chance to get anything more than belongs to them, unless it is done by commission on contracts, etc."[104]

Assembly Bill No. 396 was defeated. In two ways the balloting on it differed from that taken on Plympton's unsuccessful district bill for Hudson County. The Union measure even failed to receive enough affirmative votes for passage in the Assembly, and the voting this time was a matter of absolute party regularity. Every one of the twenty-nine yeas was Republican; all the seventeen nays were Democratic.[105]

But earlier on the same day that this partisan vote was taken, the lower house had passed without opposition another Lufberry bill that incidentally raised the number of Union County's freeholders to seventeen. Assembly Bill No. 476, amending the city charter of Plainfield, included a provision allotting that Republican municipality two freeholders of its own. This was to be in addition to Plainfield Township's freeholder, whose constituency had included the city residents. With twenty-five Republican and nine Democratic votes, the bill passed.[106] Nor was there a single nay to be heard in the Senate when seven Republicans and six Democrats voted favorably on the measure the following day.[107] Losing no time himself, the Governor approved it on the third day, which happened to be the last of the legislative session.[108]

Not until the board meeting two weeks later did the Union County freeholders discover with "considerable consternation" the effect of this act amending Plainfield's charter. Even the Democratic assemblyman elected by five wards in Elizabeth had been "so absorbed in his warfare on the Comptroller bill that he entirely lost sight of this measure," observed the *Elizabeth Daily Journal*. It correctly predicted that the board of eight Democrats and seven Republicans that had just been elected since passage of the Plainfield act would be controlled by nine Republicans after the special election for the two new freeholders before the organization meeting in May.[109] The change was hailed as "the most important victory ever achieved by the Republicans of Union County." In its jubilation the *Journal* continued, "This old Democratic stronghold is in fact revolutionized, enrolled henceforth under the Republican counties of the State,—redeemed, regenerated, disenthralled."[110]

In 1873 Union County's Republican William McKinlay introduced Assembly Bill No. 232, identical with Lufberry's 1872 bill for electing freeholders by Assembly districts, except for the dates on which the changes were to take effect.[111] An amended version of McKinlay's bill passed the lower house by a 33 to 7 vote: thirty Republicans in the majority and only two in opposition.[112] After the bill had been reported without further amendment by a Senate committee, Union County's Republican Senator J. Henry Stone observed that providing for the election of freeholders by legislative district was unknown in every New Jersey county. (Only Hudson's Jersey City was electing freeholders by aldermanic districts that were coterminous with Assembly districts.) There was no reason for making an exception in the case of Union County, he argued, and his motion to postpone the bill indefinitely was agreed to.[113] The *Elizabeth Daily Journal* maintained that the bill's defeat was "less a matter of regret than it was last year," because the "present complexion of the Board [a Republican majority] and the character of its members are such that we may expect an estoppel put to the mania for bridge building. . . ."[114] But two days later the editors noted that the McKinlay bill's defeat did "not satisfy our people" and that they were "determined to stir up this question until their rights are recognized—to fight on that line of [sic] need be for the next five years." Even if Senator Stone's "weak argument" were granted, "what then?" readers were asked. Did that prove the bill's unfairness? "Must we forever follow old customs merely because they are old?" Whether the board should have been reduced to nine instead of fifteen or the current seventeen was "a question open to discussion." But that some mode of relief from unequal tax burdens and unjust representation was demanded "neither Senator Stone nor any other candid man will deny."[115]

The day after this bill of McKinlay's was killed, he introduced Assembly Bill No. 622, amending Elizabeth's city charter to provide for the election of a freeholder from each of its wards (then eight). Until such election, the City Council was to appoint from each ward that was unrepresented on the board a person of the same political party as the incumbent councilman.[116] "Since reduction [of unjust representation and taxation] descending is unpopular let us try reduction ascending as by the present bill and increase the representation," argued the *Journal*, basing its "plea on the forefathers of the Revolution claim—that taxation and representation are inseparable."[117] Reported from committee without amendment, the bill passed, 36 to 5. Lufberry did not join in the majority with twenty-seven other Republicans, including his Union County colleagues, doubtless because his own constituency did not embrace any Elizabeth ward.[118] Once again Senator Stone's motion for indefinite postponement, this time on the day before adjournment, ended consideration of a McKinlay bill to change the number of Union County's freeholders.[119] "This course was probably taken from a want of time in the session and not from the want of merits in the bill," Elizabeth voters were advised. "The bill though killed for the present will assuredly rise again next winter and demand that its claims be recognized and admitted."[120]

By 1875 Senator Stone had "caught the spirit of the other counties" and introduced a bill providing for the annual election of three freeholders from each Assembly district in Union County.[121] Senate Bill No. 238 provided that each freeholder would be paid at a yearly salary of $500 "in lieu of all other fees, perquisites, entertainment, traveling or other expenses, or disbursements whatever." Any freeholder convicted of receiving such extra considerations would be subject to a fine not exceeding $2,000 or imprisonment up to one year, or both. Ordered to be printed without reference, the bill was read a third time only two days later. Every one of the thirteen Republicans in the Senate voted affirmatively, and the bill was passed, 16 to 0, immediately prior to the 15-to-0 passage of the Assembly-amended Abbett bill for the election of Hudson's freeholders by legislative districts.[122] In discussing the proposed changes a week before the legislative session was to come to a close, the Union County freeholder board arrived at no conclusion.[123] The judgment of an Assembly committee on the evening preceding adjournment day was adverse, and that house concurred in the report. Although, shortly thereafter, the measure was agreed to and ordered to have a third reading, it was not destined to be voted upon.[124] "The Union County freeholder bill was killed," the press acknowledged.[125]

MERCER COUNTY

By 1864, when Mercer County included nine municipalities, compared to eight at the time of its establishment in 1838,[126] the injustice of allotting two freeholders to each of them had become so pronounced that it was recognized by statute:

> . . . the population of the city of Trenton, in the county of Mercer, is nearly one-half of that of the entire county, and the quota of taxes levied upon the property and inhabitants of said city is more than one-third of the amount levied upon the entire county. . . .[127]

The remedy provided by the law was to increase Trenton's 11 percent share of the freeholders by granting the city five members who were to be elected at large. In 1866 the board's number was raised to twenty-two members, when the county seat was granted a new charter assigning a freeholder to each of its six wards; and during the following year a seventh ward with its own freeholder was created.[128] But Trenton's quota of freeholders was reduced to five, elected at large, when the representation of each of the Mercer townships was reduced to one in 1868.[129] The 1870 census statistics show that Trenton, with more than 49 percent of Mercer's residents, was entitled to elect only 38 percent of the thirteen-man governing body.

Partisan resistance resulted when Republican legislators tried in 1871 to restore to Trenton a ward-representation system and to increase at the same time the city's allotment of five freeholders. William H. Barton (R-Mercer) introduced Assembly Bill No. 490, providing that Trenton's First, Second, Third, Fifth, and Seventh Wards should each elect one freeholder, and that the Fourth and Sixth Wards *together* should elect a single freeholder.[130] When the measure was first considered on third reading, it did not receive the thirty-one-vote absolute majority required for passage, although supported by most Republicans. A motion to reconsider then was passed, and the Assembly adopted the bill, 35 to 15, with only two

Democrats in the majority and three Republicans in the minority. On the last day of the session, the Senate passed the bill, 15 to 2: twelve Republicans and three Democrats opposed by two Democrats, including one from Mercer.[131] However, Democratic Governor Theodore F. Randolph did not sign the bill, and consequently, it did not become law.

Trenton's Republican Richard R. Rogers sponsored Assembly Bill No. 384 the following year (1872) to return the city's representation quota to one from each ward. With about one-fourth of the affirmative votes cast by Democrats, the Republican lower house passed the bill, 31 to 7. No Republican was recorded in the opposition. Except for the affirmative vote of a Hunterdon Democrat, passage in the Senate, 13 to 1, was along party lines. At least five Democrats abstained.[132] This time a Democratic Governor, Joel Parker, signed the bill.[133] Thereupon, Trenton, with 49 percent of Mercer County's residents, was to elect seven of the fifteen-member board. In 1874 a sixteenth freeholder from newly incorporated Chambersburg was added to the board.[134]

PASSAIC COUNTY

Representation in Passaic County, too, was influenced by the presence of a large and growing city—Paterson. The original freeholder board of Passaic County in 1837 included two members from each of five townships.[135] Two years after Paterson became a city in 1851, it was given two freeholders for each of its three wards.[136] In 1854 a new ward was created by the legislature, and another in 1855, each with two freeholders.[137] Paterson then included more than two-thirds of the county's population but elected the same number of members (ten) as did the five townships.

While other New Jersey cities were fighting for increased county representation, Paterson actually had its share of the board of freeholders reduced. In 1858 Senate Bill No. 54, providing for one freeholder for each Paterson ward, was passed, and Paterson's allotment of freeholders (five) became half that of the five townships (ten). A proposed Assembly amendment that would also have reduced the townships' representation to one each was defeated.[138] Not until ten years later did a statute give Paterson the right once again to elect two freeholders for each of its five wards; another law approved during the following month divided the city into eight wards with *two* freeholders each.[139] Including more than 70 percent of the county's population, Paterson then elected sixteen freeholders, or 57 percent, of the twenty-eight-member board.

With equal support from Republicans and Democrats in the 1869 legislature, the representation of each Passaic County township and each Paterson ward was halved to one freeholder.[140] Now Paterson could elect eight of fourteen members. But, as in other counties, the incorporation of new municipalities worked to dilute the gains made by the large cities. After the Village of Passaic was assigned its own freeholder in 1871,[141] Paterson was electing 53 percent of the board members with its 72 percent of the county population. The Village of Passaic was reincorporated in 1873 as a city, with its three wards[142] each electing a freeholder of the new seventeen-member board. Voters in Paterson still elected only eight members, although the city comprised almost three-fourths of the county's residents.

HUNTERDON COUNTY

Special legislation passed by partisan majorities for one municipality increased the number of Hunterdon's freeholders in 1872, despite strong sentiment for abandoning the single-freeholder system and drastically reducing board membership. Senate Bill No. 246, reincorporating the Town of Lambertville as a city, was introduced into the Republican legislature by Mercer Republican Charles Hewitt; his Hunterdon colleague, David H. Banghart, was a Democrat.[143] Included in the bill was a provision for three wards, each to elect a freeholder. The 1870 census showed that Lambertville, with 3,842 residents, was the county's most populous municipality; but four others also had more than 3,000 people.[144] When Banghart offered an amendment to continue the election of one freeholder elected at large in Lambertville, six Democrats voted aye, and nine Republicans nay. Strict party regularity in the balloting for the measure's final passage, 13 to 3, was marred only by an affirmative vote by Edward H. Bird (D-Warren).[145] In the Assembly, thirty-two Republicans and four Democrats passed the Hewitt bill over the opposition of nine Democrats, including both Hunterdon representatives. The measure became law on the same day.[146]

But by 1872 the county that had been a leader of a successful effort to halve the number of freeholders was the scene of a "movement to favor the abolition of this office, and the transfer of the control of county affairs to commissioners. . . ." The following petition was circulated and "freely signed:"

To the Honorable the [*sic*] Senate and General Assembly of New Jersey: The undersigned citizens and tax-payers of the County of Hunterdon would hereby respectfully petition your honorable bodies for the passage of a law abolishing the office of Chosen Freeholder in this county, and providing for three Commissioners to perform the present duties of the Board of Chosen Freeholders; one of said Commissioners to be chosen from each of the two Assembly Districts into which the county is divided by the voters thereof, and one by the whole county, who shall (after the first term) be chosen for three years, and whose terms shall expire so that a new one be elected each year; said law to provide a fixed salary for such Commissioners, for a properly bonded security for their county, and for an annual auditing and approval of their accounts by the County Judge before the discharge of said security.[147]

No legislative action resulted from such agitation that year.

In 1875, however, the scheme outlined in the petition appeared in Senate Bill No. 205, introduced by Hunterdon's Frederick A. Potts, who had "carried the county by a good majority, being the first republican since the days of Jackson that has done so."[148] The bill embodied "a proposition which it may be well for other counties to consider favorably," declared the *Newark Evening Courier*. The newspaper predicted that the name "commissioner" would probably be changed to "supervisor" and that provision would be made for minority party representation. Readers were told that the measure included "several important provisions in relation to the construction of bridges—one prolific source of corruption and extravagance—designed to prevent waste of the public moneys and other abuses which have grown up under the present system."[149] One section required the commissioners to meet on the site of every proposed bridge costing more than $500, after ten days notice of the meeting's time and place had been advertised in two of the county's newspapers circulating in the neighborhood. Another section required that no bridge costing less than $100 could be built without the written consent of the commissioner within whose district it was proposed to be built and the written consent of a majority of the township committee where the bridge was to be located.

His bill was entirely nonpartisan in character, Senator Potts insisted during final consideration of an amended version. Because Hunterdon's twenty-one freeholders had proved to be expensive, he argued, a great many residents had long desired a change in the system. Senate Bill No. 205 was an outgrowth of the popular will, and its passage would meet with the general satisfaction of Hunterdon voters, the Senate was assured.[150] On the day before the Hudson and Union bills went unopposed through that house, nine Republicans and six Democrats passed the Potts bill without a dissenting vote.[151] Despite such success, the measure was never reported from an Assembly committee.

SALEM COUNTY

The first change in Salem County's two-freeholder-per-township system occurred when the City of Salem was authorized in 1867 to elect three freeholders by wards; but this was changed to at-large election the following year.[152] In 1871 Salem Republican John C. Belden introduced Senate Bill No. 134 ("A supplement to an Act to incorporate the City of Salem"), which included provisions reducing the number of wards to two, with a freeholder to be elected from each. It passed the Senate with the affirmative votes of eight Republicans and seven Democrats, and no recorded opposition. Two weeks later, thirty-one Republicans and two Democrats passed it over the nays of eighteen Democrats, and Governor Theodore F. Randolph signed it into law.[153] But during those two weeks Belden sponsored and saw the upper chamber pass Senate Bill No. 265, authorizing the election of only one freeholder in each of his county's townships (ten) and in each city (Salem). As in his first measure, the city would lose its extra freeholder representation. Although five Republicans and seven Democrats passed the second bill without any negative vote,[154] the Assembly's partisanship on this measure, too, was obvious. Salem Democrat John W. Dickinson moved to amend by giving each ward, rather than each city, a freeholder. Seventeen other Democrats, including his Salem colleague, John Hitchner, supported the proposed amendment, but twenty-seven Republicans defeated it. There were no defections on either side in this effort to retain extra freeholder representation for the City of Salem. But on final passage, Senate Bill No. 265 received thirty Republican and six Democratic votes; it was opposed by thirteen Democrats, including Dickinson and Hitchner.[155]

Further attempts were made to provide special representation for the city of Salem. The following year (1872) Belden sponsored Senate Bill No. 345, requiring that city to elect a freeholder in each of its two wards. Although twelve Republicans and four Democrats passed the measure in the upper chamber without opposition, the Assembly failed to act on the measure.[156] In 1873 a similar bill, Salem Republican D. P. Dorrell's Assembly Bill No. 280, was indefinitely postponed.[157]

The uniform two-freeholder-per-township system of representation had been broken in the early 1850's, largely because rapid incorporation of new townships threatened to increase board size unreasonably. During the next two decades the legislature, through the device of special legislation, grappled with problems of representation presented by the concentration of population in the cities of the State.

Clearly, the time had come for increased efforts to replace the scheme of freeholder constituencies of single municipal units. But what should be the new system? One early approach, first tried in Jersey City, was to equate city wards with townships for the election of freeholders. However, if every township, regardless of size, were to be assured of at least one freeholder, either the fast-growing cities were certain to be underrepresented, or the freeholder boards would grow to enormous size, for many city wards included far more inhabitants than some outlying townships. Newark in Essex county, Elizabeth in Union, Trenton in Mercer, Paterson in Passaic, all were growing dramatically, not only through an influx of population, but also through the annexation of pieces of bordering townships or sometimes of whole municipalities. Even alloting to each of Jersey City's aldermanic districts *triple* the number of freeholders elected by each township and each Hoboken ward had not closed the representation gap between them—and the Hudson board numbered thirty-one members! The Jersey City legislation, however, prepared the way for a different approach, for the aldermanic districts had the same boundaries as districts created for election of members of the legisture's lower house—the General Assembly. By 1875, statutes had been enacted providing for election of all Hudson freeholders from Assembly districts. Municipal representation had been ended in at least one county.

But in 1875 another event occurred. A constitutional amendment prohibited the use of special legislation to solve problems of county government representation. After that date, fundamental changes in the method of distributing freeholders in New Jersey would have to overcome the newly created constitutional obstacle.

6

GATHERING UP THE PIECES:
EARLY ATTEMPTS AT
GENERAL LEGISLATION, 1876–1883

In the years following the Civil War, the use of special legislation proliferated in New Jersey until, in 1873, Governor Joel Parker could point out that the general public laws enacted in the last session of the legislature took up only about one hundred pages of the annual volume of statutes, but special and private laws required over 1,200 pages. One outcome of this situation was the organization of a constitutional commission, which recommended a package of amendments to the state Constitution. Twenty-eight amendments were approved by the legislature and were accepted by the voters at a special election held in 1875.[1] Among the amendments adopted was one which prohibited the legislature from passing any private, local, or special laws:

... Regulating the internal affairs of towns and counties; appointing local offices or commissions to regulate municipal affairs. ... The Legislature shall pass general laws providing for the cases enumerated. ...[2]

As a result of the constitutional amendment of 1875 against special legislation regulating the internal affairs of counties and towns, two approaches to changing the system of representation on freeholder boards occupied the attention of the legislature concurrently. Before 1880 the major effort was to pass general laws ostensibly applying to all municipalities and counties in the state, but actually affecting only some of them. After that date, there were more numerous attempts to enact statutes that clearly would affect only those municipalities with specific forms of government or only those counties or municipalities within certain population groupings. Some conflicts were between urban and rural interests; others, between the two major political parties.

LEGISLATIVE JOINT COMMITTEE'S PROPOSAL FOR ASSEMBLY DISTRICT CONSTITUENCIES

In February 1876 the legislature's Joint Committee that had been established by concurrent resolution three weeks earlier "for the preparation of public laws required by the recent Constitutional Amendments" considered and amended a general bill for the government of counties.[3] It was largely the work of Union County's Republican Assemblyman Benjamin C. Vail, who had just been assigned to the subcommittee on counties, along with his party colleagues from Essex, S. V. Cortlandt Van Rensselaer and Elkanah Drake. The Joint Committee took from 8:30 until 12:30 that night to "digest" the bill.[4]

Most of what was new in the draft that was to become Senate Bill No. 55 was compared in the press to the act of 1875 reorganizing Hudson County's freeholder board; but there was an important innovation based on the 1872 statute concerning Passaic County's governing body. The proposed text reenacted the 1846 general law regarding the incorporation of counties and, in addition, divided them into three classes: first, counties with more than four Assembly districts (Essex, Hudson) to have two freeholders from each district; second, counties with more than one and not more than four Assembly districts (Burlington, Passaic, Camden, Union, Mercer, Morris, Monmouth, Middlesex, Hunterdon, Warren, Bergen, Cumberland, Somerset, Gloucester, Salem), to have four freeholders from each district; and third, all other counties (Sussex, Atlantic, Ocean, Cape May), each to elect six freeholders at large. In *every* county a freeholder who was to be the director of the board would be elected at large for a two-year term, as was then the case in Hudson. Because no director was to have the veto power, that county's presiding officer would lose his just-acquired parliamentary weapon.[5] Like Hudson's, all freeholders would be elected at the time of the General Assembly elections in November, instead of in October or in the spring, as previously required.[6] But like Passaic's board, all would serve *two-year staggered* terms. After the first election, the freeholders were to meet on the Wednesday after the first Tuesday in January and divide themselves by lot, one half to serve one year, and the other to remain in office for two. Half the board each year after

1877 would be newly elected. The compensation of each member was set at $3.00 for each day's service, but not more than $3.00 for any single day's service, which sum was to be "in lieu of all emoluments, allowances or expenses of every nature and kind whatever." In any one year the total payment of a freeholder was not to exceed $500. The director would receive an additional sum of not more than $300 per annum in first-class counties; $200 and $100 were the maximum amounts allotted in second- and third-class counties, respectively. Each board was to determine the director's salary at its first meeting.

"The attempt to produce a symmetrical system of local government for all the counties is to be commended and we hope that it may be successful," announced the *Elizabeth Daily Journal* before the bill's introduction. Basing representation on Assembly districts would do away with "disproportioned representation" that existed in some counties, notably Union. Nevertheless, the editorial argued that the division of counties into three classes with different numbers of freeholders was "an anomaly in legislation" and was "contrary to our theory of government." The "inequality" in the representation of states in the United States, which gave Rhode Island and New York the same representation, was explained by the fact that Senators represent sovereignties rather than population, "but not so with freeholders." Other features of the bill appeared "objectionable," but because the text was still in the committee, it was "premature to judge of their merits."[7]

"Insuperable objections" were put forth by Trenton's *Daily True American* to two changes in the proposed bill on the day that it was to be introduced. The newspaper considered "the questions involved in this bill to be of principle and not of partisan politics." First, it opposed the change in the time for holding elections. The bill's advocates believed that both parties would be more particular in the fall concerning the selection of nominees. But even though the purpose of the change from the spring was a good one, practice would show that better candidates for freeholder would not be secured. Instead, the office of freeholder, "minor" compared with others usually to be filled at the general election, would be used as bait to secure for the candidates for the highest positions the influence of the lower classes of voters. That is, freeholder nominations would be given to "improper persons" in order to enlist the votes and influence of these nominees and their supporters in the effort to elect candidates for the legislature and Congress. Similar circumstances had obtained in Pennsylvania, where the "evil at last became so pressing as to force the Constitutional Convention to propose, and the people of the state to compel a separation of the state and municipal elections." Trentonians were warned: "Like causes breed like results. . . ."[8]

Second, the *Daily True American* objected to the election of freeholders by legislative districts. "Population is not, nor should it be the only basis," it declared. There was not so much propriety in selecting such a basis as there would be in choosing the amount of taxable property. After all, the freeholder board's principal function was expending money for county purposes, "and those who pay the money, should have the voice as to how it should be spent." It was true that the members of the New Jersey House of Assembly and the United States House of Representatives were elected according to population, but their actions were checked by upper house members, not elected according to population. "There is no restraining power over the Board of Freeholders," the newspaper noted. Rather than just population or taxable property, the many and diverse interests of the different communities comprising a county should be represented. Such interests were "found best represented in the townships and wards."[9]

The proposed system would upset the fair representation that had resulted over the years in most of the counties, argued the newspaper. For example, Trenton, with 22, 874 of Mercer's 46,386 inhabitants (1870) and with $12,686,666 of the county's $23,861,916 in taxable property (1875), would be entitled to but four of the board's twelve members. The city would have the members of the Second Assembly District, but the 226 Trentonians in the Third District would be completely outvoted by township residents. In Union County, the case would be exactly reversed. Elizabeth, with a population of 20,832 out of 41,859 (1870) and with $14,156,900 of $27,894,567 in ratables (1875), would have the members of the First District beyond doubt and would control the Second District, with 1,537 Elizabeth residents in three city wards against 1,096 voters in Linden, Union, Springfield, and Cranford. Rahway and Plainfield would have to take their chances of getting one freeholder each in the Third District. In its practical operation, the reorganization bill would "merely make arbitrary divisions, which ignore not only population, but property and various other interests which are connected with county government." Nevertheless, there were some good features that should be legislated, such as restraint on freeholders' actions, it was conceded.[10]

On the following day the *Daily True American* could cite the Newark *Register* to support its position. According to this Essex newspaper, the election of a director at large would violate the right of every governing body to choose its own presiding officer, and the effect would be "the virtual creation of a Directory in every county." Moreover, "for the practical purposes of local government, the township is to be abolished," the *Register* contended. It noted that a county with three assemblymen would have a thirteen-member board. But as soon as its population would increase sufficiently to entitle it to four Assemblymen, the county would become first class, and its board "would be reduced to nine members." "A severe penalty to pay for greatness, certainly," the editorial warned.[11]

But the "most objectionable" feature was that the measure was "revolutionary to the last degree; and destructive of the rights of sections and minorities." The freeholder boards were "local legislatures" founded on the same ideas of representation as the State legislature or Congress. "The townships possess to a certain degree, an autonomy of their own; and their right to protect themselves in the Board of Freeholders is as inalienable as the right of a State," readers were advised. The newspaper conceded that in some counties the preponderance of the townships on the boards was too great and that the centers of population were too much under township control. "But, on the other hand, the compactness and unity of purpose usually displayed by the cities give to them the power of more efficient action," the editorial continued. Consequently, "they ought not to fully equal the townships in representation." The existing imperfections could be easily remedied by a less extreme measure. The proposed bill might have been conceived by "a monarchical supporter of the French Septennate, determined to give the least possible leeway to aggressive republicanism." But "it could never have originated in the head of a man who understands popular methods of legislation." Of course, the editorial was "not speaking with any idea that the law proposed in the Joint Committee could ever be made a statute." Still, the writer would not like to stand two years later in the boots of the country members who would vote for passage of the measure.[12]

The *Hunterdon Republican* which regarded the bill as "an unusually good and wise one" was correct in its observation that the opposition would come from the local politicians whose chances of reelection to the freeholder board would probably be affected.[13] On the very day that the bill's text was completed for introduction, its provisions were outlined in the Essex County freeholder board by Republican State Senator William H. Kirk. The board voted to instruct the county's delegation to the legislature to oppose the measure.[14] Learning of this order, the legislators from Essex became "somewhat indignant," for to them it looked as if the freeholders were "providing for themselves a home." The *Elizabeth Daily Journal* was reminded of "the action of a similar board nearer home in days gone by." That body "would send committees to Trenton, pay their expenses out of the people's money to oppose the people's wishes and thus defeat the people's measures."[15]

Other newspapers favored the bill. The *New Jersey Mirror* in Burlington County held that the reduction of the number of free-holders would be "generally approved."[16] It seemed to be a "move towards practical reform." But instead of the four freeholders that would be allotted to each Assembly district in Burlington County, plus one elected at large in the county, the *Mirror* suggested that "three for each district and one at large, or even two to the district, would be still better as tending to increase the responsibility of the officer, without diminishing the efficiency of the Board." Noting that there was "some force" in the argument against "bringing a local and purely business office too prominently into political contests" by changing freeholder elections to November, the editorial asked whether this difficulty could not be obviated by providing that no voter should vote for more than two candidates if there were to be four elected, or for one, if but two were to be chosen. By insuring the election of half the board from each of the two leading parties, and the election of the director by the majority party, the system would result in "a Board so close as to render it difficult for either party to go very far wrong in furtherance of party ends or in the abuse of power." And "the one majority would secure to the victors the offices — baring [*sic*] accidents." Readers were assured that this was not a new suggestion: several of the most important boards of Newark were said to be chosen in this way, and the system met "universal approval" there.[17]

The first section of Senate Bill No. 55 to be considered by the upper chamber was the one that deprived the townships of their separate representation. On the bill's second reading, Samuel T. Smith (D-Sussex) moved to amend by providing that one freeholder should be elected in each township, ward, or aldermanic district in all counties.[18] He was supported by William H. Kirk (R-Essex) who alluded to the difficulties that would arise in regard to bridges and who favored the amendment as giving the townships a fair representation.[19] Leon Abbett (D-Hudson) objected, pointing out that there were no wards in Jersey City, and that its aldermanic districts were coterminous with Assembly districts. Paying two-

thirds of the county taxes, Jersey City would be entitled to but six
members of a thirty-member board under the proposed change.
Smith replied that he had inserted the words "aldermanic districts"
just because there were no wards in Jersey City. Although there was
no intention to work any injustice to Hudson, he could not support
the proposition of a bill that would allow Sussex only seven freeholders for the fifteen townships covering an area of twenty miles by
thirty miles.[20] The mountain townships in his own county would be
unrepresented.[21]

Several senators sought to prevent adoption of the amendment.
William J. Magie (R-Union) favored the original text, because the
current system of freeholder representation seemed to him arbitrary,
onerous, and expensive. If all the affairs of each Pennsylvania county
could be managed by three "Supervisors," he argued, surely New
Jersey as well could manage with fewer freeholders. Magie pointed
out that one ward in Elizabeth paid ten times as much tax as did
Clark Township, although each had one freeholder. The true mode
of representation was based on population, not on area.[22] John Hop-
per (D-Passaic) said that, as nearly as he could learn, the people of
his county were favorable to the bill, except as to the election of
director at large. There was a fear that this officer would become a
sort of autocrat. The Senator thought that the existing composition of
freeholder boards was cumbersome and that these governing bodies
were run more for private emolument than for public good.[23]
Frederick A. Potts (R-Hunterdon) spoke in favor of election of
freeholders by legislative districts. His county had prepared a measure similar in principle to Senate Bill No. 55, he said.[24]

Nevertheless, by 13 to 8, the Senate agreed to the Smith
amendment, with seven Democrats in the majority and two in the
minority.[25] Seven of the affirmative votes were cast by counties in
which the status quo would be wholly maintained by its adoption.
In these counties the township form had already been electing a
single freeholder, rather than two of them. In fact, *only* those
municipalities with *township* charters were electing freeholders in
Monmouth, Somerset, and Bergen. The other four counties also
included different types of municipalities (and wards) that had been
allotted single-freeholder representation by special legislation. In
Warren, there were the towns of Belvidere, Hackettstown, and Phillipsburg (four wards), and the borough of Washington;[26] in Atlantic,
Egg Harbor City, and Atlantic City, both wardless, and the towns of
Absecon and Hammonton;[27] in Mercer, Trenton's seven wards;[28]
and in Camden County, the wardless Gloucester City and the eight
wards of the City of Camden.[29]

Also unchanged would be the *relative* voting strength of the municipal units in four other counties approving the amendment. For whereas each of the townships would lose one of its two freeholders, all towns and cities would likewise be deprived of half their membership on the county governing body. There would be only one freeholder each in Sussex County's Town of Newton; Gloucester County's wardless City of Woodbury; Cumberland County's city wards in Bridgeton and Millville;[30] and in the wardless Cape May City.

Although halving the townships' freeholders would make no difference in the relative voting power among the townships in Salem and Middlesex Counties, other adjustments would effect changes that could not be considered overwhelming. The City of Salem with two wards would receive a second freeholder that it had been seeking in 1872, and 1873.[31] The City of New Brunswick would be allowed to keep the single freeholder that had been granted to each of its six wards in 1871 and would thereafter elect 35 percent of a seventeen-member board, instead of 21 percent of a twenty-eight-man governing body.[32]

Of the eight counties recorded against the amendment, six were opposed to maintaining the system of freeholder representation of municipal units and subunits. Four of the counties would not be affected at all by the amendment. Ocean was already electing one freeholder for each township,[33] as was Burlington, where several townships included cities within their borders.[34] Passaic County was electing one freeholder from each township and one from each ward of the cities of Paterson and Passaic.[35] There was one freeholder from each Hunterdon township, from each of Lambertville's three wards, and from the Borough of Frenchtown and the Town of Clinton.[36] In Morris County, the amendment would halve the representation of each township, but the relative voting strength of each would be untouched. Union County, with its single-freeholder townships, opposed these changes that the amendment would produce: Elizabeth's eight wards would be allowed a freeholder each, instead of a total of four for the city; and Rahway's four wards would have one each, instead of a city total of two; one of two freeholders would be taken from the wardless City of Plainfield; and Plainfield Township would keep its single freeholder. Under the districting plan Elizabeth would fare better.

Two of the eight senators voted negatively in order to *preserve* the current system in their own counties. His support of the Smith amendment during debate did not prevent Essex County's Kirk, himself a freeholder, from voting against the proposed change.[37] In his view, the representation of townships in many cases was not sufficient. He apparently preferred the current scheme of *two* freeholders for each Essex township, even though halving their number would increase Newark's representation of 37½ percent of a forty-member board to a more equitable 51.7 percent of a twenty-nine-member body.[38] Hudson's senator was voting to maintain the bill's *original* text that left unchanged his county's allotment of two freeholders for each of eight Assembly districts, plus a director at large. One minor difference in the unamended bill was the omission of the requirement in the 1875 statute for Hudson that one freeholder from its Eighth Assembly District reside between the Hackensack and Passaic Rivers.

After adoption of the Smith amendment, the Senate approved Abbett's motion instructing the Judiciary Committee to provide that counties of the first class elect freeholders by Assembly districts, according to the original text.[39] The senator from Hudson then assured Camden's Republican Senator William J. Sewell that there was no doubt about the constitutionality of providing for the election of a director in one way (at large) by one class of county, and in a different way (by the board) in another class.[40] By a 13 to 8 vote, with identical groupings to those on the Smith amendment, the upper chamber disagreed to a motion by Union's Magie that counties of the second class, as defined in the bill (having more than one and not more than four assemblymen), elect freeholders by Assembly districts. Magie's second motion to have counties with more than *two* but not more than four assemblymen elect by assembly districts was also defeated.[41] After the Senate approved a Smith amendment providing for the election of freeholders at the time of the election of township and municipal officers,[42] Smith moved that in counties not of the first class, the director be elected by the freeholder board, rather than at large. It was ruled that the question of electing such an officer had been settled by the affirmative vote on the original Smith amendment concerning the apportionment of freeholders.[43] Then the bill was committed to the Judiciary Committee with instructions to change the text in accordance with the sentiment of the upper chamber.[44] With the effect of the Smith amendment now limited to counties smaller than Essex and Hudson, there were to be only two classes of counties.

Two weeks later Senator Kirk, obviously expecting his county of Essex to have more than 169,000 inhabitants, according to the 1875 state census to be promulgated in April (168,812), offered an amendment providing that any county with that amount of population should elect one freeholder for each township and ward (rather than two for each Assembly district, as would be required for "first-class" counties under the Abbett plan). Arguing that some relief from the bill's application was due to his county of Essex, he noted that most of its population was in Newark and that the entire area outside the city was to be represented by only two freeholders elected from Assembly district constituencies. To assign to these two the duty of looking after all the bridges and other matters concerning the townships seemed to him "unequal and unfair." But in order to achieve his objective of preserving the *status quo* in Essex, Kirk accepted in place of his own amendment another by Hunterdon's Potts: "That all counties having cities with aldermanic districts [Hudson] shall be of the first class." After this change was adopted, another proposed by Mercer Democrat Jonathan H. Blackwell to fix the maximum annual salary of a freeholder at $400, instead of the original $500, was lost, 7 to 11.[45]

The bill was also amended to change the uniform April election date reported by the committee[46] to provide that freeholder elections be held "at the time and places of holding the annual township, ward, or aldermanic election, as provided by law."[47] Twelve days later, the bill was recommitted to include a clause validating the recent elections in which some municipalities had elected *two* freeholders each.[48]

By the time the bill was passed, 12 to 1, it had been "amended in such a way as to be satisfactory to every section of the state, dissimilar as are their interests."[49] The "author" of Senate Bill No. 55, Union's Assemblyman Vail, was reported to be "not so especially interested in the bill since the amendments have so emasculated it that he would hardly recognize it if he stumbled against it outside the Legislature."[50]

Although the extensive modifications made in Senate Bill No. 55 had apparently made it sufficiently palatable for the Senate, the proposal achieved little success in the lower house. When the Assembly Committee on Revision of Laws reported Senate Bill No. 55 with a substitute, the report was accepted, 21 to 16. But later that same day, the bill was recommitted to the Committee on Corporations.[51] Again, two days later, a substitute was reported without recommendation, and the report was adopted.[52] On the measure's second reading, David Dodd (D-Essex) moved that at such a late stage of the session (April 18) all bills respecting counties be indefinitely postponed,[53] and the motion was carried, 30 to 17.[54]

Another unsuccessful general bill, but limited to changes in freeholder allotments, was considered late in the 1876 legislative session. On the day after the introduction of Senate Bill No. 55, Elias J. Mackey (D-Warren) had sponsored Assembly Bill No. 106, providing that only one freeholder be chosen in every township and in every ward of every incorporated city or borough.[55] Immediately, the *Evening Journal* of Jersey City protested that such an arrangement would give that municipality, with two-thirds of Hudson's population, only about one-fourth of the freeholders.[56] Four times in April the measure was laid over, and it was never brought to a vote.[57]

In 1877 Union County's Magie sponsored Senate Bill No. 21, identical to the previous year's Senate Bill No. 55, the general law for county government, in the form prepared in 1876 by the Joint Committee on Public Laws. On the measure's second reading, Essex County's Kirk, who had voted in 1876 against the original proposal for representation by Assembly districts, moved to increase the number of freeholders required by the bill to one from each ward and township, as a matter of justice and equality. In his county, he argued, the Magie bill for electing freeholders by Assembly districts would eliminate representatives from the rural areas. They were generally the best men, better acquainted with the wants of the county; they were men of property and stability, who had been on the board for years, and who were not drifting about year after year. It was because the rural sections were fully represented, Kirk claimed, that Essex was so well governed. Sussex Democrat Francis M. Ward supported the amendment. At the request of the Senate president, Hudson's Leon Abbett, the bill was laid over in order that he might draft an amendment that would meet the difficulties in his own county.[58] Again on second reading the following day, the bill was sent back to committee on Abbett's motion, with instructions to amend it so as to leave the election of freeholders as it was then in the several counties. The Senate recommitted the measure, 12 to 9, with the county groupings substantially as they had been on the general counties bill in 1876.[59] Two weeks later the Magie bill was postponed (10 to 4) for one week on motion of Camden Republican William J. Sewell and was not officially acted upon again. General laws are very pretty in theory, but they don't work profitably at times, Sewell told his colleagues. The people were satisfied with the existing law, he insisted.[60]

During the same legislative session, Marmaduke Tilden (R-Hudson) introduced Assembly Bill No. 214, providing that the governing bodies of those counties with more than 100,000 inhabitants

(Essex, Hudson) should consist of two freeholders from each Assembly district. All existing special laws relating to any particular county affected by the act would continue in force and apply only so far as consistent with the new measure. The structure of the Essex board would be changed, but not Hudson's, where presumably the at-large election of the director would continue.[61] Reported without recommendation, the Tilden bill was withdrawn at that time by its sponsor, with the approval of the Assembly.[62]

FARMERS' PRESSURE FOR ASSEMBLY
DISTRICT CONSTITUENCIES

The rapidly rising cost of government caused county reform to interest the farmers. There seemed to have been no organized effort or discussion concerning taxation from their standpoint until the Grangers took up the subject, remarked G. W. Thompson to his colleagues at the March 1877 meeting of the Middlesex Farmers' Club. But at that time his own group became possibly the first local agricultural association—and certainly the most persistent in New Jersey—to take official action. It adopted Thompson's resolution to join with the New Brunswick Board of Trade and with the Grange "to further elucidate the oppressions of the taxes under which we suffer"; and a committee was appointed to confer with these organizations.[63]

A discussion of county government preceded the vote. According to Captain Samuel Blish, who was to become a leader in the reform movement, the expenses of the freeholder board needed to be investigated in detail, as had been those of the state. Without finding fault with the board members for following the law in matters of finance, he noted that the freeholder system was very burdensome and expensive. There was no freeholder who could not be trusted to look after the repairing of small bridges himself, just as well as the entire membership of thirty. And although the account rendered by the county collector was very accurate, it puzzled a plain farmer to discover by looking through it what amount was paid to any particular freeholder or which items made up the expenses. Farmers did not object to paying fair salaries, just to exorbitant fees and salaries, Blish insisted.[64]

Freeholder extravagance was attacked by other farmers in the Club. James Neilson noted that a thorough appreciation of the matter of taxes resulted from owning a farm within the New Brunswick city limits. The county tax had been said to equal six times the state tax, and he had found that the city tax was equal to four or five times both the state and county tax. Taxpayers should organize against tax consumers, Neilson advised. A. Vermeule said that farmers were especially interested in the tax question, because their property was exposed to the assessor's view and could not be hidden like personal property. They should cease paying men for holding offices that required less work than the farmers did, at a rate enabling the officials to drive their fine teams and build cottages by the sea. It seemed to him as if even the jail inmates had more meat in their diet than many farmers had.[65] "What do we want with two Freeholders from every town when one would answer just as well?" asked Vermeule. "In Somerset county they have only one in each township, and think that is double the number they need. The study of our leaders today is to make positions and put their friends in them."[66] The remedy for high county taxes was to elect men as freeholders who would not spend money recklessly, argued John S. Voorhees. For example, there had been seven or eight freeholders from Middlesex and Somerset viewing holes in the road and building culverts, where, in each case, a plank would have been enough. (He understood that there were twenty-eight men in his township who desired to be freeholders, not one of whom he would be willing to vote for.) But the opinion that prevailed was delivered by a freeholder from New Brunswick, J. W. Pennington, in defense of his colleagues on the county board: the way to correct abuses was to change the law, not to abuse those who obeyed it.[67]

Efforts to enlist the cooperation of other groups proved fruitless. At the Club's next meeting one month later, the members who had been appointed to confer with the New Brunswick Board of Trade reported that "to both personal and written applications little or no notice was vouchsafed, and the Committee consequently concluded that the officers of the Board of Trade were unable to appreciate 'Taxation from the Farmers' Standpoint.' "[68] When the Club met again in September, there was so much interest in the subject of taxation, brought up by the Committee, that the scheduled topic, "How to increase the quantity of manure on the farm," was passed by altogether. Thompson reported that his committee, in common with other members, was "sanguine that this Club could take such action as would have an appreciable and beneficial effect in helping forward the reduction of taxation." This was "a matter in which the farmers were more particularly interested than any other class in the community, because in proportion to their profits, their taxes were larger and consequently more burdensome," he asserted. "But for some reason which did not clearly appear," the farmers were told, "there seemed to be an indisposition on the part of the committee appointed by the Board of Trade to do more than assist in their own way, and therefore no practical united action could be had." The farmers' committee was continued.[69]

The Board of Trade had definitely declined to cooperate with the Club or the Grange in any effort to reduce taxation, Thompson reported at the farmers' December meeting. Neither could the Grange join forces, he continued, because the matter of taxation had assumed a partisan character in the state.[70] Obviously, Thompson was referring to the sentence in the Declaration of Purposes, adopted by the National Grange, Patrons of Husbandry, on February 11, 1874: "No Grange if true to its obligations, can discuss political or religious questions, nor call political conventions nor nominate candidates, nor even discuss their merits in its meetings."[71] Although there was no restriction on the individual's participation in politics, Thompson even expressed doubt whether his membership in the Grange would allow him to take such action. In any case, he warned that members could not do singly all that might be accomplished.[72]

A "ripple of excitement" was created at the meeting by Vermeule's proposal that the Club petition the legislature to enact a law that thereafter the public offices in Middlesex County should be put up at auction and sold to the highest bidder, with the proceeds to be applied to the payment of county expenses. This would be one of the very best means of lightening taxes, he argued: *"It is better to sell offices in this manner than permit them to be bought in the criminal and thieving way they are secured now."* Although "no one had the courage to second the motion," one newspaper noted, several members intimated after adjournment that they would support the proposition, if it were to be renewed the following month.[73] Vermeule's proposal "seemed to meet with much approval," another local journal reported.[74]

Several days later at a meeting of the recently organized Tax Reform Association of New Brunswick, its membership adopted a report including a statement that application would be made at the next legislative session for passage of a statute providing for only one freeholder (instead of two) from each township in Middlesex County and continuing the election of one from each ward in New Brunswick.[75] This statement had not been incorporated into the report as originally presented, but was brought up at the meeting by Dr. J. L. Janeway and approved *unanimously*. With the text of applications for the other reform measures, it was referred to the Association's Council of Officers for the publication in the daily newspapers that was required in order to have the matters brought before the legislature.[76] To a member's suggestion of a plan for two freeholders from each of Middlesex County's three Assembly districts, John F. Babcock, senior editor of the New Brunswick *Daily Fredonian,* replied that such a law would be unconstitutional. He stated erroneously that New Jersey's Constitution contained a requirement that every township in the county be represented on the freeholder board.[77]

Apparently, Babcock learned that he was mistaken, because within a week his newspaper supported such an "unconstitutional" scheme to replace the existing freeholder boards. "The necessity of some change in the arrangement of these bodies is so universally apparent that nothing but the difficulty of agreeing upon an acceptable substitute for them prevents their being swept away altogether," the editorial began. It went on to suggest the election of "one County Commissioner from each Assembly District, and one from the County at-large, the latter being Chairman of the Board." They would be paid $5.00 instead of the current $2.00 rate, for every day of actual service, with no other payment or allowance, and would be relieved of a considerable part of the freeholders' work that was wasting both time and money. Every bridge costing less than $500 would be built and maintained by the *township* in which it was located. In New York something like this worked very well, readers were assured. Instead of having an entire freeholder board looking after a bridge costing at least $500, there would be a county engineer and surveyor, elected or appointed, who would (at the board's order) examine the ground, draw plans and specifications, supervise the erection of the structure, and certify its completion. In addition, he could settle "authoritatively" disputes about boundaries. For county buildings, an architect would be employed by the board and would receive the professional percentage for his service.[78]

After another week had elapsed, the *Fredonian* listed five general areas in which the advantages of adopting the "commissioner" plan would result. First, in *expense.* The board membership would be reduced from thirty to four, and fees allowed by law would be cut from $60 per day (30 × $2) to $20 (4 × $5), "a saving of four-fifths" from the actual current expenditure of $100. Second, in *efficiency.* Three or four men could be "made to agree with tolerable precision, while every one who is added to such a number is one more to object and consequently one more to convince." The promptness required in most cases of the board's business would become possible. Third, in *quality of members*. The office of freeholder was "the standing resource of the smallest kind of politicians . . . taken rather as a stepping-stone to that of Sheriff than for any other reason." For many years it had paid a "salary just sufficient to tempt its holders to steal, and they have stolen with remarkable unanimity." Reducing the number of freeholders by "nine-tenths" would "at least give the taxpayers an opportunity to save themselves if they will." Surely, one honest man of reasonable executive capacity could be found in each Assembly district at least once in three years. If the districts would select their best men, the saving to the county would be immense; but if the districts should insist upon the "present kind of stock," the less of it, the better. Fourth, in *continuity*. Because the terms of all incumbent freeholders then expired annually, a new board had "a fine opportunity to lay its shortcomings at the door of its predecessor." The county's governing body ought to be "continuous and perpetual." If its members, elected for as many years as there were Assembly districts in the county, were to leave office one by one, there would be "no break in responsibility." Fifth, in *responsibility* (in a judicial sense). How could a board of thirty members be punished? Courts stood "abashed" before them, and grand juries were composed largely of freeholders or their friends:

> To indict the Devil in a Grand Jury selected from among fallen angels by Belial or Mammon would be about as easy as to get anything more than a presentment against a body upon whom the officer who selects the Grand Jury [sheriff] depends for the allowance of his chief perquisites.

But the connections of only four men would not permeate a whole county; and these commissioners could be "brought to book."[79]

Support for the district plan was not lacking. "We are glad to say that this matter is gaining deserved prominence by discussion in the newspapers," observed a Burlington County weekly newspaper. Noting that for several years it had been urging a system of district-elected commissioners and one commissioner at large, the *New Jersey Mirror* declared that "each year's experience increases our faith in the wisdom of the proposed reform in the interest of the taxpayers."[80] In Hunterdon County, the taxpayers' Association met in Flemington and considered suggestions by a Judge Van Fleet to replace the current freeholder board (costing about $4,500) with three commissioners to be paid $500 each.[81]

Opposition to the district plan developed immediately. *The Independent Hour* of Woodbridge did not think that the scheme would be successful in Middlesex County "for local reasons, if for none other." But besides those considerations, "the proposed change looked at from any other standpoint is of doubtful advantage", it declared. The argument for efficiency of the proposed commissioners was countered with the charge that small bodies "are not truly representative in their character, and cannot understand the general wants of the several townships, unless by the appointment of subaltern officers." The argument for economy was disputed with the prediction that the commissioners would have to meet quite often, with other frequent calls upon their time, all at a per diem remuneration. Moreover, the county engineer's salary would be an additional expense. The aggregate cost to the county of the board of commissioners and the engineer might be less than the expense of the current freeholder board, "but while it would remove a burden from the County it seems to place it upon the townships, and after all it falls upon the people." Middlesex County's system was "good in itself if faithfully and honestly executed," according to the *Independent Hour.* "The Board of Chosen Freeholders is the Legislature of the County, and intended to be composed of representative men taken from the body of the people to confer the greater good to the greater number," it continued. But the suggested plan was "exactly the contrary to this system and centralizing in its tendencies." Besides, the same old corrupt influences could affect the board of commissioners. "Purge the present system of its corrupt practices and we have all the change necessary, in our opinion, for an efficient and economical administration of County affairs," the township newspaper argued.[82]

During the first week of 1878, the *Fredonian* reprinted the draft text of "An act to create a Board of County Commissioners in each of the Counties of this State," supplied by "several of our citizens" and embodying measures that it had been advocating in articles "for two or three weeks past."[83] In addition, an editorial in the Woodbridge newspaper was answered point by point. First, to the *Independent Hour's* observation that the New Brunswick journal had admitted the very satisfactory operation of the freeholder system in the past, the *Fredonian* declared: "The garment that fitted a baby to perfection, would make a very poor overcoat for him when he has become a man." The old scheme had worked well, "when we had half a dozen townships and New Brunswick was a village, half our territory a wilderness, and railroads and Life Insurance swindles and State Banks were unknown. . . ." Second, to the *Independent Hour's* objection on principle to municipal and county government by Commission (obviously the kind then appointed by the state for certain municipalities), the *Fredonian* replied: "Nobody is more thoroughly opposed to governing by Commissioners than we are." It was advocating "a Board of Audit which shall oversee and settle the accounts of the various executive officers of the county whose duties are, or ought to be, prescribed by law." Third, to the charge that the commission would be "not truly representative," the *Fredonian* held that such a body could "represent the better element of our people very thoroughly. The deuce of the present Board is, that they represent the worst element to perfection," the argument continued.[84]

"Almost our own proposition and the comment is in our line exactly," stated the *Fredonian* in making its fourth and fifth points. The *Independent Hour* had stated that the public might endorse, and good results might flow from, a law by which the commissioners should manage only the finances of the county and have jurisdiction in all matters of difference between the townships, and between Middlesex and any other county on the question of bridges. The Woodbridge weekly also asked why the townships could not control, construct, and repair their own bridges, thus relieving the county from any direct supervision or responsibility and producing better and cheaper bridges. Cost could be apportioned equitably, where a bridge involved two or more townships. There was "more of shadow than substance" in the idea of taxing the whole county for building bridges, because residents of the several townships used them to some degree. The "same logic might equally apply to the highways, which are taken care of exclusively by the townships."[85]

"One chief objection" to the *Fredonian*'s proposed plan for county government was the placing of a joint responsibility upon all the townships for bridges costing more than $500. "This might work great injustice, for it affords a decided opportunity for 'little jobs' and 'nice corners,' " argued the *Independent Hour*. To this sixth item the *Fredonian* answered: "We do not see the possibility of avoiding this exactly by providing a County Engineer and Surveyor. Large bridges must be built by the County, there is no help for it." Noting the Woodbridge newspaper's admission that if law enforcement could not remedy a corrupt system, then the system must be changed, the *Fredonian* made its seventh point by querying: "Who can bring a clean thing out of an unclean?" And last, the *Fredonian* agreed with the *Independent Hour* that Middlesex County had nothing to hope for by reducing the number of freeholders in each township (and ward) to one, as Somerset had done. "Eight or nine counties, we think, have tried 'to kill the devil by cutting off his tail' in this way, and he is an astonishingly lively corpse in every one of them," residents of the county seat were advised.[86]

On the day of this editorial, Capt. Samuel Blish, newly elected Master of Pioneer Grange No. 1, Patrons of Husbandry,[87] presented several resolutions which the Middlesex Farmers' Club agreed to discuss at a special meeting the following week. They recommended that the county clerk, surrogate, and sheriff be made salaried officers; that the "Board of Chosen Freeholders as now existing should be dispensed with, and one Commissioner be chosen from each Assembly District to perform their duties at a stated salary, without perquisites"; that state Supreme Court judges should be allowed no fees or other compensation in addition to their salaries; and that the offices of county or lay judges be abolished.[88] "Among the forty or fifty gentlemen present [at the special meeting of January 14, 1878], many of whom took part in the discussion, not one had a single word to say in favor of the Freeholder system," the *Fredonian* pointed out. Middlesex County's director of the freeholder board, J. V. D. Christopher, "delivered some telling blows at coordinate branches of the County administration, and at the individual dishonesty which is at the bottom of our troubles in this matter"; he showed that the Court of Sessions, the lay judges, the jail, and the debt were largely responsible for the increase in taxation. But Christopher "never even insinuated an opinion that he thought the Freeholder system defensible." (And, the newspaper asked, "When the Director of the Board abandons it to its fate, what can be hoped for it from others?")[89] A. S. Meyrick noted that a bill similar to that already published in the *Fredonian* had been before the legislature for two years, with the prospects of passage growing more favorable. Even if the Club could not have this kind of measure enacted immediately, there would be "such an agitation as greatly to increase the chance of its passing another year." The members approved the resolutions without amendment, with one if not both of the negative votes cast by freeholders. On motion of Thompson and at Meyrick's suggestion, a committee was appointed to prepare a bill embodying the objectives of the resolutions and to submit it at the following week's meeting.[90]

A number of prominent citizens interested in tax reduction were in attendance with the farmers on January 21. The Committee (Christopher, Blish, Vermeule) submitted nine resolutions signed by each of its members;[91] a tenth without the signature of Freeholder Board Director Christopher read:

Resolved, That the Board of Chosen Freeholders as it now exists, be abolished, and one Freeholder be elected from each Assembly District, to serve for one, two, or three years; and it shall be incumbent upon them, at their first meeting, to draw for the length of each member's term; after the first election for Freeholders they shall be elected for three years each; those having but one year to serve shall be the Director for that year; the Freeholders shall receive each $3 per day, when employed, and mileage at five cents per mile, and no other perquisites whatever for their services.[92]

With very little debate the resolution was adopted; and upon Meyrick's motion, the Club voted to have a copy of all the resolutions sent to each member of the legislature who represented Middlesex.[93] Meyrick then asked for the reading of a memorial to the Senate and General Assembly that he presented from "petitioners, residents and taxpayers in the counties of Middlesex and Somerset." It characterized the existing freeholder system as "cumbrous, uncertain and expensive, besides opening avenues to corruption, which are safely and easily followed in nearly every county in this State." The demanded remedy was enactment of "laws reducing the number of the members of these Boards very greatly, and strictly prescribing their offices, duties and emoluments." Bridges costing less than $300 could be "built and repaired better and cheaper by the townships in which they are located then by the counties at-large," and a law permitting this should be enacted. An amended version of the memorial was adopted, and a committee of Meyrick and two others was appointed to present it and the resolutions to the lawmakers.[94] In addition, the Club's members were requested to use their influence in Trenton to secure attention to the subject. In conclusion, a resolution was adopted appointing a committee composed of J. R. Russell, Captain Blish, and Lambert to attend that evening's meeting of the Tax Reform Association.[95]

About half of the one hundred persons attending that meeting were visitors in sympathy with the objects of the Association. After the Chairman of the Council read aloud the four reform bills that had been drawn up by an attorney in accordance with the notice of application approved by the membership in December, he gave assurances that the text of the freeholder measure was strictly constitutional. It required qualified voters "in the County of Middlesex to elect for each township in said County but one chosen freeholder instead of two as now authorized by law. . . ."[96] Speaking of the proposal of the Middlesex Farmers' Club for three commissioners was Russell, who had been re-elected earlier in the evening to office on the Council of the Association. He asked for the sense of the meeting as to which of the two plans would be preferred. One member declared that the three-commissioner scheme was working admirably in Cumberland County, Maine, with a population of between 80,000 and 90,000 (including the City of Portland with 30,000).[97] The President remarked that it was probable that the legislature would refuse to pass the proposed special law for Middlesex, but would enact a general statute as the result of a "general movement" to reduce the number of persons on county governing boards to three or one from each Assembly district. If such a system of representation should be authorized by the legislature, the Chairman of the Council then moved, the City of New Brunswick should heartily endorse it. The Association adopted his motion unanimously.[98]

The resolution approved by the Middlesex Farmers' Club had been "numerously signed" and forwarded to the county's senator, George C. Ludlow, reported Captain Blish at the March meeting. Expressing his approval of the farmers' spirit and agreeing with most of the details, the senator commented that some, but not all, could be accomplished at once.[99]

In 1879 taxation continued to interest the Middlesex Farmers' Club. The subject was "debated with an earnestness that ought to be productive of a rich harvest," the press reported about a special January meeting, lasting nearly three hours, that was attended by an unusually large number of members and outsiders.[100] One speaker insisted that there was sufficient justification for agitation, because taxes were then two to three times as high as they had been twenty years earlier. The county ought to receive some of the money that was going to its officials, he complained, if reports were true that a number of them were receiving $5,000, $8,000, or $10,000 a year. Another said that because the cost of living was as low as it had ever been, there was no reason why the salaries of public officials should be kept at the same figure as during high-priced wartimes. When salaries had been more moderate, officeholders were servants of the public, who were eager to please and satisfied with reasonable pay. But they had become masters of the people, because they could afford to buy their way into office.[101] To Thompson's demand for remedies, rather than further talk of the evils of taxation, Captain Blish[102] replied that he had already caused to be prepared and printed three bills tending to reduce taxation. The one providing that each county elect a single freeholder from each Assembly district was then amended on Meyrick's motion to provide that there be at least three freeholders in every county. After rejection of an amendment to have only one freeholder from each township, the draft bill was adopted. Of special interest to some members was the provision that "each Township and City shall build and keep in repair all bridges within their limits costing less than three hundred dollars." That was held essential to the success of the effort to reduce the number of freeholders. Blish, Meyrick, and others were appointed as a committee to present the Club's resolutions to the legislature.[103]

The measure was introduced the following week by Isaac L. Martin (R-Middlesex) without Meyrick's amendment, as Assembly Bill No. 86. Its preface included a declaration that the "present system of one or more chosen freeholders from each township and ward makes an explosive and unwieldy body to transact the business of the county"; it proclaimed that "the curtailment of county expenses has become a necessity." There would be one freeholder elected in November from each Assembly district, serving a three-year term (staggered with the other freeholders' terms), and receiving $3.00 for each day's work and also travel expenses at the rate of five cents per mile. Twice laid over, the Martin bill was withdrawn by its sponsor after two weeks.[104] In the interim, the Middlesex Farmers' Club continued Blish's committee, after accepting his report that the legislators were speaking favorably of retrenchment, with few in Trenton endorsing the proposed change.[105]

The need for a smaller county governing body was again expressed in May 1879 by the Middlesex Farmers' Club in both individual and collective judgments at a hearing of a commission appointed by Democratic Governor George B. McClellan to prepare a system of general laws for municipalities. Testifying in New Brunswick, G. W. DeVoe advocated the election of three freeholders in each Assembly district and one freeholder at large, none of them eligible for reelection for a second successive term. Three freeholders should be enough for an entire county, declared Vermeule, who objected *in toto* to the existing system of representation. Captain Blish presented the pertinent resolutions that had been adopted by the Club "some two years ago."[106]

PROPOSALS FOR AT-LARGE ELECTIONS AND MINORITY REPRESENTATION

At-large election of a three-member board of commissioners in each county was preferred outside Middlesex. Assembly Bill No.

308 of Silas DeWitt (D-Warren) provided in 1878 that the commissioners were to be chosen by the entire county electorate for staggered three-year terms and were to receive $3.00 for each day's service. Further consideration of the measure was indefinitely postponed after its second reading, when the sentiment of the Assembly was indicated by the passage of two amendments excepting Essex (the most populous county) and Cape May (the least populous) from the section incorporating counties. The first was carried, 29 to 23; the second, 27 to 21.[107] In 1879, DeWitt reintroduced the plan as Assembly Bill No. 45, and an amended version lost, 8 to 39. Only three Republicans voted for passage; two from Somerset and one from Morris. With twenty-five Republicans recorded in opposition, failure to pass this type of small board bill could not be attributed to the Democrats.[108]

Between actions on these two bills there was consideration of another introduced by John C. Schenck (R-Somerset). On January 21, 1879, he introduced Senate Bill No. 37, also replacing the system of freeholder representation by wards and municipalities with a board of only three freeholders to be elected *at large* within each county in November. But at the first election all the members would be chosen, each citizen voting for two persons, thus securing *minority representation.* The board members so chosen were to decide among themselves at their organization meeting who should serve for one, two, and three years, respectively. At each subsequent election in November, one person was to be chosen for a three-year term to take the place of the one whose term would expire. At any election at which a successor to the minority representative was to be chosen, no person belonging to the same political party as the majority representatives on the freeholder board would be eligible for election. Furthermore, no two freeholders could reside in the same ward or township. In counties of not more than 20,000 inhabitants, the annual salary would be $400; in counties with more than 20,000 and fewer than 75,000, $600; and in counties having more than 75,000, $800. Each board could employ a civil engineer at an annual salary not to exceed $1,000.

"The objections to such a bill are too numerous to mention," remarked the *Newark Daily Advertiser.* Taking the case of Essex as an example, the editorial pointed out that a three-member board "would be required to do more work than any men are capable of." There were "not hours enough in the day, nor days enough in the year, for them to act as anything more than a Board of Audit." Every member "would necessarily be on a dozen committees involving varied qualifications in the transaction of business and, often, real scholarship in the social sciences whose practical working they are to direct." In the *Advertiser's* judgment, neither the proposed $800 salary, nor even $8,000, could find a man competent to do the work.[109]

Even with the large Essex board capable of a liberal subdivision of labor, the argument continued, freeholder duties were found so onerous by many members that it was "not always easy to find good candidates to take the place of those who retire." The visits of freeholder committees to county institutions were "frequent, usually weekly, and not formalities." Accounts were regularly inspected; decisions on the need for repairs or alterations were made, "the discipline observed and enforced"; and then the action taken discussed in reports made to the entire county governing body. "This, with the general finance of the Board, occasions all the work that can reasonably be expected from men having other avocations in life," the *Advertiser* declared. Despite the many burdensome responsibilities of a freeholder board, it was regarded as "a local legislature . . . without executive functions." The newspaper contended that the "proposed Ring of three men would inevitably swamp all legislative action in executive function."[110]

Moreover, the three-cornered system of choosing the board was regarded as "an official recognition of the claims of the party to patronage." The people would really have no part in choosing their freeholders, when their nomination by a convention was the equivalent of election. Then the trio themselves "would be the sole arbiters of a great patronage." Also, "In a very compact little Board of three, with nobody to audit their receipts and disbursements, the temptation to steal would be irresistible."[111]

But the existing system was defended on the ground that "the office of Freeholder is regarded, in the townships always, and in the wards to some extent, as one of local trust and honor, a genuine dignity and a pleasant association." The greater care exercised in the townships in electing their best men increased the "disparity" of representation between the two members from each of these municipalities and the single member elected by each ward in the cities.[112]

Five points favoring the Schenck bill appeared in a letter reprinted by the *New Brunswick Daily Fredonian*, which "in the main" approved them. First, Senate Bill No. 37 was economical. Money would be saved directly on salaries and expenses; and also indirectly, because three men would have increased individual responsibility. They would be accountable to the entire county, rather than to a single township "which they may hold in their pockets." Since only one member at a time would be chosen after the first election, the people would be careful to examine a candidate's qualifications and character. Second, a fixed salary was "desirable because it does away with the odium and possible abuse which is attached to the per diem mode of payment, and makes it possible to get our best men to serve ..." Third, it was "both just and fair that a minority should be represented in our municipal affairs." Aside from that, a minority representative would be "a great check on the existence of rings...." Fourth, the proposed discretionary power of the freeholder board to appoint a civil engineer could prove useful in the building of bridges. Fifth, the change of election time to the fall would suit all parts of the state, and people would be better able to attend to such an important election.[113]

The bill was amended in the Senate to exempt counties with more than 100,000 population (Essex, Hudson), and, for setting salaries, to extend the group of counties with fewer than 20,000 inhabitants (Cape May, Ocean, Atlantic) to include other counties with fewer than 25,000 people (Salem, Sussex, Gloucester). In this enlarged category a freeholder's salary was lowered to $300 per year from $400 in the original text.[114] But on the following day the motion of Garret A. Hobart (R-Passaic) to reconsider the affirmative vote for the changes was agreed to in the upper chamber, and the amendments were withdrawn.[115] On the very next day Francis M. Ward (D-Sussex) offered an amendment providing that the act would not apply to those counties having a population according to the previous (1875) census of between 14,000 and 54,000. The proposed change could not be considered partisan, since the sixteen counties to be exempted were equally divided in the Senate between both major parties; and of the remaining counties, three were Republican (Atlantic, Cape May, Essex), and two were Democratic (Hudson, Ocean). As soon as the Senate agreed to the amendment, Schenck withdrew his bill.[116]

Nevertheless, the press could note the next day that the bill "had some excellent features." Articles included a financial statement, like this one supplied by Senator Schenck, for eight counties in North and East Jersey:[117]

	Expense Under Present System	Expense Under Schenck's Bill	Expense of Engineer Included	Amount Saved
Hunterdon	$ 6,179.89	$ 1,800	$ 2,800	$ 3,379.89
Mercer	4,946.90	1,800	2,800	2,146.90

	Expense Under Present System	Expense Under Schenck's Bill	Expense of Engineer Included	Amount Saved
Middlesex	$ 6,189.94	$ 1,800	$ 2,800	$ 3,389.94
Monmouth	2,861.43	1,800	2,800	61.43
Somerset	4,150.00	1,800	2,800	1,350.00
Union	4,113.26	1,800	2,800	1,313.26
Warren	4,508.00	1,800	2,800	1,708.00
Sussex	1,367.40	900	—	467.40

Loading Schenck's measure with so many amendments that it would be practically useless was "no fair way to treat the bill," argued one legislative correspondent for a New Brunswick Republican newspaper. Senators Hobart and Ward had a perfect right to oppose its enactment, "but courtesy would have demanded that it should have been done in the usual manner by letting it come up on its merits and then killing it by a majority vote if they could effect it." Although Somerset supported the bill, "Ocean didn't want it, Burlington ditto, and South Jersey generally...."[118] Yet two months later the same correspondent ("Brunswick") could attribute the bill's defeat to partisan rivalries. This time, without mentioning the views of South Jersey Republicans or of Hobart, their party colleague from Passaic, he could state that the "opposition mostly came from the Democratic side of the Senate, especially Hudson, Hunterdon, Sussex and Bergen howling against it."[119] But the legislative reporter ("Williams") for Jersey City's Republican newspaper had stated earlier that the Schenck bill "was a measure which in Hudson County at least would have been most acceptable." Furthermore, he noted that its Democratic senator, Rudolph F. Rabe, had "advocated the bill strongly."[120]

In February 1880 a "Committee of Experts" that had been appointed by a Judge Dalrimple at the request of the Taxpayers Association of Somerset County to investigate irregularities in county government reported what the resolutions committee called "a state of things even more deplorable than was anticipated." Among the resolutions adopted was an endorsement of "a bill which we learn [erroneously] is about to be introduced by Senator Schenck, changing the form of our local government from a Board of nine Freeholders to three Freeholders, to be elected by the county with a fixed salary," and forbidden to accept any other fee or reward.[121]

Township Representation Halved in Several Counties

Nevertheless, 1879 did see a reduction in the number of freeholders. On March 4 Governor George B. McClellan signed Assembly Bill No. 179, providing that in every county containing between 25,000 and 80,000 inhabitants there should be elected just one freeholder for each township and in every city or ward the same number of freeholders as had been previously authorized by law.[122] Introduced by Isaac L. Martin (R-Middlesex), who "worked most assiduously"[123] to secure its passage, the measure applied to his own county and to twelve others: Bergen, Burlington, Camden, Cumberland, Hunterdon, Mercer, Monmouth, Morris, Passaic, Somerset, Union, and Warren. But only the two-freeholder-per-township system of Middlesex, Cumberland, and Morris would be changed; the others were already electing one freeholder from each township. By a bipartisan vote of 33 to 5 (nineteen Republicans and fourteen Democrats to three Republicans and two Democrats), the Assembly passed the bill.[124] Its "devious passage through the Senate" was caused not by any apparent desire to kill it, noted a New Brunswick newspaper, but by some senators who were "exceedingly fearful that their counties would be smuggled under the provisions of the bill." Shortly after ten Republicans and nine Democrats passed the Martin bill, with no recorded opposition, that vote was reconsidered. The senators "skirmished around in a very lively manner urging upon the Senate the necessity of such amendments as would securely exclude them."[125] Accordingly, the minimum and maximum of the population figures in the bill were made those "ascertained by the *last* [1875] census."[126] By this means, apparently, the populations of Gloucester (24,486) and Sussex (24,010) were removed from imminent danger of having their freeholder systems changed. The upper chamber passed the bill, nine Republicans and six Democrats in favor; and two Democrats opposed. With no negative votes, a bipartisan majority (nineteen Republicans and twenty Democrats) in the Assembly passed the amended version.[127]

But only two days after the Martin bill became law, Assembly Bill No. 173, which Caleb C. Pancoast (R-Gloucester) had introduced a month earlier[128] for one freeholder from each township and ward throughout the state, was amended in the Senate to apply only to those counties with a population by the last state census of between 24,400 and 36,000 inhabitants. The legislature's intention in amending the bill was simply to add Gloucester (24,486) to the list of counties with single-freeholder townships. Within the specified population range, the other counties had been included in the Martin law: Bergen (35,516); Cumberland (35,511); and Somerset (27,453). Before the amendment, Pancoast's general bill for all counties had passed the Assembly by a bipartisan majority, 36 to 8. The amended version was passed with no recorded opposition in either house.[129] Governor McClellan approved the measure.[130]

The situation created by this general law with special application to a single county was further complicated in 1880 by passage of a bill to repeal it; the minimum population figure was raised from 24,400 to 25,000. Senate Bill No. 13, sponsored by Gloucester's Republican John F. Bodine, passed the Senate, 19 to 1; and the Assembly, 41 to 0.[131] But this bipartisan measure was vetoed by Governor McClellan, who had been "advised by the Attorney-General that by recent decisions of the supreme court this bill conflicts with the constitution" (presumably as special legislation regulating the internal affairs of towns and counties).[132] A bipartisan Senate vote upheld the veto, 0 to 18.[133] To insure that the residents of Gloucester County's townships could vote under a constitutionally acceptable statute and to avoid illegal proceedings by the freeholder board, its director addressed a letter to the board's solicitor concerning the constitutionality of the unrepealed law of 1879 that halved the membership of Gloucester's governing body. In the light of the recent court decisions, the solicitor concluded, the act was unconstitutional; and his opinion was endorsed by the Attorney General. Consequently, each Gloucester township was to disregard the 1879 law and continue to elect *two* freeholders.[134]

ATTEMPTS TO REGULATE MEMBERSHIP OF CERTAIN CITIES BY "GENERAL" STATUTES

The constitutional prohibition against special legislation prompted devious apportionment schemes under the guise of general statutes. Late in the 1878 legislative session, a partisan plan to increase the number of Newark's freeholders was challenged, because it depended on earlier legislation of doubtful constitutionality. On April 5 Democratic Governor McClellan signed Assembly Bill No. 422, passed by a strict party vote, thirty-three Democrats to twenty-four Republicans, in the lower chamber; and eleven Democrats to seven Republicans, in the Senate.[135] This act provided for the annual election of *three* freeholders from every ward in every city where the ward lines then or thereafter should correspond with the Assembly district lines in such city, and where no Assembly district in such city should embrace any territory outside such city. [136] Obvi-

ously intended to apply only to Newark, the measure would increase
that municipality's freeholders from fifteen to twenty-one, with
twenty-five for the remainder of Essex County. But such an arrangement was based upon two laws that had been approved by the
Governor on April 3 and 5: Chapter 177 (a supplement to the 1871
reapportionment act) creating seven Assembly districts wholly
within Newark; and Chapter 196, an act *requiring* the mayor and
common council in any city with more than two Assembly districts
where all the Assembly districts within such city were completely
and exclusively within its city limits to divide the city into wards
corresponding in number and boundaries to such Assembly
districts.[137] Under either of these two acts, the whole territory of
Newark would be embraced in seven districts, all of them exclusively within the city limits.[138] Both laws were intended to accomplish what Chapter 10, approved February 15, had failed to do. That
act, amending the charter of Newark and changing the lines of
eleven of that municipality's fifteen wards, was special legislation,
and therefore unconstitutional, according to a March 18 decision of
New Jersey's Supreme Court.[139]

Because they were public acts containing no provision concerning the time that they were to take effect, the Supreme Court held on
July 1, the two laws (for Assembly districts and wards) approved in
April could not go into effect until July 4, as provided by a statute
governing such situations. Until that time, Newark could not answer
the description of a city containing more than two Assembly districts
where all the Assembly districts in the city were completely within
its limits; and there was no duty imposed upon its common council to
divide the city into wards. It was unnecessary in this case, said the
Court, to consider the question of the constitutionality of special
legislation regulating the internal affairs of a city.[140]

Eight days later, the Court of Errors and Appeals began hearing
argument on the appeal of the case involving Chapter 10, the original
Newark ward act that had been held unconstitutional in the opinion
of a lower court. "By a tacit agreement the constitutionality of this
whole class of legislation [regulating the internal affairs of cities] was
argued before the Court of Errors, the object being to obtain, if
possible, a decision which will set the question at rest," noted one
leading newspaper.[141] In December the Court held that the constitutional provision prohibiting special legislation regulating "the internal affairs of towns and counties" embraced cities and that the
Newark ward statute of February 15 changing the boundary lines of
eleven wards was unconstitutional.[142] The number of freeholders
elected from each of Newark's wards was not increased.

Senate Bill No. 152 of 1881, introduced by William H. Francis (R-Essex), provided that "in all cities of the state where there is *now* elected but one chosen freeholder to represent said city, there shall hereafter be elected one chosen freeholder from each ward in said city [italics added]." The obvious intent was to assign an additional freeholder to the City of Salem, the only single-freeholder city that had wards (two). After passing the Senate, 17 to 2, and the Assembly, 35 to 0,[143] the bill was vetoed by Governor George C. Ludlow. He noted that limitation in application to such cities as "now" elect one member for the whole city had been held by the New Jersey Supreme Court in 1880 to make the law special and therefore unconstitutional.[144] On the motion of Quinton Keasby (R-Salem), the bill was referred to the Attorney General for his opinion concerning the measure's constitutionality.[145] After his reply the following week that the bill was "unconstitutional for the reasons given by the Governor in his message to the Senate, returning said bill without his signature," only Keasby and Isaac T. Nichols (R-Cumberland) voted to override the veto; sixteen supported the Governor with their negative votes.[146]

On the day that the veto of Senate Bill No. 152 was upheld, Francis sponsored another measure that would assign two freeholders to the city of Salem as part of a *general* plan. Senate Bill No. 258 required that not fewer than two freeholders be assigned to *every* city in the state, provided that "whenever any city shall under the provisions of this act, be represented by two freeholders, they shall not be elected from the same ward." By the time it reached third reading, the application of the bill was restricted. One amendment provided that "any city within a township, which township, as such, is represented in the board of chosen freeholders of the county in which such city is located [e.g., City of Burlington] shall not be represented as a city in said board of chosen freeholders."[147] The Senate also adopted a change providing that "any city which has not been divided into wards shall be deemed to constitute one ward for purposes of this act." Passed 15 to 0 in the upper chamber, the bill was lost in the Assembly, 18 to 21, but was subsequently passed, 33 to 4, on the same day, and approved by the Governor within another twenty-four hours.[148]

COMMISSION ON GENERAL LAWS FOR MUNICIPALITIES

In February 1880 the Commission on General Laws for Municipalities, appointed by Governor McClellan the previous year, submitted its report to him and the legislature. One of three accompanying bills recommended by the members was introduced as Senate Bill No. 158, "An act for the government of the counties of this state," read a first time, ordered to second reading, and referred to the Committee on Municipal Corporations.[149] All resort to the system of classifying counties and cities had been avoided in the drafting of general laws by the Commission. That body had "concluded that the rulings of the courts on this question are so indefinite as to make them unreliable," noted the press, "and they did not care to take the chance of having their year's work set aside on objections to any method of classification they might adopt."[150]

The proposed general county law provided for one freeholder to be elected in each township and ward, except in those counties (Hudson) in which freeholders were elected by Assembly districts, where such system was to continue. Likewise, at-large election of the director could continue where it already had been authorized (Hudson), but elsewhere the freeholder boards were to elect their own directors. Each member would receive $2.00 for every day's work. Refusing to attend stated or special meetings would entail an $8.00 fine. Every freeholder board was charged with raising money to defray court expenses; to pay the county debt; to maintain the insane in state or county asylums; to pay "for the maintenance of the poor in those counties that have assumed the burthen thereof"; to maintain prisoners in county jails; to build, purchase or repair poorhouses, jails, court houses, and other public buildings and grounds and bridges; to prosecute and defend the rights of the county; to defray the public and other necessary charges; and to execute "all the legal purposes, objects, business and affairs of such county, as they, or a major part of them, shall deem adequate or proper. . . ."

"Numerous improvements in detail and in the matter of checks in financial matters"[151] appeared in Senate Bill No. 158. Appropriations were to be specific, divided into classes, and no moneys were to be spent in any class or sub-class beyond the amounts specifically appropriated for that category. In case a freeholder should vote for or incur any liability beyond the amount actually raised for any purpose, he would become "personally bound therefor to the person with whom it shall be contracted." The whole amount of money appropriated, contracted, or expended in any one year was not to exceed three-fourths of 1 percent of the gross valuation of the taxable property in the county. No money was to be borrowed in anticipation of taxes for longer than nine months, and then not more than half the amount of the appropriation. The county auditor was to examine the county collector's books quarterly, or more often, if he should deem it necessary. Additional checks on the collector and the auditor were "very stringent, and if observed will render peculation almost impossible," observed one newspaper.[152]

SPECIAL JOINT COMMITTEE

Assembly Joint Resolution No. 8, postponing consideration of both the report of the Commission on General Laws for Municipalities and the report of the special tax commission established in 1879, was changed by a Republican Assembly to a *concurrent* resolution, requiring no signature of Democratic Governor McClellan. The preamble noted that the reports "were presented so late in the present session as to prevent the due and careful consideration which should be given" to such important measures. Provision was made for the appointment of a committee of three senators (to be named by the Senate president) and five assemblymen (to be named by the speaker) to examine the reports of the two commissions that had been appointed by the Governor and present its own recommendations on the first day of the next session (1881). For general distribution to the people, 6,000 copies of each of the bills submitted by the two commissions were to be furnished to the legislators.[153] Adoption of the concurrent resolution in the Assembly followed.[154] On the next day in the upper chamber, Hudson's Democratic Senator Rudolph F. Rabe offered a substitute resolution postponing adjournment for one week in order that due consideration might be given the bills.[155] "The absurdity of attempting to do this in even three weeks was shown by Senators Hobart [R-Passaic] and Francis [R-Essex], and the necessity of hearing more definitely from the people on these measures was urged," Newark's Republican newspaper observed.[156] By an absolutely partisan vote again, eight Democrats to twelve Republicans, a change in the resolution was defeated, and the original wording was adopted.[157]

Once more, an attempt to introduce uniformity ran into conflict with the special interests of individual counties. Among the several measures reported by the Special Committee on January 17, 1881, was one introduced that day as Senate Bill No. 14, providing for one freeholder to be elected by the voters in every township and ward throughout the state. In an effort to maintain the two-freeholder per-township system in his own county, John F. Bodine (R-Gloucester) moved, on the bill's second reading, to amend that section by adding the words, "except in such townships and wards of cities of this state where the number is otherwise fixed by law, and in these townships and wards such memberships shall continue as now fixed."[158] There followed "quite a fiery debate."[159] William B. Deacon (R-Burlington), chairman of the Special Committee, opposed the Bodine amendment on the principle that the law would not then be general, but special. Adoption of the change, he argued, would lead to other amendments of a special character in this and the other general bills. In answer, Bodine noted some special features in the bill, particularly in the seventh section, referring to the offices of county collector and county auditor. There were several counties where there was no county auditor, he pointed out. Deacon explained that this was no fault of his; he had tried to make the measure uniform in this respect, but the majority of the committee had overruled him. Speaking in favor of the Bodine amendment was Benjamin A. Vail (R-Union), who apparently did not wish to see the number of his county's freeholders increased, as individual ward representation would do. He offered a substitute amendment to give each Assembly district in the state three freeholders who should serve three-year terms.[160] John J. Gardner (R-Atlantic) asked how that would do in a county (like his own) where there was only one Assembly district. The board would consist of only three members, and they would be unable to discharge their duties properly.[161] Supporting this position was Waters B. Miller (D-Cape May), whose constituency would also be entitled to only three freeholders under such a scheme. Vail's substitute was defeated,[162] and then the Bodine amendment also lost, 8 to 12, with six Republicans favoring passage and nine opposed.[163]

Debate followed on the provision in Senate Bill No. 14 for paying a freeholder $2.00 a day for discharging his regular duties and $3.00 a day for attending board meetings. To replace the latter, Bodine made a motion (subsequently withdrawn) for payment of travel expenses.[164] Sewell offered a substitute calling for $25 annual compensation, remarking on the frequent complaints of exorbitant charges, some as high as $700 and $800, and even $1,000. The time had come to end per diem allowances and to secure a better class of representatives by making the service a matter of honor, rather than profit, he argued. If there were no compensation at all, that would be the result.[165] Opposing this point of view as an insult to men who sometimes had to travel forty miles to attend board meetings, Hobart expressed satisfaction that the annual salary given to each freeholder in his own county of Passaic had resulted in a better class of men who faithfully discharged their duties. He proposed to amend the Sewell amendment by fixing the annual salary at $150. This change was accepted by Sewell, who stated that he had no objection to giving a respectable salary.[166] But the next day Hobart withdrew his amendment and offered another that Sewell's amendment for a $25 salary, still before the Senate, should not apply to counties (Hudson, Passaic, Camden) in which the salary was fixed by law. After a "spirited discussion," the upper chamber agreed to the change, 12 to 5.[167] When Bodine reoffered his amendment to reimburse freeholders for expenses, it was opposed by some as affording an excellent opportunity for defrauding the county.[168] "So telling was their opposition," the press noted, that only two Senators voted for the change (Bodine and Gardner).[169]

On the same day, Elijah J. Paxton (D-Hudson) moved to amend the bill so that the election of a freeholder in each township and ward would apply "except in those counties wherein chosen freeholders are elected by assembly districts, where the boards of chosen freeholders shall be elected as now provided by law." Without adoption of such amendment, he told the Senate, Hudson's freeholders would be increased to more than fifty. By a vote of 13 to 3, the change was agreed to. The negative votes and those not cast at all were Republican, but that party contributed seven votes to the majority.[170]

During discussion on the bill, James C. Youngblood (R-Morris) moved that further discussion of the bill be postponed until the Senators could find out whether any existing act was modified by it,[171] and he "then went on to ridicule the notion that the Legislature would ever succeed in framing a strictly general law." The version of Senate Bill No. 14, as enacted, he said, would have to be entitled "A general act for the government of counties, providing that it does not conflict with the existing laws of any county." William J. Sewell (R-Camden) disagreed. He argued that although the diversity of interests according to the different localities might prevent passage of a law that would be absolutely uniform in its effects, the legislature could arrive at something that would closely approximate that idea. Youngblood withdrew his motion to postpone.[172]

Two more attempts were made that same day in the Senate to change the bill's provision for the distribution of freeholders. John J. Gardner (R-Atlantic) offered an amendment deleting the important provision for electing one freeholder from each ward and township and requiring that each freeholder board be "elected in such manner and at such times as is now provided by law." Eight Republicans voted against the change, but six Republicans and four Democrats agreed to it; and with the new text the bill was ordered to a third reading.[173] Later, after successfully moving for a reconsideration of that vote, Sewell moved to amend the first section of the act by adding the words, *"Provided,* that cities in any county where there is a freeholder to each township, shall have one freeholder to each ward." This was designed in favor of the City of Salem, which had yet to be assigned a freeholder. Union's Vail said that this amendment would increase the number of freeholders in his county and he must therefore oppose it. The amendment lost, 3 to 11. Only those senators (all Republicans) from Salem, Atlantic, and Camden favored it; nine Republicans voted negatively.[174]

After a week's delay, William H. Francis (R-Essex) obtained unanimous consent for reconsideration of the vote by which Senate Bill No. 14 had been ordered to third reading; and on his motion the bill was ordered to lie over for five more days.[175] Then, on the advice of several other senators, he moved that the measure be "referred to a special committee for the purpose of reconstruction." The amendments were to be drawn up in a more constitutional form, and if necessary, new amendments would be added. Because some of the amendments already adopted were certainly "unconstitutional" and would kill the bill, Deacon hoped that they would be omitted. But Francis denied any intention to destroy the measure, and his motion carried; he, Deacon, and Gardner were appointed by Senate President Hobart to membership on the committee.[176] "There was a tendency that was quite apparent among the senators to laugh as this disposition was made of the much-boasted general law," observed one correspondent. "To thus refer it back again to a committee, in order to give it a semblance of constitutionality which its champions do not claim that it really possesses," he continued, "is a pretty fair acknowlegement that the general laws are going to be a failure."[177]

When the report was presented the following week, it recommended deletion of the clause: ". . . and the said corporation shall consist of a board elected in such manner and at such times as is now provided by law." The change was agreed to, leaving the bill with no specific scheme for apportioning freeholders; those "elected in their respective counties in the manner now or hereafter prescribed by law in this state and their successors in office" were simply declared to be "a body politic and corporate in law by the names by which they are now entitled respectively." With twenty votes cast in its favor, Senate Bill No. 14 was sent to the Assembly.[178] Burlington's Deacon, who had not signed the report of the special committee, was the only senator to vote negatively on the question of the bill's passage. He maintained that the measure was no longer general.[179]

The final text of the bill as passed by the upper chamber was discussed in a leading newspaper. In answer to a charge that it had not made the measure intelligible to its readers, the *Evening Journal*'s Trenton correspondent acknowledged his failure. But he maintained "that there is no lawyer or set of lawyers in this or any other State, including Philadelphia, that could do it." Then he recounted the history of Senate Bill No. 14:

> It was drawn by a Commission, referred to a Joint Committee, who amended it right and left and reported it to the Senate, who referred it to the Committee on Municipal Corporations, who amended it a great deal and reported it to the Senate, who amended it some more and recommended it to a special committee, who did some more amending and reported it to the Senate, who tackled it again this morning and amended it a great deal more, and it is now in the printer's hands. The worst of it is that about all the amendments have been amended, which makes it pretty well mixed up.[180]

In the Assembly, after the Clerk had finished reading the bill "amidst the yarns [*sic*] and dozing of the members," J. Herbert Potts (R-Hudson) moved that the office of director at large be stricken from the measure in order to abolish that position in his home county. Allan L. McDermott (D-Hudson) opposed this, arguing that a supervisory officer should be elected outside of the board altogether and should be "amenable" to the whole county rather than to only a portion of it. In the latter case, McDermott said, the director would use his influence to be reelected. Potts then spoke of needless expenditures under the Democratic incumbent, Edward F. McDonald, and charged that this officer had paid no attention to the law taking away his veto power. Hudson's freeholders were as competent to elect a director as were board members of every other county in the state, Potts maintained; for it was useless to pay a man $2,500 a year for doing nothing. McDermott retorted by pointing out that the salary was only $1,000. Furthermore, he continued, the act divesting the director of his veto power had been declared unconstitutional by a Judge Knapp, who approved of McDonald's course.[181] After McDermott's "able defense of the Director, clearly proving it was in the interest of the taxpayers to continue his office," reported a Democratic journal's correspondent, the Potts amendment was lost. Subsequently, the bill was "numerously" amended.[182]

The amended bill passed the Assembly with the support of

twenty-one Republicans and fifteen Democrats; only two Republicans and two Democrats opposed it.[183] Upon the measure's return to the Senate, that body agreed to motions by William H. Francis (R-Essex) that the Assembly amendments be nonconcurred in and that a conference committee be created. The same Republicans (Francis, Deacon, Gardner) who had been named to the special committee previously were appointed by the Senate President as members.[184] Named as counterparts in the Assembly were William R. Williams (R-Essex), Lewis J. Martin (D-Sussex), and Charles S. Robinson (R-Mercer).[185] After agreement on a compromise, the bill was passed: 17 to 0 in the Senate; and 35 to 0 in the Assembly.[186]

Despite the long process of debate, compromise, and amendment, Senate Bill No. 14 never became law. Democratic Governor George C. Ludlow, a former Middlesex freeholder, was able to exercise his "pocket veto" power to kill the legislation. The bill was filed with the Secretary of State within thirty days after the adjournment of the legislature, and it failed to become law. Noting that the bill was in the form of a general statute, the Governor held that by provisos to nine sections it was "made special in its application to some counties and non-application to others." The general county act was "in violation of that clause of the Constitution which forbids a general law embracing any provisions of a private, special or local character," in the Governor's judgment.[187]

Senate Bill No. 14 was the only one of four general bills even to reach the Governor. Senate Bill No. 15 (cities), which included a provision for one freeholder for each ward, had been defeated 5 to 12, in the upper chamber.[188] Assembly Bill No. 21 (townships), with a section requiring one freeholder from each township, had "died" of absolute inanition."[189] According to one newspaper editorial, it had been "smothered in Committee, because it did not in all particulars suit a certain city member." But on a vote, the bill "would probably have commanded the support of three-fourths of both houses."[190] Likewise, Assembly Bill No. 20 (taxation) had never been brought to a vote for passage. As analyzed by the *Newark Daily Advertiser's* legislative reporter:

. . . The whole trouble was and is and will be that for a century or more the counties, the cities and the towns of the State have been working under different systems of law, and any attempt to unify them into one general system is sure to demand a sacrifice which they are unwilling to make and create a danger which they are unwilling to brave. The legislators found that it would be disastrous personally and perilous politically to so much as attempt the mildest system of general laws.[191]

CONSTITUTIONAL COMMISSION

"The remaining avenue of escape was a constitutional commission," the reporter continued.[192] In February (1881) a concurrent resolution providing for creation of such a body "to suggest and prepare amendments to the State Constitution for submission to and consideration by either the present or the next Legislature" had passed unanimously in the Senate and by a strict party vote of thirty Republicans to nineteen Democrats in the Assembly. Membership on the Commission would include three persons appointed by the Governor "by or with" the consent of the Senate; the president of the Senate and two senators designated by him; and the speaker of the House of Assembly and two assemblymen appointed by him. The Commission was to meet at such times and place as the Governor should designate.[193] But Governor Ludlow, who apparently believed that a convention composed of popularly elected delegates would be the proper means to revise the Constitution, was not required to sign the resolution; and he could not veto it. He simply did not comply with its provisions.[194]

To remedy this executive inaction, Senate Bill No. 247 was introduced three weeks later and passed in the Senate, twelve Republicans to three Democrats; and in the Assembly, twenty seven Republicans and three Democrats to nineteen Democrats.[195] The text, which became law without the Governor's signature,[196] provided for a nine-member commission: the president of the Senate, and two persons (not restricted to senators) to be designated by him; the speaker of the House of Assembly and two persons (not restricted to assemblymen) to be designated by him; and three persons to be appointed by the Governor. But the act also required the appointments to be made "during the current session of the legislature." In addition, the place and time of the Commission's organization meeting were now specified: the State House on or before June 1, 1881.[197] At the last moment, Governor Ludlow filed his appointments with the Secretary of State.[198]

In January 1882 Governor Ludlow transmitted the Commission's report to the legislature. It included suggested constitutional amendments that had received at least six affirmative votes from the nine-member Commission. Among the approved recommendations was one to insert in Article IV, Section VII, Paragraph 11, after the requirement for general laws, the following text:

But until general laws regulating all the internal affairs of towns and counties shall have been passed, local or special laws may be passed for that purpose (but not for the purpose of appointing local officers or commissions to regulate municipal affairs,) with the assent of three-fifths of all members elected to each house, which laws shall not take effect until they shall have been referred to the legislature then next to be chosen, and shall be agreed to by three-fifth of the members elected to each house thereof, and be then approved by the governor.[199]

When the proposed constitutional amendments were considered two months later, John S. Applegate (R-Monmouth) moved in the Senate to strike out the requirements for three-fifths majorities of each house of two consecutive legislatures, followed by gubernatorial approval. The motion lost, 7 to 9. Then Benjamin A. Vail (R-Union) moved to strike out only the provision for a three-fifths majority in both houses of a second legislature. To the same affirmative votes that had just been defeated, five were added to carry this amendment. All five nays were cast by Republicans. Finally, a motion by Garret A. Hobart (R-Passaic) to delete the whole of the proposed text of Section VII, paragraph 11 was agreed to, 13 to 3.[200]

During the same legislative session (1882), election of delegates to a constitutional convention and submission of their product to the voters for ratification was proposed in Assembly Bill No. 4. After a 25-to-31 defeat, it was amended and passed, 35 to 15.[201] As in the previous year, a bill for such a purpose was not reported from a Senate committee. In fact, no such measure was ever to pass both houses. But a statute enacted in 1882, creating four classes of cities,[202] was to be matched by such an act for counties the following year.

Attempts from 1876 through 1883 to fashion a single general pattern of representation acceptable to all counties proved fruitless. The legislature could not agree 1) on the use of Assembly districts as freeholder constituencies; 2) on having board members elected at large within each county; or 3) on providing for minority representation. Even a *state-wide* system of assigning one freeholder to each township (autonomous municipality) and ward was opposed as a diminution of rural political power. Consequently, the only steps toward uniformity were: 1) halving of the number of freeholders in the townships of certain counties; and 2) guaranteeing two freeholders to every autonomous city. Of course, these changes shored up the scheme of representation by municipal units. But just as significant was the beginning of strong partisan efforts of the legislature to manipulate the allocation of freeholders by dictating the number of their urban constituencies (wards) and by requiring that their boundaries should coincide with gerrymandered Assembly districts.

7

EFFORTS TO CLASSIFY
COUNTIES, 1883–1890

The inauguration of county classification according to population was a major milestone in the history of New Jersey's county government. Beginning in 1883, patently special legislation became ostensibly general, a concept that persists today. But any immediate upheaval in the system of apportioning freeholders was prevented by certain constitutional considerations and by the narrow partisan majorities in the legislature. Besides, the conflict over representation on the county governing bodies was primarily between urban and rural interests.

For the first time, in 1883, a specified voting population was required for each type of municipality to qualify for freeholder representation. Jesse D. Ludlam (D-Cape May) sponsored Assembly Bill No. 146, providing that "no [sic] township, city or borough in this state, entitled by law to elect chosen freeholders, polling less than two hundred votes at the last preceding election for congressman in this state, shall elect but one chosen freeholder for such township, city or borough." Despite the faulty English, doubtless due to a printing error, the sponsor intended the measure to apply to *every* township, city, or borough in the category described. "This act is a good one, and is aimed at the many seaside resorts your county is developing," the press informed Cape May residents.[1] But, in fact, it would have affected not only Cape May Point and Sea Isle City, but also the Township of Walpack in Sussex County.[2] Twenty-four Democrats and twenty three Republicans passed the bill over the nays of eight Assemblymen; and on the following day eight Democrats and six Republicans passed it in the Senate, with no recorded opposition.[3]

Subsequently, however, both houses passed a concurrent resolution requesting the Governor to return the bill to the Assembly, and he complied.[4] Over three negative votes, twenty eight Democrats and seventeen Republicans in the lower chamber then passed a bill revised in committee to provide that "no city, township or borough . . . entitled by law to elect chosen freeholders, and having less than one thousand inhabitants at the last preceding national or state census shall elect more than one chosen freeholder. . . ." The Senate in a bipartisan vote agreed to the amended version, and the Governor approved it.[5] In the County of Cape May, Sea Isle City and West Cape May each lost one freeholder;[6] and according to the terms of the new law, only one freeholder could be assigned soon afterward to Ocean City and West Cape May (1884); and Holly Beach and Anglesea (1885).[7] In Sussex, the townships of Green, Hampton, Lafayette, and Walpack had their membership on the county governing board halved.[8]

General Classification of Counties

In January 1883 William Stainsby (R-Essex) sponsored Senate Bill No. 2, providing for *three* classes of counties: first-class, to include all those with a population exceeding 150,000 (Essex, Hudson); second-class, those with not less than 50,000 nor more than 150,000 inhabitants (Camden, Passaic, Mercer, Union, Monmouth, Burlington, Middlesex, Morris); and third-class, all others. Before passage, the bill was amended to establish *four* classes of counties. The two original groupings were retained; but the third class was made to include those counties with not less than 20,000 nor more than 50,000 residents (Hunterdon, Cumberland, Bergen, Warren, Somerset, Gloucester, Salem, Sussex), and the fourth class was to include all other counties (Atlantic, Ocean, Cape May).[9] Like the 1882 law classifying cities, the county act passed both legislative chambers without recorded opposition.[10] Although two counties (Atlantic, Bergen) were later (1885, 1895) to move to a higher classification, these population divisions continued until 1901, when categories for both counties and cities were revised.[11] Only the population requirements for the three classes of boroughs, also created in 1883 without a dissenting vote,[12] were to last longer.

Assigning freeholders strictly on the basis of county classification, however, was rare in the nineteenth century. The constitutionality of the law establishing the new system was questioned by counsel in an 1883 case, but not determined by the judiciary at that time.[13] Moreover, the first two bills involving classification were opposed by Governor Leon Abbett.

One of the measures did not concern representation. In February 1884 George Hires (R-Cumberland) sponsored Senate Bill No. 112, requiring *three*-year terms for all freeholders in New Jersey. A Senate substitute, providing for *two*-year terms for freeholders elected in second-class and third-class counties only, was passed on a bipartisan basis.[14] Without amendment the bill was passed in the Assembly, 33 to 11, again with help from both parties.[15] After a week, the Senate received a long veto message from Governor Abbett, labeling the measure "a clear violation of the provisions of paragraph XI, section 7, article IV, of the constitution, because it is a local law regulating the internal affairs of counties." Noting that the present term of office for freeholders "with a few exceptions" was for one year, he charged that the framer of Senate Bill No. 112 had "sought to avoid the prohibition of the constitution by an attempted classification" based upon the 1883 statute. Failing to see any reason for excluding counties of the first and fourth classes, the Governor cited pertinent cases to satisfy the legislature that "such bills where classification is attempted to be based upon population (where the subject-matter is not one that can be properly classified upon that basis) are in violation of our amended constitution."[16] There was no effort to override the veto.[17]

Two additional counties decreased their freeholder representation in 1885 as a result of Senate Bill No. 72, introduced by Stacy L. Pancoast (R-Gloucester). Although it provided that each township and ward in counties of the third class (Bergen, Cumberland, Gloucester, Hunterdon, Salem, Somerset, Sussex, Warren) should elect only one freeholder, all these counties except Gloucester and Sussex were already operating under such a scheme. Presumably in order to retain only *two* freeholders in Gloucester's City of Woodbury with *three* wards, Pancoast's bill provided that its text should "not be so construed as to apply to such city or cities of said counties in which the manner of chosen freeholders to be annually elected is determined by their charter or charters." The measure was passed in the Senate by nine Republicans and seven Democrats, with no recorded opposition; but Lewis Cochran (D-Sussex) did not cast any vote.[18] The proviso limiting Woodbury to two freeholders was stricken from the bill in the Assembly, where it passed, 41 to 2, the negatives cast by Horatio N. Kinney (D-Sussex) and George Harrison

(R-Essex townships).[19] The amended bill then passed the Senate, 12 to 0, on a bipartisan vote, with none of the Senators from two-freeholder-township counties (Cape May, Essex, Gloucester, Sussex) casting ballots.[20] This bill became law without Governor Abbett's signature;[21] and then Gloucester elected seventeen freeholders, instead of thirty; and Sussex, fifteen freeholders rather than thirty.

AD HOC CLASSIFICATIONS

As city wards continued to grow in population at a faster rate than the outlying townships, *ad hoc* classifications were invented in attempts to have apportionment legislation upheld as general, rather than as special acts. Early in March 1884, William Harrigan (D-Essex) introduced Assembly Bill No. 402, providing that persons qualified to vote for freeholders at any municipal election in any ward of any city in the state should elect *two* freeholders whenever the population of that ward should exceed 5,000, according to the national census of 1880. In Essex, fourteen of Newark's fifteen wards and one of Orange's three wards included a number of inhabitants greater than 5,000. Also affected would be four other cities in as many counties. Seven of Paterson's eight wards; four of Camden's eight wards; three of Elizabeth's eight wards; and two of Trenton's seven wards came under the bill's provisions.[22] Edward Q. Keasbey (R-Essex), whose Assembly district included Clinton, Livingston, Millburn, South Orange, West Orange, and Newark's least populous (3,670) Fourteenth Ward, opposed the measure on the ground that it would create an additional expense to Essex County. But Herman Lehlbach (R-Essex), elected by two Newark wards, pointed out the "manifestly unfair" representation in his county's freeholder board: the Assembly district of fellow Republican George B. Harrison (Caldwell, Montclair, Bloomfield, Belleville, Franklin) had ten freeholders, while the Thirteenth Ward constituency of Republican Assemblyman Charles Holzwarth elected only one member of the county governing body.[23] By adopting an amendment lowering the population figure to 3,600, the Assembly extended the bill's coverage to include all of Newark's fifteen wards, one ward in Orange, all eight Paterson wards, all eight Camden wards, five of Trenton's seven wards, one of Bridgeton's three wards, and two of New Brunswick's six wards.[24] But at the insistence of Edward A. Armstrong (R-Camden) that the bill not apply to his county, the text was amended further to apply only to those counties in which the townships elected two freeholders. The measure now affected only Essex and Cape May, the latter with no municipalities containing wards.[25] Twenty-two Democrats and fourteen Republicans supported Harrigan's bill; five members voted against it. The Essex delegation was split, but all three Newark Democrats voted for passage. Not one assemblyman with a township constituency in Essex approved.[26]

   · The legislative committee of the Essex County freeholder board called the attention of that body to Assembly Bill No. 402 two days later. At least two freeholders supported it, objecting that the current system allowed a township with two hundred or three hundred voters to have double the representation of a Newark ward with 3,000 voters. Because the board was "too large," it was suggested that a single freeholder be given to each ward, township, and incorporated village. Action by the Essex board on the Harrigan bill was tabled.[27] "The committee were divided on this question, and as they received no instructions from the Board very little work was done," noted the Newark press, after the close of the legislative session.[28]

   Nine times the bill was ordered to lie over in the Senate before that body amended and passed it.[29] In an apparent maneuver to avoid the election of an additional freeholder by the 6,126 inhabitants of Orange's Third Ward, the Senate restricted the bill's application to Newark. The new text provided that persons qualified to vote for freeholder at any municipal election in any ward in any city of the first class (Newark) in the state were to elect two freeholders, whenever the population should exceed 3,600 according to the census of 1880; but the act was specifically *not* to apply to any city where the freeholders were elected in, by, or from districts (Jersey City).[30] By a preponderance of Republican votes (eight) in the upper chamber, the measure was passed, 12 to 3.[31] After the Assembly could muster only twenty-nine affirmative votes to twenty-four negatives for concurrence in the upper chamber's amendments, another vote was taken; and the Senate version was passed, 36 to 16, with twenty-seven Democrats on the majority side. All assemblymen from Newark (three Democrats and four Republicans) voted affirmatively this time.[32] Governor Abbett had the last word, however, as he pocket-vetoed the Harrigan bill, declaring it unconstitutional.[33]

   But the following year Harrigan offered another way to change the system of representation in Essex. Assembly Bill No. 179 of 1885 provided for only one freeholder from each township that was then electing one or more freeholders in any county in the state. When the "majority in the House were caught napping" late one morning in March, the "strong party measure" passed with a bipartisan majority,

35 to 8.[34] "Only after it was too late was it discovered that practically it was a scheme to throw the control of the Board of Freeholders of Essex into the hands of the Democrats, or at least to give them a good chance to capture it," observed the legislative correspondent of a Newark daily newspaper.[35] In the afternoon Franklin Murphy (R-Essex), who had voted with the majority, moved to reconsider the bill's passage, in order to give his Republican colleague from the Essex townships, George B. Harrison, an opportunity to state any objections that his absence during the floor discussion had prevented. A "lively cross-fire of debate among the Essex men" resulted, and the matter was postponed until the following week.[36]

When Murphy moved at that time to take from the table the resolution to reconsider the vote by which the Harrigan bill had passed, "the members of the House showed by their alertness that the subject had been made familiar to all of them by diligent lobbying."[37] In the judgment of one reporter, "Probably, no more abusive season has transpired since the session opened. . . . The Essex freeholders were charged with jobbery, corruption and what not, and the members from Essex became very wroth as they took notes for or against the measure."[38] Harrison admitted that the Newark wards had a much larger number of inhabitants than the townships, but he added that "the superiority in size of the latter and the interests therein makes it even." The townships very much feared giving control of the freeholder board to Newark, because of the effect that it would have upon the debt of the county, composed principally of war obligations. Whenever portions had come due, Harrison declared, the townships had paid promptly, not asking the legislature for permission to renew bonds, as Newark had done instead of paying every year. The townships "would regret exceedingly" placing the $300,000 lunatic asylum (already paid for) under city control, as would be done if the Harrigan bill were to be enacted. Moreover, by a bill that had just been passed in the Assembly that day, Newark would be entitled to divide two of its wards, thereby increasing its majority on the freeholder board and making the townships' representation "amount to nothing." "But the principal reason why I oppose the bill," said Harrison, "is because I do not believe that the people of the city of Newark want it themselves." They were "already disgusted with the policy of government in the city without extending it over the county."[39]

Newark's Franklin Murphy (R-Essex) denied that his city had never paid its bonds, noting that only recently $200,000 had been expended for that purpose. Except in two cases, he said, the bonds

had been paid as they came due. The township-controlled freeholder board had built thirty miles of macadamized roads, but 82 percent of the cost had been paid for by Newark. The township-
controlled freeholder board had built an asylum "which they have
no more use for than a cat has for two tails." Murphy argued: "It is a
question of representation according to taxation." Even the Harrigan
bill would "give the townships more representation than they are
entitled to for the eighteen percent of the taxes which they pay."[40]
When Harrison retorted that the lunatic asylum had been built
wholly at the instance of the freeholders from Newark, and had been
forced on the county by them, Murphy demanded to know how they
could force anything upon the county, when the townships had
double Newark's representation. But after reiterating his charge and
blaming a Newark freeholder for initiating and carrying through the
building of the asylum, Harrison argued that the roads had been
"built for the accommodation of Newark, that the city might grow."
It did not pay more than one-half of 80 percent of the cost, he said.[41]

David A. Bell (R-Essex), representing Orange and East Orange,
delivered a twenty-five-minute speech, claiming that Newark furnished the criminals for the jails and received the advantage of the
roads that were maintained by the townships. In fact, he insisted, the
city complained of the costs, but had been the gainer in all the
county's enterprises. The townships did not want to be delivered
over to the Philistines to be devoured. It was not politics, but a
question of material interest to the townships; and the right of the big
fishes to swallow the little ones should not be applied to property.[42]
The only Newark assemblyman to oppose the bill, R. Wayne Parker,
charged that the Essex freeholder board was "perhaps the most
anomalous body in the State," because there was no president and
no veto power. It was "wise as it stands at present because of the
conservative opinions of the country members," according to that
Republican legislator.[43]

"As the debate was getting hotter every moment, the members
from other counties took a hand and insisted upon a vote upon the
motion," reported the press. When the question of reconsideration
was put to a vote, "the excitement grew intense." So closely were the
assemblymen divided, with a slight majority in favor of the rural
members, that "Murphy began to kick himself, figuratively, for allowing it to be brought up again." The vote stood at twenty-two in
favor of reconsideration and twenty-one against it, when Thomas
Flynn (D-Passaic), "who was hot in the fight for Bell," tried to have
the roll call suspended. "The chamber was thrown into an uproar,

every member being out of his seat."[44] When the first call was completed, the motion had a bare majority, thirty-one votes. Both sides made strong efforts to secure the needed votes or to make changes. Those absentees who later cast ballots decided to vote against reconsideration. When one of those who had voted for reconsideration changed his vote, there was an uproar in the Assembly, and a further call of absentees was demanded. William H. Grant (R-Monmouth) changed his vote to "nay," leaving the motion for reconsideration with only twenty-nine votes and defeat. "The excitement of the members was tremendous and it was a long time before they were in any condition to proceed with routine business,"[45] the press reported. But the turmoil in the Assembly was unproductive, however; in the Senate, Harrigan's bill was never reported from committee.

The ultimate in classification, of course, would be a separate county. Immediately after the Newarkers' victory, Bell introduced Assembly Bill No. 408 to establish a new county to be called Carteret, composed of all Essex municipalities outside Newark, except Belleville and Franklin. Three Assembly districts of Essex would be assigned to Carteret County, minus the two townships and Newark's Fourteenth Ward, which were to be joined to two different districts in the existing Essex County. Until other arrangements could be made, there would be joint use of the Essex buildings. The debt was to be adjusted by nonresident commissioners on the basis of taxable property in the old county, as declared in the abstract of ratables for 1884. "This will be favored," said one press report about the bill, "because it will give the Republicans an additional senator, but the South Jersey men will oppose it, as giving North Jersey an increased senatorial representation."[46] Another newspaper remarked that it was "just possible that it may be accepted, some time, as a compromise on the demands for a Constitutional Convention." The sponsor himself was subsequently described as "sanguine of the ultimate passage of the bill." Having carefully studied the sentiment in the Assembly, Bell predicted that all the Essex members would vote for it and that there would be no opposition of any importance in the Senate.[47] But doubtless he recalled that, only three years earlier, Assembly Bill No. 331, sponsored by John H. Parsons (R-Essex) to transform the City of Newark into the County of Newark, had been passed on a bipartisan vote, 36 to 10, in the lower chamber, only to be defeated in the Senate, 6 to 15.[48]

Bell's Carteret County bill was considered for final passage in the Assembly, after it had been amended to leave Clinton in the old county and join it with Newark's Thirteenth Ward as one Assembly district.[49] During the debate, Murphy spoke against it: "I don't believe that Newark wants the bill, and I don't believe the townships want it. The latter are only incensed, I imagine, because the Freeholders bill passed, and they introduce this one in retaliation."[50] Bell retorted that a petition in favor of dividing Essex County had been signed by the best men in the townships.[51] Only after the roll had been called three or four times could the bill be passed by a bipartisan majority, 33 to 14, with the ten-member Essex delegation splitting evenly.[52] "The principal vote came from South Jersey," reported one newspaper from that county, with a good deal of exaggeration. Readers were told that the "significance of that fact was not known until a few moments afterwards, when the constitutional convention bill to change the senatorial representation was called up." After Bell failed to answer a roll call, the "State House was searched from the dome to the cellar," and a good portion of the morning was spent sending officers after him. Finally, a warrant was issued to bring Bell to the bar of the Assembly, and Murphy remarked on the floor that Bell had traded his vote on this measure for the South Jersey votes on the Carteret County bill. As soon as Bell arrived, he denied the charge.[53]

Despite its passage in the Assembly, efforts continued there to kill the bill. A resolution that the Senate be requested to return the measure to the Assembly was adopted, 31 to 16, with twenty-five Republicans in the majority.[54] Murphy had said that, if he could get Bell's bill on second reading for amendment, he would take the balance of the summer to write his additions.[55] Because it had not been reported by a Senate committee, John W. Griggs (R-Passaic) raised the point of order that the bill was not yet before the Senate. That chamber's president agreed, and the bill was reported before the Assembly's request was concurred in, 17 to 0.[56] But even then Murphy could not carry out his plan to retaliate against Bell for voting that very morning against a bill to move the state's capital to Newark. For, when Harrison deserted Bell, his Republican colleague from the Essex townships, and moved to reconsider the vote by which the Carteret County bill had passed, the speaker ruled that reconsideration at that time required unanimous consent.[57] Apparently, no one had thought of that, until some time had been spent in debate and the Assembly had become weary of the whole subject.[58] A motion to suspend the rules in order to allow reconsideration was lost, 18 to 30, and the bill went back to the Senate.[59] How Bell had managed to secure a majority to support him by voting negatively aroused much curiosity. It was understood, the press reported, that he had agreed to cease all efforts to pass his bill in the Senate, if the Assembly would relieve him of the bad position in which punitive action of that morning had placed him.[60] The Carteret County bill was not reported from the Senate committee, quite likely because Senate inaction on Harrigan's freeholder bill made a future within Essex County more acceptable to the rural townships.

GENERAL BILLS DISREGARDING POPULATION FIGURES

Another serious attempt to enact uncomplicated general legislation occurred in 1885. On the day before Assembly passage of Harrigan's one-freeholder-per-township bill, William H. Corbin (R-Union) sponsored Assembly Bill No. 351, requiring that "boards of chosen freeholders shall hereafter consist of one member from every ward and township of the respective counties of this state." The term of office would be one year. In an editorial, the *Newark Evening News* noted that insiders believed that the matter was "being engineered in the Legislature in the interest of the Republicans" and that it was "designed more particularly to have reference to Union County which has for years been governed in the board by Democrats." By such an allotment Elizabeth would double its representation on the board from the current four freeholders to eight; Rahway, from two to four; and Plainfield, from two to four.[61]

Meeting two days after the bill's introduction, the Union county board was asked by the director, C.W.L. Martino, for an expression of opinion on it. He argued that there were some townships in the state that were as large as Union County, and because it took their freeholders nearly all day to get to board meetings, each of these municipalities needed two freeholders, so that at least one of them could be available for such service. In the director's observation, representatives had never been assigned according to population or valuation of property, and this would not be the case even if Elizabeth were to have eight freeholders. Judging by the valuation of some wards in Elizabeth, Plainfield, and Rahway, he maintained that every township should have *two* freeholders. Board members were told by Martine that he had been willing at all times to do everything that was wanted for the cities and townships.[62] Some freeholders contended that increasing the membership of the county governing body might make it necessary to enlarge the room where the meetings had been held for many years.[63] At one freeholder's request, a roll call vote on the Corbin bill was taken; and those

present unanimously opposed its passage. The director announced
that he would inform Corbin of this action.[64]

Corbin argued in the press that the board's action did not reflect
the views of the county's residents. He noted that Elizabeth contained nearly 51 percent of Union's population, but elected only four
of the seventeen freeholders. Elizabeth, Plainfield, and Rahway
together included more than 77 percent of the population, but
elected only eight of the seventeen freeholders. Nine townships
with 23 percent of the population were controlling the county. From
the property point of view, the inequality was "no less striking." In
1884 nearly 47 percent of the county's assessed valuations were in
Elizabeth; together with Plainfield and Rahway, more than 76 percent. Moreover, the administration of the county funds was unfair,
Corbin charged. More than one-fourth of this money, collected for
the school tax, was apportioned by law; about one-third was used for
court expenses and could not be apportioned among the cities and
districts. By examining the greater part of the remainder, spent for
bridges, one could see how the system worked. Of the $111,315
spent for this purpose from 1877 to 1884 (excluding 1883, for which
details were "not at hand"), Elizabeth raised nearly half the money,
but received only $14,600. In no year did the city receive as much as
it had contributed. The closest approach to it had been in 1881, when
Elizabeth received somewhat more than half of what it had paid.[65]

Repeating Corbin's reasons and agreeing with them, the
Elizabeth Daily Journal declared that the only argument against his
measure that was worth talking about was the proposed increase in
board membership (to twenty-five); but other counties had tried the
bill's system and had flourished quite as well as Union. The editorial
attacked the freeholder board's "haste to resolve that the Corbin bill
is an unwise measure:"

> It seems not to have occurred to them that the people are the one's [*sic*]
> to say how many laborers they will have in the Court House vineyard rather
> than the servants themselves to declare how much supervision and assis-
> tance they need from the people.[66]

In taking exception to this sentence, particularly, when he was asked
to submit his view, Director Martine replied:

> Now, that was the reason that we *did not declare, resolve* or take *any
> official notice* of the bill. We only reasoned as tax payers and citizens, for it is
> well understood that many people, and it seems yourselves among them,
> think that when gentlemen are elected to places of public trust and take an

oath to perform faithfully all its duties, they must cease to have any interests as taxpayers or good citizens, and with folded arms let things drift until invited to express an opinion.

Under these circumstances you should not ask our views.

He noted that four votes of Elizabeth and two from Rahway plus one other vote had "controlled the county (as under the Corbin bill) one year." Of the nearly $140,000 expended upon the single item of bridges, $125,000 was spent for Elizabeth, Rahway, and Linden. "Have these gentlemen their eyes on that year?" he wondered.[67]

The Assembly adopted a committee amendment providing that the bill should take effect in Hudson County only after Jersey City should have been divided into wards, "which may never be," as Corbin observed.[68] After further amendment giving boroughs the same representation as the townships, the measure survived a motion to recommit and was passed, 32 to 17, over the "decided opposition of the rural members" (including Republicans Harrison and Bell, whose districts included Essex townships).[69] The majority included twenty-three Republicans. In the Senate, a substitute bill was reported from committee, and the new version applying only to Union County just managed to overcome dilatory tactics and to pass by a vote of eleven Republicans to three Democrats, seven Democrats abstaining. In the negative was Robert L. Livingston (R-Union).[70] On the next day, and last of the legislative session, the Assembly passed the measure, thirty-three Republicans to twenty-two Democrats and three Republicans.[71] Again, however, Governor Abbett took advantage of the end of the legislative session, and used his power to "pocket-veto" the bill.

A last unsuccessful effort to increase city ward representation was Assembly Bill No. 417, sponsored by Charles Herbert (R-Middlesex) in March 1888. It provided for the election of a freeholder in every ward "in each of the cities of the state which are now or may be hereafter divided into wards." Even after being amended to apply only to those wards that were yet to be created, the bill lost, 26 to 19. Twenty of the majority and only six of the minority were Republicans.[72]

TERMS OF ALL FREEHOLDERS EXTENDED TO TWO YEARS

In 1886 the longer term attracted equal support in the lower chamber from both political parties. It voted, 36 to 10, to pass Assembly Bill No. 281 of Roderick B. Seymour (R-Hudson), providing for two-year terms for all freeholders in New Jersey and staggering such terms in those Assembly districts, wards, and townships that were entitled to elect two.[73] As soon as the tally was completed, Philip Tumulty (D-Hudson) obtained leave to withdraw from the legislature's files his Assembly Bill No. 80, which also required that freeholders in every county serve for two years.[74] But the Senate concurred in an adverse report on Seymour's bill, and it was indefinitely postponed.[75]

With no alteration in text, Seymour's measure was introduced the following year (1887) as Assembly Bill No. 61, this time by a Hudson Democrat, Robert S. Hudspeth, rather than by a Republican from that county. The Assembly made minor changes in the text and approved it, 32 to 21, with twelve Republicans on each side.[76] Before a final vote was taken in the Senate, however, John A. McBride (D-Sussex) moved that further consideration of the bill be indefinitely postponed. John J. Gardner (R-Atlantic) noted that the prominent men of his county, irrespective of political party, favored the bill; and Frederick S. Fish (R-Essex) supported his position. In Mercer, maintained its Republican Senator John D. Rue, two-year terms for freeholder had given so much satisfaction that no one would think of asking for any change. After the motion to postpone failed, the bill was defeated.[77] But a week later the Senate voted to reconsider its action and passed the measure, 12 to 7, with seven Republicans voting affirmatively.[78] According to a Trenton newspaper, "The advocates of the bill were in a hurry to pass it in the hope that it might become law today (Tuesday) and affect the township election [by the provision that it take effect immediately]."[79] Democratic Governor Robert S. Green signed the bill on Thursday, saying that he had withheld his signature on Tuesday, because the people were voting for freeholders on that day with the understanding that the terms were to be one year only. To sign the bill at that time for two-year terms, in the Governor's judgment, would be taking unfair advantage of the citizens. But the new law was to apply to certain freeholders to be elected during the following month (April).[80] Such a system of staggered terms was regarded by many, said one newspaper, as a very good feature, because it would "never leave the Board without some members who have had at least one year's experience" and would "give new members a chance to correct any errors or extravagances that may creep into the Board without waiting two years for a change of sentiment."[81]

For two reasons there was no serious legislative effort from 1883 through 1888 to change the basic organization of freeholder boards by municipal units. Authority to enact laws that would apply to counties by population classifications had still not been defined or even declared constitutional by the judiciary. Moreover, there was an unusually close party balance during this period, even though the Senate was always Republican and the Governor Democratic. On those infrequent occasions when a majority could be mustered in each house for any measure dealing with freeholder boards, the change could be blocked by governors who made effective use of the "pocket" veto. Only relatively minor adjustments in freeholder apportionment were possible during this period.

8

PRESSURES FOR THE END OF MUNICIPAL REPRESENTATION, 1885—1892

As the construction of railroads and highways improved transportation throughout the State, new clusters of population began to develop outside the main cities of New Jersey. Scattered through the rural townships, residents of these smaller population concentrations frequently began to look for urban governmental services which the townships either were unable or unwilling to provide. The answer often was found during the late nineteenth century in the incorporation of new municipalities, known as boroughs, within the townships. At least two "boroughs" (Trenton, Elizabeth) had been formed by royal charter in colonial New Jersey,[1] and a handful of others had been created by special act of the legislature prior to 1875. But the real burst of borough incorporation began after 1878, when the enactment of a general law permitted the inhabitants of any township or part of any township, not exceeding four square miles and containing a population not exceeding 5,000, through a petition and referendum process, to incorporate itself as a borough.[2] Where in 1875 there were only a few boroughs in the state, more than 120 additional boroughs had been created by 1896.[3]

Representation of Boroughs and Towns

In 1885, Samuel D. Dickinson (R-Hudson), on behalf of the speaker, E. Ambler Armstrong (R-Camden), introduced Assembly Bill No. 31 to provide for the election of one freeholder from each incorporated borough in the state. But the bill was to apply only where "the voters in such borough do not at present vote with the township in which it is situate for freeholder." On partisan votes the bill passed the Assembly, 44 to 2 (only four Republicans not voting affirmatively);[4] and the Senate, 15 to 0 (only one Republican failing to vote favorably).[5] Without the Governor's approval, the measure became law.[6]

Apparently in order to authorize two freeholders who would be elected by the Borough of Vineland (1885 pop., 3,170), Philip P. Baker (D-Cumberland) introduced Senate Bill No. 151 of 1887, enabling the legal voters of each of the state's incorporated boroughs having 3,000 inhabitants to elect one freeholder in addition to the one freeholder to which the township in which the borough was located was entitled, and also one additional freeholder for each 3,000 inhabitants in the borough. Seven Democrats and seven Republicans formed a majority to pass the measure over negative votes from Essex and Warren.[7] But the Assembly changed the text to provide that the legal voters of *each* incorporated borough containing a population of not less than 3,000 inhabitants should elect only one freeholder. The effect would be to limit Vineland to a single freeholder separate from that of Landis Township. In this form the lower chamber voted for passage, nineteen Democrats and sixteen Republicans to two Republicans from Cumberland and Gloucester.[8] With both political parties supplying an equal number of votes, the Senate accepted the Assembly's version, 12 to 0, and it was signed into law.[9]

But the following year (1888) an effort was made to increase the representation of Mercer County's Borough of Chambersburg, which, unlike Vineland, was already electing its own freeholder. By the terms of Assembly Bill No. 116, sponsored by Lyman Leavitt (R-Mercer), whose constituency included Chambersburg, each incorporated borough in New Jersey would be entitled to a freeholder for *each* 3,000 of its inhabitants. The bill was amended to authorize an additional freeholder for such borough's population in excess of 3,000,[10] but it went on to defeat, 19 to 25. There were fourteen Republicans on each side, and nine of their party colleagues did not vote at all. In each of these groups there was one Mercer assemblyman.[11]

With few exceptions,[12] boroughs in New Jersey had not been entitled to elect their own freeholders until 1887, when a population of 3,000 was made the requirement.[13] But this law was repealed in 1891, and all borough membership on the board abolished. As before, a freeholder had to be elected "for the whole of said township including the town, borough or incorporated village situate therein."[14] In 1894 each first-class borough (more than 3,000 residents) existing within the limits of a township and incorporated under the 1878 Borough Act was made independent of its parent township and was authorized to elect one freeholder.[15] Boroughs with 2,500 inhabitants were allowed to elect freeholders, according to an 1895 statute;[16] and a revision of the Borough Act of 1897 raised the figure to 3,000.[17] By lowering this to 1,200 (according to the last preceding *federal* census) for boroughs in counties with 75,000 to 200,000 inhabitants (Passaic, Camden, Mercer),[18] the 1896 legislature had allowed the possibility that such reduced requirements would be extended to include one-third of the state's counties after promulgation of the 1900 population statistics.

Another trend in municipal incorporations began to have an impact on county freeholder boards in the 1880's. As early as 1845 (Belvidere), the legislature, by special act, had begun to issue charters for limited local governmental powers to *towns* located within townships. During and after the Civil War, more towns were created. Increased powers were granted to the governing bodies of the towns in 1884, and, in 1888, a general law was enacted providing in detail for their formation and government. Towns by 1895 had become of age as separate municipal corporations.[19]

The "Act providing for the formation of government of towns," introduced in 1888 as Assembly Bill No. 140 by E. Frank Short (D-Hudson), had been drawn and introduced unsuccessfully the previous year for the benefit of West Hoboken.[20] "It practically gives the town committees the power of [city] Common Councils," remarked Jersey City's *Evening Journal,* after an amended version passed the lower chamber, 34 to 14.[21] Further modified in the Senate, it barely passed there, 11 to 8, and then won approval again in the Assembly, 38 to 0.[22] The final text provided that "the inhabitants of any town or borough or of any township having a special charter, or of any township which has or hereafter may have a population exceeding six thousand inhabitants" could incorporate as a town governed under the provisions of the act by approving the proposal in a special election authorized by the governing body of the municipality upon petition of at least fifty resident freeholders (that is, owners of real property). If the municipality that voted favorably did not already have wards, the governing body would be required to divide it into not less than three, containing as nearly as possible an equal number of inhabitants. The law also required that "in counties in which chosen freeholders are elected by townships and wards [not Hudson] each ward of the town shall elect one chosen freeholder."[23]

The granting of separate representation on county boards of chosen freeholders to boroughs and towns re-created the potential for boards of enormous size which the state had been struggling to prevent for the previous four decades. Originally brought about by the proliferation of townships, each entitled to two freeholder representatives, the rapid growth in board membership had been checked in mid-century; first, almost accidentally, by the establishment of new counties, and later, consciously, by legislation which halved the representation of each municipal unit or even went to the length (in Hudson) of abandoning municipal representation and substituting the election of freeholders from Assembly districts. Now with the authorization of separate freeholder membership for boroughs and towns of certain populations, the freeholder boards might soon explode with new members; for the number of boroughs was to grow enormously, while the towns could increase their freeholder representation at will through the creation of new wards.

Pressure by Farmers for Optional Referenda

In the late 1880's the movement for the reform of county government was still being led by the members of the Middlesex Farmers Club, but under a new name. On November 2, 1885, the organization had resolved itself into the Middlesex County Board of Agriculture.[24] Its president, Captain Samuel Blish, presented a paper at the February 1888 meeting in Trenton of the State Board of Agriculture, arguing for the reduction in the number of freeholders. The nineteen-member governing body was currently costing his county $7,680. "We have found that in many other States, in Massachusetts and others, they have Commissioners who do the same work as this body of Freeholders and perhaps a little more work," he told the delegates. "We found in counties having double the population of Middlesex, the whole expense does not exceed $2,000 annually," Blish continued, receiving permission to read the text of a bill that had been drawn up by his local farming organization to replace the "unwieldy" and "old-fashioned" freeholder board. The plan that he wanted the State Board to urge upon the legislature required that every county elect three freeholders (at the same time as the election of members of the General Assembly), who would be paid $800 a year in counties with not more than 50,000 inhabitants; $1,000, in counties with more than 50,000 and not more than 75,000; $1,500, in

counties with more than 75,000 and not more than 100,000; and
$2,000, in counties exceeding 100,000.[25] A "somewhat lengthy dis-
cussion" followed the unsuccessful motion of a delegate from Camden that the bill lie on the table. If county affairs were to be placed in
the hands of only three men, it would be the greatest monopoly of the
age, insisted a Burlington delegate. Another from Cumberland asserted that the taxpayers in his county were not in favor of the
change; and the representative of the Essex farmers maintained that
his county was perfectly satisfied with the freeholder law as it was.
The resolution to endorse the bill was defeated.[26]

When the Middlesex County Board of Agriculture heard Captain Blish report in February on what had transpired in Trenton, the
general opinion was in favor of the bill. The members decided to
perfect the measure and to submit it to other local agricultural boards
before the next January.[27] At the October meeting, each member of
the Middlesex group had a pamphlet containing the county's financial statement which had been "dissected" by the *Fredonian*. Readers of that newspaper learned that its "crusade" against the freeholders' dishonesty and extravagance and against the "iniquity of the
system" received "hearty commendation." "One of the most
influential members" at the meeting then compared the New Jersey
system of county government very unfavorably with those in
Pennsylvania and Massachusetts. If the farmers presented a united
demand to the legislature, an Essex County freeholder told them, the
Middlesex freeholder board could be abolished. "With hardly an
exception" the farmers favored a small commission elected at large
to replace the current governing board, and they instructed their
secretary to obtain financial statements from other counties for purposes of comparison.[28] A five-man committee, including Captain
Blish, was subsequently appointed to draft an appropriate bill.[29]

But it was another member of the committee, former Judge
Woodbridge Strong, who drew up the bill for three commissioners
that was approved *unanimously* by the Middlesex County Board of
Agriculture at its meeting in December 1888. He and Blish were
included among the four members reappointed to present the measure to the State Board for its endorsement. Doubtless that would be
secured, and the bill would be introduced with very strong support
during the next session of the legislature, the *Fredonian* predicted.
According to Strong, the bill would pass the Assembly with little
opposition, because the objectionable provision making the new
system of representation *compulsory* in every county had been
eliminated, and a *local option* provision for each county included.

While preparing the draft, Strong explained, he had considered introducing a clause providing for the election of a single commissioner from each Assembly district. But he found that some counties had only two such districts and that, therefore, two of the three commissioners would have to come from the same one. If his bill were to become law, the people would certainly see the wisdom of selecting the commissioners from different parts of the county. In addition, Judge Strong made special mention of his belief that a public official should receive a salary, rather than payment by fees.[30] The draft bill, reflecting this viewpoint, was hailed by the *New Brunswick Home News* as "a measure the accomplishment of which has been long contemplated and urged, especially by the agricultural and rural property owners and taxpayers not only of Middlesex county, but throughout the entire State."[31]

After promoting its own plan for three district-elected commissioners to replace the "Two Dollar Brigade," the *Daily Fredonian* began to modify and support the farmers' scheme. "From various sections of the county opinions have been received showing conclusively that the leading agriculturalists of both parties are heartily in favor of the proposed change," the newspaper declared of the small board generally.[32] On the day that it advised Charles B. Herbert (R-Middlesex) that he "would do well to draft a bill in advance of his colleagues in the Assembly which shall cover the point raised," he was quoted as saying:

I haven't given the matter sufficient consideration as yet, to give an opinion on the subject. Of course, I would introduce such a bill as that which I understand the State Board of Agriculture will frame, should the people desire it, as I consider it my duty to carry out the wishes of my constituents. But I think that the Board of Agriculture will most likely get a member of the majority [Democratic] side to introduce their bill.[33]

Several days later the *Daily Fredonian* suggested that the bill sponsored by the Middlesex County Board of Agriculture be altered to require that one member of the governing body be of the minority party, because the "proposed commission should be also as nonpartisan as it is possible to make a board of three individual members."[34] Immediately, Herbert announced that he would support no new freeholder bill that did not provide for minority representation.[35]

In at least one other county, Captain Blish gained support for the reform ideas of the Middlesex County Board of Agriculture. Addressing a special meeting of its counterpart in Mercer on January 8,

1889, he secured favorable consideration for Judge Strong's bill. Assisting him was George O. Vanderbilt, former Democratic State Senator from Mercer, who spoke "quite at length," about the current freeholder system, expressing particular alarm that the rapid increase in the membership of his county's governing board was increasing taxes. As an example, he cited Chambersburg, which had just increased its representation from a single freeholder to one from each of three wards, established in that borough's territory after its consolidation with Trenton and Millham Township (1888). The three-member commission was not an experiment, but a plan that was operating in both North and South to the satisfaction of all concerned, the farmers were assured.[36] After Vanderbilt urged them to move at once on the legislature, they approved this resolution from a constituent group:

Resolved, That the Ewing Grange recommend the Mercer County Board of Agriculture to co-operate with other County Boards in requesting the State Board of Agriculture to petition the Legislature to reduce the representatives of Boards of Freeholders in this State to three in each county, to be known as Commissioners, with compensation sufficient to amply pay them for their services.[37]

The minority representation provision was added to the text of Judge Strong's local option bill before Captain Blish submitted it to delegates at the annual meeting of the State Board of Agriculture later that month. In addition, not more than one of the three freeholders was to be elected from any ward or township (municipality).[38] Many discussed the measure, reported a Trenton newspaper, and "sentiment appeared to be pretty evenly divided."[39] Supporting Blish were Strong himself, two delegates from Hunterdon, one from Somerset, and one from Sussex who favored the bill's main features, but thought that it would work disastrously in his county. Opposed were two members from Essex, one each from Warren, Sussex, Cumberland, and Burlington. Although the motion to support the bill was defeated,[40] the next day the delegates approved the report of the Committee on Resolutions, which recommended adoption of the Ewing Grange's resolution of January 8 for a three-member county governing body.[41]

What was doubtless the first bill for *popular* local option concerning representation in New Jersey's county governing bodies was sponsored in February, 1889 by Herbert of Middlesex. Assembly Bill No. 309 would reduce to three members the freeholder board in any county where the voters approved the plan in a referendum ordered by the county's circuit judge, after at least one hundred legal voters had petitioned him for it. No two of these board members elected at large could reside in the same ward or township, nor could more than two of them be elected from the same political party. In counties with fewer than 50,000 inhabitants the annual salary would be $600; more than 50,000 and fewer than 75,000, $800; more than 75,000 and fewer than 100,000, $1,000; more than 100,000 population, $1,500. Traveling expenses were included in these sums. Terms for the first three freeholders to be elected would be one, two, and three years, respectively, and thereafter for *three* years each.

Immediately, two Middlesex County journals endorsed the measure, soon to be joined by at least one South Jersey newspaper. "ASSEMBLYMAN Herbert has the good wishes of nearly all his constituents for the success of his bill . . . ," the *New Brunswick Home News* proclaimed. "This is a movement in the line of reform and economy," and although Herbert was "not on the side of the [Democratic] majority in the Legislature . . . that should not prevent the success of a good measure, especially, when it is needed to insure good government." Not only could three good men perform all the work currently done by the nineteen-member board in Middlesex, but they could "do it more efficiently and less expensively."[42] Equally enthusiastic was the *New Brunswick Daily Fredonian:*

It is the sincere desire of the taxpayers of this county, regardless of party, that Assemblyman Herbert's bill for the abolition of the Board of Freeholders shall become a law, and that a non-partisan County Commission, such as THE FREDONIAN recently advocated while exposing the rottenness of the present fee system shall be substituted instead.

The measure was "a fair one and should be supported by each party in the House of Assembly and Senate." Passing it "would insure a saving of at least $10,000 a year to the taxpayers of this county, besides giving the people a smaller body of county officials to handle."[43] Noting that three commissioners would get a total of $2,400 annually, instead of the nearly $5,000 then paid in Burlington, a local weekly newspaper also acknowledged "no doubt that the business of the County would be just as well looked after as at present."[44]

But opposition came quickly, too. The *Camden Courier* could "appreciate the New Brunswick FREDONIAN's interest in the bill" because of economy reasons, but did not want the bill to apply to its own county: "Things are jogging along very satisfactorily here under the present conditions, and the change would bring us no improvement." Advice was smugly offered: "The best way to remedy the alleged evils in Middlesex would be to elect better men to the board, as we have been doing in Camden for a number of years past."[45] With no pretense at nonpartisanship this time came the reply: "The esteemed Courier can well afford to compliment the Camden Board of Freeholders, that body being Republican and therefore in sympathy with law and justice. In Middlesex it is quite the reverse and likely to remain so." The local residents submitted to "being fleeced by the pernicious fee system in vogue" in government by the freeholders, and, indeed, actually reelected them. Even though Herbert's bill might not be enacted, the evidence that he would produce before the Assembly in "arraigning" the Middlesex board would "prove mighty entertaining reading."[46]

Assembly Bill No. 309 was "hardly likely to get very far on the way of realization," although its aim wasn't a bad idea by any means, judged one legislative correspondent. He held that "the attempt to provide for minority representation by only permitting a voter to cast his ballot for two members shows that those who are responsible for the plan are either politicians, or are unacquainted with the disastrous results of such legislation." Speaker Hudspeth's bill, providing for a freeholder from each Assembly district and a director at large had more chance of passage and "accomplish[ed] all the good in the Herbert proposition, without any of its bad fruits, provided it is made to take in the whole State."[47]

Exactly that scheme of representation was reported in the substitute for the Herbert bill one month later, because "the original bill was so obnoxious to certain sections of the State that it would have been strongly opposed." The salary for the single freeholder to be elected from *every Assembly district* in New Jersey was to be $600; and for the director at large, who would be the presiding officer, with no vote except in case of a tie, $1,000. All would be elected in the fall for two-year terms. Provision was made for continuing in office those freeholders who would be elected at the ensuing spring elections until the first day of the following December, when the new board would assume its duties.[48] Amended again the following week, so that it would apply only to second-class counties and would provide also for the election of a freeholder from the county at large,[49] the substitute for the Herbert bill never reached a final vote.

RENEWED AGITATION BY FARMERS

The farmers' voting inconsistency at the 1889 annual meeting of the State Board of Agriculture did not remain unnoticed. At the next meeting, the Committee on Resolutions reported without recommendation a resolution that the delegates endorse passage of the bill that had been presented the previous year by the Middlesex board.[50] A Mercer County farmer explained the measure's status:

This proposition to change the existing Boards of Freeholders to three Commissioners came up last year, and was fully discussed, some advocating it very strongly, and this board inadvertently voted both ways. It endorsed the action of the Mercer County Board, and yet, when it came up as a resolution before the State Board, they voted against the bill. This comes before the Board again, endorsed by the Mercer County Board and by the Middlesex County Board.[51]

A Burlington County delegate was the only speaker to oppose the idea of a small board. In his township alone there were more than 600 bridges; and if only three men were to be given charge of his county, from the Atlantic Ocean to the Delaware River, not one-third of the work looking after the bridges could be done for $1,000. "No honest man can do it for such a salary," he insisted, doubtless aware that freeholders elected at large in counties with Burlington's population were to receive $800, according to Assemblyman Herbert's plan. The freeholders elected from the delegate's township would not serve on a small board for one cent less than $1,000.[52]

Those supporting the resolution were led by Judge Woodbridge Strong of Middlesex, who pointed out that the proposed system was not new: "Ever since we were little children it has been done in Connecticut, Massachusetts, Pennsylvania, and in many other States, and it is therefore not impossible." Formerly a member of a large freeholder board himself, he had "seen there more jobs set up, more bidding out to other parties, and more shady transactions there, than I can conceive possible to exist under the control of three men, who are under the close supervision of the people all the time. . . ." In Middlesex County there were men willing to become freeholders for a $600 salary, the Judge assured the delegates. They adopted the resolution endorsing the small board bill, immediately after hearing Strong's concluding words:

The taxation growing out of these cumbersome bodies must be swept away; and I can see no better way to begin this than to begin at the Board of

Freeholders. I assert that it is a festering bed of corruption. It is so in many counties and I believe it is so right here in Mercer county also. With such a Board of Commissioners you know at the commencement of the year what you are paying, for this bill provides that their salary shall pay all their expenses. They can't come in with their little incidentals, and you know what you have got to pay.[53]

The farmers continued to challenge the existing apportionment of freeholders. Delegates to the next annual meeting (1891) of the State Board accepted the report of the Committee on Resolutions recommending that the three-commissioner resolution be brought again to the attention of the legislature.[54] In 1892 the Chairman of the Board's Legislative Committee reported that it had conferred with Governor Abbett and had requested him to urge the passage of a bill dividing the Tenth Assembly District of Essex, which county had been electing freeholders by Assembly districts since 1889.[55] With a population of nearly 50,000, composed in large part of farmers and including almost all the agricultural area of the county, that district would then elect two freeholders and two Assemblymen, instead of only one of each. "The apparent result of this [request] was a still further discrimination against the farmers of said county by the making of a new district in the city of Newark," the Committee's report concluded.[56]

As the last decade of the nineteenth century began, the insistence on municipal representation on the freeholder boards, increasingly impractical with the rapid incorporation of new towns and boroughs, was abandoned by organized farmers throughout New Jersey. That the State Board of Agriculture could endorse a bill permitting local referenda concerning three-member boards to be elected at large clearly indicates that the time for radical changes was not too distant. But for the next few years the urban-rural conflict would be subordinated to another type of struggle for control of the county governing bodies.

9

RISE AND FALL OF THE ASSEMBLY DISTRICT APPROACH: ESSEX AND HUDSON, 1889–1894

Partisan advantage was to become a greater consideration than maintaining the system of freeholder elections by municipal units. Controlling both legislative houses in 1889 (for the first time in eleven years), 1891, 1892, and 1893, Democrats favored the election of county board members by Assembly districts in certain counties. Under their aegis, new heights of gerrymandering were reached. As a counter move, the Republicans were forced to support the principle of at-large elections and minority representation.

REORGANIZATION ACT OF 1889

As part of a reorganization plan to give the Democrats control of the freeholder boards in both Hudson and Essex, Assembly Bill No. 329 of 1889 was introduced by William C. Heppenheimer (D-Hudson) for the Speaker, R. S. Hudspeth (D-Hudson). Besides electing a director at large, each of the two first-class counties was to elect one freeholder from each of its Assembly districts, which were about to be gerrymandered that year. The existing board would continue in office until and including November 30, 1889, no matter when its term was due to end. The new board would replace it on December 1.

"It is inevitable that such a scheme as that devised by the majority of the present Legislature to perpetuate the sway of Democracy in State and county affairs should trample roughshod the rights of localities," declared the Republican *Newark Evening News.* The Democratic gerrymander of Assembly districts also contemplated control of the freeholder boards, "a fact, when accomplished, that will leave the rich and thickly settled townships of Essex County in a hole both deep and broad." Although the current allotment of twenty-five of forty freeholders to the townships was conceded to be "unfair to the city," the proposed change to two freeholders for the area outside Newark against eight from the city would be "incomparably more unjust the other way." In that case, readers were advised, "the city would get the oyster and the townships the shell."[1]

"It is a wild and groundless argument to advance, that because this bill will be good for Hudson it will be fair for Essex," a Democratic member of the Essex board's legislative committee told the press. Besides the difference in area of the two counties (Essex, 140 square miles; Hudson, fifty square miles), he noted the contrast in the "geographical aspect of the counties." Essex was "mountainous, uneven and almost a network of streams, highways and byways," while Hudson had "the broad expanse of meadows, really a barren waste, which requires no attention from county officials." Essex had about 1,500 bridges and culverts, compared with two hundred for Hudson; and more than 1,200 of the Essex bridges were outside Newark. Although each county had ten Assembly districts, "Hudson Freeholders would earn their salaries easily, while the Essex Freeholders could hardly give the work required of them proper attention by working every day in the year." The City of Orange and the townships together would elect only two freeholders and would never elect the director at large; he would be elected by Newark, and it was "reasonable to suppose that he would be a Republican." The legislative committees of county boards were powerless to influence the Democratic legislators, who would say that they "can recognize only political grounds in their movements, regardless of public and private interests."[2]

Party regularity during final consideration of the reorganization bill was blatant. With not a vote to spare, the measure passed the Assembly, thirty-one Democrats in favor, twenty-three Republicans opposed. McDermit was the only Democrat included with the five Republicans who did not cast a ballot. Also with a bare majority, the bill passed the Senate: eleven Democrats to nine Republicans; one Republican, not recorded.[3] On the same day, John Gill (R-Essex) unsuccessfully resurrected David Ball's 1885 plan to divide his county and form a new one to be called "Carteret," this time to include the City of Orange, where he lived, and all the townships except Clinton (Assembly Bill No. 478).[4] Two days later, when

Democratic Governor Robert S. Green signed the text of the Hudson-Essex reorganization bill into law,[5] a Jersey City newspaper reported the likelihood that the constitutionality of the act would be tested by the people of Essex County.[6]

The newspaper was right. Six months later the New Jersey Supreme Court unanimously upheld the act's constitutionality (*State, ex. rel. Christian* v. *Mortland*)[7] and the decision was affirmed, 9 to 2, by the Court of Errors and Appeals in 1890.[8] Rejecting the argument that the object of the act was not truly expressed in its title ("An act to reorganize the board of chosen freeholders in counties of the first class in this state"), the state's highest tribunal held:

> . . . The title of an act is, in the constitutional sense, aptly expressive of its object if it contain a mention of the subject matter generally, together with a succinct indication of the legislation respecting it.[9]

The majority opinion rejected the contention that the act was a local and special law, regulating the internal affairs of towns and counties:

> . . . viewed from the standpoint of population, the act in question must be deemed to be general in that it reaches the one class to which the legislature has determined that it is appropriate, and that class is distinguished by those features which constitute its appropriateness from all the other counties in the state.[10]

Like the Supreme Court's opinion, this one did not decide whether Assembly districts were illegal creations, inasmuch as New Jersey's Constitution contained no mention of them:

> . . . it is sufficient to say that we are not now concerned with legality of such subdivisions of counties. The act under review refers to these districts for the purpose of defining a territorial limit. Such precincts as assembly districts do exist, whether legally or not, and to each of these *de facto* districts a freeholder is assigned. Beyond this we need not, at this time, go.[11]

By 1892 it was discovered that the 1889 reorganization statute had apparently omitted provision for ending the terms of the incumbent freeholders in first-class counties and for electing their successors. In response to these problems, Assembly Bill No. 287, extending the term of Essex and Hudson freeholders until May, 1893, was introduced by James A. Dempsey (D-Essex).[12] In addition, the bill lengthened the term of future freeholders in these counties to three years. The Assembly passed the measure, 34 to 2, with Democrats casting twenty-two of the affirmative votes. In the Senate, the vote was thirteen Democrats in favor, four Republicans, opposed.[13]

Enacted without Governor Abbett's signature,[14] the text was bitterly criticized for failing to provide machinery for the April elections of district-elected freeholders mandated by an 1891 freeholder statute.[15] To correct this oversight and to increase the term of the director at large, still elected in November, to three years, Assembly Bill No. 294 was sponsored by Joseph P. Clarke (D-Essex). According to the *Newark Evening News*, passage of the bill might be prevented by Hudson politicians who were "apprehensive that their questionable and extravagant acts may result in the election of a Republican Board of Freeholders."[16] But within a few days the bill was passed and signed into law.[17]

An unprecedented case of urban overrepresentation existed for a short time as a result of the 1889 freeholder reorganization act and subsequent legislation redistricting the Assembly.[18] Newark, with more than 71 percent of the Essex population in both 1885 and 1890, was enabled to elect eight of the ten district freeholders in 1889.[19] After the creation (1891)[20] of an additional Assembly district in the county, Newark elected nine of the eleven-member board (1893). Both times the three Republican members of the board included two from that city.[21] But the prediction that only a Newark Republican could become director at large was wrong. In 1889 and again in 1891, the voters elected Dr. Eugene Tiesler, a Democrat from Orange, the second most populous municipality in the county.[22]

In Hudson, excessive representation of the largest city was not a problem. The six freeholders elected by Jersey City districts in 1889[23] to the ten-member board constituted less than that city's proportion of the county population in 1885 (63.4 percent) and almost perfectly in line with the 1890 population (59.2 percent). With the creation of Hudson's Eleventh Assembly District (1891),[24] the six Jersey City freeholders elected in 1893[25] accounted for only 54.5 percent of the board's membership. As in Essex, two of the three successful Republicans in each election were elected by the county seat.[26] Likewise, the director at large, elected in 1889 and re-elected two years later, did not live there: August Bruggemann was a Democrat from Hoboken, the city with the county's second greatest population.[27]

FUTURE ROLE OF ASSEMBLY DISTRICTS QUESTIONED

The New Jersey Supreme Court's decision in *State v. Wrightson* (November, 1893),[28] required that the full number of assemblymen allotted to a county be elected at large within that county. This created "a great diversity of opinion among lawyers as well as laymen" concerning its effect on county government.[29] Some pointed out that the election of freeholders could be provided for in whatever way the legislature thought best, and that the decision depriving that body of the power to elect its own members by Assembly districts could not also be construed as applicable to the method of electing freeholders by those districts in Hudson, Essex, Passaic, Mercer, and Camden. This appeared to be "good reasoning," said one Passaic newspaper, but whether it was sound or not was of very little importance "because one of the first acts of the incoming legislature will be to repeal the law under which the Freeholders are elected by districts and go back to the old plan of a Freeholder for every ward and township."[30] Even among those who thought that district election of freeholders would end, there was immediate disagreement about a new plan. Hudson's Republican Executive Committee, for example, included members who believed that the freeholder board would be replaced by a County Commission of Charities and Correction appointed by the legislature.[31] But a subcommittee of Jersey City's Republican Executive Committee unanimously endorsed a scheme to abolish that municipality's aldermanic districts (coterminous with Assembly districts) and to substitute wards as freeholder constituencies.[32] Some Essex residents wished a return to the system of freeholders elected by townships and by the old fifteen Newark wards (instead of the existing nine wards).[33] The Essex Republican Executive Committee was reported as ready to endorse a board of nine members elected at large,[34] empowered to divide the county into districts from which their successors would be elected.[35] But there was strenuous opposition on the part of Essex assemblymen, subsequently, when the State Republican Committee was to consider a proposed bill providing that the legislature should name a five-member commission to lay out aldermanic and freeholder districts in the several cities and counties. Such a proposition was regarded as not in keeping with the party's pledges of home rule in the platform of the previous campaign.[36] The legislative committee of the Essex County Republican Committee recommended repeal of the 1889 act concerning district-elected freeholders in first-class counties.[37]

OLCUTT BILL VETOED

On March 22, 1894, George P. Olcutt (R-Essex) sponsored Assembly Bill No. 213, providing for the election of new freeholder boards in first-class counties on the second Tuesday in April. Each board was to consist of fifteen members elected at large in classes of five each, to serve terms of one, two, and three years, respectively, with terms thereafter to be three years. Instead of the existing position of director at large, paid $1,500 annually, there would be a director at $1,000 a year, elected by the freeholder board, and the annual $1,200 salary of each of the other members would likewise be reduced to $1,000. Hudson County was not ready for a new election, its legislative delegation maintained in its opposition to passage of the bill; but Essex representatives supported it in order to have a new governing body.[38] When the measure was reported with several unimportant amendments, the previous year's speaker, Thomas Flynn (D-Passaic) told his fellow assemblymen that "it pained him to see how Essex members were trying to ram it down the necks [*sic*] of the Hudson people." Furthermore, he protested, the Olcutt bill was "an undemocratic measure, inasmuch as it made no provision for minority representation." There were then three or four Republican freeholders in Hudson, but under the proposed law there might not be even one. One couldn't expect Hudson to sacrifice everything just to suit the desires of Essex, where the entire board might become Republican.[39] In place of the motion of Max Salinger (R-Hudson) to lay the committee report on the table, Flynn moved to recommit the bill. Charles B. Storrs (R-Essex) urged speedy passage to end the Democrats' "infamous gerrymander" of the two first-class counties. Although it looked as though this measure that "had sprung up like Jonah's gourd" meant only a local fight between Essex and Hudson, John W. Beekman (D-Middlesex) pointed out, the entire state was interested in the outcome. Flynn's motion to recommit was lost, 25 to 29. All the negatives were cast by Republicans, and the affirmatives were Democratic, except for six Republican votes from Hudson and one from Warren. After Salinger's original motion lost, the amendments to the bill were read rapidly by the Clerk "amid much confusion and considerable protest," and the report was adopted. Flynn's motion to reconsider this last vote was lost, 26 to 27. Again all the negatives were Republican; all the Hudson votes were affirmative.[40]

In another delaying tactic, Michael J. Coyle (D-Hudson) moved that the bill be reprinted as amended. The motion was adopted, 40 to 10, with all his Hudson colleagues of both parties voting with the majority. When Salinger insisted that there be a conference of Hudson and Essex members, Storrs and Olcutt replied that they had notified the Hudson legislators of the provisions in ample time during the previous week; and Storrs also asserted that the bill had been discussed at a December meeting in Newark. Salinger and other Hudson members denied this, saying that the Olcutt measure was a new one, of which they were ignorant.[41] William J. Thompson (D-Camden) even offered to bet that there were not three members outside the committee having charge of the bill that could tell its contents.[42] Finally, on Olcutt's motion and "after various dilatory and useless motions had been made," the bill was recommitted.[43]

Apparently, Thompson was right about the widespread unfamiliarity with the provisions of the Olcutt bill. In the same article that reported his comment, the *Newark Evening News* offered its readers this *erroneous* summary of the measure for electing fifteen freeholders at large:

> Take Essex County. The bill sets forth that there shall be fifteen Freeholders, and that nine of these shall be from the city of Newark, one for each ward, and six for the rest of the county. Orange is to have one Freeholder, and East Orange is to be similarly favored. Bloomfield, Belleville and Franklin are to form a sort of a Freeholder district and have one representative for the bunch; Caldwell, Verona and Livingston are to be bunched; Montclair and West Orange are to lock arms; and South Orange, Millburn and Clinton are to have one Freeholder.
>
> That is the plan mapped out. As the Freeholders are to be elected by the voters of the counties at-large, the name of the man favored by the majority of delegates from the district which he is to represent will be placed on the general ticket, . . .[44]

And as late as the following day, when a substitute bill was reported from committee, the *Newark Daily Advertiser* could present the features of the original Olcutt bill in this way:

> It gave to Newark nine Freeholders, and to the districts outside of Newark, six Freeholders. Now, for many years, the suburban districts have not received the representation in the Board of Freeholders that they ought to have, because of their deep interest in the roads, highways, bridges and other county improvements. Indeed, the Board of Freeholders is of far more importance to the agricultural and suburban communities than to the city of Newark, whose affairs come under the direction of so many municipal organizations. It was only fair, therefore, that the suburbs should be well represented on the Board of Freeholders, and this is precisely what the original bill aimed to do, by giving Newark nine and the other districts six Freeholders. Besides, the original bill was a direct embodiment of the principles and promises set forth in the Republican platform, namely, that the power of choosing the Freeholders should be lodged directly in the hands of the people.[45]

In order to insure substantial Republican membership in Hudson's freeholder board, the committee reported a substitute bill for minority representation. It provided that no party could nominate (in a county convention) more than seven candidates for membership on a twelve-man board to be elected at large. While the majority party's seven nominees would be successful, only five of the minority party would be elected. There was no requirement for representation by district. The salary of a freeholder in a first-class county would be reduced from $1,200 to $1,000, and his term would be shortened from three years to only one.[46]

On its third reading, the substitute bill was opposed by Michael J. Coyle (D-Hudson), who declared that a new election would cost the taxpayers of his county $23,000 and that the current scheme of electing freeholders by districts had saved the people $273,000 in four years. He noted that there was $1,463,000 on hand in a sinking fund to the county's credit.[47] There was no use in any Republican's trying to denounce Democrats concerning the management of Hudson's affairs, because Republican freeholders had plunged Hudson into a $250,000 debt some years earlier, added William Harrigan (D-Essex). At this point the speaker succeeded in ending debate, and a roll-call vote on the question of passage was ordered.[48] In the affirmative were thirty-two Republicans; in the negative, nine Democrats and one Republican. Assured that their county's freeholder board would have minority representation, the five of Hudson's six Republicans who cast votes were included in the majority.[49]

Swift action followed. As soon as the Assembly passed the bill, it was signed by the speaker and given to the secretary of the Senate, who ran with it to the upper chamber, where it was immediately ordered to first reading and referred to committee. An objection by William D. Daly (D-Hudson) prevented the bill's advancing to second reading on the same day, but the measure was reported without amendment on the next day and passed second reading.[50]

Without a negative vote, the Senate amended the bill to increase the board membership to twenty-five to be elected at large, after the Essex County Republican Committee and other G.O.P. leaders had refused to approve a twelve-member body on the ground that township residents were demanding "home and home Freeholders." There were to be fifteen names on each party ticket; and the expectation was that ten minority party members would be elected. To compensate for the greater number of freeholders, the annual salary was further reduced to $500.[51] "What good is $500? It is better to give them no salary at all," argued William D. Daly (D-Hudson). "It is as much as Senators get," noted Edward Stokes (R-Cumberland). "Ah! But Senators are here only eight or nine weeks. Freeholders serve all year," Daly replied.[52]

Because long discussions had led the Hudson legislators to conclude that they could expect nothing better than the amended substitute bill, their meeting with the Essex members and party leaders resulted in an agreement to let it come up for a vote.[53] On April 2 the measure barely passed the Senate, eleven Republicans to nine Democrats.[54] Immediately, it was rushed to the Assembly, which had taken a recess awaiting its arrival. To muster enough members for passage, a call of the House and a locking of doors were required. The rules were suspended by a strict party vote, and the amendments placed on third reading. After the Democrats chided their opponents for rushing the bill through without giving the minority an opportunity to be heard, the Senate amendments passed, thirty-four Republicans to sixteen Democrats and two Republicans. This time again, five of the six Hudson Republicans voted with the majority.[55]

The bill was delivered to Democratic Governor George T. Werts the next morning in the hope that he would either sign it or veto it at once, in time for the legislature to override his disapproval. But the Governor told the press that he would probably hold the measure for five days (plus Sunday) before returning it unsigned, stating that there were more Republicans opposed to it than in favor of it. He admitted telling some Republicans more than a week previously that a measure "on the line of home rule" that they had outlined for *township and ward representation* would be acted on promptly (and possibly approved), so that another bill extending the time for election might be passed. "But the bill that has just passed is bad, in my estimation, and I do not want it to go into effect in time for next week's election [April 10]," he added.[56]

On April 9 the Governor returned the substitute bill to the Assembly with a veto message condemning the scheme as "very crude and indefinite; apparently, a mere temporary makeshift, suggested by the desire of speedily attaining a partisan end." He could "perceive no good reason for arbitrarily fixing the membership at twenty-five." Although elected by the county at large, the free-holders could all be chosen from a single ward or township. Even an attempt to secure local representation through the nomination process could be defeated by the at-large election. The provision for minority representation "might or might not operate beneficially."

"Minority representation should properly be made to depend upon the relative and proportional strength of the parties," and the "proposed bill pays no attention thereto," the Governor declared. Even if the assumption that the correct basis or proportion should be fifteen members for the majority party and ten for the minority party, there could be no certainty that such a division would occur: "There might be three or more tickets of parties nearly evenly balanced, with corresponding results; and in a contest between two parties only, it is manifest that the result would as likely be thirteen and twelve as fifteen and ten." Moreover, the Governor noted a "very great" probability that two or more candidates would receive the same number of votes, rendering it impossible to determine which twenty-five were elected; or a tie might result in deadlocking the board with no remedy provided. "The existing system may (as is said) be unfair as to numerical apportionment," the veto message continued, "but it at least secures representation to defined and ascertained localities, and does not embrace the objectionable features of the substitute scheme."[57]

STORRS BILL VETOED

On the same day, an identical fate met its companion measure. Assembly Bill No. 260, introduced by Charles B. Storrs (R-Essex) five days after Olcutt's ill-fated scheme, provided for the immediate repeal of the 1889 act reorganizing freeholder boards in first-class counties and the repeal of subsequent supplements and amendments. "It was the first 'jingle bill' of the session, it having been introduced, reported, and passed in less than half an hour," observed one Trenton newspaper.[58] The vote for passage was thirty-five Republicans to twelve Democrats.[59] On the following day, there was an unsuccessful motion in the Senate that the rules be suspended and the bill taken up on third reading.[60] When it did reach that stage the next night, George W. Ketcham (R-Essex) explained that the intent was to make way for Olcutt's Assembly Bill No. 213. Suddenly, Foster M. Voorhees (R-Union) started from his seat, walked across the Senate chamber toward Edward C. Stokes (R-Cumberland), who was moving about uneasily, and whispered "Low bridge." Together the two approached Ketcham and advised him not to permit the repealer to be passed until the act providing for the election of new freeholders was in force and it was a certainty that the election would be held on April 10. There was to be no possibility of leaving Essex and Hudson without freeholders. "Like a flash" Ketcham was on his feet with a request, agreed to by the Senate, that the bill lie over until April 2, when it could be passed together with the new reorganization bill.[61] At that time, just before passing the substitute for Assembly Bill No. 213 by a bare majority, the Senate passed the Storrs bill with the minimum number of affirmative votes (eleven Republicans to nine Democrats).[62]

According to the veto message of April 9, the Storrs bill would have repealed not only the 1889 act, but ten supplemental acts as well. "The effect of the enactment of the returned bill would be the abolition of the Boards of Chosen Freeholders in first-class counties of this state, without any provision for obviating the inconvenience and perhaps, disastrous consequences thereof," Governor Werts declared. His simultaneous veto of Assembly Bill No. 213 would prevent the election of successors to the Essex and Hudson freeholders boards on April 10, the Assembly was informed.[63]

KETCHAM BILL PASSED OVER VETO

Partisan efforts to change the system of representation in first-class counties continued. At a conference on April 13 of Republican legislators and leaders from Essex and Hudson, a committee was appointed to prepare a bill ending the terms of their incumbent freeholders without incurring the trouble and expense of new elections. The general plan agreed upon called for replacing each of the two boards with one composed of a single freeholder from each city ward and township to be appointed by the governing bodies of the municipalities to serve until the spring of 1895. Other legislation would provide for the division of the cities into wards.[64] As soon as the bill had been revised four days later, it was rushed to the State House by special messenger, and delivered to Ketcham, who introduced it immediately as Senate Bill No. 152. On the following day it was reported from committee favorably.[65]

The new text provided that on the first Tuesday after the first Monday in May 1894, mayors of first-class cities (Newark, Jersey City) would each appoint one freeholder for every ward, who was to be of the political party which received the highest number of votes at the previous municipal election; mayors of second-class cities (12,000–100,000 population; Hoboken, Bayonne, Orange) would each appoint two freeholders; every township with more than 12,000 inhabitants was to have two freeholders chosen by the township committee; each township or city with fewer than 12,000 inhabitants and each "incorporated town" would have a single freeholder selected by the township committee or governing body. On the second Tuesday of April, 1895, and *every year* thereafter the people would elect a freeholder board under the same scheme of apportionment. Besides shortening the existing three-year term, the bill would reduce the annual $1,200 salary of a freeholder to $500; and instead of a director at large with veto power, who was then paid $1,500, there would be a director at $1,000 elected by the board from their own number, "who shall be the presiding officer of said board, and shall appoint the standing committees." Regardless of the time remaining to be served, the terms of all officers who had been appointed by the existing freeholder boards would expire on May 7.

On the measure's second reading, William D. Daly (D-Hudson) vigorously opposed it. First, he moved to strike out the enacting clause, claiming that the bill deprived the people of their constitutional rights. In reply, Ketcham read from the presentment of a grand jury of Essex County which denounced the corruption of recent freeholder boards there. Daly attacked the grand jury for not indicting the board and added that even though the Democrats had committed the error creating partisan freeholder boards in Essex and Hudson in former years, the Republicans would not be warranted in following such a bad example. Predicting that passage of Senate Bill No. 152 would prove injurious to the Republicans, he suggested a halt in this "headlong partisanship." But Ketcham answered by defending the grand jury as overburdened with work, and he foresaw that its successor would doubtless bring the matter to "a conclusion that would satisfy the most captious critic." The only verbal support for Daly's motion came from John Hinchliffe (D-Passaic), who counseled delay until the fall election, when the people could record their desire for a new freeholder board.[66] These two Democrats cast the only affirmative votes for the motion to kill the bill; eleven Republicans were opposed.[67] After another unsuccessful motion by Daly, requiring the concurrence of the board of aldermen in the appointment of freeholders, the bill passed to third reading.[68] Monmouth's Republican James A. Bradley felt called upon to explain that he favored passage of the bill intact, because the people of Newark and Jersey City, knowing of the efforts to enact other reorganization bills in time for the April 10 election, had "spoken with no uncertain sound" at that election. In his view, they had shown their true desire for reform in every particular and had practically patted the legislature on the back and said, "God bless you; go on your way rejoicing."[69]

Called up shortly afterward for final passage, the bill was recommitted, because Daly claimed to be too ill to debate certain of its provisions.[70] When it was again considered, the Senate accepted amendments by Ketcham providing for borough representation (later deleted), changing the minimum population of townships having two freeholders from 12,000 to 10,000; requiring that the two freeholders from each second-class city must include one from each political party; and requiring that the incumbent auditor and collector in each first-class county should continue in office until their successors would be appointed by the new freeholder boards and duly qualified.[71] The bill was changed again a few days later to exempt veterans from dismissal and to postpone the start of the term of the incoming freeholder boards by two weeks until the third Monday in May. Alteration of the date resulted from the delay in getting the bill passed and the probability that Governor Werts would hold the bill five days before vetoing it, thereby preventing its going into force on the original date (May 7).[72]

After the Governor vetoed as unconstitutional the similar bill for appointed freeholder boards in Camden, Mercer, and Passaic, there was great concern about the possibility of like treatment for Ketcham's first-class county bill. Several Senators argued that it would not receive the support of Republicans in the upper chamber. Among the most outspoken legislators on this point were Stokes and Voorhees, who opposed the selection of freeholders by officials who had not been elected for that purpose or with that possibility in view. Agreeing with the Governor's objections to the recently vetoed bill, these two Senators offered to remain as long as required to pass the proper bills for electing freeholders either at a special election or at the next regular election—even at the risk of incurring the people's condemnation for prolonging the session of the legislature.[73] The Republican leadership prepared a new amendment, accepted by the Senate, eliminating the provision for *appointing* new freeholders, making the new freeholders *elective* in November, 1894, and providing that the incumbent boards retain office until December. Freeholder terms would be *two* years.[74] Only after "considerable coaxing" induced Bradley to join them could the Republicans muster the required eleven affirmative votes from their party members to pass the amended Ketcham bill. Four Democrats voted negatively, and six were not recorded.[75] With "no debate worthy of mention," the Assembly passed it unamended on the same day, thirty-three Republicans to fifteen Democrats and one Republican.[76] Five days later Governor Werts submitted his veto to the Senate:

... A more complex and complicated scheme was never devised by partisan ingenuity. The appetite for political spoil must be absolutely uncontrollable when it compels resort to such legislation. I am at a loss to conceive (except for partisan reasons) why first class cities should be represented by wards and second class cities should not, or why second class cities should have members-at-large and first class cities should not.

The bill is not only complex and complicated, but it is incongruous and inconsistent [with regard to ending the terms of the incumbent freeholders and their appointees on Sunday, December 2, 1894, the day before the new board was to take office]. ...

The sole object of the pending bill is to obtain and retain partisan control by the devious methods therein embodied, of the boards of freeholders in the first-class counties of the State. Were a bill submitted to the Executive, providing for a fair and equitable representation upon a just and impartial basis, the present officials to be superseded at the election to be held in November next, as provided in the pending bill, no objection would be made thereto. But the proposed scheme, partisan, cumbersome, and intended to subvert and defeat the popular will, has not a single merit, and is, in every respect, worse than the system it proposes to supersede.[77]

Both houses repassed the bill: eleven Republicans to nine Democrats in the Senate; and thirty-three Republicans to fifteen Democrats in the Assembly; and it became law.[78]

EFFECT OF KETCHAM LAW MODIFIED

Because of another bill passed over the Governor's veto on the very same day, the exact number of freeholders that the first-class counties would elect in November, 1894, could not be immediately determined. The new statute provided for the mayor or chief executive officer of each first-class city to appoint five residents of that city as commissioners to divide it into wards. In order to insure some semblance of fairness, no more than three commissioners could belong to the same political party.[79] As the press had predicted might happen,[80] fifteen wards were established in the county seat of Essex. Consequently, that city's ward-elected freeholders comprised one-half of the thirty-member board. Two members were elected by Orange, a second-class city, and by East Orange Township, whose population exceeded 10,000. Each of the other eleven municipalities elected a single freeholder. Under this plan, the first county governing body in Essex included twenty-eight Republicans and two Democrats.[81]

In Hudson, matters were more complicated. When the maps defining the wards and precincts were filed in the city clerk's office in August, James F. Fielder, a Democratic commissioner, refused to sign the report, saying that the twelve new wards were arranged to give the Republicans unwarranted control. Another objection was that under this scheme Jersey City would have twelve freeholders (one for every 13,500 residents); and Hoboken, only two (one for every 20,000).[82] Wishing to avoid interfering with the filing of the maps, in case the law for dividing first-class cities should be upheld, Judge Job H. Lippincott of the New Jersey Supreme Court waited until September 1 before he granted a writ sought by a former Democratic Senator from Hudson (William D. Edwards) for a review of the statute's constitutionality.[83]

In subsequently refusing to set aside the stay contained in the writ of certiorari,[84] Judge Lippincott noted that the Supreme Court had already upheld the law in relation to the subdivision of Newark,[85] where the equality of population of the wards had been satisfactory. The allegation that such equality among Jersey City's new wards had been "disregarded to a quite serious extent," he continued, seemed to be supported by *prima facie* proof. Nevertheless, the new freeholder law ended the term of the freeholders and the director at large on December 2. If, upon review by the Court, the new wards were to be declared unequal in population and therefore invalid, the election of freeholders by those wards would "fall to the ground." Jersey City would then be entirely without representation in the county governing body for another year or until some legislative remedy were devised. (Under the earlier law, freeholders held office until their successors were elected and duly qualified.) Moreover, the judge's position was supported by the "entire feasibility" of electing freeholders under existing legislation with regard to the disputed division of the first-class city into wards. Jersey City was already divided into aldermanic districts for the purpose of municipal government, and each of these districts was a ward in the legal sense. With the rest of the county there would be no problem, because the representation was not dependent upon wards. The first-class county reorganization act could be "fully complied with."[86] Consequently, in November 1894 a freeholder was elected from each of Jersey City's six aldermanic districts, rather than from the twelve new wards, as proposed. As second-class cities, Hoboken and Bayonne each elected two freeholders; and the Town of Union and the Township of West Hoboken (both with more than 10,000 population) did likewise. The new twenty-member Hudson board remained under Democratic control, thirteen to seven.[87]

But the judiciary changed the situation. In 1895 the New Jersey

Supreme Court held that Jersey City's division into wards was illegal, because it appeared to have been made with regard to the equality of the average total *vote* of the new wards, rather than with regard to equality of *population*.[88] The Hudson freeholder board that was elected in 1896, after the establishment of *new* ward lines, was increased to twenty-seven members. Twelve of them were elected by wards in Jersey City, and one by the newly incorporated Borough of East Newark. The remainder were allotted as in 1894. For the first time in years, the Republicans were in the majority on the board: fifteen to twelve.[89]

The use of Assembly district constituencies for the election of freeholders in both first-class counties—however partisan in motivation—did introduce a note of simplicity. No longer was it necessary to weigh a city ward against a rural township or a small borough and make a judgment of their relative claims for separate representation. The elements for equity of representation according to population were present—if the gerrymandering of Assembly districts could ever be controlled. But the potential of this approach was crushed when the courts ruled in 1893 that the very existence of Assembly districts was unconstitutional. Representation on freeholder boards in Essex and Hudson was thrown into confusion compounded by partisan manipulation. Eventually, a scheme of city ward and township representation was evolved by the Republican legislative majority and made its way past a hostile Democratic Governor. Essex and Hudson thus returned to an older form of freeholder representation, though one that did give some recognition to the amount of population of the areas represented.

One of the more significant aspects of the Assembly district bill of 1889 for first-class counties was that it occasioned the judiciary's support for the concept of classifying counties by population for purposes of reasonable legislation. In turn, this decision encouraged extension of the approach to other counties and ultimately led to the breakdown of municipal representation on freeholder boards.

10

RISE AND FALL OF THE ASSEMBLY DISTRICT APPROACH: PASSAIC, CAMDEN, AND MERCER, 1892–1894

With a majority in both legislative houses in 1892, the Democrats proceeded to extend their control over several larger counties. Two ways were proposed to accomplish this; and although both were passed by the legislature, only the election of freeholders by Assembly districts was approved by the Governor.

An earlier attempt (1890) to have governing bodies of larger counties elected by Assembly districts had failed in a Senate that the Republicans controlled by a majority of one. Howell C. Stull (D-Mercer) introduced Assembly Bill No. 139, requiring the election of two freeholders at $500 a year from every Assembly district in each county of the second class (Passaic, Camden, Mercer, Union, Monmouth, Middlesex, Bergen, Morris, Burlington) and the election of a director at large at $1,000 annually in each. "Under the gerrymander of the Assembly districts the Democrats would have the Board almost all the time in Mercer and most of the other counties, and schemers and corruptionists could easily manipulate such small boards," noted the *State Gazette*.[1] This was disputed by the *Daily True American*, which noted that the director at large and the two members from the First District were sure to be Republicans, and the Second and Third Districts could go to either party.[2] But even an amended version of the bill failed to reach a vote.

PASSAGE OF LANNING LAW

Plans for making gerrymandered constituencies the basis of freeholder representation were introduced in 1892 by James W. Lanning (D-Mercer). On February 9 he sponsored Assembly Bill No. 230, providing that in each of the counties with a population of not less than 75,000 nor more than 200,000 the governing body should consist of three members from each Assembly district. By such a scheme, Passaic would have twelve freeholders, Camden nine, and Mercer nine. They were to be elected for three-year terms, beginning December 1, at the November general elections and would be paid $600 annually. All terms of incumbent freeholders that would expire before November 30 were to be extended to that date. When this bill had still not been reported from committee after three weeks, Lanning offered Assembly Bill No. 387, with the same provisions for freeholder apportionment and salaries. But the board members were to be elected at the municipal and township elections in the spring, and those freeholders who had been elected during the previous spring (1891) for two-year terms were to remain in office until May, 1893. Moreover, the $600 yearly salary would not take effect until expiration of the terms of the holdovers, when the boards should consist solely of members elected by Assembly districts.

Within two days Assembly Bill No. 387 passed both houses, but not without vigorous protest in the Assembly. Joseph M. Engard (R-Camden) asserted that a more daring attempt at the wholesale robbery of the people's rights had never been conceived, that the measure was pernicious in every sense of the word and a direct blow at the fundamental principles of the Union's form of government. Proponents of the change were "battering down the walls of home rule stone by stone."[3] William H. Cole (R-Camden) "became livid with rage when the bill came up," reported a Trenton newspaper. "He got off his usual diatribe and worked himself up to a high pitch of excitement," declaring that the bill was "undemocratic, unpatriotic, and everything else that was devilish." Under such a system with a majority of Democratic freeholders, the people would not be properly represented. Barton B. Hutchinson (R-Mercer) called attention to the population of each Assembly district, arguing that many fair-minded Democrats were opposed to this legislation, which could not result in fair representation. With much less territory than the townships, for example, Trenton would dominate the new Mercer board by electing all but two of the members. In defense of the bill, Lanning pointed out that it would save the Mercer taxpayers nearly

$10,000 a year in salaries alone. Currently, such expenses amounted to $15,000 annually, while they would be reduced to $5,400.[4] On March 2 the bill was passed in the Assembly, thirty-eight Democrats to sixteen Republicans, and in the Senate thirteen Democrats to five Republicans, despite the statements of John J. Gardner (R-Atlantic) to the upper chamber that he doubted the text's constitutionality.[5] Not until March 15 did Governor Abbett, a Democrat, sign the measure into law.[6]

By that date the election of freeholders by municipalities and wards had already been held. Along with Lanning's Assembly Bill No. 387, Democrats in both houses had passed his "chaser," Assembly Bill No. 388, fixing the second Tuesday in April for the election of all officers (including freeholders) in any municipality in any county where the freeholder board was to be elected by Assembly districts. But John Hood, a Democratic candidate for mayor of Camden, opposed the measure, maintaining that his chances would be improved if he should run on the same ticket with the city's freeholder candidates on March 8, as scheduled. At Hood's request that the bill be withheld from Governor Werts until after that election, Senate President Robert Adrain (D-Middlesex) locked it up in his desk.[7] Municipal elections were held on the usual date.[8]

On March 15, when the Governor approved Lanning's Assembly Bill No. 387 concerning the election of freeholders by Assembly districts in Passaic, Camden, and Mercer, he also signed Senate Bill No. 245, nullifying the March 8 election of freeholders by municipalities and wards in those counties.[9] Sponsored by John Hinchliffe (D-Passaic), the measure provided that counties with more than 75,000 inhabitants hold freeholder elections on the second Tuesday in April and that the election of any freeholder on any other day in 1892 be "declared null and void and of no effect whatever." Of course, the vote was partisan: thirteen Democrats to five Republicans and one Democrat in the Senate; and thirty-one Democrats and one Republican to fourteen Republicans and three Democrats in the Assembly.[10]

As intended, the April election of freeholders from gerrymandered Assembly districts increased the board membership of the Democrats; but their success was neither total nor without complications. Incumbents were to be continued in office until the expiration of their terms in 1893, and, consequently, the election of six of the nine district freeholders in Camden enabled the Democrats to capture control of the board by only one vote. There were two holdover Republicans.[11] In Mercer, the Democrats insured their recent domination by adding six of the nine district freeholders to the party's majority of the nine incumbents from the municipalities and wards.[12] But in Passaic the Republicans won eight of the twelve district-constituencies to augment their majority of four of the seven hold-over members.[13] In this county they had been challenged by successful candidates in the March 8 election.[14]

Union had not been included in any of Lanning's bills. But the *Elizabeth Daily Journal* erroneously reported that the first one (Assembly Bill No. 230) would apply to *all* counties with more than 70,000 population (even Essex and Hudson) and would, consequently, affect Union's 72,467 residents. "Thus by this iniquitous bill the Democrats [,] while casting less than a majority of the votes in the whole county, would have a two thirds majority in the Board of Chosen Freeholders," an editorial remarked, pointing out that Union's delegation to the Assembly was so constituted.[15] The freeholder board was then controlled by a Republican majority of one.[16] Only weeks later could the newspaper note that in Lanning's bill "Union County and Monmouth County [69,128] were deftly left out, because Senator [Frederick C.] Marsh [D-Union] and others feared the righteous wraths of the voters in the townships."[17] Doubtless this was true. In Passaic, Mercer, and Camden, the overwhelming majority of people lived in Paterson (74.5 per cent), Trenton (71.8 per cent), and the City of Camden (66 per cent); and these cities were, respectively, six times, fourteen times, and thirteen times as populous as their closest county rivals. But Elizabeth accounted for only 52 per cent of Union's residents and had only twice the population of Plainfield. (Monmouth's largest municipality, Ocean Township, included 10,209).[18]

Senator Marsh's partisan plan, not involving Assembly districts, was proposed to the Democratic joint caucus on March 2. Said to be approved by Governor Abbett, it would require the election of a freeholder for every 5,000 population in any city having more than 50,000 inhabitants in any county of the second class. Marsh argued that not only would Union's Republican board become Democratic, when Elizabeth's 37,764 residents would elect seven members instead of four, but the scheme would also help his party's candidates in Passaic, Mercer, and Camden. (Paterson would elect fifteen freeholders; Trenton and Camden City eleven each.) When Lanning replied that his own Assembly Bill No. 387 was completely satisfactory to Mercer, the legislators designated that one as the caucus measure and agreed simply to recommend Marsh's bill and let it take its chances without enforcement of party discipline.[19] "The chances, it was agreed, were against the measure," noted a Newark newspaper.[20]

As introduced on that same day, March 2, just before Lanning's Assembly measure was to be received in the upper chamber and passed, Marsh's Senate Bill No. 212 would apply only to Elizabeth. Any city in the state with a population by the last federal census of *not* more than 50,000 persons would be entitled to elect one freeholder for every 5,000 inhabitants and one freeholder for every fraction of 5,000 inhabitants above 2,500. (Union's county seat would have eight board members, rather than seven as under Marsh's original plan.) Nothing in the bill was to be construed to decrease the current representation of any city falling under the terms of the act, nor was the text to apply to any city where the freeholders were then being elected by Assembly districts (Hudson, Essex).[21] Under suspension of the rules in both houses, on March 7, an amended version passed the legislature. In the Senate, the vote was fourteen Democrats to three Republicans; in the Assembly twenty-nine Democrats and four Republicans to ten Republicans and three Democrats.[22] But Democratic Governor Abbett pocket-vetoed the bill, doubtless because its application to a single municipality was patently special legislation, whereas the original Marsh plan applied to all cities with more than 50,000 residents in second-class counties.

The Lanning Law provoked continued attacks by public officials on its constitutionality. For example, Passaic's county counsel "had no hesitation in saying that the bill reapportioning the representation in the Board of Freeholders is unconstitutional." In his opinion, the Lanning measure interfered with the classes of counties as then constituted, because it applied (theoretically) to counties of both the first class and the second class. (Although 150,000 population was the dividing point between the two categories, there was no county with a population between that figure and the Lanning law's upper limit of 200,000.)[23] More than a year later, a local journal was advising the City Council of Passaic "to think twice before beginning a legal fight against the Freeholders," warning that there were "at least two very good reasons" against adopting a resolution introduced earlier that week to instruct the city attorney to test the constitutionality of the 1892 statute. First, the process of litigation would take two, and possibly three, years, during which the city would incur the ill will of the freeholder board and be wholly cut off from county favors as a result. Second, even though the law might have been crudely drafted, the newspaper could "speak with the utmost assurance as to the constitutionality of the principle" involved: "The Legislature has as much right to direct how and when the Freeholders shall be elected as it has to pay the Governor's salary, or elect United States Senators." The "true remedy" for the injustice inflicted on the city "must be sought in another direction," readers were told. Instead of being "buried" in a district dominated by the Republican end of Paterson ("the source and secret of our unfortunate lack of representatives, not only in the Board of Freeholders but in the Legislature"), the City of Passaic would have to constitute or control an Assembly district. "If we were to fight at all our blows should therefore be aimed at the infamous Democratic gerrymander," the editorial argued.[24]

Repeal of Lanning Law

The Supreme Court decision (1893) ending the district election of assemblymen prompted a change in the freeholder representation of Mercer, Camden, and Passaic. With Republicans controlling both legislative houses in 1894, John Ginder (R-Mercer) sponsored Assembly Bill No. 135, repealing the 1892 act for district-elected freeholders in every county with a population of not less than 75,000 or more than 200,000 and replacing them in May 1894 with one freeholder "from each township, ward and borough possessing complete authority of local government." Each new board member would be paid $100 for a one-year term. After only a week with no recorded committee action on the measure, Ginder obtained leave to withdraw it from the files.[25] Then he introduced Assembly Bill No. 165,[26] with the same repeal clause and the same distribution of freeholders, but with a provision for two-year terms at annual salaries of $150. In addition, the incumbent freeholders, elected by Assembly districts, would be allowed to complete their terms.

At first it was thought that the legislature would pass Ginder's Assembly Bill No. 165, but then there were reports that Senator William H. Skirm (R-Mercer) would not accept anything less than a clean sweep of the incumbent freeholders.[27] On March 22 he sponsored Senate Bill No. 10, repealing the 1892 act, and providing that counties with not less than 75,000 nor more than 200,000 inhabitants elect one freeholder from "each township, ward and borough possessing complete autonomy of local government of such county." On the second Wednesday of May, the existing freeholder board in each of the affected counties (Camden, Mercer, Passaic) would be replaced by a new board, elected for two years at an annual salary of $150.

"The Skirm bill has been made a 'party measure' and will be put through both houses next week," a Passaic newspaper correctly asserted.[28] When the measure came up for final passage, Skirm maintained that it would save Mercer County thousands of dollars. Instead of the $5,400 current expense for the salaries of nine freeholders, the amount to be paid to eighteen freeholders would be only $2,700. Edward C. Stokes (R-Cumberland), speaking for Senate President Maurice A. Rogers (R-Camden), pointed out that 65,000 people in Camden had three representatives on the county governing body, while 10,000 people in another section of the same county also elected three. The existing system was "unjust and unfair." John Hinchliffe (D-Passaic) opposed the bill, and William D. Daly (D-Hudson) could see nothing but politics in it. Nine men, he claimed, could do as much work as eighteen. Elected by the people, the current boards should not be legislated out of office for a lot of place-hunters.[29] Eleven Republicans and a Cape May Democrat voted for passage; seven Democrats were against it.[30]

That same day "a very lively discussion" of the Skirm bill was held in the Republican Assembly caucus. Speaker John I. Holt announced his opposition to any change that might result in a setback in his county of Passaic, where his party dominated the freeholder board. According to a leading newspaper, "He did not seem to fear a defeat so much as he did a shakeup among office holders that might result disastrously to Republican interests later on." Men with good election-day followings might be replaced by others in the spring, and the "outs" would probably retaliate at the general elections in the fall. But Holt's argument failed to convince his colleagues from Camden and Mercer, who hoped that the G.O.P. could wrest control of freeholder boards from the Democrats in those counties. Taking his defeat "philosophically," when the bill became a caucus measure, he decided to submit to his party's decree "in this as in everything else," the press reported.[31]

During the afternoon, the bill was rushed through all its stages in the Assembly. Before the vote for passage was taken, Democratic ex-Speaker Thomas Flynn of Passaic asked "in behalf of the Republicans of Passaic" that the measure be defeated and his county spared from moving into the Democratic column. General laughter followed his "odd speech," but no one detected a smile on his face. In a similar vein, Thomas McEwan, Jr. (R-Hudson), who was the majority leader, declared "in behalf of the Democrats of Passaic" that they did not wish the Skirm bill to pass. "I have as much right to speak for the Democrats of Passaic as he has to speak for the Republicans," Mc-

Ewan insisted.[32] After opposition from Camden's only Democrat in the legislature, William J. Thompson, the bill was passed: thirty-nine Republicans and one Salem Democrat, in favor; seventeen Democrats against.[33]

But the next week the press reported that the reorganization plan was "dead so far as any effect it may have this year." Governor Werts had conferred with the clerk of Mercer County and had pointed out that the bill was so defective from a legal standpoint as to be practically worthless.[34] Becoming alarmed on learning that a veto message had been prepared for delivery to the Senate, Mercer's legislators and leaders decided to recall the bill from the Governor and amend it. "After some difficulty," a concurrent resolution accomplished the return of the measure, and the faulty wording was corrected.[35] The most important amendment was the insertion of a comma after the word "ward" in the provision for "one freeholder from every township, ward and borough having the autonomy of local government of such county." (Because wards did not possess such autonomy, passage of the original text would leave the wards of cities without any representation, the Governor held).[36] In addition, the time before an election within which certificates of nomination must be filed was shortened from eight days (as provided in another law) to three days, in an effort to make the measure's provisions effective for the following week's election.[37]

During the "lively debate" in the Senate, Skirm charged that the Governor had not kept his promise to return the bill immediately, as first passed, with his approval or disapproval. Moreover, Skirm expected the chief executive to hold the amended bill for five days, thus making it inoperative for the forthcoming election.[38] The amended bill was passed in the upper chamber, eleven Republicans to six Democrats, and rushed to the Assembly, where it was passed without debate, thirty-eight Republicans to fifteen Democrats and a Hudson Republican.[39]

Six days later the Senate received this veto message:

> ... The bill returned proposes radical changes in the government of several counties of the State, which changes are sought to be consummated at the election to held [*sic*] not more than one or two days succeeding the passage of the bill, should its passage not be arrested or delayed by Executive action. Sudden and radical changes in government should be founded upon evident public necessity. I cannot see that any such occasion exists for the hurried passage of the proposed law. Against the principle embodied in the bill no objection is made.
>
> This bill was originally received by the Executive on the 28th ult., and

but for errors that made it partially, if not wholly inoperative, would then have received prompt Executive approval. Its approval at that date would have afforded time and opportunity to have given notice of election thereunder and for the filing of necessary certificates of nomination as required by existing laws. . . .

It cannot be possible that any justification can exist for such unusual and extraordinary legislation. An election to be held without notice, and certificates of nomination to be filed up to the hour of 12 o'clock midnight, on the day preceding such unnotified election. The fact that such provisions must be inserted to render the act operative, demonstrates beyond dispute the impropriety and unwisdom of its enactment at the present time.[40]

The message was ordered laid upon the table and was not taken up until more than two weeks later. At that time its consideration was postponed.[41]

When Governor Werts seemed "bent on preventing the reform party in the Legislature from reforming the Boards of Freeholders in Passaic, Camden, and Mercer counties,"[42] the *Passaic Daily News* offered a plan that the editors had endorsed the previous year as "the best remedy we know of" for county government's faults.[43] It had been suggested by Mayor Walston R. Brown in his second annual message to the Passaic City Council in January 1893, because the taxpayers had been blaming municipal officials who were powerless to reduce the high taxes created by "exorbitant" freeholder demands. The scheme called for the freeholder board to consist of one alderman from each ward of each city and the chairmen of the township committees or other governing bodies of the townships and boroughs. Having the senior alderman in a ward serve as freeholder would produce a "perfect system of rotation." In Passaic, for example, where each ward had three aldermen elected for staggered three-year terms, the one serving his last year would have to submit to the judgment of his constituents at the end of the year. Although other cities, like Paterson, had only two aldermen elected from each ward for two-year terms, "that would not alter the conditions in the least except that the rotation would be more rapid."[44]

"The manifest advantage of having the governing body of the county directly under the control of the governing bodies of the cities and townships," readers were told, "must be apparent at the very first glance." It would concentrate responsibility and reduce expenses by eliminating one whole set of public officials "with their retinue of friends and dependents who have to be aided or supported at the public expense, as a reward for services at election time." In addition, the plan would "not disturb the partisan equilibrium," because the aldermen in each ward were "invariably of the same faith as the Freeholder." Any difference would be accidental and just as likely to occur with elective freeholders as under Mayor Brown's proposal.[45] But no other support could be found for such a change.

The Republicans were determined to alter the system in Passaic, Camden, and Mercer. "Having been thwarted in their attempt to railroad" Senate Bill No. 10 through the legislature in time for the election, the Republicans proposed another way to oust the incumbent boards in the three counties. Skirm introduced Senate Bill No. 127, for which President Maurice A. Rogers (R-Camden) was really responsible,[46] repealing the 1892 act for Assembly-district freeholder constituencies and ending the terms of the current freeholders in counties with not less than 75,000 nor more than 200,000 inhabitants on the second Wednesday in May, 1894. To replace the removed freeholders, the bill empowered the board of aldermen or common council in cities, the borough council in autonomous boroughs, and the township committee in townships to choose one person from each of the respective city wards, autonomous boroughs, and townships to serve as freeholders until the second Wednesday in May, 1895. Just prior to that day, the people would have elected members of the county governing board from these same constituencies to serve two-year terms at an annual salary of $150.

After debate along the lines of arguments on Skirm's earlier bill, the Senate passed the new one: eleven Republicans and a Burlington Democrat to two Democrats.[47] In the Assembly, thirty-two Republicans outvoted thirteen Democrats, despite Flynn's contention that Senate Bill No. 127 was unconstitutional in that it attempted to regulate the internal affairs of municipalities.[48] Immediately, the *Passaic Daily News* predicted that the Democratic Governor would veto the measure and that the "determined Republicans" would repass it over his disapproval.[49]

The prophecy was correct. In his veto message Governor Werts noted "serious constitutional objections to the proposed legislation that suggest themselves to every legal mind," and he understood that measures would be promptly taken, if the bill were repassed, to have the courts determine the matter. There were other objections which seemed to him "equally conclusive." No time was fixed within which the interim freeholders were to be appointed; nor, indeed, was their appointment mandatory. Moreover, the Governor complained that the bill did not invest the interim board with all the powers and authority that were transferred from the outgoing board to the board that was to be elected by the people in May 1895.

Consequently, the interim board would be "unable to perform any function except possibly to draw the individual salaries of one hundred and fifty dollars"; and for a year the counties would be "without any county government, with all the disastrous consequences as such a condition of affairs may entail." Even if it were constitutional, the mode of appointment was "violative of the principles of home rule that should prevail in the choice of such officials"; and such a procedure was "unprecedented and altogether unwarranted, except upon evident public necessity," which would justify a *special* election. "Aside from the desire and determination to effect a change for merely partisan purposes," Governor Werts declared, "no reason is or can be advanced for the proposed legislation."[50]

Great haste was made to repass Senate Bill No. 127, when it was considered a week later (May 8). Because it provided that the terms of the current freeholders in Passaic, Camden, and Mercer were to end at noon on the second Wednesday in May (May 9), there was some concern that the bill would be inoperative unless enacted by the noon hour of that day.[51] Only with the aid of a Burlington Democrat, Mitchell B. Perkins, could the Senate Republicans repass the measure, 11 to 6.[52] Believing that they lacked sufficient votes to pass it in the Assembly, the Republicans sought Democratic votes unsuccessfully on May 9. In order to secure three additional votes the Republicans sent messengers and telegrams "in all directions," and finally the speaker issued warrants for the arrest of his absent party colleagues. When 12 o'clock passed, the Democrats "poked fun at the discomfited [*sic*] Republicans," and some of the majority party themselves were "outspoken in their satisfaction over the failure to become law of a bill that they acknowledged was a most vicious piece of legislation, and for which they only voted because of the arbitrary power of King Caucus."[53] The Assembly recessed until 2 o'clock, and the bill was passed, thirty-three Republicans to thirteen Democrats, over the Governor's veto at 2:47 o'clock at the insistence of Senate President Rogers, who wished to dislodge the Democratic Camden board. He maintained that this new act (Chap. 165) would be valid, but others argued that still another bill would have to be passed.[54]

That is exactly what happened. On that same day (May 9) the lower chamber passed Assembly Bill No. 134 which had also been originally intended to take effect that noon (the second Wednesday of May). As introduced on February 20 by John Ginder (R-Mercer), it simply repealed the 1892 act for Assembly districts as freeholder constituencies. The vote was thirty-three Republicans, in favor; twelve Democrats opposed.[55] In the Senate, the bill was amended to take effect *immediately* and to require that "the term of office of all persons elected or appointed under the provisions of said act [of 1892] are hereby terminated."[56] With three of the bare majority of eleven votes supplied by Democrats, and with no recorded opposition, the new version of the measure passed. Under a suspension of the rules, in order to allow prompt action, the Assembly accepted the Senate amendments, thirty-six Republicans to sixteen Democrats.[57]

After a week, the Governor submitted his veto. Noting that the purpose of the bill was to end (immediately) the terms of certain freeholder boards and all their appointees and employees, he pointed out that no successors were provided to these boards, nor were their powers and duties vested elsewhere. "The bill is part and parcel of the scheme conceived by partisan ingenuity, and now being consummated by legislative act, to seize for partisan purposes wherever possible the various Boards of Freeholders throughout the State," the Governor asserted.[58] Notwithstanding his disapproval, the Assembly repassed the measure, thirty-four Republicans to fifteen Democrats and a Hudson Republican; in the Senate, a Burlington Democrat joined eleven Republicans voting for passage over the negative votes of seven Democrats.[59] Assembly Bill No. 134 became law.[60]

END OF DISTRICT SYSTEM AFFIRMED BY LITIGATION

Legal and political complications did result from the fact that the law changing the freeholder system was passed after the time that it was supposed to take effect. No effort was made to oust the incumbent board in Passaic, where it was Republican, but in Camden and Mercer the municipal governing bodies selected freeholders in accordance with the provision in the Skirm Act of May 9 for filling vacancies.[61] The Democratic incumbents who had been elected in 1892 from Assembly districts would not yield office, maintaining that their three-year terms had not yet expired. In each of these two counties there were rival freeholder boards transacting business, but the county collectors were refusing to honor the orders of either, and the banks would not discount their paper. Camden's Democratic district-elected freeholders began suit to retain control of the board, and Mercer awaited the outcome.[62] In a *quo warranto* proceeding, brought to challenge the legality of the new board's claim to power, the New Jersey Supreme Court on October 11 struck down the plea of Camden's old board, ruling that vacancies in the Camden board did exist and that the constitutionality of the 1894 legislation was not questioned at that time.[63] But that decision "only settled a technicality, and not the issue itself," the press observed, and two weeks later the situation had "taken on a new phase." The two Justices announced that they would allow the original *quo warranto* proceedings to stand and would permit the old board to file a demurrer, that is, an objection to the sufficiency in law of such proceedings.[64] Before the Court could rule on that action, the old Democratic board in *Mercer* surrendered its claim to office on the advice of counsel.[65] A newspaper in *Passaic* announced that its freeholder board would remain the *de facto* governing body and that its title would not be contested. But in the spring of 1895 the people would elect a new board by wards and townships.[66]

Camden's Democratic freeholders still did not yield. Other proceedings were subsequently begun, and Justice Alfred Reed amended his former opinion and filed a supplemental one on November 27. It acknowledged the constitutionality of the 1894 legislation creating the new (Republican) board and ending the term of the old (Democratic) one.[67] On November 30, Chief Justice Mercer Beasley, speaking for the New Jersey Supreme Court on another aspect of the case, held that the conduct of Camden's old board members had been "so plainly illegal that it is not possible to believe that in retaining their positions, they had the faintest belief that they were right in so doing." Besides granting a writ of ouster, he imposed a $200 fine on each of the district-elected freeholders who had continued to claim office.[68] The financial penalty was "something new in such cases," remarked a Passaic County newspaper.[69]

Thus ended New Jersey's experiment with boards of freeholders elected from Assembly districts. In Hudson, it had begun in 1875; in Essex, in 1889; and in Passaic, Mercer, and Camden in 1892. By 1894 the system was dead—as were the Assembly districts themselves. Almost unnoticed was the fact that this also ended New Jersey's first experience in decades with relatively small boards of chosen freeholders. In the absence of any immediately palatable alternative to the egregious evils of gerrymandering, the demise of the Assembly district system resulted in a return to representation of townships, wards, and boroughs. But the proposed methods of assigning seats on the boards by areas with fixed boundaries continued to reflect the interests of the major political parties rather than those of the taxpaying municipalities.

11

THE SEARCH FOR SMALLER BOARDS—WITH VARIATIONS: PROPOSALS FOR AT-LARGE ELECTIONS, OPTIONAL LAWS, MINORITY REPRESENTATION, 1894–1900

The end of the short-lived district system of representation in Camden, Mercer, and Passaic (as well as in Hudson and Essex) caused a reversion to the election of freeholders once again by municipalities and wards. But only one type of adjustment in the prevailing system had been eliminated. Between 1894 and 1900 at-large elections, minority representation, optional laws for county government, and even the board's replacement by a nonpolitical body were urged upon the legislature. Not until the new century began were two of these radical features to be embodied in law.

HERBERT BILL

The principle of requiring minority representation on freeholder boards elected at large, sponsored unsuccessfully for first-class counties in Assembly Committee Substitute No. 213 of 1894 (Olcutt Bill) reappeared the following year in a measure intended to apply to *all* counties. Introduced by Charles B. Herbert (R-Middlesex), Senate Bill No. 24 provided for the fall election of seven freeholders in first-class counties, five in second-class counties, and three in third- and fourth-class counties. Each political party that had been authorized by law to select candidates in convention was to nominate four, three, and two persons in these respective categories, and each voter could cast ballots for that number. In the first-class counties, freeholders would receive annual salaries of $2,000, while their counterparts in the other classes would be paid lesser amounts:

$1,200; $1,000; and $500. Members of the board would serve three-year concurrent terms.

Although supported by newspapers in Middlesex and Burlington, the Herbert Bill was opposed by New Brunswick's City Club. It was argued that the election of a new freeholder board in the *fall* would combine local with state and national politics; that the principle of minority representation was a distinct recognition of national politics in county government; that there would not be any significant decrease in the aggregate compensation of the board; and that the bill extended the terms of the current members by seven months.[1] In defense of the measure, the *Daily Fredonian* observed that sheriffs, county clerks, and surrogates were also elected in the fall and that only visionaries could contemplate filling county offices without regard to party politics. Minority representation would help to compel the parties to nominate their best men and would check the majority. The five-member board to be elected in Middlesex would receive a total of $6,000, or less than half the cost of the current governing body; and "in all probability" the bill would be amended to provide for fewer freeholders and smaller salaries. Readers were told that the City Club's objection that the bill would increase the term of the incumbent board members was "the only one of any weight" and that Herbert would amend this feature, if a satisfactory alternative could be devised.[2] After the bill had remained in committee for almost two months, the *Daily Fredonian* observed:

> . . . It will be practically impossible to pass any kind of a Freeholders bill affecting all counties because of the diversity of sentiment in different parts of the State and therefore if those counties which desire the change can be accommodated in one bill it would seem the better part of wisdom to try the experiment.[3]

Middlesex and Burlington were so nearly equal in population that there would be no trouble in framing a bill that would apply only to them, the editorial continued, and both counties would welcome the change.[4] But the Herbert bill never reached the floor of the Senate.

PLAN FOR COMMISSION OF CHARITIES AND CORRECTIONS

In January 1897 Jersey City's *Evening Journal* announced the forthcoming introduction of a bill to replace the freeholder board in each first-class county with a five-member body to be known as Commissioners of Charities and Corrections. It had been proposed to have the members of the first board named in the bill for terms of one, two, three, four, and five years; and thereafter one member would be elected at the annual general election for a five-year term.[5] A week later the legislative committee of the Hudson County Republican Committee brought "a verbose document of forty-seven typographed pages" to Trenton, and Assemblyman Elmer W. Demarest (R-Hudson) promised to sponsor it. In order to gain legislative support to offset the anticipated opposition of Essex and Union, the text had been amended to include the nine second-class counties.[6] Each five-member Board of Charities and Corrections was to be "invested with all the powers now conferred on boards of freeholders, along with others." The first group of five commissioners in each affected county would be elected by a joint meeting of the legislature, but the scheme for staggered terms remained unchanged.[7] In first-class counties, each commissioner would receive $2,500, and each director $3,000 annually; in second-class counties the salaries were to be $2,000 and $2,300.[8]

Immediate objection was made by the press in both first-class counties. The *Evening Journal* characterized the plan as "one of the crudest specimens of legislative drafting which has been seen here in years" and predicted that "if it should be enacted in its present shape it would be operative neither in Hudson nor Essex Counties [because of technical defects in the text], and would hopelessly entangle the second-class counties." On its face, the proposed bill was "unconstitutional," and its details, "almost worthless."[9] The *Newark Evening News* observed that it would take at least three years for the new boards to include majorities of popularly elected commissioners. During that time the commissioners elected by the Republican legislature were sure to be Republican, would have "full sway," and be responsible only to the Governor. "The government of Essex County would be placed in the hands of men in whose election the Senators and Assemblymen from Camden and Cape May and Sussex and Atlantic, and all the other counties, would have a share," readers were warned. The Democratic machine that Governor Leon Abbett had built up had "brought ruin on itself by insensate unfairness and greed," and Republicans should not follow that example.[10] The bill was never introduced!

However, the plan for a Commission of Charities and Corrections was expanded and altered by the *Evening Journal* in mid-1897. It demanded a law requiring the *courts* to appoint a commission with a *nonpolitical* make-up to care for all county roads, because it "would save money and save the roads, and would remove the last pretext for the existence of the Board of Freeholders."[11] According to a later editorial, the care of the county's affairs could be entrusted to either a single or plural governing authority. Hudson County's residents would be satisfied to have a county road commissioner or commission appointed by the court, and a commissioner or Commission of Charities and Corrections, appointed *or* elected. In fact, readers were told, "It would be better so far as Hudson County is concerned to consolidate the county into a single municipality and to give the Aldermen power to employ three men to care for what is now so badly done by the Freeholders." There was no need for representation of municipalities, for they "manage to struggle along with one Surrogate, one Sheriff, and one County Clerk."[12] The election of commissioners would place them under patronage obligations to the politicians, but "appointment by the court would secure competent men who would assume no obligations and for this reason the plan seems to meet general approval."[13] The *Evening Journal* refused to concur in the *Passaic Daily News*'s endorsement of the three-year-old proposal by Passaic's Mayor Walston R. Brown that a county's governing body be composed of the senior aldermen from each city ward and the chairmen of the township committees. Although the *News* contended that the plan "would provide a direct connection between the County Board and the City and Township Boards, and would enable all to watch one another and keep track of all expenditures,"[14] the *Evening Journal* insisted that it "would soon become as cumbrously and crookedly corrupt as the present system."[15]

PARRY BILL

On the day that Hudson's Demarest was to introduce his bill, William C. Parry (R-Burlington) sponsored Senate Bill No. 41, providing that five freeholders (three of one political party and two of the other) be elected at large for three-year terms at $700 per annum in each county with a population between 35,000 and 70,000 (Bergen, Burlington, Cumberland, Hunterdon, Morris, Warren). But there was "a likelihood of its being amended so as to include Camden, Mercer and Passaic," the press reported.[16] Almost two months later, a committee substitute for Parry's measure was concurred in which included *all* counties, but it was to become operative only after submission to and acceptance by the voters at a *referendum*.[17]

In subsequent debate Senate President Robert Williams (R-Passaic) took the floor, maintaining his county's opposition to the bill and arguing that the different sections of the county could not be fairly represented by five commissioners. He was followed at some length by William H. Skirm (R-Mercer), who insisted that the referendum clause would not amount to much. In his view, such an election seldom brought out a fair expression of public opinion; and the change would involve many complications, as evidenced by the mass of laws that had grown up around the freeholder form of government that had existed for generations. A distribution of authority and representation from every township would give a greater guarantee of safety than would a concentration of power. Moreover, Skirm concluded, the proposed $700 salary would be insufficient to compensate men for devoting all their time to county business, and the administration of the system would hardly be improved. Parry replied that only the notorious mismanagement of county affairs by many freeholders had prompted his bill, and that these officials were organizing to defeat an effort to introduce reform. The claim that five commissioners could not manage the interests of Mercer and Passaic would be laughable in Pennsylvania, he declared. Bucks County was larger in area than any county in New Jersey, and had more bridges and county work; yet only three commissioners managed that county's affairs to the utmost satisfaction of all. Not expecting any opposition to his measure, Parry said, he had not prepared the array of facts and figures that he could cite in its support. He told his colleagues:

I am willing to submit the question to the people, and I cannot see why there is any opposition, for if, as the Senators say, the people of their counties do not want the law, then they will not apply for it and if it is applied for, the people being opposed to it will vote it down.[18]

After further attacks on the bill by Edmund L. Ross (R-Cape May) and Herbert W. Johnson (R-Camden), it was laid over for five days to permit consideration when more senators would be present.[19]

At that time Parry developed arguments made earlier, but he met with strong opposition from Williams who insisted that the bill was not adequate for counties, like his own Passaic, with large cities; from William D. Daly (D-Hudson), who found some legal flaws; and from Skirm, who feared that under the measure cities would "be in the saddle."[20] Lacking one vote of a majority, the bill was defeated, 10 to 9. Senators from all the counties originally included in the text were among those voting affirmatively. By changing his vote to negative, Parry became entitled to move for a reconsideration of the bill's defeat.[21] Such a motion was agreed to, 11 to 4.[22] But he later moved successfully for a reconsideration of the vote by which his bill was ordered to a third reading, and the text was amended to provide that the signatures to the petition for the commission system be those of legal voters and, further, that no one should vote for more than one commissioner from any single municipality.[23]

Additional changes four days later killed the Parry bill. Skirm's amendment that the act not apply to any county having a population exceeding 80,000 (Hudson, Essex, Passaic, Camden, Mercer, Union) was adopted, and then the Senate approved an amendment, offered by Ross, to exempt counties of the fourth class (Cape May, Ocean) as well.[24] Enactment of the bill with such exclusions would be "clearly unconstitutional," noted the correspondent of one Trenton newspaper.[25] There was no further Senate action on the commission (small board) plan in 1897.

BENNY BILL

As a result of the general outcry against the Hudson freeholder board, that county's Republican Assembly candidates promised in the fall of 1897 to try to replace it with a small body to take care of county institutions. But not one Republican was elected. Early in January 1898 Hudson's Democratic members of the legislature met in Jersey City and decided to "steal Republican ammunition" by sponsoring a county reorganization plan.[26] When Allan Benny (D-Hudson) introduced Assembly Bill No. 7 two weeks later, the Republican *Evening Journal* remarked, "it was seen that the Democrats had listened to an appeal for bread, and had given a stone."[27] The measure allowed the freeholder board in any county to submit to the people the question of adopting a nine-member freeholder board elected at large for two-year terms. Each regular member was to receive $1,000 annually; the director to be elected by the board, $1,500. No person could vote for more than five freeholders from any one municipality, a "little joker" which meant simply that five board members would invariably come from Jersey City and would control all county patronage, explained the Town of Union's newspaper. "This feature of the bill is decidedly unpopular in North Hudson, and the people in Hoboken, Bayonne, and West Hoboken are not much in love with it either," the Democratic newspaper declared, noting that the plan would probably be amended or defeated.[28]

The bill was "not designed for passage" but "was only intended to 'put the Republicans in a hole,'" the *Evening Journal* maintained in January, after five days had elapsed with no committee action on the measure.[29] "It provided that the Board of Freeholders should be perpetuated, not abolished," readers were subsequently told. If the board decided to order a referendum on the acceptance of the new plan, it would be opposed in the county outside Jersey City. If the scheme were to be adopted, it would "continue in office the same kind of freeholders that the people want to get rid of." A Republican legislature that passed Assembly Bill No. 7 for at-large elections would deprive the G.O.P. of all representation on the Hudson freeholder board. Moreover, Essex and several other counties had found the bill unacceptable, and there was some question about its constitutionality:

> Any bill which will do anything less than abolish the Board of Freehold- ers will require a careful examination of the laws relating to the Freehold- ers, and these extend far back into the last century in some counties. There is no mass of legislation in greater need of codification and simplification. No one seems willing to spend time on a remedial law, though several of the smaller counties are anxious to get rid of their cumbersome Boards of Freeholders.[30]

One week later the Assembly concurred in the adverse report of the Committee on the Revision of the Laws,[31] and no further action on the bill was taken.

McDermott Bill (1899)

But Hudson Democrats in the legislature continued to lead the fight for small boards with county-wide constituencies. Allan L. McDermott (D-Hudson) introduced Senate Bill No. 6 of 1899, pro- viding that the freeholder board in each first-class county be com- posed of seven members elected at-large for two years, with no person voting for more than four freeholders. "That means that the party conventions will select practically the board, and that the voters will have no voice except in the 'turning down' of one of the eight candidates named," one newspaper noted.[32] If it were true that Essex County opposed the bill, McDermott announced, he would amend it by inserting a provision for a referendum.[33] The proposed legislation was "certainly not American!" the *Newark Evening News* protested immediately:

> If the people were too blindly partisan or too indifferent to their in- terests to elect Freeholders, School Commissioners or other local officers [,]

unrestricted suffrage would not be the bulwark of liberty and guardian of the right that the fathers of the Republic supposed it to be.[34]

At the next general election there would be a *mandatory* referendum on establishing an eleven-member freeholder board, elected at-large without any provision for minority representation, according to the committee substitute that was reported without recommendation. In first-class counties, terms of all freeholders were to expire on the first Monday in December, 1900.[35] The plan was opposed by George W. Ketcham (R-Essex), because it would affect his county, which, he assured the Senate, was well-satisfied with the current system and did not want to be disturbed by the agitation attendant on voting on the reorganization question. When William M. Johnson (R-Bergen) expressed his regret that the provision for minority representation had been dropped, McDermott replied that the change had been made in an attempt to satisfy Essex, but the bill would (actually) affect only Hudson, which was then "very badly governed." Denying that politics was involved and, indeed, declaring that he believed in divorcing local affairs from partisanship, McDermott pointed out that the Hudson board was overwhelmingly Democratic. As a member of the Hudson County grand jury, he had voted to indict freeholders of his own political party, and he had voted for the best nominees, both Democratic and Republican, in freeholder elections. McDermott maintained that his sentiment was shared by Hudson voters generally, and that his bill would compel Democrats in that county to nominate their best men.[36] With bipartisan support, the bill was passed, 12 to 0. Seven of the fourteen Republicans in the Senate, excluding Ketcham and Johnson, voted with the majority.[37]

Although Jersey City's Republican *Evening Journal* did "not pretend to like the bill," because it could "be viewed in one aspect as simply an attempt to put the Democratic party in absolute and complete control of the county," the newspaper recognized "the force of Mr. McDermott's contention that matters are now so bad that any change must be for the better." It would be easier to concentrate attention or indignation upon the majority of an eleven-member board than upon a majority of a much larger body. Another "advantage in this undisguisedly partisan act" would be that "under its operation no cloud of dust can be raised by which Democratic rascals can escape blame under the plea that they had to do thus and so because the wicked Republicans would not permit them to do otherwise." Consequently, the newspaper hoped that the Republicans in the Assembly would pass the bill.[38]

Later, in discussing why the McDermott bill was never reported
from Assembly committee, the *Evening Journal* noted that the text
required a referendum in each first-class county. There might have
been a clause giving the freeholder board in each of these two
counties the power to order the referendum, but it had been argued
that the Hudson board would not commit political suicide by doing
so. The measure might have provided that a referendum be held
only after submission of a petition to the courts, signed by a certain
number of property owners. "But the Newark people did not want a
change," readers were told, "and there was no means of assuring
them that the Democrats in Newark would not attempt to make
political capital by getting up a petition there." Consequently,
"Newark influence defeated the bill."[39]

McDermott Act (1900)

In the fall of 1899 the Hudson County Democratic platform
included a plank for the reduction of membership of the freeholder
board. "Probably the product of a Democratic belief that the
machine can handle and control five or seven members more easily
than it can control twenty-seven," the *Evening Journal* commented.
Although not endorsing the motive, it approved the idea: "Anyway
on earth that the Board of Freeholders could be gotten out of existence short of assassination, the *Evening Journal* and the people of
Hudson County would be almost ready to approve." But at the same
time, the editors did not believe that the Democrats would have
anything to do in "ridding Hudson County of this octopus, vampire,
or whatever anyone may choose to call it." Moreover, they maintained that it would be a hopeless task:

> To wipe out the Board of Freeholders means the abolition of a factor in
> the government which has existed so long, and which would effect [*sic*] so
> variously every other county in the State that there are grave doubts whether
> it can ever be done. Certainly the risk of tangling up the whole State will not
> be taken by a Republican Legislature at the request of a small Democratic
> delegation from this wicked little county, where Democratic domination is a
> perpetual menace to the whole State. This plank in the platform is pure
> buncombe.[40]

As the new century began, there was growing discontent in
Hudson as a result of the recent legislation increasing the freeholder
representation of smaller municipalities. That county's board had
been "bad enough" before the passage of the "Essex County law"

(L.1894, c. 34) allowing the election of freeholders in every incorporated municipality in Hudson, but this "severe blow" was followed by an 1895 act (c. 121) which "made Hudson's condition very much worse," the Republican *Evening Journal* complained. It pointed out that "any town having 8,000 population can incorporate itself under a general law without special legislation" and thereafter subdivide itself "without limit" into wards, each of them entitled to a freeholder.[41] And it noted that an 1889 law (c. 81) assigned two freeholders, rather than one, to every incorporated *town*, regardless of the amount of population. But a *city* required legislative permission to create new wards and could not add to its own membership on the county governing board.[42] "I do not know just how many Freeholders the present laws allow elected in Hudson County, but think the number could be made to reach forty," McDermott declared to the press before the opening of the 1900 legisla' session.[43]

"A great deal of abuse that is thrown at the Board should be directed at the system" that the freeholders had not created and were powerless to alter, this state senator asserted in his statement explaining the danger of multiplying these officials. Nothing in county government affairs demanded the attention of a very large board, he argued. Some great mercantile establishments had single employees with more work and responsibility than that of the entire freeholder board. But even following the popular belief that it should be composed on the basis of sectional representation, nine freeholders, and possibly a presiding officer elected at large, would be adequate. Although, theoretically, a candidate for freeholder was an unwilling nominee, in fact, he had to spend money and make promises of employment in order to secure his election. It was "apparent that if thirty or forty Chosen Freeholders are to be put to the necessity of providing employment and patronage, the county government must become nothing but a scramble for patronage and place." Not only was it "nonsensical to blame the members of the Board for these conditions, or for compliance with the requirements of their environment," but abusing and indicting the freeholders as a body would tend to prevent desirable men from seeking membership on it. Indeed, many Hudson freeholders, and perhaps all, were in favor of a reform in the system, and it would be achieved, if Essex County could be "induced to leave petty politics out of the question."[44]

Hudson Democratic leader Col. Samuel D. Dickinson urged a board of no more than five members, at least two of them to come from Jersey City, which paid more than half the county tax. The remaining freeholders could be divided among the second-class cities, towns, and townships. But the colonel opposed a director at large with the "autocratic" power of the veto and was also against minority representation, which merely had "the effect of giving a job to the two minority members with absolutely no say in the county's affairs." By good salaries, the right persons could be induced to serve as freeholders.[45]

Additional changes in the system were offered by the *Evening Journal*. "Probably it would be well to limit the veto power to the annual budget," stated one editorial, noting that earlier legislation had modified the "unwise" grants of power to the then defunct office of director at large. "No doubt it is a recollection of the troubles caused by the first Directors at-Large that caused Col. Dickinson to object to the proposition," readers were advised. Limitations on the bonding power and the power to increase the annual budget beyond a fixed rate based upon the aggregate of ratables were endorsed by the newspaper, as were higher salaries for freeholders.[46]

Senate Bill No. 11, introduced by McDermott, provided that each first-class county should have a freeholder board consisting of nine members elected *at-large* for two-year terms. "Every resolution providing for the expenditure of money, the appointment of officers, or employees, or otherwise affecting the interests of the county" would have to be presented in writing to the director. Without either his approval or disapproval within five days thereafter, the resolution would become effective. Six votes could override a veto. "If the McDermott bill does not please the committee that has it then the committee should report a substitute," the *Evening Journal* advised in its eagerness to remedy an evil that was "great, recognized, and growing."[47]

Certain restrictive amendments reported by the committee a month later were agreed to by the Senate. Although the text was changed to apply to *all* counties in the state, the act was to remain inoperative in any county unless it had been submitted by a resolution of the freeholder board, on or before March 28, 1900, to the voters of the county and accepted by them at the *next* regular municipal election. Only if the people approved the act, could nine freeholders be lawfully elected in November. The salary of a freeholder so chosen was to be increased to $1,500.[48]

"On its face this is a fair proposition," the *Evening Journal* concluded with regard to the freeholder board's ordering a referendum. It gave "a general character to the bill which ought to enable it to pass muster if it is attacked in court." Besides, a majority of Hudson's freeholders were in favor of reducing the board's size, the newspaper repeated, and even if they were not so inclined, they "would hardly dare to refuse to order an election in the face of public opinion." The leaders of both political parties would have sufficient influence over the existing board to cause a referendum as soon as possible. Even before the Governor could sign the McDermott bill, Hudson would have forty freeholders "drawing $500 a year each or $20,000 altogether, and one another's blood in the fight for patronage." With nine freeholders the annual expenditure for salaries would be reduced to $13,500; and "strife over places will cease," the editorial predicted.[49]

On the bill's third reading, Thomas N. McCarter (R-Essex) said that he did not know how his constituents felt about it, but the measure was so guarded that he might safely favor it in the interest of Hudson County's redemption. He also pointed out that the provision for $1,500 salaries would not be suitable for smaller counties. Mahlon Pitney (R-Morris) expressed surprise that the bill was general. When it applied only to first-class counties, he had not been interested. But now, wondering whether it might not be an unwise measure for general application, he asked for delay. In reply, McDermott explained the difficulty in framing a general bill to meet the constitutional requirements established by the state courts. With great care, the bill had been amended in order to make it apply only to Hudson County's needs, and the sponsor declared that there was practically no fear that any other county would adopt the new freeholder system.[50] The bill was passed, 12 to 5. McCarter was included in the ten Republicans voting with the majority.[51]

Still approving of the bill's "main object," the *Evening Journal* urged the elimination of the "vicious principle of election at-large, which has already made the House or General Assembly of this State non-representative, and absolutely disfranchised the minority party in every county." Otherwise, the result would be "the most aggravated case of boss rule in the affairs of the county which can possibly be conceived." But if further amendment would endanger enactment of the measure, it might be well during this legislative session not to tamper with McDermott's scheme to reform the freeholder board. After all, "The difficulty before the people has been to secure any change whatever in this ancient and ridiculous institution."[52]

The *Newark Evening News* was less happy about requiring at-large elections. Even after the Assembly passed the bill without amendment, 47 to 5, with nine of the eleven Essex Republicans voting affirmatively together with all eleven Hudson Democrats,[53] that newspaper found it "not a little surprising that the Republican majority in the Legislature should not have insisted upon amending the bill to provide for minority representation." Such denial to the Republican minority in Hudson was "little short of absolute tyranny" and certainly not justifiable on the ground that any change in the composition of that county's freeholder board would be for the better. Adoption of the McDermott system in Essex would probably cause the election of a solidly Republican board—"a result equally to be deplored."[54] But Governor Voorhees had lost no time in signing the measure.[55]

At first the understanding was that the Hudson freeholder board would meet on March 15 and order the McDermott Act submitted for the approval of the voters at the municipal elections of April 10. But on March 9 it appeared that it would be "well nigh impossible" for all the municipalities in the county to vote on the new plan before the November election, because the spring elections in Weehawken and one or two other townships were to be held on March 13, two days *before* the announced freeholders' meeting. Scheduling an extra board meeting for an earlier date would still not allow sufficient time to arrange for a referendum on such short notice, it was claimed. County Collector Robert Davis issued a public statement, as a Democratic leader, that the act would not be voted on until the November election.[56] But after regular elections had been held in two townships, he announced that only those municipalities would hold the referendum in the fall; all the others would consider the question on April 10.[57] The Hudson board unanimously approved the resolution for a referendum at the next regular elections to be held in the municipalities, and the *Evening Journal* announced the opinion of "lawyers who ought to be well informed on the subject" that it was not absolutely necessary that the McDermott Act be voted on by every municipality on the same day. The proposed method of approval would be entirely valid.[58]

In the first referendum to be held in New Jersey on the question of reorganizing county government, Hudson approved the proposal overwhelmingly on April 10, with only West New York in opposition:[59]

	FOR	AGAINST
Jersey City	12,070	2,035
Hoboken	1,643	268
Bayonne	1,528	414
West Hoboken	366	164

	FOR	AGAINST
Town of Union	282	167
North Bergen	54	8
Guttenberg	281	12
West New York	63	254
Weehawken	8	6
Harrison	194	178
Kearny	333	204
East Newark	44	0
Secaucus	43	0
Grand Total	16,909	3,710

As the first freeholders in New Jersey to be elected at large by the voters of a county, the nine Democrats who were successful in November were expected "to inaugurate a new era" in Hudson's government. Despite its earlier editorial against the "vicious principle" of county-wide freeholder-constituencies, the *Evening Journal* was jubilant:

Each one of these nine Freeholders represents 386,000 people living in Hudson, and not a constituency of personal friends in a ward or township. There are no strings upon a single one of them. There is no obstructive minority in the Board to inject politics into official action. Furthermore, these nine men are face to face with the necessity of giving good government to this county or of leaving their party wide open to public denunciation. It would be impossible for responsibility to be more centralized and more fixed than in the case of the Board, constituted as it is.[60]

KLEIN ACT (1900)

A significant development in first-class county freeholder representation in Essex County was taking place at the exact time that the future McDermott Law (applying to Hudson County) was being debated in the legislature. What was to be the Klein Act, introduced in February 1900 just as was the McDermott Law, aroused controversy on two counts: provision for a strong "director of county affairs" and changes in the basis of membership on the freeholder board.

Introduced as Assembly Bill No. 136 by John N. Klein (R-Essex), the bill provided that in first-class counties there would be one freeholder elected from each ward of each first-class city, one from each second-class city, and one from each township and incorporated town. This would reduce the number on the Essex board from thirty-three to twenty-eight members, enabling Newark's fifteen freeholders to constitute a majority. The annual salary was to remain at $500. Although opposition to this apportionment plan was likely to develop in Orange and East Orange (second-class cities then electing *two* freeholders each), "undoubtedly the greatest objection will be to the Director of County Affairs' himself," the press predicted.[61]

"Bitterly opposed to Assemblyman Klein's bill," the Essex freeholder board nevertheless recognized that there was a popular demand for its reorganization and that some limitation had to be placed on a membership that could be expanded by multiplying wards in the municipalities outside Newark. The county counsel was instructed to draw a bill providing for a board of twenty-nine members, fifteen of whom were to be elected by Newark and the remainder to be apportioned to give the large municipalities greater representation than the smaller ones. Such a plan was "only a makeshift" that did not "strike at the root of the evil," that is, at lack of "concentrated responsibility," the *Newark Evening News* protested. Even increasing the power of the current director of the board would be "open to most serious objection" that he would regard his primary allegiance to be owed to the municipality that had elected him; and in most cases the director could achieve his higher position "only through a series of deals and compacts which would be anything but beneficial to the general welfare."[62] Within two weeks Assembly Bill No. 194, sponsored by George N. Campbell (R-Essex) provided a scheme under which thirty-one freeholders would be elected in Essex, fifteen of them from Newark. But on third reading, the measure was sent back to committee in order to give the assemblymen from Essex an opportunity to discuss it together with the Klein bill.[63]

Only after the proposed power of the county executive had been lessened and the apportionment of freeholders had been amended to conform exactly to the scheme in the Campbell bill, did the Assembly pass the Klein bill, 57 to 0, "without a word of dissent."[64] Its provisions would not have to apply to Hudson, because the Governor had signed the McDermott bill into law a week earlier. Under the revised plan there was to be a freeholder from each ward of each first-class city; *two* members elected at large from each second-class city, town, or township with an official census population of at least 14,000 by the time of the general election in November 1900; and one member from each city, town, or township with fewer than 14,000 inhabitants. For purposes of representation, each borough was to be regarded as part of the municipality from whose territory it had been created. (No longer could each borough in Essex be entitled to two freeholders, according to the 1899 act.) In addition, the number of Essex freeholders was limited to thirty-one by a clause prohibiting the governing body of any municipality from making any appointment to membership on the board whereby that municipality would further increase its representation.

With little further difficulty the bill became law.[65] The Senate insisted on official recognition of the McDermott Act by providing that "this [Klein] act shall not take effect in any county [Hudson] in which the legal voters shall decide, at an election, to adopt another plan for the election of chosen freeholders." Moreover, current freeholders were to be continued in office until the expiration of the terms for which they had been elected.[66] The amended measure was passed by the Republican Senate, 14 to 0, with the affirmative votes of four Democrats.[67] Included in the majority of assemblymen who concurred in the upper chamber's amendments, 48 to 0, were fourteen members of the Democratic minority, ten of them from Hudson.[68]

McDermott Act Nullified by Court

In January 1902 Samuel E. Renner, a Weehawken Republican, began *quo warranto* proceedings to oust the nine-member freeholder board on the ground that the McDermott Act of 1900 violated the clause of the state constitution forbidding the passage of local or special laws to regulate the internal affairs of counties. He charged that the statute was in effect and substance rendered local and special by the requirement that the proceedings for its adoption in any county should be initiated by the existing freeholder board on or before March 28, 1900.[69] "Probably the most startling feature of the situation," observed Jersey City's *Evening Journal*, "is the fact that a return to the old system of electing Freeholders would give the control of the Board to the town, townships, and boroughs." According to the newspaper's calculations, there would be sixteen freeholders elected in Jersey City, Bayonne, and Hoboken to represent more than three-quarters of Hudson's population, while eighteen freeholders would be elected by the remaining one-quarter. Moreover, readers were advised of an act providing for freeholder representation for every ward in a town or township and were warned that "many of the towns have three wards and could create still more, while the law strictly prohibits any gerrymandering of [*sic*] increasing of wards in the three cities in the county except after the national census." The three cities would supply the money for county expenses, and the other municipalities would spend it.[70]

In October the New Jersey Supreme Court entered a judgment ousting the nine-member board and held that the McDermott Act was "special and therefore invalid":

> Legislation of this sort seems calculated to thwart the purpose of the constitutional prohibition of special laws, for in order to secure the successful enactment of such laws it would only be necessary that the legislature should be informed of the sentiment in any particular locality, and then should pass a statute according to that sentiment, and providing for its acceptance in so short a time that no other locality could reasonably act in the matter. So far as practical results are involved, the act might as well expressly limit the right of acceptance to the voters of that locality alone. The inevitable effect of such legislation is to confer upon localities, which in constitutional view are alike, statutory powers as diverse as the temporary sentiments of the particular places.[71]

The Court's decision "has created a decided stir in political circles and there is considerable speculation as to the exact status of the present Board; also what the city, town, towship [sic] and borough representation will be in the next Board of Freeholders," observed the *Evening Journal* two days later. Now it announced that there would be twenty-six freeholders elected in November: Jersey City twelve; Hoboken two; Bayonne two; West Hoboken two; Town of Union two; Weehawken one; West New York one; North Bergen one; Guttenberg one; Kearny one; and Harrison one. No separate representation would be given to the boroughs of East Newark and Secaucus. "The above facts will cause considerable surprise to those who have not followed recent legislation on the subject," the newspaper remarked, calling attention to the Klein Act of 1900, ostensibly reorganizing the government of both first-class counties, but passed in order to affect only Essex. Through a clause repealing all other statutes inconsistent with its own provisions, that act became applicable to Hudson.[72] Consequently, there were "already cropping up a number of candidates for the position of Supervisor, which . . . is a most important position and one that has a great deal of responsibility attached to it." The Klein Act "creates practically the position of 'Mayor of the County,' " readers were informed.[73]

Allan L. McDermott, now a congressman from New Jersey's Seventh District, denied the *Evening Journal*'s charges that he had been responsible for the unconstitutional time limitations in the act bearing his name; "they were inserted because the Republicans refused to pass the act without them," he insisted. It had been his hope "that every citizen would accept with pleasure the betterment of our system of county government, at least until the workings of the act had shown it to be one that would be beneficial to all counties." Because the two-year experience had "demonstrated the wisdom of a 'Board of nine,' " the return to the old system would be of short duration, he told the press.[74]

The continuing incorporation of new municipalities made separate freeholder representation for each less and less practical. At the same time, the disappearance of Assembly districts had removed one alternative for keeping boards at a manageable size while providing some local representation. Only two innovations gained legislative approval: passage of an optional law for the reorganization of freeholder boards, and the at-large election of *all* members of that body. Although short-lived and limited to a single county (Hudson), they represented ideas whose time had come. But not in every county!

"THE OLD ORDER CHANGETH,"
1900–1902

Culmination of more than a half-century's efforts to reform county government in New Jersey had to be based on the principle of home rule. And even then, fundamental change was not eagerly embraced by the counties. In four of the five which first voted on the plan for a small board to be elected at large, it was rejected. Nevertheless, once begun, the movement could not be stopped.

EFFECT OF THE 1900 CENSUS

Population increases presented a special threat to the *status quo* in four counties at the beginning of the twentieth century. In 1900 Union, Monmouth, Middlesex, and Bergen had surpassed the 75,000 population figure for the first time according to a *federal* census, and would, therefore, become subject to earlier legislation regulating counties with 75,000 to 200,000 inhabitants.[1] The greatest concern was shown in Union, where each city ward would become entitled to elect a freeholder. Elizabeth's twelve wards were electing a total of four freeholders; Rahway's five wards, two; and Plainfield's four, two. Moreover, some of Union's boroughs, then unrepresented separately in the county governing body, might be authorized to have their own freeholders. Instead of eighteen members, the board could have more than thirty-five, the local press warned.[2]

As a means of forestalling such changes, if they were unwanted locally, Ellis R. Meeker (R-Union) sponsored two measures in 1901, amending the 1894 act for counties with a population of 75,000 to 200,000. Assembly Bill No. 244 provided that except for those previously in this category (Passaic, Camden, Mercer), every county was to elect a freeholder from each city ward, township, and each borough possessing complete autonomy of local government. *But this could happen only after approval in a referendum that had been authorized by resolution of the freeholder board.* The *status quo* in salaries was to be maintained by the provision that $300 be paid to each freeholder, and $500 to each director, but not in those counties with fewer than 100,000 inhabitants. Board members in Passaic and Camden would thereby continue to receive the higher compensation according to an 1895 statute.[3] The bill was not reported from committee, and after nine days, Meeker introduced Assembly Bill No. 301. None of the provisions of the 1894 act "or of the several acts supplementary thereto or amendatory thereof" was to take effect in any county until after approval in a referendum authorized by a resolution of the freeholder board. But *salaries* instead of *per diem* fees could be paid to those freeholders then receiving such fees if two-thirds of the board should agree to this. The bill's text allowed Passaic, Camden, and Mercer to be excepted from its application.

As a result of textual changes, the existing apportionment of freeholders in Meeker's county was effectively safeguarded. A committee substitute for Assembly Bill No. 301 was amended to provide that it should *not* "affect or interfere" with the number of freeholders to be elected in counties "wherein the number of wards in the largest city is less than ten [Monmouth, Middlesex, Bergen]." With Elizabeth's twelve wards, Union was to be the only county that would be required to vote affirmatively in a referendum before the Passaic-Camden-Mercer allotment plan would apply to it. By a strictly partisan vote, 42 Republicans to 12 Democrats, the bill was passed.[4] The Senate vote was 16 to 0, with Democrats from Hudson, Sussex, and Essex included in the majority.[5] Because this bill applying exclusively to Union included some provisions of which he was doubtful, Governor Foster H. Voorhees allowed it to become law without his signature.[6]

Like Union, Middlesex had expected to be seriously affected by the federal census of 1900. Besides the increase in annual salaries, there would be a rise in the number of freeholders that Perth Amboy could elect. Instead of only two for the entire city, there could be one from each of the city's six wards, according to the 1894 law passed for Passaic, Camden, and Mercer. "Why should Perth Amboy, on a tax valuation of about $3,000,000, have as large a representation as the city of New Brunswick, which pays taxes on $10,000,000 valuation and has 3,000 more population than Perth Amboy?" a newspaper in the county seat could inquire late in 1901.[7] And because every borough with more than 1,200 inhabitants (rather than 2,500 or 3,000) could claim a freeholder, it appeared that Metuchen (1,786), incorporated in 1900, would be allotted one. A board member would be retained in South River borough, whose population had decreased to 2,792 from more than 3,000 at its incorporation (1898); and in Dunellen borough (1,239), which was entitled to representation as a former *borough commission* (not a borough and now an extinct form).[8]

But after passage of Assembly Bill No. 301, matters became more complicated. A change made by the Assembly extended to additional counties the application of only the *original* 1894 law (Chapter 165); mention of "the several acts supplementary thereof or amendatory thereof" had been deleted from the text as introduced by Meeker. Consequently, the 1896 supplement's population requirement of 1,200 residents for separate representation of a borough in counties with 75,000 to 200,000 residents was superseded by Chapter 161, the general act relating to boroughs (Revision of 1897). The latter's requirement for every borough in the state was 3,000 inhabitants or the inclusion of a whole township within its limits. In a political maneuver, the Middlesex board refused to seat only Metuchen's freeholder, who brought suit, later discontinued voluntarily, to have Dunellen's freeholder also denied a seat.[9] South River's freeholder decided not to become a candidate again, following the 1902 ruling of the county solicitor that the borough's population was not large enough to justify such an election.[10] But his ruling in 1901 against seating the six candidates elected by wards in Perth Amboy was disregarded. "It was explained that Judge Lyon had presented the case to Justice Fort before the nominations were made in Perth Amboy and that Justice Fort had decided that the city is entitled under the law to six Freeholders," the press reported.[11] On what grounds the challenge or the decision was made remains unclear, but the matter seems to have concerned the drawing of new ward lines in the city.

In Monmouth and Bergen change was prevented by the 3,000 population requirement for boroughs and also apparently by Chapter 30, Laws of 1897, and Chapters 52 and 53, Laws of 1899, which restricted each of certain cities in the state with less than 12,000 residents to only two freeholders.

PRECURSORS OF THE STRONG ACT

Unlike Union's Senator Meeker, Theodore Strong (R-Middlesex) was not interested in simply maintaining the existing apportionment of freeholders. He had been asked by prominent local men to promote the passage of a different kind of bill that would apply to *all* second-class counties (Passaic, Camden, Mercer, Union, Monmouth, Middlesex, Bergen, Morris, Burlington). "Crude" and "open to amendment," an early draft called for each freeholder board in these counties to consist of five members elected at large for two years. The annual salary would be $1,500; and the director would receive an additional $500.[12] Such provisions caused by this "revolt in some of the smaller counties against Freeholderism" were "very much like those of the Hudson County proposition of several years ago," Jersey City's *Evening Journal* noted. However, it continued, the second-class counties that would be affected by the substitution of "small Boards of County Trustees" had Republican majorities, and no Democrat would be elected to any of them. Consequently, there would be "a Democratic howl" when a bill of this kind would be introduced.[13]

Yet it was a Republican committee chairman who prevented the Senate from considering the Middlesex plan for a freeholder board of five members. Two days before the appearance of Meeker's second measure (Assembly Bill No. 301) for regulating the apportionment of freeholders, Strong introduced Senate Bill No. 153. It changed the draft provision for salaries, so that $1,500 salaries would be paid to regular board members; and $1,800 to directors in those second-class counties with more than 100,000 inhabitants (Passaic, Camden). In each of the other second-class counties, a freeholder would be paid $1,200 and the director $1,400. The plan was not reported from the Committee on Revision of Laws, because of the opposition of its chairman, Joseph Cross (R-Union).[14] Neither did that same committee report Senate Bill No. 216, a similar scheme that Strong introduced the following week. All counties except those of the first class would be required to have a five-member board elected at large for two-year terms and paid according to a sliding scale: $1,500, with $300 additional for the director in counties with more than 100,000 inhabitants; $1,200, with $200 additional, in counties between 50,000 and 100,000 (Union, Mercer, Monmouth,

Middlesex, Bergen, Morris, Burlington, Cumberland); $800, with $150 additional, in counties between 25,000 and 50,000 (Atlantic, Warren, Hunterdon, Somerset, Gloucester, Salem); and $500, with $100 additional, in counties with fewer than 25,000 inhabitants (Sussex, Ocean, and Cape May).

STRONG ACT: CLIMAX OF SMALL BOARD AGITATION

The following year (1902) was to become a milestone in the development of county government, largely because of the efforts of the Middlesex members of the legislature in securing the passage of Strong's Senate Bill No. 13. Originally, it provided for nine free-holders in counties with more than 200,000 inhabitants, seven in counties with 100,000 to 200,000, five in counties with 50,000 to 100,000, and three in counties with fewer than 50,000. Elected at large in the county in November, each board member would serve a two-year term at an annual salary of $1,500. The act would not take effect in any county, unless it was approved there by a *compulsory* referendum, at the first election for members of the Assembly, *or* unless it was approved at any succeeding general election, after submission of a petition for such a referendum had been signed by 5 percent of the qualified voters.

Endorsement of the plan appeared in what was possibly the only contemporary public statement by a New Jersey historian on the subject of county government reform. Francis Bazley Lee told the press:

> The proposition made by Senator Strong is directly in line with modern thought and action in dealing with the government of municipal corporations, of which class counties, scientifically, are a part.
>
> New Jersey is one of the few States in the Union where the absolute and cumbersome system of government by boards of chosen freeholders still survives. The establishment of these boards carries one to a remote period in colonial history, when the country [*sic*], particularly in the western and southern parts of the State, was practically the unit of political life.
>
> In these early times, the theory was to choose from all the freeholders of the county, a body of men, each township or constabulary, to have complete representation—particularly as local jealousies were most intense. Since then, with new agencies of association and the uniting of local interests, the county has outgrown its primitive conditions.
>
> We now find ourselves in New Jersey, with unwieldy boards transacting business, which could be more expeditiously and more cheaply transacted by a smaller number of men.

When our neighboring state of Pennsylvania changed from a system of government by boards of chosen freeholders to that of county commissioners, the result was highly satisfactory, and has stood a test of many years.

The management of the county, like that of the city, is a business proposition. It does not take much argument to convince anyone that better results can be obtained by a small board than by a large one. What with a greater speed in conducting affairs, more increased activity, and greater certainty in fastening responsibility in case of maladministration, the advantages of Senator Strong's bill are apparent.

This is a good time for a change, as the plan has back of it, a public sentiment, as vigorous as it is just. The bill certainly represents present day views upon matters of local government.[15]

Efforts were made in the Senate to change the text of the bill. The day after its passage on second reading, Edmund W. Wakelee (R-Bergen) successfully moved that the vote be reconsidered, and he offered a substitute to apply to all but first-class counties. It would allot seven freeholders to each second-class county, and five to each third- and fourth-class county. Board members in these counties were to have *three-year staggered* terms at annual salaries of $1,000. Terms of the current freeholders were extended until January 1, 1903, and new boards would be elected in the fall. But both the compulsory and the optional referendum features in Strong's bill would be eliminated. Wakelee's substitute was laid over for further consideration.[16]

When the original Strong bill came up again on second reading, Wakelee tried twice to change it. He offered an amendment to strike out the provisions for conducting referenda, arguing that freeholder boards should be reorganized by a direct mandatory act of the legislature. Strong expressed his doubt that the legislature would pass his bill without such provisions, and Charles A. Reed (R-Somerset) agreed, although he favored their deletion. Without any support at all for his own proposal, Wakelee saw seventeen Senators vote against it. After the Senate adopted amendments that had been previously offered by Strong to remove the provision for the compulsory referenda only, Wakelee proposed that the annual salary of a freeholder be fixed at $1,000, not $1,500. But this reduction in compensation was protested by Strong, and especially by Robert S. Hudspeth (D-Hudson), who said that a bill so amended would be very objectionable in his county, because the work would be arduous for nine men (then receiving $1,500 each). Wakelee's second amendment was defeated, 5 to 13.[17] On the following day, Strong succeeded in having the bill amended so that freeholders in counties with fewer than 22,000 inhabitants (Ocean, Cape May) should receive only $500 annual salary.[18]

A "sharp fight" marked the bill's third reading. Calling Hudspeth to replace him temporarily as Senate President, C. Asa Francis (R-Monmouth) told his colleagues: "There is no opposition to this bill, except from the politicians that pull our coat tails and endeavor to show us what an iniquitous measure any bill to reduce the membership of the Board of Freeholders is."[19] After Strong urged passage on the ground that every county would be saved considerable money, Herbert W. Johnson (R-Camden) opposed the measure, maintaining that the majority of the counties were not clamoring for it. Camden, with twenty-three freeholders, each paid an annual salary of $300, was satisfied with existing conditions. By requiring a board of seven men at $1,500 each, the Strong bill would increase the burden of the taxpayers, this recent freeholder argued. Johnson had little faith in the referendum provision,[20] but Wakelee replied that it protected counties that were satisfied with their boards. Reed and Francis insisted that those counties that desired a change should be given an opportunity to bring it about. Although Lewis J. Martin (D-Sussex) found much fault in the bill, particularly with salaries that appeared to be too high for his own county, he announced his willingness to vote for passage by the Senate. But he declared that he would work afterward to defeat the proposition at the polls in Sussex.[21] By 13 to 5 the bill was passed. Included in the majority were three of the Senate's four Democrats (from Hudson, Hunterdon, Sussex); negative votes were cast by a Warren Democrat and Republicans from Union, Camden, Cumberland, and Gloucester. There were abstentions by members from Passaic, Cape May, and Salem.[22]

Only "after a long-running fight in which the opposition resorted to all the familiar tricks of filibustoring and obstruction to effect its defeat," did the Strong bill pass second reading in the Assembly.[23] In Trenton at the time there were committees of Essex and Passaic freeholders who had been lobbying against the measure since its introduction. Agreeing at the last moment to help Strong, Major Carl Lentz, Essex Republican boss, advised his county's delegation that he saw no objection to legislation that could not take effect unless the voters should approve it.[24] But when the bill was reported from the Committee on the Judiciary favorably and without amendment, a minority report was also submitted by Robert M. Boyd (R-Essex) and Frederick Van Blarcom (R-Passaic).[25]

In defense of the adverse minority report, Boyd argued that the bill was against the interests of the smaller Essex municipalities. If it were to pass, Newark would absolutely control the freeholder board by electing seven, and possibly eight, of the nine members. His town of Montclair would not have a representative once in twenty years. Such a scheme was "against common sense and justice," Boyd asserted, and he did not believe that nine men could take care of the vast amount of county business in Essex. The slight saving in expense could not compensate for the change, because the incumbent freeholders were satisfactory there. "We have no scandals and they have always done their work faithfully and well," the Assembly was informed.[26] Then the legislators heard the other signer of the minority report say: "This bill strikes at the foundations of our government. It allows taxation without representation, a question settled for all time by our patriotic forefathers." According to Van Blarcom, those assemblymen who took refuge behind a referendum clause were "shirking their clear duty." He charged that it was "cowardly to vote for a bill a member knows to be bad simply because the referendum shifts the responsibility upon his constituents." William Newcorn (R-Union) also spoke in favor of the minority viewpoint.[27]

Supporting the majority report, the judiciary committee chairman and majority leader, John G. Horner (R-Burlington), argued that the Strong bill was in the interest of "progression." Other states, he noted, had "abolished the omnibus plan and would not return to it for anything." It was true that in some counties the current method of electing freeholders was not meeting with approval, and he was willing to trust the people in his county to say which plan they favored.[28] William H. C. Jackson (R-Middlesex) contended that the bill was intended primarily for his county, where the people wanted relief from an unwieldy board. Speaking at length, William T. Hoffman (R-Monmouth) agreed that the referendum made the measure safe.[29] By a vote of 22 to 28, adoption of the minority report was defeated. Among those voting affirmatively were six Essex members (four of them living outside Newark), four of the five Passaic Assemblymen present, and two of the three from Union. Then the majority report was adopted, 31 to 19, "after a fight that brought the contestants in swarms to the clerk's desk to watch the recording of the votes."[30]

Several amendments designed to obstruct passage of the bill were offered when the bill was considered on second reading that day. Van Blarcom's proposal to allot one freeholder to each town and township in second-class counties was defeated, 20 to 26, with only eight of twenty-six assemblymen from those counties voting affirmatively.[31] Edmund G. Stalter (R-Passaic) offered an amendment to fix annual salaries at $500. After Horner protested that $1.25 a day was not sufficient compensation for practically full-time work, the Assembly defeated the change, 20 to 28.[32] Considerable filibustering was followed by the defeat, *viva voce,* of Newcorn's proposal that 25 percent (instead of 5 percent) of a county's qualified voters be required to petition for a referendum.[33] By 28 to 21, the bill was advanced to third reading.[34] Throughout the day's various roll-call votes, assemblymen from Passaic, Union, and suburban Essex voted together in opposition to the original text.

Conflicts over the amendments raised doubt about securing thirty-one affirmative votes and indicated the need for additional campaigning on behalf of the Strong bill. As "the only ones particularly anxious for its passage," the legislators from Middlesex led the fight.[35] During final debate, Jackson urged approval on the ground that his county had not asked much in the way of legislation previously. "If this bill is adopted," Horner predicted, "it will be so popular, I believe, that in a few years it would be considered a misdemeanor to go back to what is now characterized as the 'rotten freeholder system.'"[36] This majority leader from Burlington claimed to have a letter from a prominent resident of another county predicting a nine-to-one popular endorsement in that county, despite the opposition of its assemblymen.[37] Leading the final effort to defeat the measure, Boyd argued that it was too soon to say that other states were having success with smaller county governing boards: "Perhaps some day, after we have seen the way it works, we may want it ourselves, but as it stands the bill is unfair to the people in small communities."[38] If the freeholder system were to be changed, its replacement should be a complete one, satisfactory to the Assembly, he insisted.[39]

Excitement ran high during the vote for passage. After Stalter ran down to the clerk's desk to keep an eye on the tally slip, the Middlesex members followed his example, and "an interesting group was soon around the desk."[40] As soon as there was a majority recorded for the measure, Horner moved that the roll call be suspended. "The ayes and noes were about equal in volume," reported one Newark newspaper, "but the speaker declared the motion carried."[41] Just before the result of the balloting was announced, John Howe (R-Essex), who had been one of only three assemblymen from his county to cast an affirmative vote, jumped to his feet and asked that it be changed to negative. The bill would be defeated by this maneuver. But Speaker William J. Bradley (R-Camden), who had voted in the negative, but who was credited with a desire for the bill's passage, ignored him and announced that the bill had passed, 31 to 24 (with not a vote to spare).[42] Party lines were "obliterated"[43] (six Democrats in the majority; seven in the minority), and county delegation solidarity was violated in some cases (Essex, Hudson, Camden, Passaic). Howe protested angrily that he had been on his feet seeking recognition before the announcement of the result, and he was then beckoned to the speaker's desk. After a short conference, Howe explained that he had traded his vote to another member in return for votes on one of the Essex bills. There had been a stipulation that if Howe's vote should be the one to pass the Strong bill, he could have the privilege of changing it. But, he continued, seeing that effort to be recognized, the Speaker said afterward that he would change his vote to "aye" if that affirmative vote from Essex were to be reversed.[44] Two days later, Republican Governor Foster M. Voorhees approved the state's first optional county reorganization act[45] that was to apply to every county.

COUNTY CAMPAIGNS AND REFERENDA RESULTS

Hudson's Democratic leader, Robert Davis, supported adoption of the Strong Act, and petitions to place the question on the November ballot were immediately circulated.[46] Receiving 4,000 signatures two weeks later, he remarked that the petitions had been "eagerly signed by Republicans as well as Democrats" and that the proposed endorsement of a nine-member board was "not a political question." In fact, he insisted, "Politics has nothing to do with it." Maintaining that only one person refused to sign, in the belief that the petition was a different document, Davis predicted the plan's approval "by a large majority."[47]

Although his forecast of the outcome was wrong, it was certainly not a division by political parties that determined the voters' rejection of the Strong Act by a vote of 12,834 to 13,571. *Every* town and township voted against the proposal, and there were even city wards that opposed it: four in Jersey City, and one each in Hoboken and Bayonne.[48] On November 25, 1902, the new board of twenty-six members and Frank McNally, elected as county supervisor on the day of the referendum, were sworn into office, effective December 1, under the provisions of the Klein Act of 1900.[49]

In April the *Bergen Evening Record* maintained that the adoption of a small board was "a matter for careful thought." With the average earnings of a freeholder approaching $300 a year (at $2.00 for every meeting attended and for each day of work, plus mileage compensation), the existing twenty-three member board would mean "an expenditure of $7,900 [$6,900?] in fees." A county commission of five members at an annual salary of $1,500 each would amount to $7,500, or $400 less. "Besides the monetary consideration we must not forget that five men, regularly salaried, would devote all their time to their offices and that there would be less chance of friction and of barter legislation," readers were advised.[50] By the autumn they were being urged to vote for adoption of the Strong Act. Now it was noted that the previous year's freeholder board had cost Bergen County $6,000 and that the proposed system would call for only $1,500 more expenditure. The existing "unrepresentative and unfair" method of apportioning freeholders was emphasized:

> Hackensack [town, co-extensive with New Barbadoes township], for instance, with a population of 10,000 has one freeholder, while Englewood [city] with 6,300, has two. Englewood Cliffs [borough] with only 200 people has one. Rutherford [borough] with 4,500 has one. And so on.[51]

In a "very small" turnout at the polls, only 2,898 approved the proposed change; 5,021 were content with the *status quo*.[52]

The *Dover Index* denied that the new plan would produce benefits for Morris County. Not only would there be "practically no saving by having five County Commissioners at $1,500 each in place of the 22 members of the present Board of Freeholders,"[53] but five men would be "easier to corral for any scheme." Reducing the representation of Morristown and Dover to a single freeholder each should be the only change in the existing system of electing members of the governing body by municipalities. In an appeal to tradition, the newspaper declared:

> For over a century Freeholders have been honored public officials in this State and it is a shame to go on and advocate its rejection for something not in line with this time-honored home rule principle of government by and for all the people.[54]

Five municipalities (Dover, Rockaway Borough, Rockaway Township, Wharton, Randolph), clustered in the center of the county, recorded pluralities in favor of the small board scheme; and it lost by only one vote in Boonton. But the total in Morris was 2,408, for; and 4,139, against.[55]

Although "the Democratic organ in this city [New Brunswick's *Daily Times*] has remained silent on the question of the proposition before the voters to reduce the number of members in the Board of Freeholders from 24 to 5,"[56] the Republican *Home News* had campaigned vigorously for its adoption in Middlesex. Besides presenting the usual favorable arguments, that newspaper had to allay fears that the plan's approval by the voters would cause candidates to be selected from New Brunswick (later mentioning Perth Amboy) without fair representation of the other municipalities.[57] Despite the legality of this type of maneuver, "the politicians would not dare attempt such a suicidal stroke as to show any preference." For that "would mean defeat in the county if the city men were nominated and disaster in the city if the men were all taken from the county."[58] Just as in the case of nominations to the Assembly, all sections of Middlesex would be represented. In addition, the *Home News* emphasized "the opportunity for the nomination of nonpartisan men for the positions."[59]

Ironically, in the county that was a leader in the movement for small freeholder boards, the proposition lost, 5,085 to 5,825, with ten muncipalities in favor and nine opposed. Largely responsible for the defeat was the negative vote (398 to 1,014) of Perth Amboy,[60] which had recently been allowed a freeholder for each of its six wards, instead of only two freeholders elected at large. Both political parties in that city opposed a small board as likely to transfer control of the county government to New Brunswick,[61] which had been permitted since 1871 to elect six freeholders. But there was another reason offered for the defeat. "Had a majority of those who did not vote one way or the other voted for the act it would have been carried," the *Home News* observed, warning the freeholder board that the voters of Middlesex might reconsider their decision.[62]

Only in Hunterdon, which had a long history of opinion favoring smaller boards of freeholders, was the Strong Act accepted. Before the referendum in Hunterdon, the leading newspapers took different positions. The *Hunterdon County Democrat* was noncommital:

While we have our own views on the subject, yet we admit that in them we may be in error, and we would like to have any of our readers lay aside party prejudices and write us their opinions on the question. This is not a question that should relate to party, or on which party lines will be drawn. . . .[63]

The *Hunterdon Republican* supported the small board plan:

> The question is not a partisan one, and it is not labelled as a Democratic or Republican measure. It is approved, and its adoption is urged, by the citizens of all political parties, and it seems to meet with the approval of all thinking men. It is a question simply of municipal administration, and is in line with the system which has been successfully used for many years in a number of other States. A careful study of the question leads one to the conclusion that it is certainly an improvement on our present system—that it will be less expensive and more efficient. . . . This is the only way our tax burdens can be lightened, and every one should support a measure which will accomplish this great need.[64]

After the proposed change had been approved, 3,245 to 2,776,[65] the *Hunterdon County Democrat* complained that apparently there had not been "a full and candid expression of the voters." The editorial management was "very sure that the question was not understood, and therefor[*sic*] many refrained from voting, and many more crossed off the wrong question, but that may have operated either way." Moreover, the analysis continued, "Many others believed that it would change the whole freeholder system and law and voted for it on that account, . . . but on finding out that it did not . . . , expressed themselves as sorry that they voted for the new law." Although the county's newspapers had been offering to print readers' views on the question during the previous six months, there had been "but little or no response." Consequently, the public's failure to understand the question was "largely their own fault."[66]

Citing an editorial from a newspaper of each major political party, the *Hunterdon County Democrat* held that "the measure seemed to be devoid of all political significance." *The Clinton Democrat* argued that the vote in Hunterdon "should be very unsatisfactory even to those who strenuously promoted it." If the question had been put in plain and simple form, it was "more than probable" that it would have been badly defeated. More than 1,600 voters, even in the light turnout of the electorate, had left the proposition blank on their ballots, and many who had intended to vote for the "present representative Board of Freeholders" had been misled by the printing and had voted in favor of the small board.[67] *The Hunterdon Gazette,* High Bridge's Republican weekly, also maintained that the vote "was not a representative one," because "the issue was not placed fairly before the people and many who desired to vote against the proposition did not vote at all on the issue because they failed to cross the clause in favor of it." It was only 3,245 voters who had decided for the 9,000 or more that they would have to submit to a serious change in the administration of county affairs, the Republican newspaper declared. Hoping that the change would be for the better, it was "willing to be convinced."[68]

CONSTITUTIONALITY OF STRONG ACT QUESTIONED

The *Hunterdon County Democrat* subsequently pointed out that the *Clinton Democrat* had even raised the question as to whether the existing large freeholder board had really been abolished by the recent election. "Did the referendum clause in the new law[Strong Act] intend that a county adopt the new law by anything short of a majority of the votes cast at the election?" was a question that might come before the courts. Possibly they would declare that those who did not participate in the referendum had been satisfied with the current freeholder system. "The whole matter plainly shows that such questions should be decided at a separate election, and not be mixed up with the ticket at our general elections," the Flemington newspaper concluded.[69]

"The petty township and ward politicians were caught napping and now seek by indirection to defeat the accomplishment of the people's desire," Warren's Hackettstown *Gazette* observed of her neighboring county. Hunterdon's politicians were "vastly more strenuous in their opposition to allowing the dissolution of the Board of Freeholders than they were before the people voted in favor of the change."[70] Obviously supporting such local interests, the *Hunterdon County Democrat* predicted that adoption of the three-member board would be defeated by more than 2,000 votes, "if the expression of the people could be taken now, after they have realized what has been done."[71] But in order to instigate action to insure continuation of the large board, that newspaper reprinted another editorial, expressing its own views "exactly," from the *Clinton Democrat:*

We think the easiest and most generally satisfactory way to dispose of what is called "The New Freeholder Law" will be to repeal it by act of the Legislature which convenes next month.

It was decisively rejected in every county where it was submitted to the people, except in Hunterdon; and here it was more than twelve hundred short of the approval of the people who voted in the election.

This fact, and the question as to whether the proposition was really legally approved under the somewhat obscure requirements of the act itself, would make its prompt repeal the proper disposition to make of it.

Senator Gebhardt and Assemblyman Willever, on the part of this county, should ask for its repeal to save the county from a radical subversion of representative government which has been only asked for by about one-third of its voters, and many of them secured by misunderstanding.

No other county's representatives could consistently oppose a repeal if Hunterdon were to ask it on so clear a claim of justice and good public policy, because no other county has given the triumvirate act even the quasi approval that is claimed for it here.[72]

The legislature of 1903 refused to act on Gebhardt's Senate Bill No. 189 "that would have settled the whole question" by providing that in the Strong Act's seventh section "the words 'majority of votes so cast' shall be taken and construed to mean a majority of all the ballots cast in such election and on which ballots the official statement of the question has not been erased."[73] At its April meeting, Hunterdon's large freeholder board passed the following resolution:

Whereas, the referendum section of the act to reduce the number of Chosen Freeholders in any county on adoption by the voters thereof in a general election—Chap. 34, Laws of 1902—makes that adoption conditional in the following words: "and if there shall be a majority of votes so cast in favor of the adoption of this act, but not otherwise, this act shall take effect in such county immediately."

And whereas, it appears that in the election to which the said act was submitted in this county "a majority of votes so cast" was not in favor of its adoption, but some twelve hundred short of that requirement, although a plurality voted in the affirmative and not in the negative.

And whereas, it is highly important to this county, for the prevention of disputes and possible litigation as to the validity of future county appropriations and tax levies, that the fact of the adoption or non-adoption of the said act to be judiciously decided with the least possible delay, since the Legislature has now adjourned without action upon it, through a committee's refusal to report the bill presented for the purpose. Be it therefore

Resolved, That the Counsel of this Board be instructed to forthwith bring such proceedings in court as shall judicially determine whether or not the said law was adopted or otherwise.[74]

Before bringing suit, it would be better first to get the legal opinion of the best authority in New Jersey, the *Hunterdon County Democrat* advised. Only if that authority judged that there was a question in the meaning of the law should the matter be brought to court.[75] *The Democrat Advertiser* insisted that any questionable legality of the referendum's result be previously passed upon by the board's counsel. He had noted that the resolution was intended to bring up the matter for further consideration; that no specific action would be taken until further discussion by the board; and that the question as to whether the expense of such legal action should be borne by the county or by the individual freeholders had not been discussed. In any event, the expense was "a very serious matter" that deserved further consideration, the newspaper declared.[76]

Constitutional grounds were cited by those who challenged Hunterdon's adoption of the Strong Act's provisions. *The Hunterdon Gazette* announced:

> We learn that the Hunterdon County Board of Freeholders will test the constitutionality of the new Freeholder law at their own expense. The point to be raised, we believe, is one that the courts have never acted upon—that is whether the Legislature has the power to delegate enacting power to the people of any county or not. It is claimed that the enacting power was delegated to the people of Hunterdon county when a majority of the votes were necessary in order to make the law effective in the county. The point is a new one and one that ought to be settled. That the Legislature has the right to make laws is not disputed of course, but many prominent lawyers question the constitutionality of enactments covered by provisions of this kind.[77]

The Clinton Democrat insisted:

> Even if the new law were adopted under its own ambiguous terms, is such a law as the Constitution says cannot be put, specially and locally, upon any one county in the State, even by the Legislature, to which all law-making power is given? That Hunterdon should not be put under an apparently unconstitutional law without testing, even if it were a law duly enacted, seems to us to be beyond dispute.[78]

Soon afterward, that newspaper stated that because steps had been taken to secure a judicial decision on the validity of the Strong Act, it would decline further discussion of the matter.[79] But within three weeks, readers of the Clinton newspaper were presented with a "head-swimming mess of legal lore" about it.[80]

The legality of the 1902 statute was not appealed to the courts, and in November 1903 Hunterdon elected a freeholder board of three Democrats to replace the governing body of fourteen Democrats and seven Republicans.[81]

Municipal representation on the board of chosen freeholders was not to be re-established in Hunterdon, as it had been previously in Hudson, Essex, Camden, Passaic, and Mercer. Within ten years a majority of New Jersey's counties was to adopt the small board plan.

13

OPTIONAL VS. MANDATORY
SMALL BOARDS, 1903–1966

Hunterdon's 1902 adoption of the Strong Act's optional small board provisions encouraged other counties to attempt the same. The lack of success in these efforts prompted demands for *mandatory* legislation, but such a compulsory law was not to be enacted for more than sixty years. During this period, forty-four referenda were held under the optional approach, all of them occurring before 1940. Finally, in 1966, partisan motivation in the legislature responded to the threat of judicial action to regulate the apportionment of freeholders in accordance with recent decisions of the United States Supreme Court.

INVESTIGATIONS AND REFERENDA

Not additional legislation, but increased popular agitation for reform became the vehicle for structural change in freeholder boards immediately after passage of the Strong Act of 1902. Now that an end to governing bodies elected by municipality and ward could be achieved by referendum in any county, there was great use of an amended 1879 statute[1] authorizing official judicial investigation into county (and municipal) financial matters upon petition of twenty-five taxpayers. In addition, the creation of new wards and the growth of population in boroughs resulted in more freeholder constituencies, thereby heightening apprehension in some counties about maintaining equitable apportionment. But the major reason that the small board was not eagerly adopted throughout the state was the fear that the minority political party would be totally unrepresented on a freeholder board elected by the county at large. After all, since 1894, assemblymen had been elected on such a basis, and the result almost invariably was a one-party assembly delegation in each county.[2]

In Middlesex and Passaic, taxpayer demands for judicial action resulted in quick approval of the small board plan. "Several matters have come up since the last election [1902] that have awakened the people of the county to the need of a commission"; and the first was a recent investigation that "showed a shameful waste of public money for worthless supervision of county work by the freeholders," announced a New Brunswick newspaper in May 1904.[3] During the previous July, New Jersey Supreme Court Justice Franklin Fort was given a copy of the presentment of the Middlesex County grand jury censuring the freeholder board for certain transactions and recommending the appointment of a commission to examine the county's fiscal affairs.[4] Along with it there was a petition from the requisite number of taxpayers seeking the same action.[5] The expert who was chosen submitted his report of April 1904 to the Justice, who noted that it showed a large number of irregularities, an amount of carelessness, and some violations of law. He directed that the text be read to the grand jury.[6] Not long afterward, petitions to require a referendum on abolishing the large board were circulating,[7] and even before the grand jury's presentment (December, 1904) had "unmercifully" excoriated the freeholders,[8] voters adopted the five-member board, 6,731 to 4,506.[9]

In Passaic, unlike Middlesex, the 1904 investigation *followed* the petition for a referendum that had been prevented previously by legal technicalities concerning proper advertising. "Many attempts have been made in Passaic county to send the official probe into the very depths of the management of county affairs, but neither grand juries nor citizens' associations have been equal to the task," the *Newark Evening News* noted in May. But this time, instead of deriding such efforts, the freeholders even ordered an investigation of their own. "How thorough this will be may be surmised when it is known that $250 has been appropriated to this end," the editorial writer scoffed.[10] This freeholder maneuver did not forestall another investigation. By September, the expert hired by the board had "thrown up the job," because it had "proved too much for him,"[11] and the expert appointed by Supreme Court Justice Mahlon Pitney was about to begin what a local newspaper predicted would be "one of the most momentous judicial proceedings in the whole history of the county."[12] After the very first day's testimony, one freeholder who had been accused of taking graft committted suicide.[13] Capital letters in large type told readers of the *Passaic Daily News* on election eve that the investigation (still in progress) had produced "REVELATIONS . . . ENOUGH TO MAKE HONEST MEN TURN IN THEIR GRAVES."[14] The large board was abolished, 8,239 to 8,095.[15]

"The chosen freeholder system dies hard in Middlesex and Passaic," the *Newark Evening News* remarked after the referendum.[16] The Democratic members of the freeholder board in Middlesex had notified the county clerk as well as the city and township clerks that the referendum was illegal, because it had not been properly advertised. Moreover, the Democrats were ready to fight the matter out in court on the ground that only about one-half the total number of actual voters cast their ballots either for or against adoption of the Strong Act.[17] In Passaic, the freeholders coupled a similar contention with a threat. Because the notice of the election had not been printed in the newspapers in four townships, the large board intended to overturn the results of the election of candidates, in addition to the outcome of the referendum.[18] But the 1905 legislature enacted Senate Bill No. 23, introduced by William H. C. Jackson (R-Middlesex), validating any previous referendum on the Strong Act "notwithstanding that notice of the submission of the adoption of said act to vote at such election shall not have been given" as provided in the 1902 law's seventh section, and notwithstanding any defect or want of compliance with that act in the manner of position in which the proposition appeared on the ballot. There were provisos that the proposition had to have appeared on the ballot and that "the sum of the ballots cast for and against the adoption of said act was, at least, fifty per centum of the entire number of ballots cast in said county for members of the general assembly in such election."[19] In Middlesex, the referendum total was 64 percent; in Passaic, 52 percent.[20]

Lack of an investigation concurrent with the referendum was one cause of Mercer's rejection of the small board in 1904. Petitions for a referendum had been submitted in October 1903, but it was not held, because no legal notice of it had been published eight days before the election, as required. Moreover, there were objections that the Strong Act failed 1) to prescribe any method by which the municipal and town clerks should receive notice of their duty with regard to publication; 2) to prescribe any method by which the county clerk could be notified as to whether the local clerks had given any notice of intended submission; and 3) to provide a method by which the county clerk should receive information authorizing him to print the proposition on the ballots.[21] In the fall of 1904, when petitions from 1903 were resubmitted, the *Newark Evening News* complained that until the end of October "not a single prominent item or editorial appeared in any of the Trenton papers with reference to this important matter."[22] In its editorial judgment, "Superficially this has the appearance of a concerted agreement to suppress all discussion of the subject, but it may not have been so intended."[23] After the referendum, the *News* again insisted, "For some reason, as yet unexplained, the Mercer County papers allowed the whole issue to go by default until it was almost time to print the tickets, and even then the advocates of the proposed change were not enthusiastically active."[24]

Voting returns indicate no great interest on the part of Mercer to change the system. Of those who cast ballots for assemblymen, not even one in four paid attention to the referendum, and it was defeated: 2,238, in favor; 3,523, opposed.[25] "If the proposition had been submitted to the Mercer county voters immediately after the Chambers street road investigation, it would have been adopted ten to one," stated the *Trenton Times.*[26] It also noted reports that if the 1904 vote in Mercer had been favorable, a question would have been raised concerning the legality of the decision, because the matter had not been submitted to the voters at the election immediately following the filing of the 1903 petition (as the law seemed to require).[27]

The 1904 referenda showed that the winner-take-all likelihood in an at-large election could result in conflict between party loyalty and the power politics of the various municipalities. After the state Supreme Court declared the election of assemblymen by districts to be unconstitutional (1893),[28] the *Trenton Evening Times* observed, ". . . in most of the counties, both of the parties, out of a spirit of fairness apportion the [Assembly] nominations according to the old district lines . . . and the county conventions have ratified the choice made by the imaginary districts." But Passaic was one of the counties where this rule had been ignored.[29] "What chance would Passaic [city] have if seven freeholders were elected from the county at-large?" inquired the *Passaic Herald.* "The party machines in Paterson would make the nominations, and, as the county is Republican, the Paterson machine would practically be in charge of the county." Readers were advised that "from a selfish reason no Democrat anywhere nor any Republican except in Paterson" should vote for the small board.[30] Aware that the freeholder board stood eleven Republicans to ten Democrats, the City of Passaic voted against the Strong Act plan; and the six townships did likewise, regardless of the party affiliations of their freeholders (half of them Republican). With five of the six Democratic freeholder ward-constitutencies voting negatively, Paterson supplied a majority of 1,287, sufficient to have the plan carry by only 144 votes.[31] Including 67 percent of Passaic County's population and paying about 80 percent of the county taxes, that city had everything to gain.[32] Even under one *unofficial* proposal for reapportionment that had been mentioned in the press, it was to choose four of seven freeholders.[33]

In Middlesex, the scandals had led voters to disregard petty municipal interests and partisan politics. Although there were only 327 more votes cast in the 1904 referendum than in 1902,[34] this time Perth Amboy, as well as New Brunswick, voted affirmatively; and only twelve townships were opposed.[35] Neither city could complain of unjust representation, since, with 25 percent and 22 percent, respectively, of the county population, each was electing one-fourth of the freeholder board. But despite probable detriment to their own party's candidates, the reported corruption caused Democrats to vote to end a system whereby only eight Republicans were included in a twenty-four-member county governing body at the same time that the state senator and three assemblymen from Middlesex were all Republicans.[36]

"There does not appear to be as much reason for a change in Mercer as there is in either Middlesex or Passaic," judged the *Newark Evening News* before the referendum. "Economical management of county affairs," rather than an end to graft and corruption, was the capital county's goal.[37] In its comparison, the newspaper neglected to note that in Mercer the *status quo* gave greater advantage to the dominant political party (sixteen of the twenty-three freeholders were Republican) and to the major city (Trenton's 77 percent of the county population elected fourteen members or 61 percent of the board).[38]

By mid-1905 the *New Jersey Law Journal* was observing: "An unusual number of what are termed 'Freeholders' Cases' have been occupying the county courts during the past few months." They include grand jury indictments and investigations demanded by taxpayers. "In our view," said the editors, "the reason for all this is that the system of county boards is a faulty one." Originally it was a good system, when the best men in the county served more for the honor than for the per diem payments. Since the office of freeholder had become "purely political," successful businessmen usually were not attracted to it. "The remedy is for each county to take advantage of the law by which, after a public vote first taken, the governing body of three [*sic*] commissioners can be substituted for the board of freeholders," lawyers were advised. "Politics is likely to stand in the way of a general adoption of the optional Act," said the *Journal*, referring to the possibility of a mandatory law establishing small freeholder boards in all twenty-one counties.[39]

As a result of litigation and also legislation discouraging investigations, their number seemed to diminish toward the end of the decade. In September 1905, two separate applications were made to Justice Johnathan Dixon for an order directing scrutiny of Hoboken's fiscal affairs. That city's corporation counsel, James F. Minturn, subsequently raised the point that the law authorizing such municipal (and county) examinations was unconstitutional, because the legislature could not delegate the power of investigation to any court. Agreeing that the objection was an important one, Justice Dixon at first refused to order the probe, but then granted a writ of mandamus against himself, so that the question could be taken to the state Supreme Court for decision.[40] Two months later, he approved the taxpayers' application and said that he would serve as the investigator himself.[41] This action was challenged by Hoboken officials on five grounds in the Supreme Court in November 1906 and was sustained on each of them. "This statute [1879, as amended] is evidently a very useful public act," the opinion read.[42]

It was "significant" that Minturn, who was serving his third term as Hudson's Democratic senator, should have introduced a repealer of the law on investigation (Senate Bill No. 19) just after the Court's ruling, the *Trenton Evening Times* observed in the early days of the 1907 legislative session. In addition, Minturn proposed a new act (Senate Bill No. 20), requiring at least one hundred property owners, instead of twenty-five, to petition for an investigation, and making them submit a $2,000 bond to defray expenses.[43] The repeal measure was enacted with its original text; but the second bill was enacted in the form of a Senate committee substitute giving a justice discretion as to whether a county or municipal investigation should be conducted at all, and requiring the applicants to furnish a bond in such amount as he might deem necessary.[44]

If more than half the state's counties had voted in favor of the small board by 1911, such positive results were hardwon and frequently temporary. From Monmouth's approval in 1905 through that of Essex in 1910, there were nine unsuccessful referenda: Bergen,

Ocean, Warren in 1905; Somerset in 1906; Burlington in 1907; Bergen in 1908; Sussex in 1909; and Somerset and Sussex in 1910.[45] In that last year Jersey City's *Jersey Journal* could inquire: "Why all of the counties have not availed themselves of the benefits of the law no one can understand, except that the politicians who benefit by the present system have enough influence to prevent action."[46] But at the end of 1910 there began in New Jersey the movement that resulted in passage of the 1911 Walsh Act for commission government of municipalities.[47] Doubtless its quick adoption by Trenton and five other municipalities before November 1911[48] helps to account for the affirmative vote that month of all six counties that conducted small board referenda. "The Progressives were among the ardent advocates of the proposition [to adopt the Strong Act]," the press observed concerning Bergen; and it is likely that they were active in the other five counties: Burlington, Mercer, Morris, Sussex, and Union.[49] Of the six counties voting affirmatively in 1911 (Bergen, Burlington, Mercer, Morris, Sussex, Union),[50] only Union had not defeated the proposal at least once, and only Sussex would not be involved in the nine additional referenda that had to be conducted by that group in order to establish legally acceptable small boards.

LEGAL TECHNICALITIES INVOLVING SECOND-CLASS COUNTIES

Immediately after the 1911 election, some lawyers expressed the belief that second-class counties had not validly adopted the small board.[51] Considerable confusion arose over an amendment[52] to the Strong Act passed by the 1908 legislature lengthening the terms of the freeholders to three years and making such terms overlapping. In the Senate, a proviso had been added that "this act shall not apply to counties of the second class."[53] As the *Trenton Evening Times* observed, "The latter clause was probably inserted by representatives of some of the second class counties that had already adopted the act." The word "act" was "blunderingly" used where "section" had been undoubtedly intended.[54] Nevertheless, it was not clear whether the words "this act" meant the amendatory act of 1908 in which those words appeared, or whether they referred to the original optional small board act of 1902.[55] In the opinion of some, the amendment made the original act unconstitutional by making the title and body of that act contradictory.[56] Moreover, the amendment itself could be unconstitutional, because its object (in regard to second-class counties) was not expressed in its title.[57] Further complicating the situation was a recent decision by the Court of Errors and Appeals that every law was to be presumed to be constitutional until declared otherwise by a court of competent jurisdiction. The practical application of such a decision, it was argued, would be that all members of *existing* small freeholder boards in second-class counties (Passaic, Middlesex, Monmouth) would be only *de facto* officers.[58] Those five second-class counties that had just adopted the small board (Union, Bergen, Mercer, Morris, Burlington) but had not yet elected new members would have to look to the legislature for remedy of their problem.

Indeed, "a fearful maze of Freeholder bills,"[59] some of them later found to be invalid in a state Supreme Court case (1913) involving Union's referendum, was passed during the 1912 legislative session. The first, sponsored by Griffith W. Lewis (R-Burlington), provided for boards of nine, seven, five, or three members, to be elected for staggered three-year terms. In order to maintain the seven-member board in Passaic (215,902 pop.), the number of inhabitants required for the election of nine members was increased to 300,000. Of greater significance was Section 2, which provided that in all second-class counties that had "heretofore" cast a majority vote for the Strong Act of 1902, the freeholder board should consist of five or seven members, according to the original act's population groupings (changed only for Passaic). Enacted as Chapter 181, Lewis's measure was held by the judiciary to be inapplicable to Union, because the title of the act that had been approved in that county's 1911 referendum was inaccurate, and because the question on the ballot there had been worded incorrectly.[60]

In the same case, the Court struck down Chapter 314, a substitute for a Senate bill introduced by Harry D. Leavitt (R-Mercer). That act validated elections where the 1902 act and its supplements and amendments had been approved by a majority of the county's voters "notwithstanding any irregularity in the submission of the question of the adoption of said act." But the Court's opinion noted that the second-class counties had voted for the superseded act of 1902 alone, *without* any supplement or amendment. The Leavitt Act seemed "intended to cure only irregularities in the submission of the question," and it was "much more than a mere irregularity when the voters are given no opportunity to express their opinion upon the supplements and amendments to the act."[61]

Also declared invalid was Chapter 274, introduced into the Senate by James A. C. Johnson (D-Bergen), which amended the Strong Act to provide that counties with 125,000 to 141,000 (Union, Bergen, Mercer) could have small freeholder boards without the necessity of referenda. "Obviously, the legislature cannot, in legislation that relies for its becoming effective upon a popular vote, deprive those counties of the same right that is conceded to other counties," said the Court.[62]

Nor was a fourth 1912 statute, the Gill Act revising the 1902 Strong Act, accepted by the judiciary as sufficient validation for the newly approved small boards. "We cannot hold that Chapter 355 applies to Union county," the opinion read. "To hold otherwise would violate the fundamental principles of what is now called direct legislation"; and voters of every county were entitled to an equal chance to express their will. Like the Strong Act, Chapter 355 (Assembly Bill No. 399, sponsored by John E. Gill, R-Mercer) provided for adoption of small boards by referendum, but such requirement of a *referendum* was *not* to apply either to counties which had already adopted the 1902 law and had organized according to its provisions, or to counties that had already adopted the 1902 law and in which no board had been elected in the new way. In all those counties, including Union, the provisions of the Gill Act of 1912 were *mandatory*. Voters in Union would, therefore, "be subjected to its operation without having any opportunity to vote thereon, while other counties which had not already gone through the form of an invalid referendum would have the privilege of accepting or rejecting the act of 1912." Union had voted in 1911 for the original Strong Act, providing for two-year concurrent terms, but the Gill Act of 1912 prescribed three-year overlapping terms. As observed by the Court, "The evil of this [type of discrimination] appears strikingly in the case of the Mercer county freeholders argued at the time with the present." Because the population categories established by the Gill Act were different from those that had been voted on in 1911, Mercer would be forced to elect five members, instead of the seven-member body that it had approved, the opinion noted.[63] But although the opinion held the Gill Act to be inapplicable in validating Union's 1911 vote, that law's constitutionality was not to be determined until 1915.

In another 1912 legislative effort to reduce the size of freeholder boards in second-class counties, application of the principle of the Walsh Act of 1911 for commission government of municipalities[64] was proposed by Charles O. Hennessey (D-Bergen) in Assembly Bill No. 94. The seventeen-page measure provided that 1,000 legal voters could petition for a referendum, to be held the third Tuesday from the date of filing, on the adoption of a commmission of five persons. Each candidate would be nominated by a petition of one hundred voters, and there would be *no political party designation* appearing on either the primary or the general election ballot. The name of every candidate would be printed on all party tickets, "thus practically establishing the open primary in the selection of the freeholder candidates."[65] Of the ten candidates receiving the highest number of votes, five would be chosen at the general election for three-year terms. *Initiative, referendum,* and *recall* would be authorized for county affairs. But this Hennessy measure was never called up for a vote.

ATTEMPTS AT MANDATORY LEGISLATION

With the 1912 acts validating the small board referenda in second-class counties held ineffective by the courts, the 1913 legislature was to seek other methods to accomplish this. Mandatory legislation for all counties was to be urged, not only to deal with the complicated legal technicalities involved, but also to impose reform.

Home rule for counties in the matter of representation had been coming under increasing attack by proponents of the small board. "There is a demand from several counties, in which Mercer seems to be taking the lead, to have the Strong county commission law amended next winter so that it will be mandatory in all counties," observed the Somerville *Unionist Gazette* in 1907.[66] After Mercer had shown so little interest in abolishing the large board (1904), the *Trenton Evening Times,* indeed, began a vigorous campaign to make the 1902 act "compulsory in all of the counties of the State,"[67] and it was to persist for some time. After all, experience had demonstrated the value of the small board, which was opposed only by the incumbent freeholders and their would-be successors, the *Times* declared in 1907, "and if the referendum could be submitted to a vote of the people of the State, separated from all other issues, it would be adopted by at least five to one."[68] At the end of 1911, the newspaper was still demanding passage of a mandatory law: "When more than one-half of the counties in the State have voted in favor of a proposition, it is time for the Legislature to take official notice of the fact." Besides, now there was an additional reason: "A general, mandatory act will get rid of the confusion that exists over the blundering amendment made to the Strong Act in 1908."[69]

Support for a mandatory law had come from other Republican newspapers in counties where the optional change had been defeated by the voters or frustrated by legal technicalities. For example, the *Lakewood Times and Journal* said in 1906: "Some kind of

legislation should be devised this winter at Trenton which will put
not only the Ocean County Board of Freeholders out of existence,
but every other board which is not operating under the Strong Act,
also."[70] Five years later, Burlington County's *New Jersey Mirror*
declared, "There should be uniformity in county government, and it
is plain that the day of the freeholders is over."[71]

Efforts in 1912 to establish a small board of freeholders in Hudson (a first-class county) without any referendum at all brought the
concept of home rule for all counties under attack. *Mandatory* legislation to replace the thirty-one-member governing body with nine
members to be elected for staggered three-year terms in first-class
counties was introduced by James F. Fielder (D-Hudson) as Senate
Bill No. 31. (Essex had voted in 1910 to replace its thirty-two-
member board with such a system).[72] Immediately, Jersey City's
Jersey Journal began a vigorous campaign against *compulsory* reduction in the number of freeholders and claimed later to have been
"alone among the newspapers of New Jersey, opposed to that feature."[73]

When the Senate passed the Fielder bill, 19 to 0, only eight days
after its introduction, "after practically no discussion whatever on
the floor and no committee hearings at all,"[74] protests developed
among Hudson's political clubs, civic improvement associations,
and public-spirited citizens.[75] Many pointed out that "the Legislature would not dare foist a new charter on any municipality without
first submitting the charter to the people for a vote" and that Senate
Bill No. 31 was "practically a new charter for the county" without the
referendum feature.[76] "I'll bet $50 that Senator Fielder's bill to wipe
out the present Hudson County Board of Freeholders will never get
through the House of Assembly," predicted that chamber's minority
leader, Thomas F. Martin, also a Hudson Democrat.[77] Demanding
the insertion of a referendum provision, he insisted that the original
bill should not be smothered in committee, but should be killed on
the floor of the Assembly.[78]

Fielder, who was to become champion of the cause of *mandatory* small boards throughout the state, defended his single-county
measure. "I know public sentiment on this subject and I know that a
majority of the people of Hudson County want the bill and want it
without the referendum," he announced. The demand for a popular
vote emanated "from enemies of the bill who can't defeat it on its
merits in the House and who are anxious to have it changed so that
they will have more opportunity to defeat it at the polls."[79] To the
Jersey City Board of Trade, the Senator wrote his objection to a

special election for a referendum vote, "because of the expense involved and also because it is exceedingly difficult to get the vote out at a special election." And at a November election, "candidates would be seeking election to the board under the present law, and each candidate of the several parties and all their friends and political organizations would be working 'tooth and nail' against the adoption of the act."[80] Denying a charge that his bill discontinued the office of county supervisor (which was expected to be maintained by a general clause in Section 5), Fielder, nevertheless, sponsored Senate Bill No. 82, specifically providing for such a position.[81]

The mandatory feature proved unacceptable to the legislature. After the Assembly Republican caucus declared, 27 to 5, in favor of Martin's proposal for a referendum at the primary election in May for Presidential delegates, Fielder's Senate Bill No. 31 was reported favorably with such an amendment.[82] There followed a "two hours debate full of hot forceful and sometimes bitter talk."[83] On the 39-to-11 vote to adopt the Martin amendment, seven Democrats were to be found on each side (in the negative, all from Hudson).[84] But on the vote for final passage, there was "a grand rush to get on the home rule band wagon":[85] only two Hudson Democrats voted negatively, while fifty Assemblymen approved.[86] Before the Senate re-passed the amended bill, 16 to 0, with "no debate," Fielder was the only one to speak. Maintaining that such legislation would be unconstitutional, he announced his support for the measure as the best that he could get.[87] Two days later, Fielder introduced Senate Bill No. 259, drawn along what he considered strictly constitutional lines.[88] The Martin amendment was "adhered to in nearly all the essentials," except that the phraseology was "changed in a few particulars," the *Jersey Journal* reported. Authorization for a referendum in either May or November was the most significant alteration.[89]

Senate Bill No. 31 was vetoed "because and only because, in the opinion of the Attorney-General a portion of the contents does not correspond with the title." In his message to the legislature, Democratic Governor Woodrow Wilson said, "I greatly regret this apparently conclusive constitutional objection to the bill, because in the purpose and provisions of the act I heartily concur." He was "gratified to learn that a bill with exactly the same object in every respect has been presented to the Senate and will be pressed for passage through both houses."[90] Fielder's Senate Bill No. 259 with two possible referendum dates was passed without dissent in either chamber and signed by the Governor.[91] Within ten minutes after it was filed, Assemblyman Martin started a petition for a referendum in

Hudson at the May primary elections, and "hustling over to the Senate gave Senator Fielder the honor of being the first one to sign the petition."[92] The small board was adopted by more than two to one (26,207 to 11,137) with every subdivision in the county voting affirmatively, except North Bergen, Harrison, and Jersey City's Second Ward, "where Frank Hague and his cohorts stood by the machine in its efforts to throttle the new law."[93]

Even before argument was heard on the 1913 case concerning the effect of the 1908 second-class county amendment on the 1911 adoption of small boards, additional legislative attempts were made to validate them. But the state Supreme Court held that such enactments by the first legislature since 1893 to be controlled by Democrats in both houses were ineffective to legitimatize those governing bodies. Chapter 2 of the Laws of 1913, sponsored as Assembly Bill No. 12 by John W. Zisgen (D-Bergen), counsel to his county's recently elected small board, was declared inapplicable, because it "applies only to elections theretofore held and attempts to cure only defects in the notice of election, in the calling of same and in the manner of submission or certification thereof."[94] Chapter 4, sponsored as Assembly Bill No. 108 by Hugh J. McLaughlin (D-Union), applied only to freeholders elected pursuant to the 1912 Gill Act and not to previously elected freeholders;[95] and Chapter 5 (McLaughlin's Assembly Bill No. 109) validated all elections "heretofore held" at which an existing law was adopted. But according to the Court, "The act of 1902 [Strong Act] was not law in 1911; it had been essentially modified in 1908, was no longer applicable to second-class counties, and the amendments of that year were never voted on." Even if the 1911 referendum on the adoption of small boards were to be validated," it could do no more than make effective the act as it then was, and that act was repealed in 1912 [by the Gill Act, the legislature's latest revision of the optional small board law].[96]

In order to remedy the effect of the March 1913 decision in this case, *mandatory* legislation was passed to establish small boards in counties with more than 50,000 inhabitants. Assembly Bill No. 648, introduced by John J. Griffin (D-Union), but drawn by former Governor John Franklin Fort,[97] *required* the same number of freeholders as listed in the Gill Act of 1912: nine members in counties with more than 300,000 residents; seven in counties with 135,000 to 300,000; and five in counties with 50,000 to 135,000. In any county with less than 50,000 population, there could be a three-member board after approval by a *referendum* initiated by a petition signed by at least

5 percent of the qualified voters. Within two days, the Assembly passed the bill, but the Senate accepted an amendment by Walter E. Edge (R-Atlantic), excepting from the mandatory provisions those counties which had not *previously* adopted the small board (Camden, Atlantic, Cumberland).[98] Another amendment adopted was one offered by Carlton B. Pierce (R-Union) that would allow a petition by 5 percent of the qualified voters, one year after the act should become effective in a county, to initiate a referendum on whether that county should return to the large freeholder board plan.[99] But the upper chamber barely defeated (9 to 9) another Pierce proposal, taking much of its text from Assembly Bill No. 722, sponsored by Joseph A. Delaney (D-Passaic), that had been narrrowly defeated the previous week.[100] This amendment would have required the presiding judge of the Court of Common Pleas in each affected county to appoint a three-member bipartisan commission to divide that county into the appropriate number of freeholder districts.[101] In the last hours of the legislative session, the Assembly concurred in the Senate amendments, 35 to 7.[102] Because of the exceptions of Camden, Atlantic, and Cumberland, Acting Governor Fielder pocket-vetoed the measure. In a memorandum, he referred to the Attorney General's opinion expressing doubt concerning the Griffin bill's constitutionality.[103]

Acting Governor Fielder did not let the situation rest. On April 14 he issued a proclamation convening the legislature in special session on May 6 to pass reform measures concerning jury selection; to call a constitutional convention; and to give "prompt relief" to those second-class counties that had adopted small boards in 1911.[104] In his message, read on the session's opening day, senators and assemblymen heard Fielder's appraisal of the counties' predicament:

The government of our counties by large boards of freeholders is archaic. Through many members, responsibility is divided and can be shifted from one group to another, until the average citizen grows weary in attempting to locate the blame for county misgovernment. Hasty or misguided legislation, designed to permit the adoption of small board government has resulted in defective laws, and the expressed desire of several counties to govern themselves by a small board has been defeated, and their affairs are left in an unsettled condition. This subject directly affects many thousands of our citizens, and can and should be remedied.[105]

Fielder "was not at all pleased" with the results of the session, noted the press.[106] The only freeholder measure to pass was Hennessy's Special Session Assembly Bill No. 12, introduced primarily to correct the situation in the sponsor's home county of Bergen. Enacted as Chapter 21, this amendment to the Gill act provided that the small board could be adopted in any county at any special election called solely for the purpose of submitting that proposition or at any special election held thereafter. In Bergen there was to be a special election in July for the selection of a successor to the late Rep. Lewis J. Martin in the Sixth Congressional District. Affirmative results in the referendum would permit the election of small board members in the regular November election, saving a year in the process.[107]

Only one other small board bill came to a vote during the special session. Griffin reintroduced the *original* text of his Assembly Bill No. 648 as Special Session Assembly Bill No. 8, *requiring* governing bodies of five, seven, or nine members in counties with more than 50,000 population and *allowing* the other counties to conduct referenda on whether to establish three-member boards. Once again the bill was amended to provide for freeholder districts (and this time also to increase Mercer's membership from five to seven).[108] With only one vote to spare, the Griffin bill passed, 32 to 4.[109] But when it became evident that the Senate would not approve mandatory adoption of small boards, "the bill was allowed to die."[110]

Three county bills were considered by the Assembly on the last day of the *second* special session that Acting Governor Fielder convened on August 5 to amend the Walsh Act for municipalities and to ratify the commission government in Jersey City.[111] Second Special Session Assembly Bill No. 7, introduced by Arthur M. Agnew (D-Bergen) to validate his county's second adoption of the small board in July, 1913, was passed, 42 to 0, but did not come to a vote in the Senate.[112] Next to claim the lower chamber's attention was Zisgen's Second Special Session Assembly Bill No. 6, intended to correct the failure of the recently passed Hennesy Act to provide specifically for the county clerks' calling of elections. This proposal would make the small boards *mandatory* in second-class counties.[113] There were 761,000 persons affected in counties that had been frustrated in their efforts to adopt small boards, Zisgen argued, and it was "every bit as important that they secure relief as it is that the 272,000 residents of Jersey City shall be permitted to have the government which they desire."[114] But the Assembly acceded to Zisgen's request that his bill be allowed to lie over, after it had been sharply attacked by Majority Leader Emerson L. Richard (D-Atlantic), who maintained his county's opposition to small boards, and by Edward L. Neighbour (D-Morris), who favored freeholder districts.[115]

Immediately, Griffin's Second Special Session Assembly Bill No. 8 was taken up and "aroused much opposition," including arguments from John B. Kates (R-Camden), representing a large-board, second-class county.[116] The bill was "practically the same as the Zisgen measure," except that it provided for freeholder districts, instead of at-large elections.[117] Even Neighbour abandoned his support for the Griffin bill, when he learned that it was mandatory.[118] The vote was eight in favor, twenty-nine opposed.[119] (On that very day, Burlington voted to return to its thirty-three-member board, after having but seven months' experience with only five freeholders.)[120]

Compulsory legislation fared no better in the 1914 legislature, like its predecessor controlled in both Houses by Democrats. The Assembly was not eager to accept Governor Fielder's argument in his Inaugural Address that it was "the duty of the Legislature to pass a mandatory bill which will give a small board government to all counties."[121] Not until almost a month had elapsed did Griffin (D-Union) sponsor Assembly Bill No. 345 to make seven-member boards *compulsory* in counties with a population of 135,000 to 300,000 (Passaic, Camden, Union, Bergen). Only after the Attorney General's department had rendered an opinion that such a measure was probably unconstitutional[122] did Griffin sponsor another, Assembly Bill No. 419, making small boards mandatory in all counties. As in the optional Gill Act of 1912, still not reviewed by the judiciary, there would be nine members in counties with more than 300,000 inhabitants; seven members in counties with 135,000 to 300,000; five members in counties with 50,000 to 135,000; and three members in all other counties.

Before long, the character of Griffin's Assembly Bill No. 419 was to be changed drastically. Hennessy (D-Bergen), who had introduced Griffin's earlier bill as Senate Bill No. 149, was warning of a movement to defeat that Griffin Bill concerning the more populous counties by "the indirect process of attaching to it impossible amendments." He referred to an amendment proposed by a Camden Republican which would insure the retention in office of the county engineer and other officers and employees. This "would, of course, defeat the primary object of the legislation, which is to give the people a new deal with new men and new methods," the senator from Bergen maintained.[123] With such an amendment by Hervey S.

Moore (R-Mercer) added to a committee substitute bill for Assembly Bill No. 419 for all counties, the lower chamber narrowly rejected (24 to 25) an amendment by John B. Kates (R-Camden) to require a referendum in those counties, like his own, that were then electing large boards.[124] After that defeat, the Republican Assemblymen held a conference at which it was agreed to support Assembly Bill No. 419, if *both* the Moore and the Kates amendments should be incorporated into it.[125]

Governor Fielder was insistent on passage of the original *mandatory* Griffin measure. In a message to the Democratic members of the legislature he said:

It is most astonishing to me that a Democratic Legislature should hesitate to pass this bill. Every county having the small board is satisfied that it is better than the large one. It is my understanding that every county save two where the question of adopting the small board has been submitted has voted in favor of it. Legislation on this subject, providing for a referendum, has become so complicated and has so often been set aside by the courts—that the only safe way is to compel all counties to accept the kind of board which has been found satisfactory wherever tried.[126]

But the Governor's viewpoint was not to prevail. Despite adverse parliamentary maneuvers, the referendum amendment, offered this time by Garfield Pancoast (R-Camden), was adopted, 30 to 15.[127] Noting that there already existed the Gill Act to permit counties to vote on the small board plan, the *Trenton Evening Times* declared that the "emasculated" Griffin bill "may as well be abandoned."[128]

The Governor became furious, as evidenced by the tone of his message to the Assembly one week later:

If what I have heretofore communicated to you on the subject of small boards of freeholders has not impressed you favorably, it seems idle to say anything further; and yet, believing it my duty to do so, I am constrained to make another attempt to point out to you the obligation I consider you are under to pass a mandatory bill for all counties before final adjournment. It is the general sentiment of the State that such a law should be enacted, and you have but to refer to the large number of votes cast in counties where the proposition has been submitted at elections to be convinced that I am asserting a fact. Why is it that this legislation, promised before election from many a platform, is now denied? Why is it that the majority of your body accepts amendments to a mandatory bill which make it obnoxious to this large body of voters? Why is it that members from counties where small boards are given complete satisfaction, by their votes in connection with this measure, make it difficult for other counties to secure the kind of govern-

ment they enjoy? Those who want this legislation find in the course you have
pursued no satisfactory answer to these questions, and I warn you that your
failure to pass a mandatory bill will be taken as a betrayal of trust I feel is
imposed on you.[129]

But the Griffin bill was neither repaired according to the Governor's
wishes, nor, indeed, even considered for final passage in its
amended form with the referendum feature.

The only pertinent legislation in 1914 was an amendment to the
Gill Act which permitted a small board referendum at a special (or
general) election and provided the procedural details that were
omitted in the Hennessy Act of 1913. This new statute also was
sponsored by a Bergen Democrat, Arthur M. Agnew.[130] And in 1914,
Ocean's voters defeated the small board proposition.[131]

Defenders of home rule had to contend the following year (1915)
with another *mandatory* bill for freeholder districts as well as small
boards. Senate Bill No. 15, sponsored by Charles A. Rathbun (R-
Morris), called for a Supreme Court justice to appoint a three-
member commission of county residents, two of them belonging to
the county's dominant political party, to divide that county into
freeholder constituencies. But a committee substitute bill suspended the operation of the plan until it should be approved in a
referendum; and, in addition, the population figures dividng
categories of counties (which differed from the groupings in the Gill
Act) were changed from 200,000, 100,000, and 50,000 to 300,000,
200,000, and 50,000. Passaic would not be assigned nine freeholders
along with Hudson and Essex; but it would be the *only* county to
have seven. The number of counties electing five freeholders was to
be increased to ten. Even then the substitute measure was barely
defeated on third reading, 5 to 6. When the Senate exempted counties with more than 300,000 inhabitants (Hudson, Essex) from the
districting bill's provisions, it passed,[132] but never came to a vote in
the Assembly.

It remained for a judicial decision on the constitutionality of the
Gill Act of 1912 to clarify the muddled situation that had existed for
four years, and to end the serious demand for mandatory changes to
small freeholder boards. On August 30, 1915, Supreme Court Justice
Francis J. Swayze heard argument on a rule to show cause why a writ
of mandamus should not be issued compelling the county clerk of
Bergen to refrain from printing on the primary ballot the names of
candidates for membership on a small board. Two days later the
Justice upheld the constitutionality of the Gill Act with the result

that Bergen's small board adoption in November, 1914, for the third time was validated.[133] Because it excepted from its provisions those counties which had already adopted the 1902 Strong Act (thereby creating two classes of counties), the Gill Act had been challenged as special legislation. "But the constitutionality of an act of the legislature is not to be determined by verbal or rhetorical niceties; the act must be judged on a broader basis and according to its effect as a whole," Swayze declared.[134] In his opinion, the rule that must govern was:

If the effect of the act is to remove existing differences, and to subject the internal affairs to the operation of a general law, then it is not prohibited by the constitution, but is in strict accordance with the command of that instrument, which expressely enjoins upon the legislature the passage of general laws for such cases.[135]

Moreover, Swayze rejected his own previous suggestion that the clause in the Gill Act which provided for the repeal of legislation inconsistent with it might have the effect of repealing the Strong Act and its amendments, thereby destroying existing governments in counties like Middlesex and Monmouth. "Upon reflection, I think such could not have been the legislative intent," he said.[136]

The decision did not validate the successful small board referenda of 1911, prior to passage of the Gill Act with its provisions for new population categories and different terms of office. But, as noted by the Trenton press, "The voters of Mercer County [and other counties] may adopt the small board of freeholders act with the assurance that it is legal in the eyes of the Supreme Court."[137]

OPTIONAL LEGISLATION, PROPOSED OR PASSED

Even though the validity of optional small boards had been settled, serious argument over at-large elections versus district constituencies for freeholders was to continue. In 1916, Harold Wells (R-Burlington) sponsored Senate Bill No. 131, providing that a petition of 5 percent of a county's qualified voters on a resolution of the freeholder board could place the district proposition on the ballot. An affirmative vote would authorize the local judge of the Court of Common Pleas, the sheriff, and the county clerk to divide the county into districts. After changes were made to follow the population categories of the Gill Act and to establish three-year staggered terms, a committee substitute was passed, 13 to 0, but lacked three votes of passage (28 to 16) in the Assembly.[138]

The following year (1917), the text of the committee substitute for the Wells measure was introduced as Assembly Bill No. 34 by another Burlington Republican, Emmon Roberts. But it was amended so as not to apply to counties with more than 300,000 residents (Hudson, Essex) and to require 15 percent of the qualified voters to place the proposition before the electorate. On Roberts' motion the bill was amended further to have the *Governor* appoint three commissioners who would district a county and file their report with the county's judge of the Court of Common Pleas (rather than with a Supreme Court Justice).[139] The *Bound Brook Chronicle* declared: "There appear to be few if any flaws in the Roberts bill. Nor is it arousing much opposition. It is adequate and it is fair." Rural readers were assured, "All the interests of the separate townships and boroughs are safeguarded."[140]

Despite such a glowing endorsement, the Roberts bill was never considered for final passage. Burlington, Atlantic, and Union were said to be in favor of it; and probably the small board counties would be willing to accept the scheme for new constituencies, "if it could be inaugurated," the *Trenton Evening Times* observed.[141] But it went on to remark that "the district plan does not appear to be practical under the present constitution" which required every male citizen to be "entitled to vote for *all* officers that are now, or hereafter may be elected by the people [italics added]." It was a "perfectly safe assumption that if the Legislature lacked the right to form Assembly districts, it also lacked the right to provide for freeholder districts."[142]

But the demand for districts had not quite subsided. If the Gill Act were to be adopted in Burlington's 1918 election, declared the *New Jersey Mirror*, "a determined effort should be made at the next session of the Legislature to secure amendment of the Small Board act so that in 1919 the five members of the new Board should be representative of as many districts, equably arranged."[143] After all, during the small board's "brief tenure [in 1913]" said the newspaper, "a narrow strip contiguous to the Delaware river front, into which is crowded the densest population, supported a slate which gave to that area all five of the Commissioners."[144] Following the affirmative vote on the proposition in 1918, the Mt. Holly newspaper recognized the apparent constitutional obstacle to districting and called for fair distribution of freeholder candidates by the political parties, that would be "in effect, district representation."[145] Before Union's unsuccessful referendum of 1920, it was recalled by the county treasurer that the small board of 1912 had included five members from Elizabeth and two from Plainfield, "thereby depriving the other nineteen municipalities of representation."[146] With some degree of realism, Assemblyman Arthur N. Pierson (R-Union), who also supported the large board, remarked that the uncertainty of passing a districting law *after* adoption of a small board "sounds a great deal like Mr. Wilson's and Mr. Cox's reasons for adopting the league covenant and then amend it to make it workable."[147]

With districting unattractive to the legislature, certain changes in the small board law were tending in the direction of making its adoption more difficult. In 1917 a supplement to the Gill Act, sponsored by Lewis T. Stevens (R-Cape May) had raised from 5 percent to 10 percent the number of qualified voters required to sign a petition for a referendum that could thereafter be held only at a *general* election.[148] In 1921 Union's Pierson unsuccessfully sponsored another supplement which prohibited the resubmission of the small board proposition in any county for a period of five years after it had been rejected by the voters in a referendum.[149]

The appropriate number of freeholders was always a subject of controversy. After the Gill Act's constitutionality was upheld, the *Trenton Evening Times* declared:

Hudson and Essex Counties have as little need of nine members of the small Board of Freeholders as Bergen, Mercer, Passaic and Union have for seven members. The fact that the municipal governments of Jersey City and Trenton are being carried on by five men is proof of this; and both cities spend several times as much money per year as the counties in which they are situated.[150]

Doubtless the politicans had created the maximum representation in order to provide more jobs, the newspaper argued, but the Gill Act should be revised and the number of freeholders reduced for reasons of economy and efficiency. "The classifications of 300,000, 135,000, 50,000 and less than 50,000 are unsubstantial, and they should be changed," the editorial concluded.[151]

There were no further serious technical difficulties concerning small board referenda after 1915. Of the eleven conducted between 1915 and 1921, four were unsuccessful: Ocean, 1915 (defeated 1905, 1914); Cape May, 1916; Union, 1916, 1920.[152] But both seaside counties subsequently voted to reduce the size of their boards: Ocean, 1918; Cape May, 1921.[153] In addition, three counties re-approved the small board proposal: Mercer, 1915 (defeated 1904; approved 1911); Morris, 1916 (defeated 1902, approved 1911); Burlington, 1918 (defeated 1907, 1913; approved 1911).[154] For the first time the small board was approved in Warren, 1916 (defeated 1905) and Somerset,

1919 (defeated 1906, 1910).[155] Not until the 1930's were other referenda on the question to be held.

From the *Trenton Evening Times*, which had been constantly urging mandatory legislation concerning county organization, came support in 1920 for an *optional* law to reduce the number of freeholders in fifteen counties, because it "embodies the home rule principle."[156] Sponsored by S. Roy Heath (D-Mercer), Senate Bill No. 117 would allow any county of less than 170,000 population to limit the county governing body to only *three* members, stagger their terms, and raise their salaries. The intention was to forestall passage of Senate Bill No. 79, introduced by William B. Mackay, Jr. (R-Bergen), that provided for *mandatory* increased salaries of $4,000 for each freeholder in counties with more than 500,000 residents (Essex, Hudson); and $3,000 in counties with less population. After the Mackay bill barely passed the upper chamber, 11 to 3, the Heath reorganization measure was amended "to apply more directly to county affairs the principle of commission government which has proved such a success in Trenton."[157] From the amended version (1917) of the 1911 Walsh Act for municipalities, the county bill took the system of preferential voting, by which the voters' second choices (or third choices, etc.) of candidates are considered, if first-choice votes are not sufficient for a majority. But unlike the municipal system, the bill would allow political party designations to appear with the candidates' names. In addition, provisions were included for setting a *special* election date for a referendum on whether to elect three freeholders (for staggered terms) five weeks thereafter. Passed 12 to 0, the measure was "bottled up" in Assembly committee for three weeks.[158] Even after the Mackay salary bill had been approved by Democratic Governor Edward I. Edwards, the Trenton newspaper refused to give up its fight for fewer freeholders. "As the latest expression of legislative will, the Heath measure would control," readers were assured.[159] But the Assembly committee submitted an adverse report.[160]

Even a demand for increased board membership could not produce mandatory legislation. An *optional* law[161] was passed in 1923 to enlarge the freeholder board in Cape May, which had voted in 1921 to reduce the size of its fourteen-member board. As introduced by Lewis T. Stevens (R-Cape May), Assembly Bill No. 273 amended the Gill Act to *require* any county that had a population of less than 50,000 and was, in addition, a fourth-class county (less than 20,000) to elect five (rather than three) freeholders. "By reason of the conditions arising from greatly increased population in the summer, the duties of the board are such that they cannot be performed by the smaller number," read the statement appended to the bill; and "the many diverse interests will be better served by a greater representation." The measure was enacted with an Assembly committee amendment making necessary its adoption in a county-wide referendum, initiated by petition of 10 percent of a county's qualified voters.[162] A companion measure by Stevens, Assembly Bill No. 274, was enacted with its original *mandatory* provision, halving a freeholder's salary to $1,500 in counties of the fourth class.[163] "This act applies only to Cape May County," the bill's statement baldly proclaimed.

Before the referendum in November 1923, the Cape May County *Gazette* noted that the two laws were "separate and distinct acts" and had "no connection whatever one with the other, although it is believed that seventy-five percent of the voters of this county are under the impression that in order to reduce the salaries they must vote to increase the membership of the board."[164] Moreover, the *Ocean City Ledger* pointed out that the law for lower compensation would go into effect in 1925, regardless of the number of men on the board. "There will be a saving, with more effective work by a three-man board of freeholders," it insisted.[165] To the argument that a five-member board would be more representative than a three-member body, an editorial offered this classic reply:

... If the number of freeholders were increased so as to make it possible for one to be elected from every precinct in the County, there will be those who will argue that there should be a representative for every block or street. The day when all men are persuaded they have adequate representation upon any administration will not dawn until after the millenium—doubtful even then. If this is the sole charge against a small board, why did we change from the old system?[166]

Unconvinced by this reasoning, the voters of Cape May approved the increased membership.[167]

The last small board referenda to be held in New Jersey resulted ostensibly from the vigorous demand for economy during the Great Depression. But, as usual, partisan considerations and glaring inequities in the allotment of freeholders both played important roles. Union, in its fourth referendum on the size of its governing body, voted in 1932 to reduce the membership to nine from twenty-four (about to become twenty-five).[168] The Democratic minority had pointed out that Elizabeth was allowed to elect only four freeholders, although it included three-eighths of Union's population and paid about one-third of the county taxes.[169]

In their first official expression on the subject (1939), Camden's voters approved an end to their thirty-eight-man board[170] (New Jersey's largest in the twentieth century, surpassed only by the forty freeholders elected by Essex before 1892). The movement for such a change to seven freeholders had been "inspired and supported by the Republicans, who in 1938 had lost control of the board to the Democrats for the first time in 75 years."[171]

But in 1935 Atlantic had refused to reject its thirty-four-member board, despite "the fact that the combined morning, evening and Sunday newspaper, a tabloid weekly, and the Chamber of Commerce Committee campaigned for the change in representation."[172] Fearing domination by Atlantic City,[173] every municipality, except Folsom Borough (pop. 219) with no freeholder of its own, responded negatively. By almost two to one,[174] Atlantic City voted to maintain a system in which it elected only four freeholders, although it included considerably more than half the county's inhabitants and paid about two-thirds of the county taxes.[175] The reason for such a victory was simple: County Republican leader Enoch L. ("Nucky") Johnson had made support for the *status quo* a test of his political strength.[176]

By 1940 more than 92 percent of New Jersey's residents were governed by small freeholder boards. In only Atlantic, Cumberland, Gloucester, and Salem were freeholders elected by municipalities and wards.

FIRST MANDATORY SMALL BOARD LAW

The "one man-one vote" decision of the United States Supreme Court on June 14, 1964[177] was not only to cause the mandatory reorganization of the four large-board counties but allow establishment of a state commission to study the structure and functions of all twenty-one counties. As a result of that decision, New Jersey's highest tribunal ordered that the 1966 legislature be the first one in the state's history to have both its houses apportioned on the basis of population.[178] No less important for county government was the fact that the legislature was the first since 1914 in which both the Senate and Assembly (and the Governor) were Democratic.[179]

Court actions were started by residents of Gloucester and Cumberland to have the laws which provided for their large boards

(twenty-three and twenty-six members, respectively) declared unconstitutional as violative of the equal protection clause of the Fourteenth Amendment of the United States Constitution. Afterwards,
Salem (fifteen freeholders) entered as the third-party defendant.
(Atlantic, with thirty-five board members, was not a party to the
action.) In deciding that the boards in those counties were "clearly
malapportioned," Superior Court Judge John B. Wick also held in
the spring of 1965 that the size of the new boards should not be
decided by the judiciary.[180] For more than fifty years there had been
authority to select small boards, noted the Court, citing the Gill Act
of 1912 (and ignoring the Strong Act of 1902). Consequently, there
was a presumption that citizens in the three counties desired to
retain their large governing bodies. "For this Court to order a county
to change its form of government deprives the citizens thereof of the
right to select their own form," the opinion continued, and would be
"a more serious deprivation of rights than the denial of the right of
equal representation."[181] "Political solution of the matter" would be
awaited in the form of a referendum on a small board or the passage
of a proper reapportionment law concerning freeholders. If neither
should occur, the Court's hearing of argument for appropriate relief
would be held on February 21, 1966 (on the assumption that the
legislature would amend its 1965 law requiring June primaries for
general elections and would re-establish the April primary); or else
on April 11.[182] As it happened, by April 1966 the legislature was
planning to postpone primary elections from June to September, and
the Attorney General's office petitioned Judge Wick to extend the
April 11 deadline for congressional redistricting. He set July 1 as the
new date for that purpose,[183] and Senate Bill No. 390, introduced in
May, noted in an appended statement that the "Superior Court had
set a deadline of July 1, 1966 for the reapportionment of large
boards, failing which the court itself will take affirmative action."

Partisan motivation was obvious in the text of Senate Bill No.
390, sponsored by John A. Waddington (D-Salem, Cumberland) to
require the election *at-large* of seven-member freeholder boards in
all four large-board counties. Of these, only the governing body in
his original single-county constituency of Salem was Democratic
(eight to seven).[184] Republican Senators Frank S. Farley and John E.
Hunt, both representing the Atlantic-Cape May-Gloucester district,
declined to co-sponsor the measure.[185] In fact, Hunt was trying to
advance his own Senate Bill No. 285, requiring each large board to
establish by resolution after each national census either single-
member *districts,* multimember *districts,* or both. Each was to be

"contiguous and compact and follow municipal lines insofar as practicable." The number of freeholders to be apportioned among the
districts was not to be less than the total to which the board would be
entitled at the time of the resolution's adoption. But in the opinion of
the Salem County counsel, such a plan would be held unconstitutional, because the courts had ruled that a malapportioned body
cannot reapportion itself.[186] The counsel had advised against officially submitting the scheme devised earlier by a bipartisan citizens'
committee in Salem creating a district of approximately 4,000 inhabitants for each of that county's fifteen freeholders. It would be
inappropriate to bring the plan out when the legality of the large
boards was under litigation.[187]

In the legislature's consideration of the *mandatory* small-board
bill, partisan opportunism could not successfully be disguised.
Waddington asked that his measure be approached as "governmental problems not as partisan or party politics"; and, indeed, it was
attacked only as an infringement of home rule. "Nothing has developed which could pass this legislature on the court's requirements except my bill," he insisted.[188] But Farley argued that the
Court "did not mandate the legislature to act" and that the people
should "decide by petition what size they want the board to be in
their county."[189] Hunt said that Waddington (who defended "as a
compromise" his proposal for seven-member governing bodies) had
"chosen a Las Vegas number for the counties—seven is famous all
over the world as a gambler's number . . . we have rolled the dice and
come up with seven. . . ."[190] From Senate Minority Leader William
E. Ozzard (R-Somerset) came a request that the upper chamber not
violate its long-standing policy of respecting the wishes of an individual county when there was no matter of state or party policy
involved. "Once this precedent is broken, it will stay that way," he
warned. "Why can't Waddington amend his bill to apply only to
Salem?" the Senators were asked.[191] The only one to support the bill
in debate was Nicholas T. Fernicola (D-Essex), who argued that if
Farley and Hunt were sincere, they could have taken steps during
the previous fourteen or fifteen months to give the counties self-
determination procedures.[192] But in the temporarily-reapportioned
Senate, now with twenty-nine members, all nineteen Democrats
supported the measure with their votes, opposed by eight Republicans (with two Republican abstentions).[193] In the Assembly the next
week, this strict party voting was not to be changed by repetition of
the same arguments or by the denial of John B. White (R-Glouce ster)
and Benjamin Rimm (R-Atlantic) that Judge Wick had imposed a

deadline for reorganization of large freeholder boards.[194] With only
one vote to spare, the Waddington bill was passed, thirty-two Democrats to fifteen Republicans.[195]

With the four affected counties about to lose a total of seventy-
one freeholders (reducing the state total to 129), the new law[196]
continued under attack. Its mandatory uniformity outraged the president of the state freeholder association. As Passaic Democrat John
Jay Sullivan observed at its June convention: "I don't believe it's
right for someone to come in and tell us how to run our county
government." That was "usurping home rule."[197] It was not only
local Republican politicians who were insisting that passage of the
small board law was "a result of the Democrat party's domination of
the New Jersey Legislature."[198] United States Senator Clifford Case
told fellow Republicans before the November elections that the
Waddington bill had been passed by Democrats so that they could
gain control of the four large-board counties in South Jersey.[199] But in
every one of their freeholder boards, the political complexion was to
remain the same. Salem was still narrowly controlled by Democrats
(four to three); and Republicans maintained domination of Cumberland (six to one); Atlantic (seven to none); and Gloucester (seven to
none.)[200]

The first eight years of experience under the optional Strong Act
had not been encouraging to the advocates of small boards of chosen
freeholders, elected at large. Of sixteen referenda, only four resulted
in a change. It appeared for a time that only the existence of indictments or grand jury presentments could move the voters to accept a
change in the *status quo.* Then, in 1910, Essex voters abandoned
their thirty-two-member board, and in the following year, six counties voted for smaller boards. In five of the six, the question had been
defeated earlier and, because of defective statutory language, all five
second-class counties in the 1911 group would have to reaffirm their
action through some later referendum. But with the votes of 1911,
large boards of freeholders, with the members elected from individual municipal constituencies, were on the way out in New Jersey.

During the early years of the century, as voters showed a reluctance in approving small board referenda, advocates of change re-
peatedly moved for mandatory legislation to abolish large boards of
chosen freeholders. But with greater popular acceptance of the
small-board idea, the use of optional legislation (such as the Strong
Act and its successor, the Gill Act) became intrenched in New Jersey
practice.

By 1940, only four South Jersey large-board counties still held out. Atlantic, Cumberland, Gloucester, and Salem continued to elect their county governing bodies through the old methods until the "one man-one vote" judicial decisions of the 1960's cleared the way for mandatory legislation imposing on them a system of small boards of chosen freeholders. At the end of that decade, and for the first time in New Jersey history, every county was served by a small board of chosen freeholders, of three to nine members, all of whom stood for election in a countywide constituency. But sentiment for local option would not be long in passing legislation permitting changes in county government more sweeping than the simple assignment of freeholders to small boards.

14

DIRECTORS OR DICTATORS? EXPERIMENTS WITH EXECUTIVE OFFICERS

The widening scope of county government in the last quarter of the nineteenth century and the concurrent opportunities for corruption led to the first attempts to provide a new focus for executive leadership in New Jersey counties. Although some experiments were made before 1900, almost all freeholder board directors prior to the twentieth century were simply one of the municipally elected freeholders named by their colleagues to do little more than preside at board meetings. Not until the 1930's did the emphasis in New Jersey county government shift away from a search for equity of representation toward a quest for more concentrated executive authority and responsibility.

Against the entire background of freeholder apportionment schemes one can understand the parallel development of the county executive. Separate treatment of the office of this at-large representative is required by its intermittent existence, its restricted application, and its protean powers. As in many other facets of county reorganization, Hudson led the way—but the road was rough.

FIRST DIRECTOR AT LARGE: HUDSON, 1875–1877

Not until the autumn of 1874, apparently, was there any demand for the election of a single county executive. But scandals in the Hudson County freeholder board prompted Jersey City's *Evening Journal* to claim that everyone, except possibly some incumbent freeholders or those persons with contracts to swindle the county, favored the reduction of the board to one member from each of Hudson's eight Assembly districts, and a director elected at large. "The election of a Director by the people would relieve him from all obligations to the members and leave him free to appoint the committees without bargain, fear or favor," readers were told. An act to effect such an organizational change would be demanded from the next legislature.[1] Two months later, the *Palisade News* of West Hoboken vigorously endorsed the *Evening Journal's* plan.[2]

That second editorial referred to the grand jury's recent presentment concerning charges of fraud on the part of Hudson County's freeholder board. The investigating panel did not find any indictment but charged that freeholders had enriched themselves by means of acts that were "if not actually criminal, . . . highly reprehensible." Some freeholders had been personally involved in contract negotiations with the county, and the grand jury recommended immediate court actions of debt to recover from those members the money that had been expended. According to a law of 1869 regarding municipal officers and public contracts, no other penalty could be sought. The grand jury charged further that "goods and especially liquors, have been furnished to the institutions at Snake Hill, apparently enormous in quantity and exorbitant in cost"; that members of the various committees had annually squandered thousands of dollars "for the purchase of champagne, costly wines and segars, which were used for the gratification of their own and friends ['] appetite"; that county property had been removed from Snake Hill by various freeholders for their own use; but that in some cases the evidence was too indefinite to warrant indictments, and in others, the matters testified to had occurred more than two years earlier. It was recommended by the grand jury that "the constitution of the Board of Chosen Freeholders of this county, and the rights, duties and privileges of the members and their relations to the Board and to the county shall receive the attention of the Legislature."[3]

The result was Chapter 189 of 1875, "An Act to reorganize the Board of Chosen Freeholders of the County of Hudson," providing for one freeholder to be elected from each Assembly district and one director at large to be elected by the voters of the entire county. Although this law gave the director at large no vote except in the case of a tie vote of the board, he would have to give written approval to "every *resolution* of the said board affecting the interest of the county [italics added]" before that resolution could take effect. After ten days of his failure or refusal to do so, a two-thirds vote of the entire membership could override his veto. (By contrast, a simple majority of both legislative houses could pass an act over the Governor's veto). Any appointment by the board would have to be approved in writing by the director at large (or the acting director).[4]

Presiding at his last meeting as director (elected by the board membership) in November 1875, E.F.C. Young submitted a report showing that for the previous six months the county's expenses had been cut 20½ percent over the corresponding half year in 1873, and 28½ percent over that period in 1874. He then introduced David Halsted, soon to take office as director at large, who told the board that its proceedings for the six months just completed appeared to have been very satisfactory to the people of Hudson and that an examination of the official minutes had convinced him that Young had performed his duties well. But, Halsted remarked, the minutes showed that bills, contracts, and other matters had been frequently referred to the director with power to take care of them; and this was illegal and could not continue. The board was told that the new director at large had no voice in its proceedings and could not control its actions; and that both he and the board had individual responsibilities which could not be shifted from one to the other. Halsted assured the county's governing body that he would endeavor to perform his duties impartially with regard to sections and freeholders.[5]

One week later Halsted presided at a board meeting for the first time. In addressing the members, he mentioned his duty to define his position and noted the peculiar coincidence that just one year earlier, to the day, he was one of a committee of the grand jury which met to prepare a presentment against the board's irregularities. That document was the cause of the legislature's passage of the reorganization act for Hudson County, he maintained; and it was "rather singular" that he should be the one particularly required by the people to carry out the wishes of the legislature and the grand jury. When the audience applauded Halsted's reading aloud a section of a parliamentary practice manual dealing with his powers, "he arose as if insulted." Putting on a "tragic air," he said of the demonstration: "I have the prerogative of the veto power and I forbid it." According to the *Evening Journal*, "The whole act was so ridiculously dramatic that it made much amusement." But the reporter could see nothing funny in Halsted's vehement declaration that there was no appeal from his decision to entertain a certain resolution. That no appeal could be made from the director's action on opposing or vetoing *actions* of the board was acknowledged. Yet the newspaper article went on to insist, "The idea that there is no appeal from his *rulings* in the meetings of the Board is a power never possessed by any presiding officer, and is preposterous [italics added]."[6]

Halsted's first veto message, submitted at the board's next meeting, concerned one motion to table a majority report and another to table a minority report of the select committee that had been appointed, before he assumed office, to investigate reports, charges and accusations against the warden of the Hudson County Penitentiary at Snake Hill. Both reports, argued the director, had shown that the accusations against the warden were "apparently unsubstantiated" and "should not be suppressed by being 'laid on the table,' but should receive the continued, careful and unbiased consideration of your whole Board."[7] On the following day the press printed a scathing editorial demanding

to know by what rule he [Halsted] assumes to know for how long a time any motion may be laid upon the table and how he, having no vote in the Board, except a casting vote in case of a tie, can have the power to call that from the table against the wish of the Board.[8]

Readers were asked whether there was anything ever more absurd, except perhaps Halsted's other ruling that there was no appeal from his decision while in the chair. The newspaper also objected to the director's insistence that the law of 1875 reorganizing Hudson's freeholder board required the election of all officers and employees to be by a *viva voce* vote. This entirely ignored "the sacredness and right of all bodies to vote by ballot." In the statute there was no mention of a *viva voce* vote, but of an "affirmative vote," it was pointed out; and such a vote could be given by ballot, as well as by voice. The editorial concluded:

It is really surprising to see sixteen men, all supposed to have good sound judgment, submit without even protest to such ridiculous ruling, and it is a matter of surmise how long they are going to do it. Already County matters are beginning to get muddled on account of it, and it will, in the interest of the County become of necessity one of the first duties of the Legislature to veto this parliamentary prodigy.[9]

Further disagreements between the director and the board occurred at the next meeting. One of the disputes was prompted by his communication refusing to approve the appointment of a jailer. When Halsted's reasons were demanded, he replied that the members had not told him why they had voted for the appointment; and that he had the right to the same privacy in regard to his disapproval. The director declared out of order a motion to refer his own communication right back to him. At that point, a freeholder maintained that the only course for the board to pursue was to adopt the resolution that he offered: "That a committee of three be appointed to ask the aid of the Legislature in our present embarrassed and helpless condition." If that freeholder were in such a suffering condition, he could be excused to go home, Halsted said. To the cheers of the audience the freeholder retorted:

> It is you whom we want to get rid of. We are helpless because we have a Dictator instead of a Director. We are being humbugged and are not allowed to attend to the business of the County, and we will be compelled to go to a Republican Legislature to get power to exercise our rights as Democrats.

In answer to repeated calls for the question of passing the resolution, Halsted said that he couldn't understand its meaning and declared it out of order. He ruled similarly on two others. One resolution would require the appointment of a committee of three to go to Trenton with a view to modifying the powers of the director at large. The other asked the opinion of the board's counsel as to whether there was an appeal from the director's decision; whether passage of a resolution required a majority vote of all the board members, rather than a majority of a quorum; and whether a recess of the board could be prevented by the objection of only one member. "After nearly an hour spent in senseless motions in an effort to tire out the Director," reported the local press, the board adjourned.[10]

The office of director at large came under attack late in the 1876 session, when it appeared that there would be no passage of the general county bill (Senate Bill No. 55), requiring that each county elect freeholders by Assembly districts and also a director at large *without* veto power. David Dodd (D-Essex) introduced Assembly Bill No. 379, requiring that in all counties freeholders were to be elected "as now provided by law, except that so much of any law now providing for the election of a chosen freeholder at large in any county [Hudson] be and the same is hereby repealed."[11] The measure passed the Assembly, 34 to 5, with half the Hudson delegation voting affirmatively,[12] but it never came to a vote in the Senate.

One bill that did become law in 1876 was also intended to change not the distribution of freeholders, but the balance of power in Hudson County. In April, Hudson Republican Alexander Jacobus introduced Assembly Bill No. 342, abolishing the office of director at large of the board of chosen freeholders where it existed in any county (Hudson), as soon as the incumbent's term should be completed. For the first time, it would be specifically provided that during the continuance of the director's term, any *ruling* that he might make could be appealed from by any two members of the board and could be overruled by a two-thirds vote of all of the regular members. The director's veto of a *resolution* could still be overridden only by a vote of two-thirds of the membership. Before time for final passage, the abolishment of the office of director at large was deleted, but his appointment power was made subject to a two-thirds vote, "*provided* action be taken on said veto by said board at the same meeting such veto is received by the board, or at the next regular meeting thereafter."[13] The bill passed, 40 to 4 in the Assembly; and 12 to 0 in the Senate.[14]

Nearing the end of his term in November of 1877, Halsted defended his administration. In the performance of duty, the director admitted, he had to be what the reporters and others termed "arbitrary." The circumstances under which he took office were not generally known and never would be, board members were told. The office was new; there were no rules to guide him; and there was a hostile majority of the members who refused to adopt any rules. Halsted maintained that he was first opposed by the board's clerk, who did all that he could to obstruct him. Anyone imagining that the director's seat was a bed of roses was greatly mistaken, the incumbent declared, predicting that his successor would find it a bed of thorns. The director-elect had said that he would not exercise the prerogatives of the office; but without them, Halsted warned, the position was nothing.[15]

In February 1877 Halsted had been arraigned in Oyer and Terminer Court for malfeasance in office, along with twelve regular members of Hudson's freeholder board.[16] He (and the county collector) had approved a resolution on December 16, 1876, passed two days previously by the board, for purchasing a new court house site in Jersey City at a cost of $225,720 to be paid for by county bonds issued to the owner out of the appropriation of the following fiscal year, beginning December 1, 1877. The bonds were issued. But taxpayers who objected to the purchase brought about the indictment of Halsted and the regular members of the freeholder board under an act of 1876 (Chap. 3), which made it a criminal offense for any freeholder or member of a county, or municipal governing body, or board of education to "disburse, order, or vote for the disbursement of public moneys" in excess of the appropriation to such body or to "incur obligations in excess of the appropriation and limit of expenditure provided by law. . . ." The appropriation beyond a single fiscal year could not be exceeded.[17] During the trial there was an unsuccessful motion to quash the indictments on the ground that they did not charge criminal intent on the part of the accused.[18] But before the trial continued, the New Jersey Supreme Court, on writs of certiorari, ruled in June that the motion should be denied, holding that where a statute specifically defines which act constitutes a misdemeanor, it was sufficient in the indictment to bring the defendant within the statutory description of the crime.[19] In May 1878 members of the jury in the Court of Oyer and Terminer found Halsted guilty without even leaving their seats, after hearing the presiding judge's charge that the state had completely proved its case and his intimation that they find accordingly.[20]

After another motion to quash the indictment on new grounds had been denied during the trial, Halsted's counsel asked the state Supreme Court to rule on the matter (so that he could take it still higher on appeal).[21] In the Court of Oyer and Terminer, the defense had maintained that the director at large had not voted at all for the resolution and could not vote except in the case of a tie.[22] The office, according to this argument presented to the New Jersey Supreme Court, was the same in essence as that of Vice-President of the United States or Lieutenant-Governor of the State of New York, each of whom presided over a Senate, without being a member of such a body.[23] When the Court of Errors and Appeals affirmed the conviction of Halsted and Abraham Speer (representing the indicted freeholders) and sentenced each of them to pay a fine of $1,000 and costs, counsel for both officials presented writs of error to that court.[24] (The other indicted board members pleaded guilty in the Court of Oyer and Terminer.)[25]

Again the decision was adverse to Halsted. In December 1879 the highest state court held *unanimously* that Halsted had, indeed, participated in incurring the illegal obligation as a member of the freeholder board.[26] Despite the different status of the director at large (such as greater salary, the right to vote only in the case of a tie, "and sundry expressions in the act [1875] that seem to indicate that his is a separate and independent office"), there was a provision of the Hudson County statute "which clearly makes the director a part of it." That "statute in express terms declares that the board shall *consist* of a director and the other chosen freeholders," the Court declared.[27] In response to the argument that no guilty intent had been shown on Halsted's part, reported the press, the opinion "defined elaborately" the distinction between cases where the guilty motive must be shown, and where it was unnecessary.[28] The question was the intent of the legislature; the "sole business of the court is to find the meaning of this law [L. 1876, c. 3] and then give it effect in that sense." Whether it worked hardship to the individual was not a question for the Court, but for the legislature.[29]

Only Halsted would have to pay the $1,000 penalty, the press pointed out.[30] Deciding the "curious case" of Speer's appeal at the same time, the Court of Errors and Appeals unanimously reversed a lower court decision.[31] That freeholder's plea of guilty to having voted moneys in excess of the appropriations for the following fiscal year was held to be an absurdity. No man, said the Court, could know what the appropriations for the next fiscal year would be, and, consequently, he could not be guilty of any offense in saying that he had so voted.[32] "Queer thing, law is, sometimes, when it gets started," Hudson County readers were reminded.[33] But in April, 1880 the Court of Pardons granted Halsted a full and unconditional pardon and remitted the amount of the fine, after a petition for such action had been submitted by numerous owners of extensive property in Hudson County "who had been most active in the prosecution of the case against Mr. Halsted and the Freeholders."[34]

EXECUTIVE'S POWERS CHANGED BY LEGISLATION AND LITIGATION, 1878–1882

Only months after the next director at large, Edward F. McDonald, took office, the *Evening Journal* almost despaired of his relationship with the board. "The Director lectures and scolds the members and gets mad when the won't comply with his demands," noted a front-page editorial. Objecting to McDonald's open accusations of mismanagement and crookedness on the part of the committees, the freeholders were annoying and thwarting him in many ways. If matters were to continue in such a state a little while longer, "the conflict between the Director and a portion of the Board will soon be pronounced and bitter as that which marked the turbulent reign of 'King David' [Halsted]." When McDonald had been a candidate, and again at his inauguration, voters were reminded, he deprecated the use of the extraordinary veto power and said that he should not feel disposed to use it. But the new director at large was "already using it in quite as arbitrary and dictatorial a fashion, as his predecessor, and without the latter's cool self-possession." It was, for example, "manifestly unwise" for McDonald to prevent adjournments that had been voted by a majority of the board. These freeholders had some rights, "and if they had the ability and pluck they ought to have, they would make the Director appreciate that fact." Still, the Jersey City newspaper could "most fully sympathize with all Mr. McDonald's desires and efforts to put a stop to jobbery and waste and to save the money of the County." In this regard, the director "could have great influence and would be sustained by public sentiment." But if McDonald should antagonize the board "on other and minor and petty issues, he will soon render himself unable to checkmate or resist the schemes of unworthy members of the Board," the press warned; and he would "put himself on the wrong side of popular favor."[35]

By sponsoring a radical proposal in 1879 to give more power to the directors in the other twenty counties, Terrence J. McDonald (D-Hudson) tried to alter that of his own county's chief executive. Assembly Bill No. 263 would still prohibit "the director or director at-large of each and every board of chosen freeholders of this state" from voting, except in the case of a tie. But each of them was to appoint all committees provided for by his board, by resolution or otherwise; sign or countersign all warrants or orders for the payment of money; and veto "*any action* of the board within ten days thereafter [italics added]." Worded this way, the time limit would prevent indefinite inaction by the director in the matter of approving appointments. Moreover, the written veto would have to be submitted to the board at its next general business meeting, and it could be overridden by a *majority* of all the members, rather than by the two-thirds then required in Hudson. An *amended* version applying to "the director at large of each and every board of chosen freeholders of this state," that is, *only to Hudson*, was defeated in the Assembly, 24 to 31, on a bipartisan vote.[36] But two days later the amended bill was passed, 38 to 3, after two Hudson Republicans, Samuel W. Stilsing and John H. Tangemann, had supported its reconsideration and its sponsor had stated that the incumbent director at large favored it.[37] In the Senate, the measure was amended, at the insistence of Hudson Democrat Rudolph F. Rabe, to restore the existing requirements of *two-thirds* of the board's membership to override a veto.[38] The upper chamber passed the bill, 17 to 0; and the Assembly agreed to the amended version, 34 to 1, with all but one of Hudson's legislators voting affirmatively. With the Governor's signature, it became law.[39]

In January 1880 J. Herbert Potts (R-Hudson) introduced Assembly Bill No. 100, abolishing the office of director at large, and it was reported without amendment. "The passage of this bill is sought by a band of men in Hudson County of both political parties as a part of their plan for the robbing of Hudson County," contended Allan L. McDermott (D-Hudson). They had "been trying a couple of years to have the office abolished for this purpose." In reply, Potts maintained that the measure was intended "to abolish an office with more power than the Governor of this State."[40] After recommitment on the motion of its sponsor, the bill was reported by him with a substitute.[41] It provided that the director at large could *not* vote in the appointment of any person to any position under the freeholder board; could *not* veto any appointment made or employment ordered by the board; could *not* remove any member from a committee, except for cause (submitted to the board in writing, and entered in full upon the minutes); could *not* change or alter the committees, except by the concurrence of a majority of the board members; and could *not* vote even in the case of a tie vote on appointment to office or employment. Except for resolutions dealing with the subject of working for the county, all other resolutions could be vetoed within ten days and could be overridden by a *majority* of all the board members.

On the substitute's third reading, "Mr. McDermott attacked the bill savagely, and claimed vehemently" that it destroyed the veto power of the director at large. Denying this, Potts said that, in deference to McDermott and his friends, he had withdrawn the original abolishment bill and that he wanted this substitute to pass. McDermott retorted that his colleague's action seemed to be caused by a petition from Hudson County's principal Republicans. Moving to strike out the entire section which excepted from the veto power any matter of appointment to office, McDermott made a "spread eagle speech" against the measure and in favor of the office of director at large. Potts argued against the McDermott amendment on the ground that the director at large had the power to carry around his veto of any appointment for a year, if he wanted to do so, and no one could see that veto. The new text was intended to force him to act in accordance with the principles of common usage and common sense. When Thomas O'Connor (D-Essex) asked whether any colleague from Hudson could tell the tax rate before and after the election of the incumbent director at large, McDermott, "who had arranged this," replied instantly. He "created a sensation," telling the Assembly that the rate before 1876 was $5.20 per $1,000; in 1876, $6.30; in 1877, $6.00; in 1878 (the first year of McDonald's term), $4.00; and in 1879, $2.40. Potts attacked O'Connor's supporting speech with claims that the decrease in the tax rate was due to the reduction of expenses in Jersey City and in the county, and he differed with Patrick Sheeran (D-Hudson), who maintained that Jersey City's tax rate had not decreased. Finally, McDermott withdrew his amendment and moved that the veto could be overridden by a two-thirds vote of all the freeholders, rather than by a majority as provided in the bill. The Assembly agreed to the change.[42]

McDermott quickly proposed an amendment to strike out the third section prohibiting the director at large from changing the membership of a committee, removing a member from a committee, or voting in the case of a tie in the matter of appointments. When Potts objected, McDermott read a statement on the removal of the Hudson board's committee on county institutions by the incumbent director at large and claimed that the committee was discharged for robbing the county. There was laughter in the Assembly chamber when Samuel W. Stilsing (R-Hudson) favored McDermott's amendment, because Hudson's freeholder board and the committee under discussion were both composed of Democrats, forcing the Democratic director at large to replace them with Republicans. After further debate, the Republicans defeated the amendment on a party vote. Only Stilsing defected to the Democrats in voting affirmatively. Then McDermott's motion to strike the enacting clause lost by a strictly partisan vote: seventeen Democrats in favor, thirty Republicans opposed. A motion by Patrick Sheeran (D-Hudson) to lay the bill over was followed by a speech of David W. Lawrence (R-Hudson) on how the director at large could currently veto appointments and not have them overridden by any vote of the board. After Sheeran's delaying tactic proved unsuccessful, there was "a series of filibustering motions all along the Democratic line," equally futile, before the bill was amended and ordered to a third reading.[43] It was subsequently recommitted on Potts's motion, and reported with further restrictive amendments that were agreed to. They provided that the director at large could *not* veto or disapprove of any resolution fixing the salary or compensation of any employee of the freeholder board.[44]

When the measure came up again for final passage, "Mr. McDermott sprang to his feet, clinched [*sic*] his fist and, raising his voice sixteen tones above concert pitch, made a lunge into the bill." Calling the *Jersey City Argus* "that sheet which is supposed to represent the Democracy of Hudson county," he said that it had assailed Director McDonald every day for a year with the result that McDonald was elected by a larger majority than before. Then

McDermott attacked "the thieves who oppose this man—thieves whom his watchfulness has prevented from robbing the county." After reiterating his arguments about the decrease in Hudson's tax rate, he "wound up with a discharge of Gattling [sic] gu[n]s in all directions." In reply, Stilsing and Potts said that the bill would not interfere with McDonald's saving the county's money, but would cut off his despotic power of nullifying every non-Democratic appointment and of manipulating committees to suit himself.[45] The bill was passed, thirty-four Republican votes to twenty-four Democratic; and then was passed without amendments by the Senate, twelve Republicans to seven Democrats.[46]

But there remained the constitutional rule against special local laws, a barrier to so much county-oriented legislation in the 1870's and 1880's. Assembly Bill No. 100 was vetoed along with others in a single message by Democratic Governor George B. McClellan, because he had been "advised by the Attorney-General that, by recent decisions of the Supreme Court, all these bills conflict with the Constitution."[47] On the day after the Assembly received the message, Potts moved that the veto be overridden. "Mr. McDermott went at him and worked like a Trojan, to say nothing of a Stentor," trying to prove that the Attorney General's opinion made it useless to pass the bill. Potts "made a gallant defence" of the measure, claiming that it was general, applicable to every county in the state. If it so happened that only one county had a director at large, he argued, that did not make his bill a special one. If it was unconstitutional, then the Supreme Court should say so; the Governor's saying it did not make it so. The Governor had vetoed the bill, because it affected a Democratic officer, Potts charged, noting that McClellan had signed a similar measure (Assembly Bill No. 263) the previous year. Potts was supported by Harrison Van Duyne (R-Essex), who reminded McDermott of several decisions by the Attorney General which were not sound, and who suggested that if that legal officer were to decide all constitutional questions, the Supreme Court might as well be abolished. "After some more sparring," the Assembly overrode the veto, thirty-four Republicans to twenty-one Democrats.[48] By a bare majority (eleven Republicans in favor; seven Democrats opposed), Assembly Bill No. 100 became law on the following day.[49]

The power of the director at large had now been curtailed by this 1880 statute, although a two-thirds vote of the freeholder board would still be required to override his veto. No longer could he veto resolutions making appointments to office or to county employment; nor could he even vote on them in case of a tie vote. In addition, the director at large was specifically forbidden from vetoing resolutions fixing the compensation of county officers and employees. Only with the approval of the board majority, and for "cause which shall be submitted to the board in writing" could he remove a freeholder from a committee or alter the committees. Any change of a freeholder's assignment would also require the concurrence of a majority of the board.

By increasing the $1,000 salary of the director at large, Hudson Democrats tried in 1882 to strengthen his office. Elijah T. Paxton (D-Hudson) introduced Senate Bill No. 196, authorizing freeholder boards in all counties to fix the annual salary to be paid to the director, director at large, or presiding officer, provided that such payment should not exceed $2,500, and that it should be in lieu of all other compensation then allowed by law. Amended to apply only to a director elected by the *people* (Hudson's), the measure was passed by seven Democrats and seven Republicans over the nays of two Republicans.[50] In the Assembly, a motion by David W. Lawrence (R-Hudson) to amend by setting the salary at the current amount of $1,000 was defeated: twenty-five Republicans and one Hudson Antimonopolist to twenty-nine Democrats. But the lower chamber did reduce the proposed annual salary to $2,000, at the urging of Paxton and the Antimonopolist, Thomas V. Cator.[51] With no votes to spare and with ten Republican ayes, the bill was passed 31 to 9.[52] On the day before the legislative session ended, the Senate considered the amended bill and refused to concur in the Assembly's salary change. Even Paxton voted negatively. Later that day, however, the measure was passed with a minimum of affirmative votes (six Democrats and five Republicans) over the opposition of six Republicans.[53] Because the legislature's adjournment prevented Democratic Governor George C. Ludlow from returning the bill to the Senate with his veto, he simply filed it with the Executive Department, and it failed to become law without his signature. "There is but one county to which this bill can apply, and it is, therefore, special and local," the Governor wrote.[54]

By 1882 *The New Jersey Law Journal* could say of Hudson County's freeholder board:

It is impossible in the space at our command to note the various difficulties into which it has been plunged or to explain the complicated litigation in which it has become involved. There are suits between rival Clerks, several cases against the Director, an application for a mandamus and suits by members of various committees against the Board and apparently questions as to the legality of the acts of everybody concerned. . . . Some new legislation is certainly needed.[55]

In that year, the New Jersey Supreme Court heard arguments on three related cases, caused by a Republican takeover of a Democratic board.

In the first case[56] the Court considered competing claims for the clerkship of the board based on the board's power to override rulings by the director at large regarding procedure. When the governing body of twenty regular members had met with Director at Large Frederick P. Budden, on May 18, 1882, he declared out of order a motion to proceed to the election of clerk. Thirteen members voted to sustain an appeal from this ruling, but the director at large decided that his decision could not be set aside by less than a two-thirds vote. A freeholder named Baldwin stated that since the director at large had refused to perform his duty, he (Baldwin) would put the motion and proceed with the roll call. Doing just that, he declared the motion carried. When the director at large refused to call for nominations, Baldwin did it, and Charles A. Billings was nominated. When the director at large refused to call for a vote, Baldwin called for the ayes and nays. After five names had been called, a motion to adjourn was made and seconded. Baldwin stopped to await the vote on the motion; but the director at large called for a *viva voce* vote and, in what was to be another crucial ruling, declared the motion to adjourn carried, although thirteen members protested. After the director at large and seven regular members left the room, followed soon after by one of the thirteen, the remaining twelve freeholders elected Baldwin *acting* director. He took his chair, and then Billings was elected clerk. But Democrat George B. Fielder refused to relinquish that position. In May, 1881 he had been elected by the board to serve as clerk for one year, and on April 20, 1882, prior to the incoming of the newly elected Republican board, he resigned; his resignation was immediately accepted; and he was re-elected for a one-year term.

In deciding against Billings, the Court held that the tenth section of the 1875 act (Chap. 189), providing that the Hudson board should "have power to appoint such officers, agents and employees as may be required to do the business of said county, and fix their compensation and term of service," did not authorize the election of a clerk of the board. That officer was to be elected annually by virtue of Section 8 of the *general* act incorporating the several freeholder boards (*L.* 1846, c. 10), and consequently, a *majority* vote of the board was, indeed, sufficient for his election *without* the approval of the director at large. But the Court based its decision on the fact that the "power of obstruction" granted to the director at large was "very great." Even in the case of his temporary absence from a board meeting, no authority had been conferred upon the board to elect a replacement to act with the full power of that popularly elected official. Only in the event of a vacancy could the board fill the office, and then it would have to be for the unexpired term. After Director at large Budden made the "erroneous" and "arbitrary" ruling that the board, by its vote, had agreed to an adjournment, "a majority of the board could not do, indirectly, by reorganizing after he left, what they could not have done directly at the meeting when he was present [*i.e.*, proceed to the election of a clerk] by less than a two-thirds vote." Claiming the power to correct any unlawful action on the part of the director at large, and also the means to require him to exercise the functions of his office, the Court held that Billings could properly test Fielder's title to the clerkship by instituting *quo warranto* proceedings.[57]

The second decision[58] also arose from the tenth section of the Hudson County act of 1875. At the beginning of the official year (May 1881), the freeholder board had appointed sixty-eight persons for one year at a certain compensation. In April 1882 each person in the group resigned, his resignation was accepted, and the board reappointed each to the same position for one year from the time of his new appointment—in some instances at an increased compensation. Immediately, the director at large approved the resolutions, in writing. The Court held that the last appointments were valid, but were subject to the power of the new board to annul them and to reappoint, whenever it should choose to do so. It was also declared that the increase of salary was illegal, because of the last clause in Section 10 of the 1875 act which prohibited such a rise.

The third decision[59] concerned the validity of the action of the director at large in appointing standing committees and in designating certain freeholders as members of such committees. There had been a deadlock between the director at large and the board members. They could take no successful action in opposition to him without a two-thirds vote, which they could not muster; and he was powerless without the support of a majority, which he could not obtain. In this situation the director at large appointed a number of committees under the rules of previous boards. Ruling on the validity of these appointments, the Court held that because the new board had not adopted any rules, the only authority which the director at large could invoke for such action did not exist. Therefore, all his appointments were set aside.

OFFICE OF DIRECTOR AT LARGE ABOLISHED, 1885

In February 1885 two Republicans from Hudson County introduced bills attacking the office of director at large. Cornelius R. See's Assembly Bill No. 226 was to abolish the position, and Samuel D. Dickinson's Assembly Bill No. 227 would deprive the director at large of most of his exceptional privileges. The second measure would give every freeholder *board* in the state the power to designate any and all committees, to define their duties, to determine the number of members on each committee, and to discharge any committee that the board had created. The "officer who may lawfully be entitled to preside over the meetings of the board of chosen freeholders of any county in this state," whether he was elected by the governing body itself or by the county at large, could still name the individuals to the committees and could still discharge members with the consent of a board majority. But the presiding officer would have no veto over appointments (also prohibited in the 1880 statute), removal from office, and abolishment of positions. All these actions would require a majority vote of all the board members. Dickinson's bill made no mention of the right of the director at large to veto those other resolutions "affecting the interests of the county."

By almost identical votes, the two bills were passed in both houses. See's abolishment measure received thirty-three Republican ayes and twenty-two Democratic nays in the Assembly.[60] Reported adversely in the Senate three weeks later, Assembly Bill No. 226 was placed on the calendar by a vote of nine Republicans to eight Democrats and barely passed on the following day, eleven Republicans to eight Democrats.[61] Dickinson's bill, considered in the Assembly five days after See's bill, provoked more debate there. Edwin O. Chapman (D-Hudson) objected to the section which transferred control of the committees to a board majority. In his opinion, this would permit all sorts of narrow-minded, petty party dickerings; and besides, it was bad in principle. The bill sought to overturn the system of twenty counties for the benefit of one. Defending Dickinson's bill, See retorted that the bill was intended to accomplish just the opposite: to make the system in Hudson like that in all the other counties. The result of the "quite long and lively" argument was passage of Assembly Bill No. 227, thirty-four Republicans to twenty-two Democrats, five days after the lower chamber had agreed to its companion measure.[62] And like that bill, it passed the Senate on the same day with no votes to spare: eleven Republicans to nine Democrats.[63] Both bills were vetoed the next week by Governor Leon Abbett, a Jersey City Democrat.

Assembly Bill No. 226 "is local and special, and attempts to regulate the local affairs of the county of Hudson, and is therefore unconstitutional," declared the Governor in the exact wording of the accompanying opinion of Attorney General John P. Stockton.[64] In that document, which had been directed to the Senate's Judiciary Committee a week earlier, Abbett noted, it was pointed out that the general law incoporating freeholder boards in the various counties left the method of electing their members to the laws creating their respective townships, precincts, and wards in the counties. Subsequently, special legislation had been obtained by certain counties, including Hudson (before the 1875 constitutional amendment prohibiting this). Since the Court of Errors and Appeals had decided in *Halsted* v. *State* (1878) that the director at large was, indeed, a member of the freeholder board, the veto message continued in the very words of the Attorney General's text, Assembly Bill No. 226 "simply repeals one of the special provisions of a special act relating to a particular county, and fails to bring the method of electing members of the respective boards of chosen freeholders of this state into harmony." One member of the Hudson board was being legislated out of office, while the others were permitted to remain.[65]

In vetoing its "companion bill" sponsored by Dickinson, the Governor observed that the "object of both bills is to reach the board of chosen freeholders of Hudson county." Assembly Bill No. 227 was intended to deprive the director at large of all his principal powers, if abolishment of his office should be held by the courts to be unconstitutional. "In both cases the legislation is purely partisan," Abbett declared. Examining the origin of the office of director at large, he noted that the "condition of affairs in Hudson County in 1875 was such that this change was demanded by the best men of both political parties; it was passed by a Republican Senate and a Democratic House of Assembly." The new position that had "remained in force for ten years with the approval of the people of the county" had "secured efficiency and honesty" and had "prevented jobbery in the administration of county affairs." Assembly Bill No. 227 was "not asked for by the people at large," and it was "so purely special in its partisan effects, applying only to the county of Hudson" that the Governor "deemed it a grave question as to whether or not any court would sustain its constitutionality." But even if it were constitutional, it "ought not to receive the sanction of fair men of any party;" it was "in marked contrast to the principles and actions that now govern and control the administration of national affairs." Transferring control of political patronage from an official representing a majority of the people to others representing only a minority was "unfair" and could "lead only to retaliatory acts when another political party is placed in power," Abbett warned.[66] He was obviously referring to the fact that although the predominantly Democratic Hudson County had invariably chosen Democratic directors at large, it was not unusual for the Republicans to elect a majority of the board members from freeholder districts.[67]

On the day after the Assembly received the Governor's message, it was read, and the vetoed bills were debated. Edward S. Savage (D-Middlesex) maintained that Assembly Bill No. 226 should not pass until some of the lawyers in the chambers had replied to the Attorney General's arguments pronouncing the measure unconstitutional. In answer to a query by the bill's sponsor about why such an unrequested opinion had been submitted at all, Savage quoted the text that stated the demand for it by the State (Senate?) Judiciary Committee. After reiterations of each party's position, See's abolishment bill, Assembly Bill No. 226, was repassed, thirty-three Republicans to twenty-two Democrats.[68] Then a motion to defer consideration of Dickinson's Assembly Bill No. 227 until the next day was defeated, eighteen Democrats to thirty-one Republicans, and the measure was barely repassed, thirty-one Republicans to twenty Democrats and one Essex Republican.[69] Also by the minimum number of votes, both bills were repassed in the Senate: eleven Republicans to seven Democrats.[70] Both became law.[71]

That very day, an *Evening Journal* reporter was told by a Democratic freeholder in Hudson County that the Republican majority of the board would reorganize at its next meeting by ousting Patrick Govern, the director at large, and would remove all the Democratic employees of the county, replacing them with Republicans. In an interview with the press, Govern admitted hearing of a plan to elect some one else to preside over the board. He said:

I shall take everything in a quiet way; I will treat all the members like gentlemen, but will stand up for my rights. There will be no fuss over the matter as I don't want the county's credit injured no matter how it may result. I propose to appeal to the Supreme Court and am confident of winning. Not only have I the opinions of the Attorney General and the Governor declaring the recent act of the Legislature abolishing the office of Director at-large as unconstitutional, but also of Republican lawyers, and the private opinion of Gov. Abbett himself. The matter will be tested in the courts quietly, so as not to injure the county. This thing must not be done violently, or else it will work great harm to our finances, etc. I am perfectly willing to go into the contest, and shall do so in a good-natured, friendly manner.[72]

When the newly elected freeholders convened in May, Govern assumed the chair without objection from the board, called the roll, and proceeded to transact business. After that meeting he claimed to be acting as a member and director at large of the board under authority of the 1875 statute reorganizing Hudson's governing body. For some reason, the same Attorney General Stockton who had written the opinion against the constitutionality of the abolishment law brought an action on behalf of a chosen freeholder filing as a taxpayer to oust Govern. The director at large took the position that the 1885 abolishment law was special and local, and, therefore, unconstitutional, because it attempted to regulate the internal affairs of counties, because no public notice had been given of the intention to apply to the legislature, as required in the case of a special act, and because the object of the law was not expressed in its title: "An act concerning the constitution of the boards of chosen freeholders of this state and to make uniform the selection and duties of directors of such boards."[73]

Govern's arguments did not persuade the Supreme Court, New Jersey's second highest tribunal. In a 2-to-1 decision on December 21, 1885, it held that

> . . . whenever an act of the Legislature is general in its terms, and its only effect is to remove in some degree the differences existing in the various regulations of the internal affairs of towns or counties, and to subject those internal affairs to the operation of a general law, then the act is not prohibited by the constitution, but is in strict accordance with the command of that instrument, which expressly enjoins upon the legislature the passage of general laws for such cases.[74]

The constitutional requirement that the object of every law should be expressed in its title, the opinion continued, is satisfied when the title fairly indicates the statute's general object, even though it does not indicate the means of attaining that object.[75] In a related case, the Court decided on the same day that the election of a new county collector was valid, even though the board had not first chosen one of its own members to preside, but had permitted Govern to act as a presiding officer. "The acquiescence of the board in Mr. Govern's presidency, and its proceeding to business with him in the chair, gave him an appearance of title sufficient to render him president *de facto*," said the Court.[76]

Govern carried the matter to the Court of Errors and Appeals, whose 8-to-1 ruling of July 19, 1886, affirmed that of the Supreme Court.[77] (Its decision in the county collector's case was upheld on the same day, 9 to 0.)[78] "Merely the fortunes of war and politics," Govern commented, predicting that within a year Hudson's taxpayers would be very sick of the 1885 law and the latest judicial devleopment. Without the veto power, the new director would be only "a figurehead."[79]

WEAK DIRECTOR AT LARGE IN FIRST-CLASS COUNTIES WITH DISTRICT-ELECTED FREEHOLDERS—BOTH NEW TO ESSEX, 1889

In 1889 two efforts were made to re-establish the defunct office of director at large; the first was unsuccessful. According to Assembly Bill No. 179 of James F. Norton (D-Hudson), there would be such a position established in each first-class county (Essex, Hudson) for a two-year term at an annual salary of $2,000. The director at large would be the freeholder board's presiding officer, with all the powers and duties then vested in directors of the county governing bodies, except the right to vote on any question. In addition, his written veto of "any resolution, appointment, motion or other proceeding," submitted to the clerk of the board, within ten days of its action, could be overridden only by a two-thirds vote of the membership. Before starting his term, the director at large would have to take an oath of office before a justice of the state's Supreme Court and give the county a bond of $20,000, approved by that justice, for the faithful performance of duties. The bill was reported favorably from committee and passed second reading.[80] But just after it was reported to be correctly engrossed, another measure, subsuming Norton's, captured the Assembly's attention, and his bill was never called up for a vote.

As part of a reorganization plan to give the Democrats control of the freeholder boards that would be elected by Assembly district constituencies in both Hudson and Essex, a director at large was provided for in Assembly Bill No. 329 of 1889, introduced by William C. Heppenheimer (D-Hudson) for the Speaker, R. S. Hudspeth (D-Hudson). In Essex and Hudson, the director at large would vote only in case of a tie, but would be empowered to appoint all committees and to veto any measure, subject to an overriding vote of two-thirds of the freeholder board's membership. He was to receive an annual salary of $2,000 and the other members $1,200, all for two-year terms. From the director at large a bond for $25,000 for the faithful performance of his duties would be required; from each of his district-elected colleagues, a $15,000 bond.

On the bill's second reading, Speaker Hudspeth left the chair to defend the new county reorganization plan. He said that it was a caucus measure agreed to, with certain amendments, by the Hudson and Essex members, which Adrian Riker (R-Essex) and Frank M. McDermit (D-Essex) both denied. Announcing that he would do nothing to reduce the number of freeholders in Essex, the latter moved to postpone further action on the bill until the next day. When the motion lost on a tie vote (twenty-seven Republicans and two Democrats to twenty-nine Democrats), Hudspeth offered amendments previously agreed to in conference, taking away the extra prerogatives of the director at large. Without opposition, the changes were accepted.[81] As one Jersey City newspaper observed, "The Democratic members from Essex County would have none of it unless that officer's powers be restricted to presiding over the meetings of the Board and casting the deciding vote in case of ties." They argued that in their county a Republican director was always certain to be elected, and if he were to be given the veto power, a board without a Democratic majority of two-thirds would become "practically Republican."[82]

The reorganization bill ultimately passed both houses and was signed into law in April, 1889. The office of director at large had been re-established in Hudson and instituted in Essex, but without great power. He was simply to "be the presiding officer of the said [freeholder] board, and perform all the duties of a presiding officer, excepting that the standing committees of said board shall be appointed by the membership of said board." When the statute's constitutionality was challenged, the act was upheld by the Court of Errors and Appeals in 1890.[83]

POWER OF DIRECTOR AT LARGE STRENGTHENED, 1891–1893;
OFFICE ABOLISHED, 1894

The powers of the director at large were soon afterward increased. In 1891 *The New York Times* printed this exaggerated report: "The new Freeholders' act, which is in the hands of Gov. Abbett, revives the autocratic Director at large, or presiding officer of the board, who used to rule affairs in Hudson with an iron hand."[84] In the original text of Assembly Bill No. 321, introduced by Andrew J. Boyle (D-Hudson) there was no such provision or intention. But the substitute bill that was reported from committee included a provision, ignored by the *Times*, depriving the director at large of the right to vote, except in the case of a tie, yet giving him the power of veto over every resolution or act of the board. The vote of *one-half* the membership, which was required by the new version to override the veto, was amended by the Assembly to require a *majority* of the membership.[85] Noting that years earlier a two-thirds vote had been needed for this purpose, the *Times* asserted: "Still, the veto prerogative is an important one, and will give the director at-large a prestige he does not now enjoy."[86] The lower chamber passed the substitute bill, thirty-one Democrats and seven Republicans to four Republicans. Included in the majority were all eight Hudson Democrats, all six Essex Democrats, and even one Essex Republican. The Senate vote was twelve Democrats in favor; five Republicans opposed.[87] It became law.[88]

Assembly Bill No. 287 of 1892 sponsored by James A. Dempsey (D-Essex) lengthened the terms of future freeholders in Essex and Hudson to three years without extending the terms of the directors at large. But it was characterized the following year (1893) as "one of the most defective acts passed," because it did not clearly specify how the April elections were to be conducted, and because the three-year term in Essex and Hudson was not to apply to the directors at large.[89] Consequently, Joseph P. Clarke (D-Essex) sponsored Assembly Bill No. 294, "a curative measure" that would provide the machinery for holding the election in the spring and would extend the terms of the directors at large by one year and lengthen the term of their successors to three years.[90] Hudson's Democrats wanted to amend the text to require a two-thirds vote to override the veto of the director at large, whom they believed they could elect.[91] A conference of party leaders from Essex and Hudson had the bill amended to provide that the director at large, serving for three years, should have a vote, not only in the case of a tie, but on *all* matters, including appointments and dismissals from any office under the jurisdiction or control of the freeholder boards. But a *majority* of the members would still be able to override his veto.[92] Laid over late in the session, the bill appeared to have no prospects of passing even the house in which it originated. Only the assistance that Camden Democrat William J. Thompson gave to his party colleague from Essex, William Harrigan, enabled passage, 38 to 3.[93] Although thirteen Republican assemblymen voted with the majority, none of their party contributed to the 11-to-0 victory in the Senate.[94] Within two days the Governor gave his approval.[95]

But the offices of director at large and freeholders elected by Assembly districts were ended in first-class counties by the Ketcham Law (1894), after the judiciary held that the election of state legislators by Assembly districts was unconstitutional.[96] In Essex and Hudson, chosen freeholders again represented wards and municipalities.

COUNTY SUPERVISOR CREATED FOR ESSEX, 1900

"A most radical departure from every system of county government existing in the East," according to the *Newark Evening News,* was Assembly Bill No. 136 of 1900.[97] Sponsored by John N. Klein (R-Essex), it provided for freeholder representation by city wards and municipalities and required that in each first-class county there was to be a "director of county affairs," elected at large, who would be the county's "chief executive officer." Instead of the current annual salary of $1,000 paid to the board's director, his yearly compensation would be $2,500. The "director of county affairs" was to recommend the passage of necessary measures; present a general statement of the condition of county affairs, with pertinent recommendations, to the freeholder board at its first annual meeting in each year and at other expedient times; and "be vigilant and active in causing the laws and ordinances of the county to be executed and enforced." With the advice and consent of the board, this official would appoint the county counsel, county auditor, county collector, county physician, county engineer, warden of the penitentiary, warden of the county jail, superintendent of the county almshouse, superintendent of each county hospital, physician of the penitentiary, a physician for the county jail, and the physicians for the county hospitals. Exercising "a constant supervision over the conduct of all subordinate officers," the "director of county affairs" could suspend or remove those whom investigation showed to have violated or neglected their duty. He was to be given the veto power over the freeholder board's resolutions and ordinances, subject to being overridden by a two-thirds vote of that governing body. "In fact, it is not known that anywhere in the United States is there such a county official as the 'Director of County Affairs' contemplated in this bill," Newark residents were advised.[98]

Criticism of both the proposed system of representation and the role assigned to the executive led to changes in the Klein bill. It was amended in the lower chamber to conform exactly to the apportionment scheme of Assembly Bill No. 194, sponsored by George N. Campbell (R-Essex).[99] In the version that became law, the title of the executive was changed to "county supervisor," and he was deprived of the power to appoint county officers.[100]

Extended to Hudson in 1902,[101] the office of county supervisor was to be established in no other county. In view of the experience with nineteenth-century directors at large and with municipal rivalries, the notable resistance to such a leadership change is hardly surprising.

INCREASING DEMANDS FOR EXECUTIVE LEADERSHIP

The idea of a county executive, which was urged outside New Jersey about the time of World War I, was not even to be promoted seriously in the state until the 1930's. About six years following the establishment of the first *city* manager in Staunton, Virginia (1907),[102] a *county* manager plan was being urged nationally by Richard S. Childs of the National Short Ballot Association and by William S. U'Ren and his Oregon Progressives.[103] Likewise, the Association's executive seretary, H.S. Gilbertson, and the secretary of the Citizens' Federation of Hudson County, Winston Paul, argued that the office of county supervisor in Essex and Hudson was "full of possibilities" that had "seldom been realized, partly because the supervisor is independently elected and only theoretically responsible to the board of chosen freeholders."[104] These commentators told members of the American Political Science Association at their December 1913–January 1914 meeting:

We would, therefore, abolish the office of county supervisor and substitute for it that of county manager, the latter office to be filled by the board of chosen freeholders, the incumbent to receive a salary determined upon by them and hold office during their pleasure. He would be expected to give his entire time to his public duties, and the board would be expected to select for this position, not a politician, but an expert administrator. This suggestion is in line with an important recent development in American city government which is currently known as the city manager plan.[105]

But such a scheme was greeted with indifference in New Jersey, which, even Gilbertson acknowledged, included "apparently the only counties in the country which are operated under the slightest semblance of a single executive head."[106]

No further significant permissive legislation concerning county organization was seriously proposed until 1931, when the Commission to Investigate County and Municipal Taxation and Expenditures recommended that counties should be allowed the same options as those that it suggested for municipalities: a commission form, a strong mayor-council form, or a manager form of government with the existing board of freeholders.[107] But the direction of agitation was definitely to be toward strong executive leadership that had been authorized by the Municipal Manager Form of Government Act of 1923 and that had already been adopted by Cape May City (1924), Keansburg Borough (1925), and Teaneck Township (1930).[108] Proposals for such legislation were to be offered by two Democratic Senators from Bergen, which had just overtaken Passaic to become the state's third most populous county.

Senate Bill No. 102 of 1934, by William H. J. Ely (D-Bergen), "would abolish completely the present methods of county government and set up a system of a new Board of Freeholders, with a county manager holding extensive power," the press reported.[109] Appointed by the county governing body (to be known simply as the "county board") to serve at its pleasure, he would supervise the budget, execute ordinances and regulations, conduct investigations, and direct personnel. The board would consist of three, five, seven, or nine members, elected for three-year terms, with categories divided by populations of 50,000,[110] 200,000, and 500,000. Annual salaries were to range from $500 to $3,000. At a primary election, the number of candidates equal to twice the number of places to be filled, who should receive the highest number of votes, would be nominated for board membership. "No bracketing of names, party or policy designated" was to appear on the ballot. Adoption of the plan would require a petition signed by 15 percent of the persons voting at the previous general election, plus approval in a referendum with at least 30 percent of the previous year's voters casting affirmative ballots. Should the proposition be defeated, two years would have to elapse before it could be resubmitted. But only after six years' trial could any county operating under the new plan move for a referendum on a return to the former system, which would require a petition signed by 20 percent of the voters. The same number could petition at any time for the recall of any board member.

That such a "radical recasting" of the county governmental system was being urged "in the presence of no little popular support may serve as a constructive warning to the irresponsible groups which have brought county rule to the low status which it occupies at the present time," observed the *Trenton Evening Times*.[111] Its prediction that the Ely bill would "be strenuously opposed by the intrenched politicians"[112] was proved accurate when the measure failed to be considered on third reading. But the newspaper was to show increasing support for so changing the nature of county organization. By 1936 Mercer readers were being told:

There is a growing conviction in informed circles that the county manager plan offers a scientific, economical road to sound administration. That it represents the most forward-looking solution of county problems would seem evident in its endorsement by the Westchester [County, New York] commission of inquiry.[113]

Impetus to the county manager movement in New Jersey had come as well from the "outstanding success" of municipal manager government in Teaneck and other municipalities in the state, noted an article in the *National Municipal Review* that same year.[114] Its author was a Teaneck councilman, who, with fellow officials of the township, had drafted Senate Bill No. 97 (1936), sponsored by Winant Van Winkle. Differing significantly from Ely's 1932 measure, the new plan provided for a county *council* (rather than a county board) consisting of five, seven, or nine members (no three-member councils), according to categories divided by populations of 100,000 and 500,000, and elected for *four*-year terms, instead of three-year terms, with the *same* $1,000 annual salary to be paid in *every* county operating under the proposed act. No bracketing of names, party, or policy designation would be allowed on the ballot, and there would be no primary election. Any person could be a candidate upon submission of a petition on his behalf signed by 0.5 percent of the voters at the previous general election. Signatures of 5 percent (rather than 15 percent) of such voters would be required on a petition for a referendum on adoption of the plan, and a simple majority of votes cast would decide the outcome. Unlike the Ely bill, Van Winkle's included no provision for reverting to the freeholder system, nor was there any authorization for recall of a councilman.

More important, the county council and the county manager whom it would appoint to serve at its pleasure were specifically given all the powers and duties of the sheriff, surrogate, county clerk [all of them constitutional officers], coroner, and register. Neither those five officers nor "any of their appointees, deputies or assistants shall receive any salary or emolument whatsoever," the Van Winkle bill's text declared. The county council and county manager were to exercise and perform "all powers and authority delegated to, exercised or performed by, or conferred upon such county and any executive or administrative official, board, body or commission of such county by any other act, general or special," provided such powers were not inconsistent with the proposed act. According to the *Review* article, the county manager acting under the direction of the council would be enabled to "consolidate or eliminate departments, commissions, or other special county agencies, in any way that in his judgment would eliminate waste or duplication of effort and promote efficiency and economy."[115] But the council would require the manager's recommendation to establish departments in addition to the three named in the bill (finance, public works, public welfare) and also to reassign any activity from one department to another.

"Enactment of permissive legislation for establishment of the county manager plan of government offers about the only real hope of scientific revision of the county administrative structure," the *Trenton Evening Times* was proclaiming during the 1936 legislative session.[116] An editorial could point out that for the first time in the nation's history "the number of communities functioning on the basis of city management exceeds that of cities employing the commission form."[117] But the Van Winkle bill was not even reported from committee, and only after another generation had elapsed was the manager plan to be seriously considered for New Jersey counties.

If New Jersey was unenthusiastic about authorizing a new type of county executive, so were the other states. Not until 1930 did the National Municipal League begin its campaign by drafting a Model County Manager Optional Law, the same year in which Durham County, North Carolina, became the first county in the nation to adopt the principle.[118] By January 1, 1966, the movement toward such a change in the nation's 3,000-plus counties could not be characterized as dynamic. Only thirty-six of them were recognized by the International City Managers' Association as having a valid council-manager plan, although some 203 counties had reported having some type of *appointed* county administrator in 1964.[119] Of the 253 counties then reporting the election of a county executive, only eleven counties had established such a position by charter (as legally separated from the county's governing body) after the first one in 1936 (Nassau County, New York).[120] "In some states the [elected] county clerk is tending to become the de facto chief executive officer of the county, as his numerous functions bring him into official contact with all branches of county administration," a 1930 textbook on county government noted, expressing a preference for filling such an office by appointment.[121] New Jersey's only positive action in this direction before the 1960's was the 1952 resolution of the Bergen freeholders giving their *appointive* board clerk the additional title of "executive administrator" and assigning him increased responsibility.[122]

New Jersey's experience in the early 1960's with legislation providing for county executive leadership dealt with mandatory rather than with optional requirements. Depending on the individual county, such compulsory legislation establishing executive leadership for freeholder boards could be either successfully resisted or vainly sought. When Bergen's population reached 780,255 in 1960, thereby thrusting it into the first-class county category (more than 600,000 residents), it was about to be required to make organizational changes including the election of a supervisor with veto power. Opposing such upgrading on the ground that it would add $300,000 in unnecessary costs, the Bergen County Chamber of Commerce supported Assembly Bill No. 492 of 1961, sponsored by Pierce H. Deamer, Jr. (R-Bergen).[123] It would prevent any change in the classification of a second-class county to a first-class county by reason of the federal census of 1960, unless that county's voters should approve such reclassification in a referendum initiated by at least 5,000 registered voters of the county or by resolution of two-thirds of its freeholders. By a bipartisan vote (nineteen Democrats and eighteen Republicans to three Democrats and three Republicans), the Assembly passed the permissive measure.[124] But three weeks later, just after the Deamer bill was ordered to a third reading in the upper chamber, a *mandatory* bill was introduced there by Frank S. Farley (R-Atlantic) for Walter H. Jones (R-Bergen) and passed as an emergency measure on the very same day, 16 to 0, also with equal support from both political parties.[125] A major provision of this Senate Bill No 215 was that the office of county supervisor should not come into being after June 1, 1961, in any county in which the office did not exist on that date. On May 31 the Assembly passed the bill on a bipartisan basis, 34 to 3, but with only five of a possible twenty affirmative votes from the first-class counties of Essex and Hudson.[126] The signature of Governor Robert B. Meyner insured that no other populous county would elect an executive.[127]

Mandatory legislation was introduced in each of the following three years (1962–64) for the establishment of a type of county supervisor in large-board counties having between 100,000 and 150,000 inhabitants. Applying only to Gloucester (134,846) and Cumberland (106,858) and sponsored by Democrats from both counties (Thomas F. Connery and Robert H. Weber, respectively),[128] these Senate bills would require the election at large of a "county co-ordinator" with a veto power that could be overriden by a two-thirds vote of all the members of the freeholder board. But he would have a longer term (five years) than the supervisor in first-class counties, and his salary was to be fixed by the board at not less than the salary set by statute for the county clerk. In none of the three years did the bill reach second reading. (Nor, in fact, did the bills introduced during those years by the same senators to require only 1,000 qualified voters for a referendum on a small board in Gloucester and Cumberland, rather than the specified 10 percent for any county).[129]

In 1967 the legislature *enabled* the freeholder board in any county that did not have a county supervisor to create by resolution the office of county administrator "to act as the executive officer for the board" and to perform such duties "as may from time to time otherwise be directed by the board by resolution." The term was to be three years.[130] Assembly Bill No. 85 (1968) to have the county administrator serve "at the pleasure of the board" was passed but not signed by the Governor.[131] By the end of 1969 five counties (Bergen, Somerset, Camden, Burlington, Mercer) had appointed such administrators,[132] and by the end of 1973 there were such officers in six more (Passaic, Atlantic, Gloucester, Ocean, Cumberland, Morris).[133]

Like many other innovations in nineteenth-century New Jersey county government, the idea of a freeholder board director, elected at large and having special powers, owed its origin to the reaction against Hudson County corruption. From the beginning, the office was enmeshed in partisan bickering, but, even though abolished in 1885, the concept established roots. Four years later the office of director at large that was re-established in Hudson and instituted in Essex was to last until 1894, only to disappear when the system of electing the other members of the board from Assembly districts was ended by a judicial declaration that such districts were unconstitutional. But the groundwork had been laid. In 1900 new legislation revived the idea of an individual county elective office, this time with many of the prerogatives of the earlier director at large, plus substantial (for that time) executive powers dealing with the administration of county affairs. The officer was now to be called a "county supervisor," and establishment of the position in Essex and Hudson was regarded even sixteen years later as representing the only examples in the nation of single county executive heads. Attempts to provide optional plans for appointed county managers were unsuccessful in the 1930's, but the growth of county government activities over the next three decades made some executive assistance for the elected boards of chosen freeholders far more palatable. Instead of providing for a new statutory office with specified powers and responsibilities, the approach of the 1960's was to authorize the boards to provide by resolution for their appointment of "county administrators," who could perform such duties as each board itself might assign. Whether this was sufficient to meet the executive needs of New Jersey counties was to be an issue for the future.

In the 1970's the demand for *optional* legislation to provide more county executive leadership was not to be ignored. But neither would such a law be passed without concerted opposition from entrenched politicians and considerable disagreement on just which forms the alternative should take.

15

TOWARD OPTIONAL COUNTY CHARTERS

With most counties having opted for small boards, other basic reforms were demanded. Early attempts were limited to revising and systematizing pertinent legislation on the counties' powers. But subsequent efforts at drafting a new state constitution in the 1940's produced the first significant movement for county home rule and optional county charters. The work of two state commissions and the unflagging interest of a single legislator for more than a decade culminated in a law increasing the number of alternative types of county organization and permitting the enlargement of the powers of counties.

HOME RULE ACT OF 1917

Before America's entry into World War I, the home rule movement was to affect, but not reorganize, New Jersey's local governments. In 1916 the McCran Act established a three-member commission to "revise and codify the statutes of this State relating to cities and other municipalities and to prepare bills delegating additional powers thereto" with "the largest possible measure of home rule, consistent with constitutional limitations."[1] Limiting the meaning of "municipalities," as far as the act was concerned, to townships, boroughs, villages, towns, and four classes of cities,[2] the Commission's work produced the Home Rule Act of 1917,[3] which Republican Governor Walter E. Edge said "places upon the statute books of New Jersey the first real measure of home rule in the history of the State."[4] But it did not provide for any change in the governmental structure of any of the municipalities. "In fact, it does not seem to be the intent of the act providing for the commission that it should attempt any such change," the Commission report held.[5] As for counties, it concluded:

> It may, in the near future, be considered a wise policy in this State to grant to the counties certain powers which are now only vested in municipalities. We do not consider this a violation of the principle of home rule when the powers transferred relate to matters which are really of county-wide interest.[6]

According to the Commission, "public opinion was not sufficintly [*sic*] formed in this subject to permit of any legislation carrying into effect these subjects at this time."[7]

But it immediately became the counties' turn for attention. The Commission was continued by Joint Resolution No. 8 of 1917, noting that it was "deemed advisable that said commission should continue the work of revising and codifying the statutes of this State relating to counties. . . ." In his annual message of 1918, Governor Edge expressed his pleasure that the previous legislature had "greatly extended the power of home rule in the municipalities of our State and thus relieved future legislatures of much detail labor." Urging "further legislation along these identical lines this year," he carefully pointed out that the term "municipalities" included counties.[8] On the same day, Commission-produced measures were introduced into the Senate that resulted in the 57½-page "County Home Rule Act," enumerating county powers and providing that "in construing the provisions of this act, all courts shall construe the same most favorably to counties."[9] Its companion was a 24½-page act repealing 124 other statutes regulating counties.[10] In neither of the two new laws was the basic structure of the New Jersey county altered.

DEMANDS FOR CONSTITUTIONAL GUARANTEES

By the 1940's "optional plans of organization and government for counties" (and other local units) were being urged on framers of a proposed new state constitution. Besides requiring such alternatives, the draft submitted unsuccessfully in 1944 by the New Jersey Committee for Constitutional Revision provided that in any county (or other local unit), a two-thirds vote of the governing body or the submission of a petition by 10 percent of the qualified voters could place on the ballot the question of whether a charter commission should be elected. Such a commission could write a charter "subject only to such specific limitations or requirements as may be imposed by this constitution or by general law," and an affirmative majority of those voting on the text at a referendum would be sufficient to adopt it.[11] For the 1947 Constitutional Convention, John E. Bebout, of the same New Jersey Committee, offered a revised draft in which the requirement for securing a referendum on establishing a charter commission was reduced to a *majority* of the governing body or only 7 percent of the registered voters.[12]

Others submitting statements to the delegates had similar, if not identical positions. Henry W. Connor, director of Newark's Bureau of Municipal Research, Inc., acknowledged that the possible real need for "flexibility in form and powers of counties in the future" could be "provided under the existing Constitution by the passage of optional forms of county government or by permitting the voters of counties to frame their own charters."[13] But, noting that the term "home rule" in connection with counties had a more limited meaning than when used in regard to cities, he held that a constitutional provision might "also grant the *Legislature* authority to adopt optional charters for counties [italics added]."[14] Proposed changes by the New Jersey State Industrial Union Council, Congress of Industrial Organizations included: "Home rule: *guarantee* counties, cities and other local units the right to choose their form of government by framing their own charters or choosing among *optional* plans provided by the Legislature [italics added]."[15] The New Jersey State League of Municipalities offered this: "The Legislature shall enact general laws, which *may* provide optional plans of governmental organization for the government of counties and municipalities and for the support of same . . .[italics added]."[16] But the League provision[17] that was accepted by the Convention (and included in amended form in the new Constitution[18] that was subsequently adopted) stipulated that when a freeholder board (or municipal governing body) should petition for a special or local law, the legislature could pass such by a two-thirds vote of each House. The delegates ignored the resolution of the New Jersey Association of Chosen Freeholders requesting that "the offices of the county freeholders . . . shall be hereinafter made and declared . . . to be an office of guaranteed constitutional responsibility. . . ."[19]

REPORT FROM LAW COMMISSION;
DEMANDS FOR STUDY COMMISSION

Only after reform of state government in 1947 and the passage of the Optional Municipal Charter Law of 1950 did attention turn once again to county reorganization, and that began in routine fashion. In 1956 a noncontroversial legislative act[20] established a County and Municipal Law Revision Commission that was to prepare a proposed revision of the statute law governing local political subdivisions of the state, according to Title 40 of the Revised Statutes, and other pertinent enactments. Conflicting and overlapping provisions were to be reconciled; confusing and redundant expressions were to be excised; and the statutes were to be "made as uniform as possible with respect to matters of basic policy and statutory provisions."[21] On the basis of two commission members for the prevailing majority political party to one member for the minority party, the Governor was required to appoint three state senators, three assemblymen, and three citizens of New Jersey. He was also permitted to appoint "an advisory and consulting committee of such number as he may designate from among citizens of the State."[22] Technical matters of form, style, and arrangement of material were to be the responsibility of the existing Law Revision and Legislative Services Commission.

But even before the Commission's first report was issued in March 1960 with four chapters of a proposed Title 40A (Municipalities and Counties) that concerned general provisions, a local bond law, a local budget law, and a fiscal affairs law,[23] there was some legislative demand for a different type of official study of county government. As sponsor of the many unsuccessful resolutions for studies of municipal consolidation, William V. Musto (D-Hudson) introduced Assembly Joint Resolution No. 22 of 1959, calling for a Counties and Municipalities Study Commission "to study the subjects of modernization of county government and the relationship of county governmental functions to State and municipal governments and of the consolidation of municipalities including a study of the constitutional provisions and statutes of the State relating to said subject matters."[24] Specific changes in the state constitution and statutory law could be recommended by the commission. Its members would include some to be appointed by the Governor: three nominees of the New Jersey Association of Chosen Freeholders; three nominees of the New Jersey State League of Municipalities; three citizens named from the state at large. In addition, three members of the Senate would be appointed by the president of that body; and three members of the Assembly would be named by the speaker. In the case of the citizen members and legislative members, not more than two of each group could belong to the same political party. No funds would be appropriated.

By the following year (1960), Musto had changed the text of his resolution on the subject of county government, appending to the new version a statement of his reason. Despite passage by both legislative houses and subsequent gubernatorial approval of his Assembly Joint Resolution No. 9 of 1959, creating a commission to study municipal consolidation, Governor Meyner had appointed no members. Consequently, Musto expressed a belief that "the aforesaid resolution [of 1959], and others proposed but not adopted, have been too restricted in their areas of inquiry." The purpose of his new Assembly Joint Resolution No. 34 would be "to study local government in all its aspects and interrelationships," the statement read.[25] This time a fifteen-member County and Municipal Government Study Commission, appointed according to Musto's 1959 plan, would be appropriated $25,000 and would be "authorized, empowered and directed to study the structure and functions of county and municipal government including their constitutional and statutory bases."[26] Moreover the commission was

directed further to inquire into the structural and administrative streamlining of county and municipal governments as proposed in New Jersey and other states, including consolidation, federation, special districts, contract purchase of services and abolition or strengthening of existing forms of government, to determine their applicability in meeting the present and future needs of the State and its political subdivisions.[27]

The Musto proposal was soon to gain the support of his colleagues in the lower chamber. As Assembly Joint Resolution No. 12, it was passed, 37 to 0, in 1961,[28] but did not reach third reading in the Senate. Although an identical proposal failed to come to a vote at all in 1962,[29] the lower chamber passed it, 47 to 0, in May 1963.[30]

Musto had not been alone during this period in sponsoring such propositions. But the other resolutions contrasted with his own in their terse charges to the proposed commission. In November 1959 and again in 1960, Joseph W. Cowgill (D-Camden) offered Senate Joint Resolutions to establish a body simply "to study the subjects of county government and the county functions."[31] The commission would include three senators and three assemblymen, to be appointed by their respective presiding officers; as well as three citizens to be selected by the Governor. Without freeholder membership the county would get a "better break," the state Association of Chosen Freeholders was told by Cowgill, himself a former freeholder, former county counsel, and currently a member of the state's County and Municipal Law Revision Commission.[32] Neither of his identical resolutions was reported from committee.

Even more concise in assigning responsibility was the text of Senate Concurrent Resolutions by Nelson F. Stamler (R-Union) in 1960, 1961, and 1962: "The commission is authorized, empowered, and directed to study New Jersey's county government." But, surprisingly from one who was soon to become a severe critic of county government, there was a lengthy preamble that mentioned the "general agreement that the county is destined to plan an increasingly important role in the nation's governmental structure." Also noted were the facts that "the Federal Government has said that the county is the ideal political unit for the administration of certain grant-aided national health, welfare, and education programs," and that "municipalities which lack the resources often turn to the county for help in providing services demanded by the public." Of course, Stamler did observe that the "centuries-old county apparatus cannot efficiently assume these new responsibilities because of the inherent weaknesses of its commission form."[33] His County Government Study Commission would include two senators and two assemblymen, appointed by their presiding officers on a bipartisan basis; and one person to be selected by the Governor from each group of nominees to be submitted by the New Jersey Association of Chosen Freeholders, the League of Women Voters of New Jersey, the New Jersey Taxpayers Association, the New Jersey State League of Municipalities, and the County Officials Association of New Jersey. In none of the three years did the Senate vote on the resolution.

Concurrent with these legislative resolutions were the staff drafts of the Law Revision Commission, then concentrating on "County Forms and Structure." Although the text of July 11, 1960, offered only a few minor changes on that subject,[34] the preliminary draft of June 1961 would give to the director elected by the freeholder board in every county those powers then exercised only by the county supervisor in Essex and Hudson.[35] In that case, the staff added parenthetically, "perhaps the selection [of the director] should be made by the voters themselves."[36] Besides dealing with the elected county executive system, the report then in preparation would include material on the county manager form, said Clive S. Cummis, commission counsel. There would be no recommendations for either form, he told the press.[37]

But the staff's introduction to the draft of September 1962 did, indeed, include such a recommendation. At first it insisted: "Short of home rule, modernization of county government can be substantially accomplished by providing for an administrative head of county affairs in the form of the office of a county executive."[38] Then the introduction added: "Evaluation of various types of county executive plans seem to favor 'county manager' as the most desirable."[39] As explained to the reader, the proposed County Manager Law that was to be submitted for consideration "authorizes the board to appoint a county manager, specifies his duties and sanctions a referendum to compel the appointment of a manager in counties where the freeholders have not exercised their discretion in this regard."[40]

Another alternative to the staff-revised chapter on County Forms and Structure (with the annual election of a freeholder director having the powers of a county supervisor) was the draft of an Optional County Government Law, also provided by the Commission staff. It offered "four different forms of government, each of which can be modified by alternative provisions dealing with the number and manner of election of members of the board of chosen freeholders and with the powers of the county executive."[41] The plans included: 1) a county manager, appointed by the freeholders and removable by them on five days' notice; 2) a county supervisor with no veto power, popularly elected for a four-year term; 3) a county superintendent with veto power, appointed by the freeholders; or 4) a county administrator with veto power, elected for a four-year term. Each executive was to have broad powers of appointment.[42] Varying in size (three, five, seven, or nine members), the freeholder board would be elected at large or by election districts established by the county board of elections.[43]

In discussing the text of the proposed Optional County Government Law, the Commission staff offered significant comments on approaches to reform. The omission of an article specifying the mechanics of adopting any one of the alternative forms was noted: "This ministerial aspect of the statute can be added at a later date and should follow the procedure set forth in the Faulkner Act."[44] In providing for a charter commission to study the various types of government, the introduction said, the draft should permit that body to reject all alternatives and to devise a special charter for its own county.[45] In that event, the law should require the freeholder board to petition the legislature for adoption of that charter according to Art.4, Sec.7, Par.10, of the state constitution.[46] Moreover, the staff continued, "consideration should be given to a constitutional amendment permitting counties to draft their own charters encompassing legislative, administrative and organizational provisions."[47] And the desirability of a strong administrative head should recommend consideration of a constitutional amendment eliminating the requirement that the county clerk, the surrogate, and the sheriff be elected.[48]

Heavy fire greeted the preliminary draft at the Twelfth Annual Conference in Atlantic City of the New Jersey Association of Chosen Freeholders in June 1963. Democratic Governor Richard J. Hughes "twice emphasized his confidence in Freeholder boards."[49] In the stronger message at the closing conference banquet, he said ". . . County business is very well conducted under the existing system of Freeholders we have in New Jersey. . . . To mind any change in county government would need quite a bit of proving. . . ."[50] Senator Frank ("Hap") Farley (R-Atlantic) warned the freeholders to be "cautious and careful" on the optional charter proposal. "Professional theorists are trying to take over powers which constitutionally and rightfully belong to elected officials responsible directly to the voters," he insisted.[51] Anthony J. Grossi (D-Passaic), Senate minority leader, who had just been honored by the freeholders as "Legislator of the Year," announced his support for the county home rule concept of giving freeholders more, not less, voice in running county government.[52] In response to continuous criticism from freeholders and other county officials, the Commission's counsel, Clive S. Cummis, declared: "I would say the optional charter recommendations would appear to have no future. Chances of enactment are very dim indeed."[53] While awaiting further developments on these, he added, the Commission would continue its study of the role of autonomous agencies in the counties.[54]

As Cummis observed,[55] the freeholder association did recognize the need for "substantial" changes in the existing Title 40 laws concerning county government. Passaic Freeholder John Jay Sullivan, chairman of the Association's special committee to review the proposed Commission draft, indicated that his organization might suggest: 1) strengthening the existing position of freeholder director in carrying out policies set by the board; 2) giving freeholders greater controls over budgets of autonomous bodies, such as welfare boards; 3) appointment by a freeholder board of an administrator; 4) creation of a supervisor with veto powers in counties other than Essex and Hudson.[56]

Within two weeks of the 1963 Atlantic City Conference, the Commission members agreed "to scrap" the tentative report. After a June 25 meeting at the State House, the members emphasized that its "preliminary" staff report "had not been submitted for approval or acted upon by the commission." Moreover, "any further study of county government is to await the recommendations of the freeholders' study committee and related groups," it was announced.[57] By February of the next year (1964), the freeholder association was "sponsoring"[58] Assembly Joint Resolution No. 17, introduced by Musto; Frederick H. Hauser (D-Hudson), a member of the Law Revision and Legislative Services Commission since 1960; and Albert S. Smith (R-Atlantic), a former freeholder (1943–1960) and a former board director (1952–1960). The text was identical to Musto's earlier resolutions, except that the appropriation was not to be $25,000, but $50,000; and the proposed County and Municipal Government Study Commission would be authorized to secure the professional services of a "qualified national foundation or research institute" which would also contribute $50,000. When the resolution did not reach third reading, the legislature passed Senate Bill No. 360,[59] transferring to the Law Revision and Legislative Services Commission the property, unexpended funds, and certain powers and duties of the County and Municipal Law Revision Commission. In September, the latter's chairman, Senator Richard R. Stout (R-Monmouth), was saying that the body (now without a staff of its own) did not plan to do anything about county government for a long time and would concentrate entirely on municipalities.[60]

SPECIAL CHARTER FOR A SINGLE COUNTY

Before further developments were to occur concerning general organizational changes in the counties, the legislature was forced to deal with a local problem of major significance: Was the principle of home rule strong enough to allow a single county to determine its own form of government? The 1947 New Jersey Constitution had provided for just such a procedure,[61] and Bergen would be the first to test the Legislature on the question. Because their landslide victories in the general elections of 1965 "gave the Democrats control of the county for the first time in modern times,"[62] the idea of structural change was to become more attractive locally to both major political parties.

Discussion of the possibility of a county's obtaining a special charter took place in December 1966 during the Forum for Freeholders. It was pointed out to participants that a 1948 statute authorized a county to petition the legislature for a special charter that would be effective if approved by a two-thirds vote of each house, and subsequently by a referendum in the affected county. At the request of the freeholders' association, the Rutgers University Bureau of Government Research prepared two papers, one on county classification and one on special charter procedure.[63]

Subsequently, the Bergen County Republican organization issued a sixty-eight-page report on April 26, 1967, calling for a two-part program for "an on-going reorganization, reorientation, and modernization of county government."[64] The first step would be the immediate creation and filling of the position of county manager, which the text claimed could be effected "now" by the freeholder board's "adoption of an appropriate RESOLUTION comprehensively and properly drawn."[65] By 1970 the second step, creation of a separate "legislative and governing branch," could be completed.[66] The "whole proposal might best be seen as the strong application to county government of many of the salient features of PLAN-B of the Faulkner Act" for municipalities, "passed under the auspices of a great Republican Governor, Alfred E. Driscoll."[67] "There is no doubt that new enabling legislation will be needed to effect such a reorientation of our county board," the text acknowledged, insisting that the county Republican organization would be its sponsor and champion, even if constitutional amendments should be required first. "Indeed, we will not hesitate to call for a state constitutional convention, if need be . . . ," readers were told.[68] It would be asked to "address itself to redefining and clarifying state-county-municipal relationships, with primary consideration to be given to the largely undefined role of county government."[69]

In two ways the plan was retrogressive: It suggested 1) a *larger* board in order "to give the results of its deliberations the support of majority votes both numerically large as well as broadly representative geographically;"[70] and 2) the election of freeholders by *district*, when the last four boards to be elected by municipalities and wards had just been abolished in the state. Specifically, the Republican organization proposed that the freeholder districts be coterminous with Bergen's five newly created Assembly districts, and that one freeholder could be allocated for every 50,000 residents within each district. (In that case, Bergen would have a nineteen-member governing body). Within one year after each federal decennial census, the board's size would be redetermined, but it would always be kept odd-numbered.[71] Freeholders would be elected for staggered terms of three (or four) years and would not hold any other elective or salaried public office.[72] In an apparent effort to gain quick endorsement by the freeholders, it was proposed that the board be allowed to establish the salary of the members "by an ACT of that body" (without legislative limitation, apparently).[73]

Despite initial displays of partisanship, the movement for change was soon to be supported by both Republicans and Democrats. It was a Democratic freeholder who introduced a resolution only one week later (May 3, 1967) to create a seven-member Bergen County Charter Committee to draft a charter for a county manager form of government. It was to study 1) the specific duties of the board and the "County Manager;" 2) the size, term of office, and method of selecting the board; and 3) the advisability of making appointive the offices of county clerk, surrogate, sheriff, and coroner. The committee would be authorized to employ the services of experts and consultants up to the amount of $20,000, and the report was to be due August 15, 1967.[74] By a partisan vote, six Democrats to three Republicans, the board voted to suspend the rule requiring twenty-four hours' notice of a resolution.[75] The Democratic director's statement that the Committee would be composed of "non-political citizens" prompted one of the minority-party freeholders to demand that the proposed group consist of the three Democratic freeholders and three Republican freeholders (including himself) who were not candidates that year. Furthermore, he insisted, "We should follow the Republican lead; . . . this is a 100% Republican program sponsored by this body."[76] With one Democrat voting with the Republican minority on the ground that the board itself should consider a county charter, the resolution was passed 5 to 4.[77] But the director's appointment of a chairman was *unanimously* carried at that meeting,[78] and during the following month the other committee members were approved *without objection.*[79] In September the board voted *unanimously* to employ a management consulting firm "to make a comprehensive study of any change in the structure of county government" and to prepare a county charter (at a cost not to exceed $17,000).[80] In October the freeholders *unanimously* voted to employ a legal consultant.[81]

The 164-page *preliminary* report of the *consulting firm*, released in January 1968 for public discussion without any endorsement at all by the study committee, proposed that the freeholder board continue to have nine members, but that one freeholder be elected from each of the county's five Assembly districts and the other four elected by the county at large. If the number of legislative districts were to be increased to six, then the nine-member board would continue "with one more freeholder elected by district and one less at-large." Should the number of Assembly districts increase to seven (or eight), the charter would provide for an increase in the board's size to eleven members, with seven (or eight) of them elected by district, and the balance elected at large.[82] The current three-year term would be extended to four years.[83] Leadership would be divided between a county administrator (appointed by a simple majority vote of the freeholders; removable by a two-thirds vote) and a board chairman with responsibilities exceeding those of the current freeholder director.[84] Neither would have a veto over the board's actions.

A variety of structural forms was provided in the *study committee*'s report and recommendations for a new county charter, submitted in April 1968. Alternative A was basically the same as the current system in Bergen: a board of nine freeholders elected for three-year staggered terms. Alternative B was the same, except that it provided for four-year terms and biennial elections. Alternative C provided for both of these features and followed the scheme submitted by the consulting firm for a mixed system of district and at-large elections. But enlargement of the board would have to halt at thirteen members (instead of eleven). When that number would be otherwise exceeded, the freeholder board was to provide (within thirty days of the federal decennial census) for division of the county into not more than six freeholder districts composed of contiguous and compact territory and as nearly as possible equal in the number of their inhabitants. In no case was the population of the largest district to exceed the smallest by more than 10 percent. Each district would elect one freeholder; the remainder of the board would be elected at large.[85]

No chance to change either the number of freeholders (nine) or the system of electing each of them by the entire county electorate was to be offered to Bergen's voters. By the fall of 1968, the new draft charter included amendments "worked out by a consultant at the request of the Board of Freeholders."[86] Instead of electing some freeholders by districts, for example, the entire board was to be elected at large. "Perhaps something can be done about this later," said an editorial in *The Record*.[87] After conducting public meetings, adopting the various modifications of the April draft, and then holding two additional hearings, the Bergen freeholder board approved a resolution on December 27, 1968, petitioning the legislature for enactment of a law permitting Bergen to conduct a referendum on the adoption of a charter. The vote of the freeholders was both *unanimous* and bipartisan: six Republicans and three outgoing Democrats.[88]

Not partisanship, but fears that a strong central county government would set a precedent and threaten municipal home rule determined the fate of the proposed Bergen charter in the overwhelmingly Republican legislature of 1969. Without opposition, all nine Democrats in the upper chamber joined twenty-eight Republicans in January 1969 to pass Senate Bill No. 325, placing the charter on the ballot in Bergen.[89] But the measure was not to be that attractive to the Assembly, where it reportedly received only nine favorable votes in a caucus of the fifty-eight-member Republican Assembly majority.[90] Joining Speaker Peter Moraites (R-Bergen) in a subsequent effort to win enough votes for passage was Democratic Governor Richard J. Hughes, whose personal counsel, Joel Sterns, lobbied for the bill in a Democratic minority caucus.[91] After "some of the most spirited debate of the 1969 session,"[92] the bill received forty-one Republican and seven Democratic votes, six short of the fifty-four votes required for a two-thirds majority. Eight of the ten negative votes were cast by a solid Hudson Democratic delegation.[93] When adoption of a motion to reconsider offered another chance for passage of the bill on March 10, it fared even worse. Only twenty-eight Republicans and six Democrats voted in favor; eight Republicans and seven Hudson Democrats opposed.[94] Even with the existing scheme for at-large election of freeholders unaltered, the legislature was not yet ready to authorize special charters.

FINAL DRIVE TO FRUITION

A fortuitous series of events enabled Musto, the champion of county reorganization, to accomplish passage of an optional county charter law. The malapportioned large boards were declared unconstitutional; Bergen County was pressing for its own special charter; and control of both houses of the legislature passed to the Democrats for the first time since 1914.

After the Superior Court decision in the spring of 1965 against preservation of the remaining large boards, Musto tried a new tactic. There had been no action on his usual *resolution* for creation of a fifteen-member County and Municipal Study Commission (designated that year as Assembly Joint Resolution No. 5).[95] Consequently, in May he became cosponsor of an Assembly *Bill* No. 704,[96] assigning substantially the same purpose to the County and Municipal Law Revision Commission and reallocating its membership. Within two weeks, on the same day that this body's number was increased from nine to ten and required to include equal numbers of Republicans and Democrats, the lower chamber passed the bill as an emergency measure, 59 to 0.[97] In November, Richard J. Coffee, president of the New Jersey Association of Chosen Freeholders, wrote to the *Newark Evening News:* "Presently we are pressing for passage of Assembly Bill No. 704. . . ."[98] But even though the Senate session did not adjourn until January 11, 1966, no vote was taken on the measure.

With the Democrats in two-to-one control of a newly apportioned 1966 legislature in which he had just been elected to the upper chamber, Musto could abandon bipartisan sponsorship of the plan for even representation of the political parties. He joined with his two Democratic Hudson colleagues (William F. Kelly, Jr. and Frank J. Guarini) in sponsorship of Senate Bill No. 64 for the type of fifteen-member study commission that he had long been urging to "study the structure of county and municipal government, the interrelationship of State, county and municipal governments, and their present and future problems."[99] Without a negative vote, the measure was passed by sixteen Democrats and eight Republicans. Only the proposed appropriation had been reduced from $25,000 to $5,000.[100] In the Assembly, Benjamin A. Rimm (R-Atlantic) charged that the Musto plan's commission would be weighted ten to five in favor of the Democrats, and he tried unsuccessfully to have the Senate bill laid over and his own Assembly Bill No. 361 passed instead.[101] Cosponsored by fellow Atlantic Republican Albert S. Smith, it was identical to the amended version of 1965's Assembly Bill No. 704 for *equal* membership of both political parties on a reconstituted ten-member County and Municipal Law Revision Commission. But once again demonstrating support by both political parties, the vote on the Musto bill was thirty-four Democrats and seventeen Republicans, in favor; one Democrat and one Republican, opposed.[102] Within a month, Democratic Governor Hughes signed the measure,[103] and by August the membership had been appointed.[104] But the original date (January 1967) set for filing the commission's report was subsequently postponed by statute to January 1968 for the *first* report. "As soon thereafter as practicable" would follow submission of the final report, which could include recommendations for constitutional and statutory changes.[105]

Now that every freeholder in New Jersey was elected at large within his own county, the attention of the Musto Commission (unofficially called after its chairman) with regard to counties was not to be concerned primarily with insuring fair systems of representation on their governing boards. The first interim report of March 11, 1968, recommended "providing the means for reorganizing the structure of county government by giving it more flexibility, a degree of home rule and central political and professional leadership."[106] It was "probable" that the Commission would propose constitutional changes to fulfill the "clear" need for home rule and optional structure, readers learned.[107]

Specific options similar to those available to municipalities under the Optional Municipal Charter Act of 1950 (Faulkner Act) were recommended in the second report (April 28, 1969). The choices included: 1) an elected executive, with powers of appointment and proposal of legislation (similar to the executive in Nassau, Suffolk, and Westchester counties in New York); 2) a strong manager, hired by the freeholder board, with powers of appointment and proposal of legislation (similar to certain municipal managers in New Jersey); 3) an elected supervisor with veto power (similar to the current Essex and Hudson officials), but with the addition of a board-appointed administrator; and 4) a board president with executive duties (similar to the current director in nineteen counties, except for the specific provision for a board-appointed administrator).[108]

"District representation by the Freeholders has much to recommend it," the report declared, noting that "in spite of what the textbooks say, under our current at-large elections, Freeholders do not and cannot always represent all the interests of the county equally, and may in fact represent none."[109] Saying that it did not expect the county political organizations to accept this notion, the Commission even discarded another plan for "a legislative body of mayors who would act as a 'second chamber' of the county legislature" in order to represent better "many of the county's constituents and clients."[110] Besides the "obvious political and administrative objections to such an unwieldy procedure," there were "staggering" problems in structuring such a body within the precepts of recent court decisions on reapportionment.[111] Consequently, the Commission said that in its final charter proposal it would consider as an alternative to district representation the possibility of establishing a county advisory body or a "restraining panel" with veto power or with the authority to review fiscal decisions. Such a body would be composed of a few mayors who would each represent several communities similar to his own or who "would each represent his own area in a county where municipalities were relatively similar but had varied needs depending on the section of the county in which they were located."[112]

This scheme was not among the types of governing bodies presented in the proposed optional charter law introduced by Musto and others[113] in January 1970 as Senate Bill No. 513. In addition to recommending that a freeholder board be composed of five, seven, or nine members elected for three-year terms (either concurrent or nonconcurrent), a county's elected charter study commission could recommend that all freeholders be elected 1) at large, 2) by districts, or 3) both at large and by districts. In the case of a combination system, a simple majority (three, four, or five members respectively) would be elected by district. The members of the county board of elections, together with the county clerk, would constitute the district commissioners, who would fix the boundaries so that each district would be formed of compact and contiguous territory and so that the districts would be as nearly equal as possible in population. After each decennial federal census, the same procedure would be repeated.

If choosing the right kind of freeholder constituencies did not attract the most controversy, it was because the political power of the current type of freeholder boards was threatened with diminution and was defended on the ground of home rule. For one thing, the proposed charter law provided for initiative and referendum. Fifteen percent of a county's registered voters could submit an ordinance to the freeholder board for adoption or rejection at the polls. Moreover, any elective officer would be subject to removal from office for cause, if he had served one year, upon the filing of a recall petition by 20 percent of the voters and the affirmative vote of those casting ballots on the question. But it was the matter of executive leadership that prevented Senate Bill No. 513 from being discharged from committee, despite unanimous support for the plan at a public hearing. Reportedly, Frank S. Farley (R-Atlantic) opposed it in the upper chamber's majority caucus as an opportunity for the proposed executives to usurp the authority of the freeholders.[114] Musto offered a vigorous defense in the press, emphasizing the *permissive* nature of the bill and the option of writing a special county charter. Only the county manager plan, he noted, would give significant power to an appointed official—and, even then, the board could dismiss the manager by a simple majority vote. To those who opposed the measure as a threat to (municipal) home rule, Musto pointed out the denial of such a charge by the New Jersey State League of Municipalities. As for the freeholders, with no legislative power then, with not even the right to reorganize agencies without special legislation, they did not really have county home rule to defend, Musto observed.[115]

Almost fourteen months after the introduction of Musto's Senate Bill No. 513 into the 1971–72 legislature, the identical text was sponsored in the lower house as Assembly Bill No. 2450 by eleven Republicans and a Hudson Democrat[116] on April 29, 1971. Only four days later, the committee on county government "unexpectedly" reported the bill with amendments that were immediately adopted.[117] But even though it was said to be on the Governor's list for passage and on the Republican leadership's list,[118] the bill did not reach third reading.

Musto's tactics in 1972 were more effective and circumstances more favorable for passage of the amended text, prefiled as Senate Bill No. 283. According to legislative sources, his technique was similar to the one he had used to secure enactment of New Jersey's new lottery law.[119] Instead of being the prime sponsor himself, Musto allowed that distinction to go to Republican William Schluter (Hunterdon-Mercer), who had served as prime sponsor of the 1971 Assembly version. This newly elected Senator, a member of the Musto Commission, was made chairman of the upper chamber's county and municipal committee to which the bill was referred. (Fortunately for the bill's supporters, two of the committee's other four members were Musto and Jerome Epstein, a Republican freeholder in Union from 1968 to 1970). In addition, Musto enlisted the support of Republicans representing a broad cross section of the state. Six of the eight original sponsors were members of that party, as were three of the four sponsors added by Senate resolution.[120] But more important, Senator Farley, the chief opponent of optional charters, had just been defeated in Atlantic by Dr. Joseph L. McGahn, who was the other original Democratic sponsor in 1972 besides Musto. Also, John V. Kenny, Hudson's Democratic leader, had made his political demise as a result of his indictment and his hospitalization for failing health, the press noted.[121]

Although Musto subsequently was to give credit for the bill's passage to a Republican Governor and a Republican legislature,[122] members of the majority party did not provide overwhelming support for the proposed optional charters. In the 29-to-9 Senate vote in April, all the negative votes were cast by Republicans, including the Senate majority leader, Alfred N. Beadleston, of Monmouth; Richard R. Stout, of Monmouth, a member of the Musto Commission; and Raymond H. Bateman, of Somerset, Senate President.[123] (The latter explained that he would have concurred with a bill applying only to first- and second-class counties.)[124] Thirty-one of the forty-five affirmative votes in the Assembly were supplied in mid-May by Democrats, and only five of the twenty-seven negatives.[125] During the debate, the strongest opposition came from Monmouth, which did not account for a single vote in favor of the bill in either house, and from the Bergen delegation,[126] which was split on the issue, as it had been in the Senate. That county's seven Republican assemblymen produced only the single affirmative vote of the majority leader, Richard W. DeKorte. (The three Bergen Democrats joined him). Somerset's Republicans did not contribute at all toward the bill's enactment.[127]

But victory for proponents of the optional county charter law was not yet complete, since the expected gubernatorial approval of the bill[128] was to be delayed in an apparent effort to prevent its use by the counties in 1972. In a mid-July meeting of the state freeholder association, Senate Bill No. 283 was vigorously attacked by the Monmouth delegation, led by its director, Republican Joseph Irwin. This former state association president objected to 1) full control of county government by an executive; 2) authorization for a county to abolish certain agencies, while it would continue to be responsible for providing the agencies' services; 3) absence of additional powers for freeholders; 4) provision for recall of an official after he had served one year. The bill was also opposed by delegations from Somerset, Essex, Ocean, Burlington, and Hunterdon. Still taking no formal position, the association sent a hand-carried letter to Governor William Cahill, asking him not to sign the measure until a newly formed committee of freeholders should present its views.[129]

One week later, the current association president, George J. Otlowski, a Middlesex Democrat, said that the bill had "certain technical difficulties which we feel will require amendment." Referring to two more of Irwin's objections, he observed that the freeholders were upset, because the bill on the Governor's desk would require a county to keep a newly approved form of government for five years, instead of for a shorter period of time. Also, the association feared disruption of county operations if efforts to change the type of county organization were to be undertaken every year, as apparently permitted by the bill.[130]

Suddenly a completely new controversy involving home rule surfaced. At an association meeting in August with Pierre Garven, the Governor's counsel, spokesmen for the thirteen county delegations that attended argued that the chief executive should return the bill with a conditional veto and that he should propose several amendments that they supported. Every voting delegate there approved a resolution in favor of amendments giving to the counties broad legislative powers in the fields of health, welfare, safety, and planning. But Garven noted that one of the reasons that the legislature had passed Senate Bill No. 283 was the clear stipulation in it that "nothing in this act shall be construed to impair or diminish or infringe on the powers and duties of municipalities. . . ." The text stated further, he continued, that "municipalities are and shall remain the broad repository of local police power in terms of right and power to legislate for the general health, safety, and welfare of their residents." In the opinion of some observers, such a recommendation by the Governor for broadening the powers of counties might well kill county government reform, because municipalities would unite in a massive lobby to defeat the bill.[131]

Besides urging the election of every freeholder at large within a county, the association recommended 1) a hiatus of three years after charter approval (instead of five years) before a new charter could be voted upon; 2) a requirement of 15 percent or 20 percent of a county's registered voters (rather than 10 percent) for a successful petition for a charter study or referendum; 3) authorization for freeholder boards to place a charter question on the ballot directly, thereby thwarting any citizen petitioners who might want a different charter; 4) denial of the vote (but not the veto) to county supervisors or executives; and 5) three-year appointments for county counsels, rather than their serving at the pleasure of the boards.[132]

Rejecting the suggestion that the freeholders continue to be elected on the recently established uniform county-wide basis, Cahill said that he found only two of the association's recommendations acceptable: a three-year period of trial for a new county governmental form and a three-year waiting period (instead of one year) after defeat of a proposed change.[133] They would be introduced in supplementary legislation, he announced before approving the Optional County Charter Law on September 19, 1972 (too late for its use during that year).[134] "This law makes New Jersey a leader among the states of the nation in giving voters greater control of and participation in the operation of their county governments," he declared during the signing ceremonies.[135]

As promised, the supplementary legislation was introduced on November 13 by nine Republicans and four Democrats,[136] with Schluter the principal sponsor. Besides including the two amendments that the Governor had endorsed, Senate Bill No. 1149, as immediately amended, would repeal the provisions in the Optional County Charter Law for the method of putting one of the charter plans on the ballot by a direct petition of the voters. All charter questions were to be the subject of a charter study. Within a week, the upper chamber passed the bill, 32 to 0, with bipartisan support.[137]

Given a second reading in the Assembly in February 1973, it was sent back to committee and reported favorably in March with an amendment reducing the number of elective members on a charter study commission to five and requiring that two members be *appointed* by each of the two county chairmen of the major political parties. The amendment was immediately adopted,[138] but the bill did not reach final vote during the 1973 legislative session.

But on November 6, 1973, charter study commissions were elected in *every one* of the nine counties (Essex, Bergen, Hudson, Middlesex, Union, Passaic, Camden, Mercer, Atlantic)[139] in which the proposal was placed on the ballot by freeholder resolution. They included seven of the eight most populous counties and two-thirds of New Jersey's population. A recommendation for no change at all was submitted (6–3) only by the Essex commission, which was also the only one that did not hire a consulting firm to provide professional guidance.[140] In other counties neither the supervisor plan nor a specially fashioned charter was recommended.

Only half of the eight referenda on November 5, 1974, were successful. Three of these four plans were variations of the county executive form: Hudson, with nine freeholders to be elected by districts; Mercer, with seven freeholders to be elected at large; and Atlantic, with five freeholders to be elected by districts and four to be elected at large. Union approved a county manager form with nine freeholders to have countywide constituencies. Three of the four rejections by the voters applied to similar plans: a county manager with seven freeholders to be elected at large in Camden and in Middlesex; and a county executive with five district-elected freeholders and four at-large freeholders in Bergen. The board president plan with seven freeholders elected at-large could not gain the favor of the Passaic electorate.

To some extent the wide range of voter sentiment toward the proposed charters reflected the final degree of solidarity within each charter commission. Of the four successful charters, two (Atlantic, Union) had been approved originally by unanimous (9–0) votes and another (Hudson) by a 6–3 vote that was changed to 9–0. In Mercer the recommendation was submitted by eight commissioners, with one abstention, even though two commissioners filed separate statements. Three of the four rejected charters had been approved by split votes (Bergen, 7–2; Camden, 5–4; and Middlesex, 6–3) that remained unaltered. Only the failure of Passaic's 6–3 report, later made unanimous, broke the pattern.[141] Every municipality in Hudson and all but one township in Atlantic voted for approval, while every municipality in Passaic and Middlesex was in opposition.[142] Percentages of affirmative votes of those persons expressing a preference were: Atlantic, 68 percent; Hudson, 62 percent; Mercer, 54 percent; Union, 52 percent; Bergen, 48 percent; Camden, 46 percent; Passaic, 38 percent; and Middlesex, 37 percent.[143] Reasons offered for the defeat in the latter four counties "ranged from the subliminal effects of Watergate [fear of a strong executive] to lukewarm organizational support and a poor selling job by good government groups on what were extremely complicated propositions."[144]

The movement authorizing optional charters for all counties in New Jersey is a relatively recent development. Even when provision for special legislation to be designed on a single-county basis was included in the 1947 Constitution, more than twenty years were to elapse before the only (unsuccessful) application for such an enactment. But the fact that Bergen bill almost achieved a two-thirds affirmative vote in each house indicated that the time was ripe for re-organization. Opposition by certain counties and officeholders to permissive legislation was difficult to maintain on the ground of "home rule." In 1972 that concept was allowed to become a fact. After almost three generations of simply deciding whether to abolish the large board for a smaller one, the people were allowed to end this structural rigidity and, even more, to extend the powers of the county. Four counties with more than one-fifth of the state's population did so at the very first opportunity.

CONCLUSION

If the movement for optional county charters in New Jersey is a relatively recent development, the demands for alternative forms of organization and "strong policy leadership from an elected official"[1] have long historical roots. Since their incorporation in 1798 with identical systems of representation, boards of chosen freeholders have come almost full circle!

Although it is not generally recognized, the vigorous movement for small boards of chosen freeholders in New Jersey predates the Progressive Era, with its emphasis on commission government for municipalities, by at least a half-century. In addition, Hudson was perhaps the second county in the nation authorized to elect a single executive with veto power[2] (stronger even than the Governor's). That increasing urbanization should give rise to such demands for structural change was inherent in the functionally weak nature of county government. But the alterations were made piecemeal and usually for partisan political advantage.

Only in light of the historic status of New Jersey's townships and their meteoric population growth can the constantly changing organization of freeholder boards be properly understood. Since the eighteenth century, every square inch of land in the state has been part of one of the self-governing, incorporated municipalities (originally all townships). This contrasted markedly with the situation in other states, where one-quarter of the counties contained no incorporated place at all, as late as 1870.[3] In that year, Essex and Hudson were each more populous than any of twelve states; New Jersey ranked fourth nationally in population density; and its six leading municipalities contained almost one-third of the state's residents. Five years later, each of those cities accounted for more than half the inhabitants of their respective counties. And while all twenty-one New Jersey counties in 1900 had at least one municipality with more than 2,500 inhabitants,[4] probably one-half of the nation's counties did not.[5]

The "pure democracy" of the township overshadowed the "simple representative government" of the New Jersey county, which, unlike its counterpart in the South, was important politically only as the unit of representation in the legislature. Because municipalities could be allowed to proliferate without increasing the number of legislators as in New England, the number of locally elected freeholders multiplied. But until the 1870's their responsibilities did not increase significantly; and (along with maintaining the courts) the most important and visible duty was the building and repair of bridges. Unlike the boards of supervisors in the State of New York, the freeholders were not concurrently officials of their respective townships, where the really vital services were being performed. Nevertheless, members of New Jersey's county governing bodies, often allocated by laws regulating individual municipalities, came to be regarded as township officials, with whom they were usually elected in the spring.

Compared with township government, the organization of the freeholder board had to cause inefficiency and popular mistrust. In a county body with as many as forty members, the individual could hide his responsibility; but not in a township committee of five. The freeholder, elected from a subdistrict (municipality, ward, aldermanic district, Assembly district) of the area that he was to govern, was encouraged to be parochial in his outlook; the township committeeman was elected at large. While the county board could "vote, grant, and raise" money without a direct vote of approval by the people, such appropriations for the township were made until well into the nineteenth century by the inhabitants themselves. The freeholders were assigned both executive and legislative duties, in contrast to the early township committeemen, who were only to "examine, inspect, and report" to the town meeting and to "superintend the expenditure of any moneys raised by tax for the use of the township." Moreover, the board served as an agency of the state, while the townships did not. Finally, the state policy of uniform treatment of counties that prevailed until mid-nineteenth century with regard to representation on the freeholder boards persisted, for the most part, into the twentieth, so far as their functions were concerned. On the other hand, various forms of municipalities were incorporated much earlier with different types of charters to reflect local conditions.

The system of apportioning representatives to these municipalities became unequal, uncertain, and complex, after the halving of the number of freeholders in Monmouth and Hunterdon and the granting of two freeholders to each of Jersey City's four wards in 1851. Until that time, there had been a single scheme throughout the state: two members of the board elected from each township. More than two-thirds of the counties had escaped from this rigid requirement by 1875, when an amendment to the New Jersy Constitution prohibited special laws regulating the internal affairs of counties and towns. By then, partisan legislation had assigned freeholders to the wards of certain types of cities, and not to others; had created new wards that were allotted freeholders; and had even used Assembly districts as freeholder constituencies. In the following quarter-century, the legislature found additional variables, besides gerrymandering, that could be used to control the political composition of the board: classification by population of municipalities and (by location as well) counties; and ostensibly general legislation regulating the types of municipal government, like boroughs and towns.

Uncertain also was the proper role of a chief executive chosen by a county-wide electorate and existing intermittently only in the two most populous counties. The director was first among equals who were elected by municipalities or wards until 1875, when a director at large was created for Hudson, with a vote that could be overridden by a two-thirds vote of the board. Because uncertainties and deadlocks arose over the nature of this power, it was withdrawn in the matter of appointments and salaries; and the office itself was abolished in 1885. Four years later, a director at large who was to be simply a presiding officer, unable even to appoint standing committees, was established in both Hudson and Essex. The veto power was restored, subject to a *majority* vote even over patronage, before the position was discontinued again in 1894.

The twentieth century began with dramatic changes: a Hudson board of nine members elected at large, including a director with increased veto power; a new Essex system of municipal- and ward-elected freeholders, plus a county supervisor with increased veto power and additional responsibilities. When Hudson's scheme was declared invalid in 1902, the one in Essex replaced it; and until 1972 the significant extension of executive powers had been resisted by passage of simply permissive legislation for board appointment of county administrators with powers limited by the freeholders.

But more important in 1902 was the passage of the first optional small board law (Strong Act) to apply to *every* county (according to its population classification). Only four of the first sixteen referenda conducted before 1909 resulted in change, but by 1912, twelve of the twenty-one counties with four-fifths of New Jersey's population had voted affirmatively (though sometimes invalidly). During this century's second decade, the concept of home rule was strong enough to defeat enactment of mandatory legislation to abolish large freeholder boards. Only when the judiciary's "one man-one vote" decisions required changes in the malapportioned governing bodies in Atlantic, Cumberland, Gloucester, and Salem were small boards to be elected at large established *without* a direct vote of the people. For the first time since 1851 the system of electing freeholders would be uniform.

In the Optional County Charter Law of 1972, two of the foremost issues are lack of executive leadership and uniformity of organization. The voters' opportunity for effecting fundamental changes in its structure and powers removes from county government the "spirit of negation" of which it has been accused and the element of "democracy via complication" by which it has been characterized.[6] For the first time the number of a county's freeholders does not have to be determined by the number of municipalities in that county or by population statistics of any kind. Atlantic and Hudson will elect the same number to their respective governing bodies. And equal opportunities for the selection of types of executives and constituencies have opened New Jersey's part of "the dark continent of American politics" for exploration.

CHRONOLOGY

MILESTONES IN NEW JERSEY
COUNTY GOVERNMENT

1798   Incorporation of boards of chosen freeholders in the then thirteen counties.

1851   First deviations from the uniform system of electing two free-holders per township:

Hunterdon, Monmouth—one freeholder per township

Jersey City (Hudson)—two freeholders from each of four wards.

1857   Last county (Union) established.

1871   First election of freeholders by aldermanic districts that were coterminous with Assembly districts (Jersey City).

1875   First election of all freeholders in a county by Assembly districts (Hudson).

First county-wide election of a director (director at large) of a board of chosen freeholders (Hudson).

New Jersey Constitution of 1844 amended to prohibit state legislation regulating the internal affairs of towns and counites.

1883   First general classification of counties (by population).

1885   Office of director at large (Hudson) abolished.

1889   Office of director at large provided for Hudson and Essex; *both* counties to elect freeholders by Assembly districts.

1892   Election of freeholders by Assembly districts in Passaic, Camden, and Mercer.

1893   New Jersey Supreme Court decision ending election of assemblymen by districts and casting doubt on election of freeholders by such districts.

1894   Election of freeholders by assembly districts ended in Hudson, Essex, Passaic, Camden, and Mercer.

1900   First successful referendum for small board (nine members) elected at large (Hudson).

Office of county supervisor established in Essex.

1902   First optional law (Strong Act) to provide for referenda in *all* counties on small boards.

First small-board referendum passed (Hunterdon) under Strong Act.

Hudson's small board declared unconstitutional.

County supervisor established in Hudson.

1911   Adoption of small boards in referenda in certain second-class counties considered of doubtful validity because of effect of 1908 amendment of 1902 Strong Act.

1912   Passage of new optional law (Gill Act) for small boards.

1915   Gill Act upheld as constitutional by New Jersey Supreme Court.

1939   Last successful referendum to abolish a large board (Camden, thirty-eight freeholders).

1947   New state Constitution authorizing a procedure for adoption of special legislation regulating the internal affairs of counties (and municipalities).

1948   Statute implementing new constitutional provisions for special local legislation.

1964   "One man-one vote" decision of United States Supreme Court.

1965   Large board held "malapportioned" by New Jersey Superior Court.

1966 First mandatory small board law; abolishment of last four large boards (Atlantic, Cumberland, Gloucester, Salem); thereafter all freeholders in state to be elected at large.

County and Municipal Government Study Commission (Musto Commission) established.

1967 Statute authorizing creation of a county administrator by freeholder board in any county except those (Hudson, Essex) with county supervisors.

1969 Failure of proposed special charter for Bergen County to win required two-thirds vote of each house of legislature.

1972 Optional County Charter Law enacted.

1973 Referenda for county charter study commissions successful in nine counties; members of these commissions elected in nine counties.

1974 Charters approved in Atlantic, Hudson, Mercer, and Union.

Charters rejected in Bergen, Camden, Middlesex, and Passaic.

Essex County Charter Commission recommends no change.

SMALL BOARD REFERENDA

These figures indicate the number of freeholders on a board at time of referendum. Gray figures represent passage. Black figures represent defeat.

	1902	1903	1904	1905	1906	1907	1908	1909	1910	1911	1912	1913	1914	1915	1916	1917	1918	1919	1920	1921	1923	1932	1935	1939
ATLANTIC																							35	
BERGEN	23			23			25																	
BURLINGTON						32				33		33				37								
CAMDEN																								38
CAPE MAY															12					14 *				
CUMBERLAND																								
ESSEX									33															
GLOUCESTER																								
HUDSON	26										31													
HUNTERDON	21																							
MERCER	24		23							23				23										
MIDDLESEX	24		24																					
MONMOUTH				24																				
MORRIS	22									24					26									
OCEAN				14									14	14										
PASSAIC		21															14							
SALEM																								
SOMERSET					10				12									12						
SUSSEX								16 16	16	20														
UNION															21				23			24		
WARREN				27											28									

* Cape May board increased from 3 to 5 members.

NOTES

1

TOWNSHIPS AND COUNTIES: FROM PURE DEMOCRACY TO REPRESENTATIVE GOVERNMENT

1. *NJL*, 22nd (1797–98), 2nd sit., p. 298. (The abbreviation *NJL*, referring to the Session Laws of New Jersey, together with the numerals indicating the session and sitting at which the law was enacted, will be used for legislation prior to 1852, when chapter numbers came into general use.) Significantly, this was not a law regulating county government, but "An Act Incorporating the Inhabitants of Townships, designating their Powers and Regulating their meetings." For a discussion of property qualifications of a freeholder, see Francis B. Lee, "The Origin of New Jersey's Boards of Chosen Freeholders," *New Jersey Law Journal*, XXI (January, 1898), 10–12.

2. Thomas F. Gordon, *A Gazetteer of the State of New Jersey* (Trenton: Daniel Fenton, 1834), p. 57.

3. N.J. Department of State, *Compendium of Censuses, 1726–1905* (Trenton: 1906), *passim*.

4. *NJL*, 22nd (1797–98), 2nd sit., pp. 297–298.

5. Gordon, *loc. cit.*

6. *NJL*, 58th (1833–34), 2nd sit., p. 117. Paterson Township, for example, voted to conduct its annual town meeting of 1835 by ballot. William Nelson (ed.), *Records of the Township of Paterson, New Jersey, 1831–1851* (Paterson, N.J.: Evening News Job Print, 1895), p. 31.

7. Paterson Township elected 32 persons to office at its 1834 town meeting: moderator, town clerk, assessor, collector, judge of election, chosen freeholders (2), township committee (5), surveyors of the highway (2), judges of appeal (3), constables (5), poormasters (2), school committee (3), overseers of the highway (4), and poundmaster, Nelson, *op. cit.*, pp. 27–28.

That freeholders were considered by some to be township officials is apparent from the following resolution adopted at Paterson Township's annual meeting of 1835: "Resolved, that the Chosen Freeholders be and are hereby instructed to make all necessary enquiries from our neighboring Counties and States, as to the actual result of the County poor house system, compared with other systems of supporting paupers, the difference of cost and the effect the various systems have on the pauper, and to report the same to the next Annual Town Meeting," *ibid.*, p. 32.

8. A. S. Meyrick, Letter to the Editor, *Monmouth Democrat* (Freehold), April 15, 1880.

9. *NJL*, 62nd Sess. (1837–38), 2nd sit., p. 150.

10. *L.* 1860, c. 256, pp. 670–672; *L.* 1861, c. 81, p. 182; *L.* 1862, c. 123, pp. 244–245. (Beginning with 1852, *Session Laws of New Jersey* will be designated by the abbreviation *L.*, followed by pertinent chapter and page numbers.)

11. *L.* 1866, c. 406, pp. 921–928; *L.* 1868, c. 460, pp. 979–982; *L.* 1868, c. 564, pp. 1210–1211.

12. *L.* 1876, c. 124, p. 167; *L.* 1876, c. 184, p. 297.

13. A. S. M. [Meyrick], Letter to the Editor, *Newark Daily Advertiser*, March 16, 1880.

14. *L.* 1880, c. 151, pp. 199–201.

15. *NJL*, 22nd Sess. (1797–98), 2nd sit., p. 299. For a discussion of township development, see Stanley H. Friedelbaum, "Origins of New Jersey Municipal Government," *Proceedings of the New Jersey Historical Society*, LXXIII (January, 1955), 4–5.

16. *L.* 1899, c. 169, pp. 372–376.

17. *Newark Evening News*, February 16, 1899.

18. Gordon, *op. cit.*, p. 57.

19. *Compendium of Censuses*, p. 41.

20. Gordon, *op. cit.*, pp. 181, 146 *et passim*.

21. For a discussion of county government in colonial New Jersey, see James Collier, *County Government in New Jersey* (New Brunswick, N.J.: Rutgers University Press, 1952), based on his Ph.D. dissertation of the same title, Rutgers University, August 1951.

22. *NJL*, 22nd Sess. (1797–98), 2nd sit., p. 272. This text, continued in the *Revision of 1877*, p. 127, was repealed by *L.* 1918, c. 189, p. 629 and replaced by *L.* 1918, c. 185, pp. 567–568.

23. A township committeeman could receive $1 for each day engaged in fixing fences, and fifty cents for each half-day so spent, *NJL*, 23rd Sess. (1798–99), 2nd sit., p. 431. But he could receive nothing for performing his other duties, until a $1 *per diem* payment was authorized, *NJL*, 68th Sess. (1843–44), 2nd sit., p. 231 (and increased to $2, *L.* 1868, c. 374, pp. 840–841).

24. Herbert Sydney Duncombe, *County Government in America* (Washington, D. C.: National Association of Counties Research Foundation, 1966), pp. 21–22; William C. Morey, *The Government of New York; Its History and Administration* (New York: The Macmillan Co., 1902), pp. 99–101; Friedelbaum, *op. cit.*, pp. 1–2.

2

COUNTY RESPONSIBILITIES CHANGE
AND GROW: 1798–1902

1. *State* v. *Hudson County*, 30 N.J.L. (New Jersey Law Reports) 137, 146 (1862).
2. *Ibid.*, p. 146.
3. *Ibid.*
4. Nevill's *Laws*, Vol. II, Chap. 154, pp. 355–356.
5. *Ibid.*, pp. 357–358.
6. Allinson's *Laws*, Chap. 589, Act of March 11, 1774, pp. 386, 396.
7. Secs. 21–22.
8. *State* v. *Hudson County*, 30 N.J.L. 137 (1862).
9. *NJL*, 22nd Sess. (1797–98), 2nd sit., p. 272; *ibid.*, 23rd Sess. (1798–99), 1st sit., pp. 415–416.
10. *NJL*, 69th (1845), pp. 139–140.
11. There were only four exceptions to this general law. When the membership of the freeholder boards in Monmouth and Hunterdon was halved in 1851, so was the number of freeholders required for action on bridge repair costing between $50 and $500, *NJL*, 75th (1851), pp. 241–242. A supplement allowed the board's director in Sussex to appoint a committee of from five to nine freeholders to decide upon bridge expenses of more than $500, *L.* 1873, c. 562, pp. 651–652. A special law for Morris changed the categories of 1845 for that county to expenses of more than $1,000; those between $250 and $1,000; and those less than $250, *L.* 1873, c. 590, pp. 691–692. After township representation by freeholders was ended in Hudson (1871), a law was passed providing for its governing body to contract for work on bridges "in such manner as the said board may elect," *L.* 1871, c. 198, pp. 506–507.
12. *L.* 1898, c. 188, p. 437.
13. James Leiby, *Charity and Correction in New Jersey: A History of State Welfare Institutions* (New Brunswick, N.J.: Rutgers University Press, 1967), p. 19.
14. *NJL*, 23rd Sess. (1798–99), 2nd sit., pp. 449–502.
15. *NJL*, 20th Sess. (1795–96), 2nd sit., p. 85.
16. *State* v. *Ellis*, 26 N.J.L. 219 (1857). The differences are discussed in this opinion.
17. *NJL*, 71st (1847), pp. 144–145; *ibid.*, p. 175.
18. "Memorial of the New Jersey Prison Reform Association, in Relation to the Improvement of County Jails, January 25, 1850" in Harry E. Barnes, *A History of the Penal Reformatory and Correctional Institutions of the State of New Jersey, Analytical and Documentary: Report of the Prison Inquiry Commission*, Vol. II [Trenton: State of New Jersey, 1917], p. 637; Martin W. Stanton, "History of Public Poor Relief in New Jersey, 1609–1934." (Unpublished Ph.D. dissertation, Department of Sociology and Social Service, Fordham University, 1934), p. 43.

19. Barnes, *op. cit.*, p. 334.

20. *L.* 1857, c. 19, pp. 40–44. Although the ninth section allowed the freeholder boards of the several counties in the state to adopt all the provisions of the act, such action in 1884 by Camden's board was declared by the state Supreme Court to be repugnant to the constitutional requirement that every law should embrace but one object, which should be expressed in the title, *Daubman* v. *Smith*, 47 N.J.L. 200 (1885).

21. *L.* 1874, c. 273, pp. 313–315.

22. Barnes, *loc. cit.*

23. *L.* 1887, c. 30, pp. 42–44.

24. *L.* 1894, c. 253, p. 597; *NJAM*, 118th, May 14, 1894, pp. 909, 922. (The abbreviation *NJAM*, followed by a numeral, refers to the *Minutes of the Votes and Proceedings of the New Jersey General Assembly* for a designated session. Similarly, the abbreviation *NJSJ* will be used to refer to the *Journal of the Senate of New Jersey*); *NJSJ*, 118th, May 16, 1894, p. 702.

25. For a discussion of classification of counties, see pp. 124–127.

26. *NJAM*, 118th, May 14, 1894, p. 911; *L.* 1894, c. 254, p. 378.

27. *L.* 1894, c. 348, pp. 534–535; *L.* 1900, c. 184, p. 474.

28. *Virtue* v. *Freeholders of Essex*, 67 N.J.L. 139, 141–143, 147–148 (1901).

29. *NJL*, 71st (1847), pp. 25–28.

30. *NJL*, 73rd (1849), pp. 267–268.

31. *NJL*, 74th (1850), p. 157.

32. "Fourth Report of the Managers of the State Lunatic Asylum", in *NJSJ*, 75th, 1851, p. 53.

33. Leiby, *op. cit.*, p. 124.

34. *Evening Journal* (Jersey City), September 9, 1869.

35. *Ibid.*, January 13, 1870.

36. "Report of the Joint Committee on the State Lunatic Asylum to the Legislature of New Jersey," *New Jersey Legislative Documents*, 94th (1870), Doc. 17, pp. 336–337. (Hereafter cited as *N.J. Leg. Docs.* with the number of the legislative session and the year.)

37. *Evening Journal* (Jersey City), September 9, 1870.

38. "Superintendent's Report, Annual Report of the Managers and Officers of the New Jersey State Lunatic Asylum at Trenton for the Year Ending 1872," *N.J. Leg. Docs.*, 97th (1873), Doc. No. 5, p. 10.

39. Leiby, *op. cit.*, p. 112.

40. Charles H. Winfield, *History of the County of Hudson, New Jersey From Its Earliest Settlement to the Present Time* (New York: Kinnard & Hay: 1874), p. 322.

41. "Report of the Joint Committee of the Lunatic Asylum to the Legislature," *N.J. Leg. Docs.*, 97th (1873), Doc. 29, p. 4.

42. *New York Times*, April 12, 1873.

43. *L.* 1873, c. 564, p. 138.

44. "Report of the Joint Committee on Treasurer's Accounts . . . ," *N.J. Leg. Docs.*, 98th (1874), Doc. 2, pp. 97, 102; *ibid.*, 101st (1877), Doc. 2, pp. 110, 111, 119, 127, 130.

45. "Second Annual Message, January 9, 1877," *N.J. Leg. Docs.*, 101st (1877), Doc. 1, p. 13.

46. U.S. Census Office, Dept. of the Interior, *Compendium of the Tenth Census* (June 1, 1880), Part II, p. 1680.

47. Leiby, *op. cit.*, p. 114.

48. *L.* 1888, c. 20, pp. 32–33.

49. "Report of the Board of Managers of the New Jersey State Hospital at Trenton," *N.J. Leg. Docs.*, 127th (1902), II, Doc. 16, p. 9; "Report of the Board of Managers of the New Jersey State Hospital at Morris Plains," *ibid.*, Doc. 15, p. 13.

50. William Nelson, "Passaic County Roads," n.p., n.d. ("This piece . . . was intended to be included as part of the printed report of the Board of Chosen Freeholders, but the entire printing, with the exception of a few pamphlets, stitched and delivered to Wm. Nelson, was destroyed in the great Paterson fire of 1904"—notation on copy in Rutgers University Library.)

51. Wheaton J. Lane, *From Indian Trail to Iron Horse: Travel and Transportation in New Jersey, 1620–1860* (Princeton, N.J.: Princeton University Press, 1939), pp. 35–37.

52. Nelson, "Passaic County Roads," *loc. cit.*

53. Lane, *op. cit.*, p. 38.

54. *NJL*, 32nd Sess. (1807), 1st sit., pp. 70–72. Forty years later the required majority in the case of a road laid out in three counties would have to include one to the two freeholders appointed from each of them. *ibid.*, 71st (1847), p. 119–120.

55. *NJL*, 35th Sess. (1810–11), 2nd sit., p. 322.

56. *L.* 1860, c. 227, pp. 601–603.

57. *NJL*, 42nd Sess. (1817–18), 1st sit., p. 49.

58. *L.* 1868, c. 525, pp. 1146–1150.

59. *L.* 1869, c. 359, pp. 957, 967–969.

60. *L.* 1881, c. 10, pp. 19–20.

61. *Poinier* v. *Schmidt*, 44 N.J.L. 433 (1882); *Morris* v. *Harrigan*, 44 N.J.L. 437 (1882); *Summers* v. *Wildey*, 44 N.J.L. 437 (1882).

62. *L.* 1868, c. 147, pp. 310–311.

63. *L.* 1869, c. 273, pp. 790–805.

64. *New York Times*, August 12, 1873; *L.* 1870, c. 429, pp. 906–907.

65. *New York Times*, August 12, 1873.

66. *Evening Journal* (Jersey City), March 15, 1873.

67. *L.* 1873, c. 606, pp. 697, 713–714.

68. *State, Gaines, pros.* v. *Hudson County Avenue Commissioners*, 37 N.J.L. 12 (1874). The act was repealed, and the freeholder board was ordered to pay certain salaries, *L.* 1874, c. 482, pp. 567–568.

69. *L.* 1876, c. 210, pp. 385–388, *et seq.*

70. *Evening Journal* (Jersey City), January 3, 1877.

71. *Ibid.*, January 12, 1877.

72. *Ibid.*, January 22, 1877.

73. *Ibid.*, January 26, 1877. Only one of the eight Assembly districts (in Jersey City) voted affirmatively. The worst defeat (261 to 1,283) was in the district that included all of North Hudson, except Hoboken, *ibid.*

74. *L.* 1883, c. 179, pp. 225–226; *Freeholders of Hudson* v. *Buck*, 49 N.J.L. 228 (1886).

75. *L.* 1886, c. 257, pp. 369–383; *Bray* v. *Buck*, 51 N.J.L. 82 (1887).
76. *Evening Journal* (Jersey City), November 1, 1886.
77. *L.* 1887, c. 105, p. 138; *Freeholders of Hudson* v. *Buck*, 51 N.J.L. 155, 159 (1888).
78. *Evening Journal* (Jersey City), November 1, 1888.
79. *L.* 1888, c. 274, pp. 397–399, *et seq.*
80. *Evening Journal* (Jersey City), November 1, 1888.
81. *Ibid.*, November 12, 1888.
82. *Ibid.*, November 16, 1888.
83. *Noonan* v. *Freeholders of Hudson*, 51 N.J.L. 454 (1889); *Noonan* v. *County of Hudson*, 52 N.J.L. 398, 402 (1890).
84. *L.* 1889, c. 41, pp. 58–63.
85. *Home News* (New Brunswick), September 27, 1889.
86. *New York Times*, December 26, 1888.
87. Quoted in *ibid.*
88. *Elizabeth Daily Journal*, January 14, 1889.
89. *Ibid.*
90. *New York Times, loc. cit.*
91. *Elizabeth Daily Journal*, March 19, 1889.
92. *Ibid.*, February 4, 1889.
93. *Ibid.*, February 16, 1889.
94. *Evening Journal* (Jersey City), February 25, 1889.
95. *L.* 1889, c. 41, pp. 58–63
96. *Daily True American* (Trenton), March 19, 1889.
97. *Evening Journal* (Jersey City), March 19, 1889.
98. *Miles* v. *Freeholders of Bergen*, 52 N.J.L. 302, 304–305 (1890).
99. *L.* 1894, c. 76, pp. 128–129. Expenditures for roads appear in "Statements of the Financial Condition of the Several Counties, Cities, Townships, Towns, Boroughs and Villages of the State of New Jersey," included in the "Annual Reports of the Controller of the Treasury of the State of New Jersey," *N.J. Leg. Docs.* 114th–127th (1890–1903). Cf. also "Ninth Annual Report of the Commissioner of Public Roads," *ibid.*, 127th (1902), III, Doc. No. 32, pp. 13–15, 18, 57.
100. "Report of the Committee on County Board Reports," in "Seventeenth Annual Report of the State Board of Agriculture, 1889–90," *N.J. Leg. Docs.*, 114th (1889), II, Doc. 14, p. 137.
101. "Minutes of the Annual Meeting," in *ibid.*, p. 123.
102. "Address by Judge William M. Lanning to New Jersey State Road Convention, January 21, 1892," in "Nineteenth Annual Report, New Jersey State Board of Agriculture," *N.J. Leg. Docs.*, 116th (1891), IV, Doc. 21, pp. 598–600.
103. *Revision of 1877*, pp. 990–991.
104. "Address by Judge William M. Lanning," *loc. cit.*
105. *L.* 1888, c. 186, pp. 240–243.
106. *L.* 1891, c. 84, pp. 137–140.
107. "Minutes of the Annual Meeting," in "Eighteenth Annual Report of the State Board of Agriculture," *N.J. Leg. Docs.*, 115th (1890), IV, Doc. 23, pp. 215–218.
108. *L.* 1891, c. 201, pp. 378–389.

109. "State Road Convention," "Nineteenth Annual Report, State Board of Agriculture," *N.J. Leg. Docs.*, 116th (1891), IV, Doc. 21, p. 604.

110. *L.* 1892, c. 215, pp. 346–351.

111. *L.*1894, c. 276, p. 409.

112. *Evening Journal* (Jersey City), March 4, 1898.

113. *Ibid.*, March 9, 1898.

114. *Ibid.*, March 4, 1898.

115. *Ibid.*, March 18, 1898.

116. *Ibid.*, March 22, 1898.

117. *L.* 1898, c. 106, pp. 173–177.

118. H. S. Gilbertson, *The County, the "Dark Continent of American Politics,"* (New York: The National Short Ballot Organization, 1917), p. 38.

119. *McArdle* v. *Jersey City*, 66 N.J.L. 590 (1901); see p. 26.

120. *Evening Journal* (Jersey City), July 3, 1901.

121. *Humble Oil & Refining Co.* v. *Wojteycha*, 48 N.J. (New Jersey Reports, Supreme Court) 562 (1966).

122. Hudson County Park Commission, *Report, June 23, 1903 to June 23, 1908*, pp. 12–14; *L.* 1888, c. 128, pp. 166–174.

123. *Evening Journal* (Jersey City), June 5, 1901; *ibid.*, March 7, 1893. Nearly 300 Passaic County taxpayers, representing $4,000,000 in property, had petitioned for the appointment of a park commission. But legal action to prevent this was instituted by the city counsel of Paterson, when that city's aldermanic board was pressured by a group of land speculators afraid of possible diversion of population from their land, *ibid.*, December 29, 1891. See also *New York Times*, December 29, 1891.

124. *L.* 1893, c. 247, pp. 429–430.

125. Frederick W. Kelsey, *The First County Park System* (New York: J. S. Ogilvie Publishing Co., 1905), pp. 12 ff.

126. *L.* 1894, c. 166, pp. 229–230.

127. Kelsey, *op. cit.*, pp. 49–50.

128. *Newark Daily Advertiser*, February 6, 1895.

129. Kelsey, *op. cit.*, p. 54.

130. *NJSJ*, 119th, February 26, 1895, p. 289; *NJAM*, 119th, February 27, 1895, p. 405; *L.* 1895, c. 91, pp. 169–185; *Newark Evening News*, April 13, 1895. Hudson County was unaffected. The State Supreme Court held, *obiter*, that the judiciary "would probably deem the provision for submission at the 'next election' directory only, designed to secure prompt submission, but not to limit the right of acceptance," *Renner* v. *Holmes*, 68 N.J.L. 192, 195 (1902).

131. *Evening Journal* (Jersey City), February 5, 1901.

132. *Ibid.*, February 11, 1901.

133. *NJAM*, 125th, March 6, 12, 1901, pp. 263, 341; *NJSJ*, 125th, March 17, 1895, p. 319; *L.* 1901, c. 64, pp. 117–135.

134. *McArdle* v. *Jersey City*, 66 N.J.L. 590 (1901).

135. *Evening Journal* (Jersey City), July 3, 1901.

136. *L.* 1901, c. 204, pp. 408–411.

137. *McArdle* v. *Jersey City, loc. cit.*

138. *Evening Journal* (Jersey City), June 5, 1901.

139. *Ibid.*, July 3, 1903.

140. *Ibid.*
141. *L.* 1902, c. 277, pp. 811–822.
142. *Evening Journal* (Jersey City), November 15, 1902. The official canvass showed returns missing from districts in every municipality except Jersey City and Hoboken.
143. *Schwartz* v. *Dover*, 68 N.J.L. 576 (1902). This case and the following three are discussed in Hudson County Park Commission, *Report, 1903–1908*, pp. 7–8.
144. *Diehl* v. *Blair*, 55 At. Rep., 1133 (1903), cited in Hudson County Park Commission, *Report, 1903–1908*, p. 8.
145. *Ross* v. *Board of Chosen Freeholders of Essex County*, 69 N.J.L. 143 (1903), affirmed 69 N.J.L. 691 (1903).
146. *Diehl* v. *Blair, loc. cit.*
147. Hudson County Park Commission, *Report, 1903*–1908, p. 8.

3

THE PUBLIC IMAGE: CRITICISM OF FREEHOLDERS' PERFORMANCE

1. A.S.M., Letter to the Editors, *Daily Fredonian* (New Brunswick), September 4, 1874.
2. A.S.M., Letter to Sheriff John D. Bucklew, in *ibid.*, December 22, 1871. The statute (*L.* 1869, c. 68, p. 108) applied to municipal governing bodies, as well.
3. *Weekly Fredonian* (New Brunswick), December 20, 1877.
4. A.S.M., Letter to the Editor, *ibid.*, February 7, 1867.
5. *L.* 1867, c. 446, p. 30. The law was not applicable to Camden. See p. 34.
6. *Our Home* I (June, 1873), 280. This was "a monthly magazine of original articles, historical, biographical, scientific and miscellaneous, mostly by Somerset and Hunterdon County writers, and on subjects largely pertaining to these counties. . . ." Ed. by A. V. D. Honeyman (Somerville, N.J.: Cornell and Honeyman, 1873). Only issues for January through December 1873 were published.
7. *Ibid.*
8. "The Somerset 'Tweed'," Art. VII, in *Extra No. 2 of The Somerset Gazette*, containing all the articles on county affairs published in *The Gazette* from June 19 to October 1, 1879 (Somerville, N.J.: The Somerset Gazette Steam Printing House, 1879), p. 59.
9. "Who Is To Blame?" Art. XIV, *ibid.*, p. 43.
10. Table XI, *ibid.*, p. v.
11. "Hotel Bills & Per Diems," Art. IX, *ibid.*, p. 35.
12. *Salem Sunbeam* (City of Salem), as quoted in *Burlington Gazette* (City of Burlington), February 7, 1874.
13. *State* v. *Crowley*, 39 N.J.L. 264, 268 (1877).
14. A.S.M., Letter to the Editors, *Daily Fredonian* (New Brunswick), September 14, 1874.
15. *Ibid.*, September 4, 1874.

16. *Ibid.*, September 14, 1874.
17. *Ibid.*, September 4, 1874.
18. *Ibid.*, September 14, 1874.
19. *Daily Fredonian* (New Brunswick), November 20, 1879.
20. *Ibid.*
21. *Ibid.*, November 20, 1879.
22. *L.* 1880, c. 213, pp. 315–316.
23. *L.* 1882, c. 137, p. 194.
24. *L.* 1879, c. 114, pp. 199–200.
25. *L.* 1858, c. 173, pp. 437–438.
26. *L.* 1874, c. 499, pp. 720–722.
27. *L.* 1875, c. 189, p. 326.
28. *L.* 1892, c. 69, pp. 125–127 applied to counties with 75,000 to 200,000 inhabitants. See p. 166–167.
29. *L.* 1894, c. 234, pp. 355–358.
30. *New Jersey Mirror* (Mt. Holly), November 28, 1872.
31. A.S.M., Letter to the Editor, *Weekly Fredonian* (New Brunswick), September 22,1870.
32. "Hotel Bills & Per Diems," *op. cit.*, pp. 31–33.
33. "The Dictator Again," Art. XVIII, in *Extra No. 2 of the Somerset Gazette*, p. 66.
34. *Daily Fredonian* (New Brunswick), May 2, 1865.
35. *NJL*, 46th (1846), p. 192.
36. *Daily Fredonian* (New Brunswick), May 2, 1865.
37. *L.* 1865, c. 514, p. 955.
38. *L.* 1872, c. 500, p. 71.
39. *Daily Fredonian* (New Brunswick), August 20, 1879.
40. *Sussex Register* (Newton), quoted in *ibid.*, February 6, 1880.
41. *L.* 1879, c. 141, pp. 230–231.
42. *L.* 1882, c. 175, p. 244.
43. *L.* 1874, c. 8, p. 174.
44. *L.* 1874, c. 157, p. 244.
45. *L.* 1875, c. 171, p. 308.
46. *L.* 1870, c. 190, p. 451.
47. *L.* 1874, c. 175, p. 255.
48. *Daily Fredonian* (New Brunswick), August 3, 1883.
49. *Central New Jersey Times* (Plainfield), quoted in *ibid.*, August 14, 1883.
50. *L.* 1886, c. 154, p. 216.
51. *L.* 1889, c. 202, p. 325.
52. *L.* 1893, c. 282, pp. 493–494.

4

A UNIFORM REPRESENTATIVE
SYSTEM UNDER STRESS, 1798–1852

1. *Guardian or New Brunswick Advertiser*, February 13, 1798.
2. *NJL*, 22nd (1797–1798), 2nd sit., p. 278.

3. *NJL*, 22nd (1797–1798), 2nd sit., p. 298. The first boards under this statute included 30 freeholders in Sussex; 22 in Burlington; 20 each in Hunterdon and Gloucester; 18 in Salem; 16 in Middlesex; 14 each in Cumberland and Bergen; 12 each in Monmouth, Essex, Somerset, and Morris; and 6 in Cape May. The total was 104 freeholders.

4. These figures were developed from the data about township incorporations, *Compendium of Censuses*, pp. 37, 22–23. Gloucester County's area appears in Gordon, *op. cit.*, p. 146.

5. *Proceedings of the New Jersey Constitutional Convention of 1844*, comp. and ed. by N.J. [Federal] Writers Project, with "Introduction" by John Bebout (n.p., 1942), June 7, p. 273; June 13, p. 384; June 20, p. 508. Bebout comments: "The treatment of county government by the convention illustrates the fact that constituion makers are generally guided by a desire to meet specific problems rather than by any inclination to write a 'model constitution' completely consistent in its inclusions and exclusions. This helps to explain why the constitution does not mention boards of chosen freeholders, which we think of as governing bodies of the counties and which, in 1844, already had a long history behind them. The selection of representatives of the towns to perform certain fiscal functions of the county goes back to the days of the proprietors; but the convention, finding no fault with the statutory provisions for boards of freeholders, saw no reason for dealing with them," p.c.

6. *Proceedings . . . 1844*, pp. 120–124, 436–444; Richard P. McCormick, *The History of Voting in New Jersey* (New Brunswick, N.J.: Rutgers University Press, 1953), pp. 134–135.

7. *NJL*, 69th (1845), p. 249.

8. *NJL*, 70th (1846), pp. 193 ff.

9. *State Gazette* (Trenton), March 21, 1845.

10. *Ibid.*, April 9, 1845.

11. The author compiled these statistics from *NJL*, 22nd (1797–1798), 2nd sit., pp. 289–296; *Compendium of Censuses, passim;* "Abstract of the Census of the State of New Jersey for the Year 1875," in *N.J. Leg. Docs.*, 100th (1876), pp. 7–36.

12. The author compiled these statistics from *Compendium of Censuses, passim*. Before 1876, freeholders were assigned to four municipalities in this group: Rahway (city), 1891; Woodbury (borough), 1870; Chambersburg (borough), 1872; and Plainfield (city), 1872.

13. For example, Atlantic City (1854); Frenchtown Borough (1867); and Hackettstown (1853).

14. *State, Pancoast* v. *Troth, et al.*, 34 N.J.L. 377, 387. This decision was reversed, *State, Rogers* v. *Troth*, 36 N.J.L. 422, but on other grounds.

15. "Annual Message, 1872," *N.J. Leg. Docs.*, 96th (1872), Doc. 1, p. 11.

16. McCormick, *op. cit.*, pp. 89–90.

17. *Newark Daily Advertiser*, March 3, 1852. This newspaper provided other percentages of increase.

18. McCormick, *op. cit.*, p. 122.

19. *Compendium of Censuses, passim*.

20. At the start of the 1844 legislative session, before the erection of Camden County from Gloucester County, there were 18 counties with

freeholder boards of the following sizes: 26 members in Essex; 22 in Burlington and Sussex; 20 in Hunterdon, Morris, Warren, and Gloucester; 18 in Mercer and Salem; 16 in Cumberland; 14 in Monmouth, Middlesex, Somerset, and Bergen; 10 in Passaic, Atlantic, and Hudson; and 8 in Cape May. At its creation later in 1844, Camden County had 14 freeholders representing six townships formerly from Gloucester plus the newly created Delaware Township; and Gloucester then elected 10 freeholders, two of them from the just-incorporated township of Spicer (which changed its name to Harrison in 1845). In 1844 there were four townships created outside these two counties, also, *ibid.*

21. *Journal of the Proceedings of the Legislative-Council of the State of New-Jersey*,68th, February 23, 1844, p.284 (This publication afterward became the *Journal of the Senate of the State of New-Jersey*); *Newark Daily Advertiser*, February 24, 1844.

22. *NJAM*, 68th, February 23, 1844, p. 493.

23. *Hunterdon Gazette* (Flemington), February 12, 1845.

24. *NJSJ*, 69th, February 4, 11, 14, 18, 19, 20, 25, 26, 1845, pp. 299, 324, 475, 485, 495, 498, 516, 530.

25. *NJSJ*, 69th, February 7, March 5, 1845, pp. 321, 568–569. Party affiliations appear in *Newark Daily Advertiser*, January 13, 1845.

26. *Compendium of Censuses*, pp. 30–31, 24, *et passim*.

27. *NJAM*, 72nd, January 13, 21, 27, 1848, pp. 83, 329, 376. The texts of all legislative bills discussed in this volume were supplied by the New Jersey State Law Library, unless otherwise indicated. *State Gazette* (Trenton), January 28, 1848, in reporting on the amendments erroneously states that the bill applied to Hunterdon as well as to Monmouth.

28. *NJAM*, 72nd, February 3, 10, 1848, pp. 431, 608; *State Gazette* (Trenton), February 4, 11, 1848.

29. *NJAM*, 72nd, February 15, 1848, p. 651; *State Gazette* (Trenton), February 16, 1848.

30. *Newark Daily Advertiser*, February 17, 1848.

31. *Ibid.*

32. *NJAM*, 72nd, February 16, 1848, pp. 677–678. Party affiliations appear in *State Gazette* (Trenton), January 6, 1848.

33. *NJSJ*, 72nd, February 25, 1848, pp. 625–626.

34. *NJSJ*, 72nd, February 29, 1848, pp. 651–652.

35. *NJAM*, 73rd, February 1, 1849, pp. 525–526.

36. *NJAM*, 73rd, January 30, February 2, 1849, pp. 493, 543; *NJSJ*, February 14, 1849, p. 681.

37. *NJAM*, 73rd, January 31, February 6, 7, 1849, pp. 508, 559, 576.

38. *NJAM*, 73rd, January 31, February 6, February 7, 1849, pp. 515–516; *NJSJ*, 73rd, February 22, 1849, p. 756; *Newark Daily Advertiser*, February 7, 1849. Party affiliations appear in *ibid.*, November 27, 1848.

39. *Hunterdon County Democrat* (Flemington), February 12, 1851.

40. *Ibid.*, February 19, 1851.

41. *Ibid.*

42. *Ibid.*

43. *Ibid.*, March 12, 1851.

44. *Ibid.*

45. *Ibid.*

46. Pennsylvania Historical Survey, *County Government and Archives in Pennsylvania* (ed. by Sylvester K. Stevens and Donald H. Kent) (Harrisburg, Pennsylvania: Historical and Museum Commission, 1947), p. 97.

47. John A. Fairlie, *Local Government in Counties, Towns and Villages* (New York: The Century Co., 1906), pp. 29–30.

48. *County Government and Archives in Pennsylvania, loc. cit.*

49. *NJAM*, 74th, January 10, 1850, p. 83.

50. *NJAM*, 75th, February 12, 1851, p. 640; February 13, 1851, p. 649; *State Gazette* (Trenton), February 13, 1851. Party affiliations for both houses of the legislature appear in *Newark Daily Advertiser*, January 14, 1851.

51. *NJSJ*, 75th, February 25, 1851, p.553.

52. *NJL*, 75th (1851), p. 97.

53. *Compendium of Censuses*, p. 24.

54. *NJL*, 75th (1851), p. 394.

55. *Ibid.*, pp. 444–459; *Compendium of Censuses*, p. 34.

56. *L.* 1853, c. 44, p. 119.

57. *Compendium of Censuses*, pp.20–21.

58. *NJSJ*, 76th, January 14, 1852, pp. 13–14.

59. *NJSJ*, 76th, January 27, 1852.

60. *Newark Daily Advertiser*, February 3, 1852.

61. *NJL*, 75th (1851), p. 445; *ibid.*, 60th (1836–37), p. 188.

62. *NJSJ*, 76th, January 28, 1852, pp. 90–91. Party affiliations appear in *State Gazette* (Trenton), January 1, 1852.

63. *New Jersey Journal* (Elizabeth), February 3, 1852.

64. *Ibid.*, February 10, 1852.

65. *Ibid.*

66. *Ibid.*

67. *Newark Daily Advertiser*, February 21, 1852.

68. *NJAM*, 76th, February 20, 1852, p. 419.

69. *NJAM*, 76th, February 12, 20, 23, 1852, pp. 310–311, 407, 424.

70. *Newark Daily Advertiser*, February 24, 1852.

71. *NJAM*, 76th, February 26, 1852, pp. 479–480; *Newark Daily Advertiser*, February 27, 1852.

72. *NJAM*, 76th, February 27, 1852, p. 490; *NJSJ*, 76th, March 3, 1852, p. 418; *L.* 1852, c. 63, pp. 141–143.

73. *NJL*, 75th (1851), p. 93. Property qualifications for voting had been effectively removed by *NJL*, 68th (1843–44), 2nd sit., p. 256. See McCormick, *op. cit.*, p. 128.

74. *State Gazette* (Trenton), May 7, 1850.

75. *NJAM*, 73rd, January 18, 19, 1849, pp. 269–270, 275. County collectors were also to retain the freeholder requirement, according to a Senate amendment, *NJSJ*, 73rd, February 22, 1849, pp. 760–762.

76. *NJAM*, 74th, February 1, 1850, pp. 508–509.

77. Twenty-nine Democrats, 1 Independent, and 18 Whigs voted affirmatively; 6 Whigs, negatively, *NJAM*, 75th, February 7, 1851, p. 478; *State Gazette* (Trenton), February 7, 1851.

78. Voting in favor of the property qualification amendment were 8 Whigs; opposed, 9 Democrats and 2 Whigs. Only 2 Whigs voted for passage of the bill, *NJSJ*, 75th, February 26, 1851, pp. 574–576. The 6 Whigs who

voted against the measure were "not opposed so much to the principle of the bill, as to the 2d section which provides that jurymen may be selected indiscriminately without reference to their property, or permanence of residence," *Newark Daily Advertiser*, February 28, 1851.

79. See Harris I. Effross, "Origins of Post-Colonial Counties in New Jersey," *Proceedings of the New Jersey Historical Society*, LXXXI (April, 1963), 103–122.

5

THE SYSTEM FRAGMENTS: PRE-1876 SPECIAL LEGISLATION

1. *L.* 1855, c. 244, p. 704; *L.* 1871, c. 87, p. 318; *L.* 1871, c. 131, pp. 403–404; *L.* 1873, c. 147, p. 314.

2. *L.* 1868, c. 100, pp. 218–219; *L.* 1868, c. 171, p. 389.

3. *L.*1858, c. 173, p. 437; *L.* 1857, c. 99, pp. 292–293; *L.* 1869, c. 282, p. 789.

4. *L.* 1857, c. 52, p. 124; *L.* 1862, c. 120, p. 238; *L.* 1861, c. 170, p. 508; *L.* 1871, c. 79, p. 306; *L.* 1864, c. 321, p. 539; *L.* 1866, c. 54, p. 117.

5. *NJL*, 75th (1851), p. 394; *L.* 1853, c. 44, p. 119; *L.* 1858, c. 173, p. 437; *L.* 1860, c. 124, p. 289.

6. *L.* 1855, c. 162, p. 450; *L.* 1860, c. 3, p. 7.

7. *L.* 1862, c. 120, p. 238; *L.* 1864, c. 279, p. 445; *L.* 1864, c. 321, p.539; *L.* 1865, c. 153, p. 274; *L.* 1866, c. 170, p. 367; *L.* 1866, c. 54, p. 117; *L.* 1867, c. 109, p. 192; *L.* 1871, c. 79, p. 306; *L.* 1872, c. 205, p. 480; *L.* 1872, c. 349, p. 825; *L* 1873, c. 414, p. 486. Atlantic City was to elect a freeholder to each of its only *two* wards, *L.* 1864, c. 303, p. 513, but the freeholders were elected at large when the city's revised charter did not provide for wards, *L.* 1866, c. 147, p. 315.

8. Camden, Newark, Orange, Hoboken, Jersey City, Trenton, New Brunswick, Paterson, Elizabeth.

9. Millville, Bridgeton, Phillipsburg.

10. Passaic, Lambertville. Salem County was to have a system of one freeholder per township and city (1871). See p. 82.

11. A list of Hudson County freeholders from 1840 to 1873 appears in Winfield, *op. cit.*, pp. 344–354. The municipalities' proportions of representation on the freeholder board are calculated from this.

12. *NJL*, 75th, Act of March 18, 1851, pp. 392–425; Winfield, *op. cit.*, pp. 345–346. The voters of both municipalities signified approval of the union as required by the act: in Jersey City, 489 to 3; in Van Vorst township, 377 to 47. Daniel Van Winkle, *History of the Municipalities of Hudson County, New Jersey, 1630–1923*, I (New York: Lewis Historical Publishing Co., Inc., 1924), p. 114.

13. *L.* 1855, c. 162, pp. 448, *et seq.*

14. *L.* 1857, c. 99, pp. 292–293.

15. *L.* 1861, c. 51, pp. 96–99; c. 53, pp. 104–107; *L.* 1867, c. 178, pp. 357–359; *L.*, 1864, c. 279, pp. 444–448; *L.*, 1865, c. 153, p. 274; *L.* 1866, c. 379, p. 871; *L.* 1869, c. 153, p. 411.

16. *L.* 1870, c. 511, pp. 1172, 1174.

17. *Evening Journal* (Jersey City), January 23, 1875.

18. Alan Shank and Ernest C. Reock, Jr., *New Jersey's Experience with Assembly Districts, 1852–1893* (New Brunswick, N.J.: Rutgers University, Bureau of Government Research, 1966), p. 77.

19. *Evening Journal* (Jersey City), April 10, 1871.

20. *Ibid.*

21. *NJAM*, 95th, April 5, 1871, p. 1401. Party affiliations appear in *Newark Daily Advertiser*, January 9, 1871.

22. *Evening Journal* (Jersey City), April 10, 1871.

23. *L.* 1871, c. 424, pp. 1099–1102.

24. *L.* 1871, c. 281, pp. 48–51.

25. According to one legal view, the City of Bayonne and the Township of Greenville were entitled to elect no freeholders, because they were then included in the Sixth Assembly District, together with a part of Jersey City. *Evening Journal* (Jersey City), April 28, 1871.

26. *NJSJ*, 95th, April 6, 1871, pp. 1423–1424.

27. *NJAM*, 95th, April 6, 1871, pp. 1434–1435. It became *L.* 1871, c. 606, p. 1526.

28. The freeholder bill made what proved to be a critical change in dates. Spring elections for freeholders were to continue. But the altered text prescribed that the freeholders' terms should commence on the Tuesday after the first Monday in May in each and every year, rather than on the second Wednesday in May, as had been specified since the general law of 1798 incorporating boards of chosen freeholders. The incumbent board members were to continue in office until their successors would be elected. All general laws relating to freeholder boards that were not inconsistent with the text were declared applicable to Hudson County, but all previous acts and parts of acts that were inconsistent were to be repealed, *L.* 1871, c. 606, p. 1526. The new Jersey City charter had already been passed on March 31 over the veto of Democratic Governor Theodore F. Randolph, *Evening Journal* (Jersey City), April 10, 1871. In this act replacing 16 wards with the six aldermanic districts, there was a provision that appeared to conflict with the new Hudson freeholder law. Section 10 of the city charter dealing with the time of municipal elections and the compensation of election officers provided "that for the purpose of any other election which under any law of this State should be held in said city, each election precinct shall be considered a township, and said judges and clerk of election shall be considered as township judges and clerk of election. . . ." *L.* 1871, c. 424, pp. 1098–1099. According to the *Evening Journal*, the only way to avoid the election of 52 freeholders (39 from Jersey City precincts plus 13 from the other municipalities) would be for the persons who might be elected to agree among themselves that only a certain number, like 16, of the 39 Jersey Cityites, should qualify, *Evening Journal* (Jersey City), April 10, 1871. On April 11 the county held freeholder elections, and the following day the press announced receipt of information that the Governor had previously signed the Hudson freeholder reorganization bill in the form passed by the legislature on the last day of the session. The local newspaper predicted that this fact would nullify the elections in Jersey City by precinct-

constituencies and would continue in office the existing board, *ibid.*, April 12, 1871.

Two groups claimed to be the legitimate Hudson County Board of Chosen Freeholders following the April 11 election. One of them included those Jersey City candidates who had been elected under the new city charter from individual *precinct-constituencies* within the aldermanic districts that were provided by the Hudson freeholder act passed after the charter. This new group organized on May 10, which was the day (second Wednesday) specified for this purpose in the long-standing general act incorporating all freeholder boards, *ibid.*, May 10, 1871. The election's legality with regard to Jersey City was denied by the incumbent freeholders from that municipality who had been elected in 1870 by voters of the *now-defunct wards*. In the opinion of Attorney-General Robert Gilchrist, the legally elected freeholders should be chosen from Jersey City's new aldermanic districts, and, as previously, from the wards and municipalities (including Greenville and Bayonne) outside the county seat, *ibid.*, May 1, 1871. "The remainder of the opinion was so complicated as not to be understood by some members of the board," and without dissent on May 1 that body accepted the opinion of its own counsel, William Brinkerhoff, that those persons elected from outside Jersey City should yield to the newly elected freeholders and that the ward-elected Jersey City members should retain their seats, *ibid.*, May 2, 1871. The latter were to serve, the board resolved, "until the whole matter be determined by a court of competent jurisdiction in the premises." "Official Proceedings of the Board of Chosen Freeholders, County of Hudson, May 1, 1871," in *ibid.*, May 3, 1871. Complying with the new freeholder statute's specification of the date for organizing Hudson's governing body, the board met again on May 2 (the first Tuesday after the first Monday), adjourned, and reorganized as the board of 1871–72, *State, Feury, Clerk & c., pros. v. Roe, late Clerk & c.*, 35 N.J.L. 123, 125 (1871).

Settlement of the controversy required two rulings from the New Jersey Supreme Court. On July 5 it held that the old board was the only authorized board; that it had rightfully transacted all freeholder business; that the old board had been correct in organizing "with an admitted majority of Freeholders legally elected to office" on the new date set for Hudson (May 2, the Tuesday after the first Monday), and that the clerk of the old board, and not the new, was the legally authorized one. But the Court at this time would not enter into the question of whether the election of certain members chosen from precinct-constituencies in Jersey City was void, *ibid.*, pp. 124–126; *Evening Journal* (Jersey City), July 6, 1871.

In subsequent litigation the freeholder board, which included nine ward-elected holdover members from Jersey City, insisted that the April 6 act concerning Hudson's freeholders had not been signed by the Governor when the April 11 election took place, and that, whether or not the act had been signed, the election in Jersey City had not been held under its provisions, but under the new charter, and was therefore void. But because the Court could find no source of information sufficient in law to show that the freeholder statute had no existence at the stated date of approval, the judges regarded such act binding as law from April 6 and presumed that the April 11 election had been held under it. Consequently, on November 9 the Court declared void the official statement of the Board of City Canvassers that there had been 39 freeholders elected from precinct-constituencies. The Canvassers' supporting statement supplying official voting returns by precincts was reinterpreted by the Court to elect three freeholders from each aldermanic district. A peremptory writ of mandamus was issued to install those candidates whose seats on the Hudson board were being filled by holdovers elected from ward-constituencies, *State ex rel., Love, et al. v. Freeholders of Hudson Co.*, 35 N.J.L. 269, (1871); *Evening Journal* (Jersey City), November 10, 1871. Greenville and Bayonne elected separate freeholders in 1872. *Evening Journal* (Jersey City) April 10–11, 1872.

29. *Evening Journal* (Jersey City), March 7, 1872.

30. *NJAM*, 96th, March 20, 1872, p. 997; *Evening Journal* (Jersey City), March 21, 1872. The party affiliations appear in *Daily Fredonian* (New Brunswick), March 17, 1875.

31. *NJSJ*, 96th, March 22, April 2, 3, 4, 1872, pp. 893, 1086, 1095, 1153, 1186. The vote on Assembly Bill No. 384 concerning Trenton appears in *ibid.*, March 19, 1872, p. 783.

32. *Evening Journal* (Jersey City), January 22, 1875. A membership list of Hudson's freeholder board for 1874–1875 appears in William H. Shaw (comp.), *History of Essex and Hudson Counties, New Jersey*, II (Philadelphia: Everts & Peck, 1884), p. 949.

33. "Official Proceedings," February 4, 1875, in *Evening Journal* (Jersey City), February 11, 1875.

34. *Ibid.*

35. "Presentment to the Court of Oyer and Terminer and General Jail Delivery of the County of Hudson," reprinted in *Evening Journal* (Jersey City), February 15, 1875.

36. *Evening Journal* (Jersey City), February 19, 1875; "Official Proceedings," February 18, 1875, in *ibid.*, February 27, 1875.

37. *Evening Journal* (Jersey City), January 12, 1875.

38. *Ibid.*, February 11, 1875.

39. *NJSJ*, 99th, February 15, 22–24, 1875, pp. 177, 236, 250, 286; *Evening Journal* (Jersey City), February 25, 1875.

40. *Evening Journal* (Jersey City), February 25, 1875; *NJAM*, 99th, February 25, 1875, p. 488.

41. *NJAM*, 99th, February 25, 1875, p. 490.

42. *Evening Journal* (Jersey City), February 25, 1875.

43. *NJAM*, 99th, February 25, 1875, pp. 490–492. The official vote is listed as 34 to 21, but not so many names were recorded. Party affiliations appear in *Daily Fredonian* (New Brunswick), March 17, 1875.

44. *Evening Journal* (Jersey City), February 25, 1875.

45. *Ibid.*, February 26, 1875.

46. *NJAM*, 99th, February 25, 1875, pp. 519–521. The official vote is listed as 18 to 31, but fewer names are recorded.

47. *Evening Journal* (Jersey City), March 3, 1875.

48. *Newark Daily Advertiser*, March 3, 1875.

49. *NJAM*, 99th, March 2, 1875, p. 571.

50. *Evening Journal* (Jersey City), March 2, 1875.

51. "Report of the Director, Official Proceedings," in *ibid.*, March 10, 1875.

52. "Official Proceedings," in *Evening Journal* (Jersey City), March 10, 1875; *ibid.*, March 5, 1875.

53. *Evening Journal* (Jersey City), March 9, 1875.

54. *Newark Daily Advertiser*, March 11, 1875. The general act to reapportion the State's Assembly districts, *L.* 1881, c. 129, pp. 148–154, increased the number of Hudson's Assembly districts to ten and dismembered the Eighth District. Part of it remained in a new district called the Eighth; part was included in another called the Tenth. Consequently, in 1884 the New Jersey Supreme Court held that freeholders in the new districts would have to be chosen at large. *Mulligan* v. *Cavanagh*, 46 N.J.L. 45 (1884).

55. *Evening Journal* (Jersey City), March 11, 1875; *Newark Daily Advertiser*, March 12, 1875.

56. *NJAM*, 99th, March 17, 1875, p. 822; *NJSJ*, March 17, 1875, p. 525; *L.* 1875, c. 189, pp. 324–330.

57. "Official Proceedings," regular adjourned meeting, March 25, 1875, in *Evening Journal* (Jersey City), March 31, 1875.

58. "Official Proceedings," regular adjourned meeting, April 29, 1875, in *Evening Journal* (Jersey City), May 4, 1875.

59. *Compendium of Censuses*, pp. 20–21.

60. *Ibid.*, pp. 30–31.

61. *NJL*, 60th (1836–37), 2nd sit., p. 188.

62. *NJL*, 72nd (1848), pp. 133–134; *ibid.*, 75th (1851), pp. 232–233; *L.* 1853, c. 104, pp. 232–234, *et seq.*; *L.* 1854, c. 117, p. 304, *et seq.*

63. *L.* 1856, c. 43, pp. 78–79, *et seq.*; c. 80, pp. 158–159, *et seq.*

64. *Newark Daily Advertiser*, January 6, 1857.

65. *Ibid.*

66. *Ibid.*, February 4, 1857.

67. *NJAM*, 81st, February 4, 1857, pp. 288–289. For a discussion of the Opposition party, forerunner of the Republican party, see McCormick, *op. cit.*, pp. 123 *et seq.*

68. *NJAM*, 81st, February 5, 1857, pp. 304–305.

69. *Newark Daily Advertiser*, February 13, 1857; *NJAM*, 81st, February 19, 1857, p. 495.

70. *NJSJ*, 81st, March 4, 1857, pp. 426–427; *NJAM*, 81st, March 5, 1857, pp. 721–722; *L.* 1857, c. 52, pp. 116–175.

71. Because Newark's five freeholders were not to be chosen until October, 1857, or to take office until May, 1858, there were only 16 members of the Essex freeholder board after the election of April 1857. *L.* 1857, c. 82, pp. 244–256; c. 52, p. 124; *Newark Daily Advertiser*, April 13, 1857.

72. *L.* 1860, c.11, pp. 35–39; *L.* 1861, c. 65, pp. 143–146; *L.* 1860, c. 3, pp. 6–7; *L.* 1861, c. 114, pp. 299–302; *L.* 1862, c. 87, pp. 178–180. Fairmount's name was changed to West Orange the following year, *L.* 1863, c. 149, pp. 279–282.

73. *L.* 1862, c. 120, p. 238; *NJAM*, 86th, March 13, 1862, p. 527; *NJSJ*, 86th, March 18, 1862, p. 235. Party affiliations appear in *Newark Daily Advertiser*, January 13, 1862.

74. *Pierson's Newark City Directory for 1864–5* (Newark, N.J.: Chas. H. Folwell & Co., 1864), p. 39.

75. 72.72% in 1860; 70.24% in 1865, *Compendium of Censuses*, pp. 20–21.

76. *L.* 1871, c. 361, pp. 353–356; c. 294, pp. 716–719.

77. *Newark Daily Advertiser*, January 29, 1874. An incomplete list of the board members appears in *ibid.*, April 15, 1873.

78. *Ibid.*, March 5, 1874.

79. *NJAM*, 98th, February 9, 23, 26, 1874, pp. 400–401, 440, 1293. Party affiliations appear in *Manual of the Legislature, State of New Jersey, 1874*, pp. 59–91 (hereafter cited as *N.J. Leg. Manual* with the appropriate date).

80. *L.* 1874, c. 49, pp. 191–194.

81. *NJAM*, 98th, March 26, 1874, p. 1328 records the vote as 26 to 25, but lists only 24 negative votes. *Newark Daily Advertiser*, March 27, 1874 says the vote was 26 to 24.

82. *Newark Daily Advertiser*, April 1, 1875. The population of Newark in 1875 was later declared to be 123,310. *Compendium of Censuses*, p. 20.

83. *NJAM*, 99th, April 1, 1875, p. 1117. The official vote is recorded as 12 to 29, but fewer names are listed.

84. *Newark Daily Advertiser*, April 2, 1875; *NJAM*, 99th, April 1, 1875, p. 1122.

85. *NJAM*, 99th, April 1, 1875, p. 1123 lists the official vote as 13 to 19, but fewer names were recorded.

86. *NJAM*, 99th, April 1, 5, 1875, pp. 1123–1124, 1141.

87. *Newark Daily Advertiser*, April 8, 1875; *NJAM*, 99th, April 7, 1875, pp. 210–211. One person is recorded with both the affirmative and negative votes.

88. *Newark Daily Advertiser*, April 8, 1875; *NJAM*, 99th, April 6–7, 1875, pp. 1156, 1212.

89. *Compendium of Censuses*, p. 39.

90. *L.* 1860, c. 124, pp. 288–289.

91. *L.* 1865, c. 290, p. 499.

92. *NJAM*, 92nd, February 18, 1868, p. 271; *NJSJ*, 92nd, March 11, 1868, p. 408.

93. *L.* 1868, c. 171, p. 389.

94. *L.* 1869, c. 211, pp. 538–542.

95. *NJAM*, 95th, February 21, 1871, p. 429.

96. *Ibid.*, March 1, 1871, p. 561.

97. *L.* 1871, c. 173, pp. 476–483.

98. *New Jersey Journal* (Elizabeth), April 4, 1871.

99. *Ibid.*, October 13, 1871.

100. *NJAM*, 96th, February 27, 1872, pp. 499–500.

101. *Elizabeth Daily Journal*, March 1, 1872.

102. *New Jersey Journal* (Elizabeth), April 16, 1872.

103. *Elizabeth Daily Journal*, March 1, 1872.

104. *Rahway Democrat*, quoted in *Elizabeth Daily Journal*, March 18, 1872.

105. *NJAM*, 96th, April 2, 1872, pp. 1276–1277. Party affiliations appear in *Newark Daily Advertiser*, November 8, 1871.

106. *NJAM*, 96th, April 1, 1872, p. 1246.

107. *NJSJ*, 96th, April 3, 1872, p. 1160.
108. *L.* 1872, c. 511, pp. 1134–1162.
109. *Elizabeth Daily Journal*, April 19, 1872.
110. *Ibid.*, May 8, 1872.
111. *NJAM*, 97th, February 5, 1873, p. 193.
112. *NJAM*, 97th, March 4, 1873, pp. 588–589. The vote was recorded as 34 to 8, but fewer names were listed, one of them both affirmatively and negatively.
113. *Elizabeth Daily Journal*, March 25, 1873; *NJSJ*, 97th, March 24, 1873, p. 769.
114. *Elizabeth Daily Journal*, March 25, 1873.
115. *Ibid.*, March 27, 1873.
116. *NJAM*, 97th, March 26, 1873, p. 1077.
117. *Elizabeth Daily Journal*, March 27, 1873.
118. *NJAM*, 97th, March 26, April 1, 1873, pp. 1105, 1248.
119. *NJSJ*, 97th, April 2, 1873, p. 1021.
120. *Elizabeth Daily Journal*, April 3, 1873.
121. *Ibid.*, March 16, 1875.
122. *NJSJ*, 99th, March 15, 17, 1875, pp. 468, 524.
123. *New Jersey Journal* (Elizabeth), March 30, 1875.
124. *NJAM*, 99th, April 8, 1875, pp. 1269, 1284.
125. *Newark Daily Advertiser*, April 9, 1875.
126. Seven municipalities were to comprise Mercer County, *NJL*, 62nd (1837–38), 2nd sit., p. 99. Princeton Township was added five days later, *ibid.*, pp. 209–210.
127. *L.* 1864, c. 246, p. 612.
128. *L.* 1866, c. 170, pp. 364–367; *L.* 1867, c. 240, pp. 496–498. For an historical account of Trenton's wards, see Leon D. Hirsch, "Municipal and Corporate History from the Charter of 1792," *A History of Trenton, 1679–1929*, I, ed. by Trenton Historical Society (Princeton, N. J.: Princeton University Press, 1929), pp. 356–358.
129. *L.* 1868, c. 100, pp. 218–219.
130. *NJAM*, 95th, March 13, 1871, p. 758. See party affiliations, *supra.*
131. *NJAM*, 95th, March 24, 1871, pp. 1066–1067; March 28, 1871, pp. 1120–1121; *NJSJ*, 95th, April 6, 1871, pp. 1406–1407.
132. *NJAM*, 96th, March 13, 1872, p. 806; *NJSJ*, 96th, March 19, 1872, pp. 783–784.
133. *L.* 1872, c. 315, pp. 742–743.
134. *L.* 1874, c. 432, p. 519.
135. *NJL*, 61st (1836–37), 2nd sit., p. 98.
136. *NJL*, 75th (1851), pp. 444–445; *L.* 1853, c. 44, p. 119.
137. *L.* 1854, c. 69, pp. 159–169; *L.* 1855, c. 125, pp. 335–336.
138. *L.* 1858, c. 55, p. 120; *NJAM*, 82nd, February 19, 1858, p. 484.
139. *L.* 1868, c. 28, p. 59; c. 200, pp. 449–451.
140. *L.* 1869, c. 282, p. 789; *NJSJ*, 93rd, March 16, 1869, pp. 503–504; *NJAM*, 93rd, March 24, 1869, p. 954. Party affiliations appear in *Holbrook's Newark City Directory, 1870* (Newark, N. J.: A. Stephen Holbrook, 1869), pp. 691–692.
141. *L.* 1871, c. 259, p. 620.
142. *L.* 1873, c. 414, pp. 484–486. A brief account of freeholder distribu-

tion in the county appears in William Nelson (comp.), *Historical and Statistical Memoranda Relative to Passaic County, New Jersey* (Passaic, N.J.: Passaic Herald Printing, 1876), p. vi. See also W. Woodford Clayton and William Nelson, *History of Bergen and Passaic Counties, New Jersey* (Philadelphia: Everts & Peck, 1882), p. 347.

143. *N.J. Leg. Manual, 1874,* p. 63.

144. Alexandria (3,341); Clinton (3,134); Lebanon (3,561); and Readington(3,070).

145. *NJSJ,* 96th, March 13, 1872, p. 654; *ibid.,* March 22, 1872, p. 889.

146. *NJAM,* 96th, March 26, 1872, p. 1106; *L.* 1872, c. 349, pp. 824–828.

147. *Evening Journal* (Jersey City), January 16, 1872.

148. *N.J. Leg. Manual, 1874,* p. 63.

149. *Newark Evening Courier,* March 3, 1875.

150. *Daily Times* (New Brunswick), March 18, 1875.

151. *NJSJ,* 99th, March 16, 1875, p. 484.

152. *L.* 1867, c. 109, p. 192; *L.* 1868, c. 250, pp. 557–558.

153. *NJSJ,* 95th, February 1, 14, 1871, pp. 171, 350; *NJAM,* 95th, March 1, 1871, p. 570; *L.* 1871, c. 103, pp. 340–342.

154. *NJSJ,* 95th, February 16, 28, 1871, pp. 397, 564.

155. *NJAM,* 95th, March 7, 8, 1871, pp. 649, 682. It became *L.* 1871, c. 131, pp. 403–404.

156. *NJSJ,* 96th, March 22, 1872, p. 887.

157. *NJAM,* 97th, March 6, 1873, pp. 664–645.

6

GATHERING UP THE PIECES: EARLY ATTEMPTS AT GENERAL LEGISLATION, 1876–1883

1. Bennett M. Rich, *The Government and Administration of New Jersey* (New York: Thomas Y. Crowell Company, 1957), p. 18.

2. *Constitution of New Jersey* (1844), Art. IV, Sec. VII, par. 11, as amended September 7, 1875.

3. *NJSJ,* 100th, January 10, 1876, p. 73; *NJAM,* 100th, January 10, 1876, p. 93.

4. *Newark Daily Advertiser,* February 10, 1876; *Evening Journal* (Jersey City), February 10, 1876.

5. After much discussion, the Joint Committee had defeated, 6 to 7, Leon Abbett's motion to make each director like Hudson's, with a veto power that could be overridden by a two-thirds vote of the freeholder board, and with power to vote only in the case of a tie. *Daily Fredonian* (New Brunswick), February 11, 1876.

6. Essex County's municipalities and city wards, for example, were about to vote on at least four different dates that spring (March 13, 14; April 4, 10) and one in October, *Newark Daily Advertiser,* March 2, 1876.

7. *Elizabeth Daily Journal,* February 11, 1876.

8. *Daily True American* (Trenton), February 14, 1876.

9. *Ibid.*

10. *Ibid.*
11. Quoted in *ibid.*, February 15, 1876.
12. *Daily True American* (Trenton), February 15, 1876.
13. *Hunterdon Republican* (Flemington), February 17, 1876.
14. *Newark Daily Advertiser*, February 10, 1876; *Sentinel of Freedom* (Newark), February 15, 1876.
15. *Elizabeth Daily Journal*, February 16, 1876. Some of the members angrily returned their letters of instruction to the board, *Evening Journal* (Jersey City), February 16, 1876. See also *Newark Daily Journal*, February 15, 1876.
16. *New Jersey Mirror* (Mt. Holly), February 17, 1876.
17. *Ibid.*, February 24, 1876.
18. *NJSJ*, 100th, February 29, 1876, pp. 195–196.
19. *Daily Fredonian* (New Brunswick), March 1, 1876.
20. *Daily True American* (Trenton), March 1, 1876.
21. *Daily Fredonian* (New Brunswick), March 1, 1876.
22. *Daily True American* (Trenton), March 1, 1876; *Newark Daily Advertiser*, February 29, 1876.
23. *Daily True American* (Trenton), March 1, 1876; *Newark Daily Journal*, February 29, 1876.
24. *Daily Fredonian* (New Brunswick), March 1, 1876.
25. *NJSJ*, 100th, February 29, 1876, p. 195. One commentator, "John," in Hunterdon's *Clinton Democrat*, March 10, 1876, remarked on the amendments made that day: "Had the bill been carried forward in its original form, there would have been less than half a dozen Democratic Boards in the State, if that many. It was a purely partisan measure in its effects, and deserved 'killing' about as much as anything that has yet showed its hydra head."
26. *L.* 1852, c. 62, pp. 141–143; *L.* 1853, c. 133, p. 346; *L.* 1872, c. 205, p. 480; *L.* 1875, c. 375, pp. 564–565; *L.* 1868, c. 41, p. 77.
27. *L.* 1873, c. 148, p. 314; *L.* 1872, c. 105, p. 302.
28. See above, p. 79.
29. *L.* 1858, c. 173, pp. 437–439; *L.* 1868, c. 44, p. 104; *L.* 1871, c. 39, p. 215.
30. Each Cumberland city was divided into three wards that were entitled to elect two freeholders apiece, *L.* 1864, c. 321, pp. 538–539; *L.* 1866, c. 54, pp. 116–117.
31. See above, p. 82.
32. *L.* 1871, c. 70, p.306.
33. *L.* 1855, c. 244, p. 704.
34. *L.* 1852, c. 63, p.141.
35. See above, p. 80.
36. *NJL*, 75th (1851), p. 97; *L.* 1872, c. 349, pp. 824–825; *L.* 1867, c. 299, p. 659; *L.* 1865, c. 431, p. 780.
37. Kirk was a freeholder representing Newark's Fourteenth Ward. Holbrooks *Newark City Directory*, 1876 (Newark, N.J.: A. Stephen Holbrook, 1875), p. 907; *NJSJ*, 100th, February 20, 1876, p. 195.
38. *Newark Daily Advertiser*, March 2, 1876, observed that the bill's *original* text would reduce Newark's freeholders by three, but would give it twice the power of the other parts of Essex. That county would have a

director at large and 18 district-elected freeholders (12 from Newark and 6 from the townships). But Kirk was correct: only two Assembly districts were not controlled by the votes of Newarkers.

39. *NJSJ*, 100th, February 29, 1876, p. 196.

40. *Daily True American* (Trenton), March 1, 1876.

41. *NJSJ*, 100th, February 29, 1876, p. 196.

42. The sponsor of this motion was not recorded in the *NJSJ*, 100th, (1876), but appears in *Daily True American* (Trenton), March 1, 1876.

43. *Daily Fredonian* (New Brunswick), March 1, 1876.

44. *NJSJ*, 100th, February 29, 1876, p. 196.

45. *Newark Daily Journal*, March 16, 1876; *Newark Daily Advertiser*, March 15, 1876. The change in designating first-class counties was included under "sundry amendments," *NJSJ*, 100th, March 15, 1876, p. 268, which did report the proposed salary change.

46. Amendments to Senate Bill No. 55, N.J. State Law Library.

47. This change was included under "sundry amendments," *NJSJ*, 100th, March 15, 1876, p. 268; *New Jersey Mirror* (Mt. Holly), March 23, 1876.

48. *NJSJ*, 100th, March 27, 1876, p. 343; *Daily True American* (Trenton), March 28, 1876.

49. *Evening Journal* (Jersey City), March 31, 1876.

50. *Newark Daily Advertiser*, March 31, 1876.

51. *NJAM*, 100th, April 4, 1876, pp. 619, 638.

52. *NJAM*, 100th, April 6, 1876, p. 709.

53. "This will have been the longest session ever held by a New Jersey Legislature, with one exception, that of 1861, which because of the exigencies of the war, was extended until May 10," *Daily Times* (New Brunswick), April 18, 1876.

54. *NJAM*, 100th, April 18, 1876, p. 887.

55. *NJAM*, 100th, February 15, 1876, p. 80.

56. *Evening Journal* (Jersey City), February 15, 1876.

57. *NJAM*, 100th, March 30; April 4, 5, 11, 1876, pp. 591, 640–641, 689, 761.

58. *Newark Daily Advertiser*, February 21, 1877.

59. *NJSJ*, 101st, February 21, 1877, p. 212; *Daily Times* (New Brunswick), February 22, 1877; *Elizabeth Daily Journal*, February 23, 1877.

60. *NJSJ*, 101st, March 7, 1877, p. 357; *Evening Journal* (Jersey City), March 8, 1877.

61. *Newark Daily Advertiser*, February 27, 1877.

62. *NJAM*, 101st, February 28, 1877, pp. 372–373.

63. *Daily Fredonian* (New Brunswick), March 6, 1877.

64. *Ibid.*

65. *Ibid.*

66. *Daily Times* (New Brunswick), March 6, 1877.

67. Pennington argued: "These Freeholders are represented as rogues, but I can tell you that if you approach any one of these men you will find that they are out over $100 a year in their expenses which is their own loss. As to bridges, they are demanded by the people and a great many considerations enter into their purchase, as in the case in the one at South River owned by two widows," *ibid.*

68. *Daily Fredonian* (New Brunswick), April 10, 1877.

69. *Ibid.*, September 7, 1877.

70. *Ibid.*, December 4, 1877.

71. Quoted in Harry B. Weiss, *The New Jersey State Grange, 1873–1954* (Trenton, N.J.: New Jersey State Grange, 1955), p. 10; Fred A. Shannon, *The Farmer's Last Frontier, Agriculture, 1860–1897* (New York; Farrar & Rinehart, Inc., 1945), p. 309.

72. *Daily Times* (New Brunswick), December 5, 1877; *Daily Fredonian* (New Brunswick), December 4, 1877.

73. *Daily Times* (New Brunswick), December 5, 1877.

74. *Daily Fredonian* (New Brunswick), December 4, 1877.

75. *Ibid.*, December 8, 1877. New Brunswick had been allotted three freeholders by *L*. 1861, c. 170, pp. 507–513; and, subsequently, one freeholder for each of its six newly created wards, *L*. 1871, c. 79, pp. 306–310.

76. *Daily Fredonian* (New Brunswick), December 8, 1877.

77. *Daily Times* (New Brunswick), December 8, 1877.

78. *Weekly Fredonian* (New Brunswick), December 13, 1877.

79. *Ibid.*, December 20, 1877.

80. *New Jersey Mirror* (Mt. Holly), December 20, 1877.

81. *Middlesex County Democrat* (Perth Amboy), December 15, 1877.

82. *Independent Hour* (Woodbridge), as quoted in *Daily Fredonian* (New Brunswick), December 22, 1877.

83. *Daily Fredonian* (New Brunswick), January 3, 1878.

84. The editorial in the *Independent Hour* (Woodbridge) is reprinted and discussed in *Daily Fredonian* (New Brunswick), January 7, 1878.

85. *Daily Fredonian* (New Brunswick), January 7, 1878.

86. *Ibid.*

87. *Daily Times* (New Brunswick), December 27, 1877.

88. *Daily Fredonian* (New Brunswick), January 9, 1878; *Daily Times* (New Brunswick), January 8, 1878.

89. *Daily Fredonian* (New Brunswick), January 17, 1878.

90. *Ibid.*, January 15, 1878.

91. *Ibid.*, January 22, 1878.

92. *Daily Times* (New Brunswick), January 22, 1878.

93. *Daily Fredonian* (New Brunswick), January 22, 1878.

94. *Daily Times* (New Brunswick), January 22, 1878.

95. *Daily Fredonian* (New Brunswick), January 22, 1878.

96. *Daily Times* (New Brunswick), January 22, 1878.

97. *Daily Fredonian* (New Brunswick), January 22, 1878.

98. *Ibid.; Daily Times* (New Brunswick), January 22, 1878.

99. *Daily Fredonian* (New Brunswick), March 6, 1878.

100. *Daily Times* (New Brunswick), January 14, 1879.

101. *Daily Fredonian* (New Brunswick), January 15, 1879.

102. Blish was now master of the newly formed Pomona Grange, Patrons of Husbandry, and Thompson was a member of its executive committee, *ibid.*, March 19, 1878.

103. *Ibid.*, January 15, 1879.

104. *NJAM*, 103rd, January 27, February 4, 10, 1879, pp. 128, 200, 261.

105. *Daily Fredonian* (New Brunswick), February 5, 1879.

106. *Ibid.*, May 19, 1879. Meyrick was reported as advocating one

freeholder for each township, *ibid.*, but he denied this as "a great many more than is needed," in a letter to the editor, *ibid.*, May 23, 1879.

107. The eight (of nine) Essex assemblymen who voted approved the first amendment, *NJAM*, 102nd, March 26, 1878, pp. 991–993.

108. *NJAM*, 103rd, March 4, 1879, p. 557.

109. *Newark Daily Advertiser*, February 12, 1879.

110. *Ibid.*

111. *Ibid.*

112. *Ibid.*

113. *Daily Fredonian* (New Brunswick), February 19, 1879.

114. Sections 1 and 3, Reprint, Senate Bill No. 37, N.J. State Law Library, provided for *nine* freeholders in every county with less than 100,000 population, but other language in sections 3, 5, and 7 indicate that the word "nine" was an error. No newspaper account that was examined reported any number except three.

115. *NJSJ*, 103rd, February 18, 1879, p. 251.

116. *NJSJ*, 103rd, February 19, 1879, pp. 263–264.

117. *Daily Fredonian* (New Brunswick), February 20, 1879; see also *Newark Daily Advertiser*, February 20, 1879.

118. *Daily Fredonian* (New Brunswick), February 20, 1879.

119. *Ibid.*, April 17, 1879.

120. *Evening Journal* (Jersey City), February 26, 1879.

121. *Daily Fredonian* (New Brunswick), February 24, 1880. Another resolution "heartily" approved of Schenck's Senate Bill No. 73, as amended, authorizing *townships* to construct bridges costing less than $100, *ibid.*

122. *L.* 1879, c. 57, pp. 83–84.

123. *Daily Fredonian* (New Brunswick), March 5, 1879.

124. *NJAM*, 103rd, February 24, 1879, p. 417.

125. *Daily Fredonian* (New Brunswick), March 5, 1879.

126. *Ibid; NJSJ*, 103rd, March 4, 1879, p. 416.

127. *NJSJ*, 103rd, March 4, 1879, p. 417; *NJAM*, 103rd, March 4, 1879, pp. 584–585.

128. *NJAM*, 103rd, February 4, 1879, p. 196.

129. *NJAM*, 103rd, February 25, 1879, pp. 433–434. Before the amendment was adopted, a motion by Gloucester's Republican John F. Bodine to strike the enacting clause lost, 6 to 11; *NJSJ*, 103rd, March 6, 1879, p. 568; *NJAM*, 103rd, March 12, 1879, p. 799.

130. *L.* 1849, c. 170, pp. 275–276.

131. *NJSJ*, 104th, January 27, 1880, p. 96; *NJAM*, 104th, February 4, 1880, p. 199.

132. Veto message, *NJSJ*, 104th, February 10, 1880, pp. 229–230.

133. *NJSJ*, 104th, February 16, 1880, pp. 259–260.

134. *Newark Daily Advertiser*, February 21, 1880.

135. *NJAM*, 102nd, April 2, 1878, p. 1108; *NJSJ*, 101st, April 5, 1878, pp. 1010–1011.

136. *L.* 1878, c. 212, p. 326.

137. Pp. 266–284; pp. 311–312, repealed by *L.* 1879, c. 23, pp. 36–37; c. 21, pp. 34–35.

138. See also *L.* 1878, c. 211, pp. 324–325 requiring the mayor and common council of any city with a population of 120,000 "by resolution to

divide such city into wards, corresponding in number and boundaries to the assembly districts or parts of assembly districts within the limits of such city." Repealed by *L.* 1879, c. 20, pp. 31–33.

139. *Pell* v. *Newark,* 40 N.J.L. 71 (1878).

140. *Gardner* v. *Newark,* 40 N.J.L. 297 (1878).

141. *Newark Daily Advertiser,* July 10, 1878.

142. *Pell* v. *Newark,* 40 N.J.L. 550 (1878).

143. *NJSJ,* 105th, February 28, 1881, pp. 431–432; *NJAM,* 105th, March 1, 1881, p. 565.

144. *NJSJ,* 105th, March 7, 1881, p. 538. The case was *State ex rel. Richards* v. *Hammer,* 42 N.J.L. 435 (1880).

145. *NJSJ,* 105th, March 15, 1881, p. 676.

146. *NJSJ,* 105th, March 21, 1881, pp. 808–809.

147. *L.* 1881, c. 198, pp. 252–253, as compared with original text of the bill.

148. *NJSJ,* 105th, March 23, 1881, p. 881; *NJAM,* 105th, March 24, 1881, p. 1803; *L.* 1881, c. 198, pp. 252–253.

149. *NJSJ,* 104th, February 23, 1880, pp. 327–328.

150. *New York Times,* February 24, 1880.

151. *New Jersey Mirror* (Mt. Holly), quoted in *Daily Fredonian* (New Brunswick), February 11, 1880.

152. *Ibid.*

153. *NJAM,* 104th, March 9, 1880, pp. 137–138.

154. *NJAM,* 104th, March 10, 1880, pp. 761–763.

155. *NJAM,* 104th, March 10, 1880, pp. 699–706.

156. *Newark Daily Advertiser,* March 11, 1880.

157. *NJAM,* 104th, March 10, 1880, p. 700.

158. *NJSJ,* 105th, February 1, 1881, p. 120.

159. *Newark Daily Advertiser,* February 2, 1881.

160. *Daily Fredonian* (New Brunswick), February 3, 1881.

161. *Daily True American* (Trenton), February 2, 1881.

162. *Daily Fredonian* (New Brunswick), February 3, 1881.

163. *NJSJ,* 105th, February 1, 1881, p. 120.

164. *Evening Journal* (Jersey City), February 2, 1881.

165. *NJSJ,* 105th, February 1, 1881, p. 121.

166. *Evening Journal* (Jersey City), February 2, 1881; *Daily Fredonian* (New Brunswick), February 3, 1881.

167. *NJSJ,* 105th, February 2, 1881, p. 132; *Evening Journal* (Jersey City), February 3, 1881.

168. *Daily True American* (Trenton), February 3, 1881.

169. *Evening Journal* (Jersey City), February 3, 1881. The vote was 2 to 18, *NJSJ,* 105th, February 2, 1881, pp. 132–133.

170. *NJSJ,* 105th, February 2, 1881, pp. 136–137; *Daily True American* (Trenton), February 3, 1881.

171. *Newark Daily Advertiser,* February 3, 1881.

172. *Daily True American* (Trenton), February 3, 1881.

173. *NJSJ,* 105th, February 2, 1881, p. 137.

174. *NJSJ,* 105th, February 2, 1881, p. 144; *Daily True American* (Trenton), February 3, 1881.

175. *NJSJ,* 105th, February 9, 1881, p. 222.

176. *NJSJ*, 105th, February 14, 1881, p. 240; *Daily True American* (Trenton), February 15, 1881; *Daily Times* (New Brunswick), February 15, 1881.
177. *Daily Times* (New Brunswick), February 15, 1881.
178. *NJSJ*, 105th, February 21, 1881, p. 334; *ibid.*, February 22, 1881, p. 361; *ibid.*, March 2, 1881, p. 507.
179. *Daily True American* (Trenton), February 22, 1881; *Daily Times* (New Brunswick), March 3, 1881.
180. *Evening Journal* (Jersey City), February 23, 1881.
181. *Ibid.*, March 9, 1881.
182. *Daily Times* (New Brunswick), March 9, 1881; *Evening Journal* (Jersey City), March 10, 1881.
183. *NJAM*, 105th, March 17, 1881, p. 950.
184. *NJSJ*, 105th, March 21, 1881, p. 777.
185. *NJAM*, 105th, March 21, 1881, p. 983.
186. *NJSJ*, 105th, March 24, 1881, p. 933; *NJAM*, 105th, March 24, 1881, pp. 1076–1077.
187. *N.J. Leg. Docs.*, 105th (1881), I, Doc. 26, n.p.
188. *NJSJ*, 105th, March 15, 1881, pp. 688–689. For the texts, see *N.J. Leg. Docs.*, (1881) 105th, I, Doc. 43, pp. 5–167.
189. *Newark Daily Advertiser*, April 9, 1881. See *N.J. Leg. Docs.*, (1881) 105th, I, Doc. 43, pp. 5–167.
190. *New Jersey Mirror* (Mt. Holly), March 30, 1881.
191. *Newark Daily Advertiser*, April 9, 1881.
192. *Ibid.*
193. *NJSJ*, 105th, February 22, 1881, pp. 373–374; *NJAM*, 105th, February 24, 1881, pp. 500–501.
194. *Newark Daily Advertiser*, April 9, 1881.
195. *NJSJ*, 105th, March 16, 1881, p. 721; *NJAM*, 105th, March 17, 1881, p. 954.
196. *NJSJ*, 105th, March 23, 1881, p. 868.
197. *L.* 1881, c. 150, p. 187.
198. *NJSJ*, 105th, n.d., p. 1197.
199. *NJAM*, 106th, January 11, 1882, pp. 75–77.
200. *NJSJ*, 106th, March 8, 1882, pp. 624–625.
201. *NJAM*, 106th, February 6, 1882, p. 222; *ibid.*, March 15, 1882, p. 792.
202. *L.* 1882, c. 46, pp. 47–48.

7

EFFORTS TO CLASSIFY COUNTIES, 1883–1890

1. *Cape May County Gazette* (Cape May Court House), February 3, 1883.
2. *N.J. Leg. Manual, 1883*, pp. 204, 230.
3. *NJAM*, 107th, February 5, 1883, p. 232; *NJSJ*, 107th, February 7, 1883, p. 294.
4. *NJAM*, 107th, February 12, 1883, p. 302, 313; *NJSJ*, 107th, February 12, 1883, pp. 334–335.

5. *NJAM,* 107th, February 25, 1883, p. 496; *NJSJ,* 107th, March 6, 1883, p. 650; *L.* 1883, c. 66, p. 83.

6. Lewis Townsend Stevens, *The History of Cape May County, New Jersey From Aboriginal Times to the Present Day* (Cape May City, N.J.: Lewis T. Stevens, 1897), p. 439.

7. *Ibid.*

8. *Sussex Independent* (Deckertown), March 21, 1884.

9. *L.* 1883, c. 11, pp. 20–21.

10. *NJSJ,* 107th, January 24, 1883, p. 149; *NJAM,* February 6, 1883, p. 242.

11. *L.* 1901, c. 113, p. 250; c. 46, p. 78.

12. *L.* 1883, c. 126, p. 157; *NJSJ,* 107th, March 21, 1883, pp. 882–883; *ibid.,* March 22, 1883, p. 952.

13. *Siedler* v. *Board of Chosen Freeholders of Hudson County,* 45 N.J.L. 462 (1883).

14. See substitute for Senate Bill No. 112, N.J. State Law Library; *NJSJ,* 108th, February 26, 1884, p. 456.

15. *NJAM,* 108th, March 4, 1884, pp. 603–604.

16. *NJSJ,* 108th, March 10, 1884, pp. 624–626.

17. *NJAM,* 108th, March 18, 1884, p. 793.

18. *NJSJ,* 109th, February 17, 1885, p. 227.

19. *NJAM,* 109th, February 24, 1885, p. 371.

20. *NJSJ,* 109th, February 24, 1885, p. 299.

21. *L.* 1885, c. 40, p. 48.

22. "1880 Census," *N.J. Leg. Manual, 1881,* pp. 138–146.

23. *Newark Evening News,* March 11, 1884.

24. *NJAM,* 108th, March 11, 1884, p. 705; *Evening Journal* (Jersey City), March 11, 1884.

25. *Elizabeth Daily Journal,* March 12, 1884.

26. *NJAM,* 108th, March 11, 1884, p. 713.

27. *Sentinel of Freedom* (Newark), March 11, 1884.

28. *Newark Evening News,* April 25, 1884.

29. *NJSJ,* 108th, March 26–April 15, 1884, *passim.*

30. *NJSJ,* 108th, April 16, 1884, p. 1143; *Sentinel of Freedom* (Newark), April 22, 1884.

31. *NJSJ,* 108th, April 16, 1884, p. 1166.

32. *NJAM,* 108th, April 17, 1884, pp. 1207, 1208–1209.

33. *Newark Evening News,* April 25, 1884.

34. *Ibid.,* March 4, 1885; *NJAM,* 109th, March 4, 1885, p. 447.

35. *Newark Evening News,* March 4, 1885.

36. *NJAM,* 109th, March 4, 1885, p. 448; *Sentinel of Freedom* (Newark), March 10, 1885; *Evening Journal* (Jersey City), March 5, 1885.

37. *Sentinel of Freedom* (Newark), March 17, 1885.

38. *Evening Journal* (Jersey City), March 12, 1885.

39. *Newark Evening News,* March 12, 1885. Assembly Bill No. 287, providing for the division of wards, was passed by votes of 31 to 18 and 12 to 1; but Democratic Governor Leon Abbett pocket-vetoed it, *NJAM,* 109th, March 12, 1885, p. 534; *NJSJ,* 109th, March 31, 1885, p. 639.

40. *Newark Evening News,* March 12, 1885.

41. *Ibid.*

42. *Sentinel of Freedom* (Newark), March 17, 1885.
43. *Newark Evening News,* March 12, 1885.
44. *Ibid.*
45. *Sentinel of Freedom* (Newark), March 17, 1885.
46. *Daily Home News* (New Brunswick), March 12, 1885.
47. *Newark Evening News,* March 24, 1885.
48. *NJAM,* 106th, March 29, 1882, p. 1008; *NJSJ,* 106th, March 30, 1882, pp. 1015–1016.
49. *Sentinel of Freedom* (Newark), April 7, 1885.
50. *Newark Evening News,* March 26, 1885.
51. *Sentinel of Freedom* (Newark), March 31, 1885.
52. *Newark Evening News,* March 26, 1885; *NJAM,* 109th, March 26, 1885, p. 725.
53. *Newark Evening News,* March 26, 1885.
54. *NJAM,* 109th, April 1, 1885, p. 807.
55. *Newark Evening News,* April 2, 1885.
56. *Daily True American* (Trenton), April 2, 1885; *NJSJ,* 109th, April 1, 1885, p. 670.
57. *Newark Evening News,* April 2, 1885; *Daily True American* (Trenton), April 2, 1885.
58. *Sentinel of Freedom* (Newark), April 7, 1885.
59. *NJAM,* 109th, April 1, 1885, p. 816. The vote is recorded as 19 to 30, but only 18 members are listed as voting affirmatively.
60. *Sentinel of Freedom* (Newark), April 7, 1885.
61. *Newark Evening News,* March 7, 1885.
62. *Elizabeth Daily Journal,* March 6, 1885.
63. *Newark Evening News,* March 7, 1885.
64. *Elizabeth Daily Journal,* March 6, 1885.
65. *Ibid.,* March 9, 1885.
66. *Ibid.*
67. *Ibid.,* March 14, 1885.
68. *NJAM,* 109th, March 9, 1885, p. 478; *Evening Journal* (Jersey City), March 10, 1885; *Daily True American* (Trenton), March 20, 1885.
69. *Daily True American* (Trenton), March 20, 1885; *NJAM,* 109th, March 11, 19, 1885, pp. 531, 634–635.
70. *NJSJ,* 109th, March 31, April 2, 3, 1885, pp. 531, 711, 761; *Sentinel of Freedom* (Newark), April 7, 1885.
71. *NJAM,* 109th, April 4, 1885, p. 911.
72. *Daily True American* (Trenton), March 23, 1888; *NJAM,* 112th, March 22, 1888, p. 697.
73. *NJAM,* 110th, March 17, 1886, p. 553.
74. *Ibid.*
75. *Ibid.,* March 23, 1886, pp. 502–503.
76. *NJAM,* 111th, February 1, 23, 1887, pp. 160, 278.
77. *NJSJ,* 111th, March 2, 1887, p. 132; *Daily True American* (Trenton), March 3, 1887.
78. *NJSJ,* 111th, March 8, 1887, p. 147.
79. *Daily True American* (Trenton), March 9, 1887.
80. *New York Times,* March 11, 1887.
81. *Home News* (New Brunswick), March 10, 1887

8

PRESSURES FOR THE END OF
MUNICIPAL REPRESENTATION,
1885–1892

1. John P. Snyder, *The Story of New Jersey's Civil Boundaries,* Bulletin No. 67 (Trenton: N.J. Bureau of Geology and Topology, 1969), p. 8.
2. *L.* 1878, c. 260, p. 403; Friedelbaum, *op. cit.,* p. 8.
3. Snyder, *op. cit.,* p. 23.
4. *NJAM,* 109th, January 28, 1885, p. 142 records the vote as 43 to 2, but lists 44 names in the majority.
5. *NJSJ,* 109th, February 9, 1885, p. 169.
6. *L.* 1885, c. 20, p. 29.
7. *NJSJ,* 111th, March 22, 1887, p. 292.
8. *NJAM,* 111th, April 5, 1887, p. 684, records the vote as 33 to 2, but 35 members are listed as voting affirmatively.
9. *NJSJ,* 111th, April 6, 1887, p. 493; *L.* 1887, c. 107, p. 140.
10. *Daily True American* (Trenton), March 1, 1888; *Daily State Gazette* (Trenton), March 1, 1888.
11. *NJAM,* 112th, February 29, 1888, p. 488.
12. For example, Frenchtown (1867) in Hunterdon; and Washington Borough (1868) in Warren, both with special charters.
13. *L.* 1887, c. 107, p. 140.
14. *L.* 1891, c. 75, pp. 121–122; *L.* 1893, c. 52, pp. 101–102, noting in its preamble that "doubts had arisen" about the meaning of the 1891 act, clarified the intent of that statute.
15. *L.* 1894, c. 88, pp. 138–139.
16. *L.* 1895, c. 107, pp. 210–211.
17. *L.* 1897, c. 161, p. 285.
18. *L.* 1896, c. 30, p. 57; see below Chap. 10, n. 54.
19. *L.* 1845, p. 108; *L.* 1884, c. 213, pp. 326–331; *L.* 1888, c. 325, pp. 43–44; *L.*1895, c. 343, pp. 690–691.
20. *Evening Journal* (Jersey City), March 31, 1888.
21. *Ibid.,* February 28, 1888; *NJAM,* 112th, February 28, 1888, p. 443.
22. *NJSJ,* 112th, March 1, 20, 1888, pp. 457, 568; *NJAM,* 112th, March 26, 1888, p. 725.
23. *L.* 1888, c. 325, pp. 483–487.
24. *Home News* (New Brunswick), November 3, 1885; *Daily Times* (New Brunswick), November 3, 1885.
25. "Minutes of Annual Meeting, Fifteenth Annual Session of the New Jersey State Board of Agriculture, Trenton, N.J., February 1, 1888," in "Fifteenth Annual Report of the State Board of Agriculture," *N.J. Leg. Docs.,* 112th (1888), II, Doc. 13, pp. 25–26.
26. *Ibid.; Daily True American* (Trenton), February 3, 1888; *Daily State Gazette* (Trenton), February 3, 1888.
27. *Home News* (New Brunswick), February 21, 1888.
28. *Daily Fredonian* (New Brunswick), October 8, 1888.
29. *Ibid.,* December 3, 1888.

30. *Ibid.,* December 1, 3, 1888.
31. *Home News* (New Brunswick), December 14, 1888.
32. *Daily Fredonian* (New Brunswick), December 12, 1888.
33. *Ibid.*
34. *Ibid.,* December 15, 1888. It reprinted the following editorial from the *Unionist Gazette* (Somerville) without commenting on the many previous efforts of the Middlesex Farmers' Club: "The Middlesex Agricultural Association has at last awakened to the present cumbersomeness and irresponsibility of the form of government which has obtained in New Jersey for nearly two hundred years. They have discovered that to elect a Board of Freeholders, consisting of a member from each township, upon the two-dollar-per day system has long outlived its usefulness, and if it does not tend in every locality to the robbing of the treasury, does lead to a slack and inefficient oversight of county expenditures and of county improvements," *ibid.*
35. *Ibid.,* December 17, 1888.
36. *Daily True American* (Trenton), January 9, 1889; *Daily State Gazette* (Trenton), January 9, 1889; "Report of the Secretary, Mercer County Board of Agriculture, Special Meeting, January 8, 1889," in "Sixteenth Annual Report of the State Board of Agriculture," *N.J. Leg. Docs.,* 113th (1889), I, Doc. 9, p. 541. The tripling of Chambersburg's board membership resulted from the legislature's overriding of two vetoes by Democratic Governor Robert S. Green. *NJAM,* 112th, March 29, 1888, pp. 775, 800; *NJSJ,* 112th, March 30, 1888, p. 794; *L.* 1888, c. 230, c. 231, pp. 330–337, 585. He wrote: "The origin, treatment and passage of those bills prove them to be dual parts of a single scheme—the one part [Assembly Bill No. 353] designating a special locality to be consolidated and not providing a means for consolidation; the other [Assembly Bill No. 352] providing a method of regulating the internal affairs of towns and counties, but without designating any locality to which it shall apply. . . ." They had been passed at "the instance of interested parties; by the consideration of partisan [Republican] advantages expected to be derived; under the guidance and control of a party caucus, and against the express opposition of the local respresentative." *NJAM,* 112th, March 28, 1888, p. 775.
37. "Report by the Secretary, Mercer County Board of Agriculture, Sixteenth Annual Report. . . ," *N.J. Leg. Docs.,* 113th (1889), I, Doc. 9, p. 541.
38. See text, "Minutes of Annual Meeting, January 30, 1889, Sixteenth Annual Session of the New Jersey State Board of Agriculture, Trenton, N.J.," in "Sixteenth Annual Report . . . ," *N.J. Leg. Docs.,* 113th (1889), I, Doc. 9, pp. 13–15.
39. *Daily True American* (Trenton), January 31, 1889.
40. "Minutes of Annual Meeting, January 30, 1889, Sixteenth Annual Session of New Jersey State Board of Agriculture, Trenton, N.J.," in "Sixteenth Annual Report . . . ," *N.J. Leg. Docs., loc. cit.*
41. *Ibid.,* January 31, 1889, p. 51.
42. *Home News* (New Brunswick), February 26, 1889.
43. *Daily Fredonian* (New Brunswick), February 25, 1889.
44. *New Jersey Mirror* (Mt. Holly), March 6, 1889.
45. Quoted in *Daily Fredonian* (New Brunswick), February 28, 1889.
46. *Daily Fredonian* (New Brunswick), February 28, 1889.

47. *Home News* (New Brunswick), March 1, 1889.
48. *Ibid.*, April 5, 1889.
49. *Daily Fredonian* (New Brunswick), April 11, 1889.
50. "Minutes of Annual Meeting, January 31, 1890, Seventeenth Annual Session of the New Jersey State Board of Agriculture, Trenton, N.J." in "Seventeenth Annual Report . . . ," *N.J. Leg. Docs.*, 114th (1890), II, Doc. 14, p. 125.
51. *Ibid.*
52. *Ibid.*, p. 126.
53. *Ibid.*, pp. 127–128.
54. "Minutes of the Annual Meeting, January 27, 1891, Eighteenth Annual Meeting of the New Jersey State Board of Agriculture, Trenton, N.J." in "Eighteenth Annual Report . . . ," *N.J. Leg. Docs.*, 115th (1891), IV., Doc. 23, p. 299; *Daily True American* (Trenton), January 28, 1891.
55. See pp. 149–151. On the subject of gerrymandering, see Shank and Reock, *op. cit.*
56. "Minutes of the Annual Meeting, January 19, 1892, Nineteenth Annual Meeting of the New Jersey State Board of Agriculture, Trenton, N.J.," in "Nineteenth Annual Report . . . ," *N.J. Leg. Docs.*, 116th (1892), IV, Doc. 21, p. 329. The Annual Report of the Essex County Board of Agriculture stated: "We want equal representation as well as equal taxation. Since the late gerrymander of our County Board of Freeholders, the farming townships of this county are totally deprived of representation in the county government, and we want this piece of political trickery rectified," *ibid.*, p. 449.

9

RISE AND FALL OF THE
ASSEMBLY DISTRICT APPROACH:
ESSEX AND HUDSON, 1889–1894

1. *Newark Evening News*, March 13, 1889.
2. *Ibid.*, March 14, 1889.
3. *NJAM*, 113th, March 26, 1889, pp. 590–591; *NJSJ*, 113th, April 1, 1889, p. 550.
4. *Newark Evening News*, April 2, 1889; *NJSJ*, 113th, April 1, 1889, p. 627. The bill was amended on April 18, but never came to a final vote.
5. *L.* 1889, c. 114, pp. 163–166.
6. *Evening Journal* (Jersey City), April 3, 1889.
7. *New York Times*, October 16, 1889.
8. *Mortland* v. *Christian*, 52 N.J.L. 521 (1890).
9. *Ibid.*, p. 537.
10. *Ibid.*, p. 539.
11. *Ibid.*
12. *Evening Journal* (Jersey City), February 17, 1892.
13. *NJAM*, 116th, March 1, 1892, p. 503 lists one member on both sides; *NJSJ*, 116th, March 2, 1892, p. 431.
14. *L.* 1892, c. 57, pp. 91–92.

15. *Newark Evening News*, March 6, 1893; *L.* 1891, c. 246, pp. 469–471. According to *Evening Journal* (Jersey City), February 26, 1891, the bill's sponsor "thinks that if the freeholders are voted for at the municipal elections the trading which it is claimed was indulged in at recent elections will be rendered impossible."

16. *Newark Evening News*, March 6, 1893.

17. *L.* 1893, c. 143, pp. 258–260.

18. *L.* 1889, c. 181, pp. 115–130.

19. *Newark Evening News*, November 11, 1889.

20. *L.* 1891, c. 182, p. 346.

21. *Newark Evening News*, November 11, 1889; April 15, 1893.

22. *Ibid.*, November 11, 1889; *Evening Journal* (Jersey City), November 4, 1891; *Newark Evening News*, October 25, 1889.

23. *Evening Journal* (Jersey City), November 11, 1889.

24. *L.* 1891, c. 182, p. 354.

25. *Evening Journal* (Jersey City), April 15, 1893. In an election dispute between candidates in the Eleventh Assembly District, the County Board of Canvassers decided in favor of the Democrat, *New York Times*, April 16, 1893, and the board's director at large ordered him seated, *Evening Journal* (Jersey City), May 10, 1893.

26. *Evening Journal* (Jersey City), November 11, 1889; April 15, 1893.

27. *Ibid.*, November 9, 1889, November 4, 1891; The Evening News, *The Evening News and Hoboken* (Evening News: Hoboken, 1893), p. 148.

28. 56 N.J.L. 186 (1893).

29. *Newark Evening News*, November 11, 1893.

30. *Passaic Daily News*, November 17, 1893.

31. *Evening Journal* (Jersey City), December 22, 1893.

32. *Ibid.*

33. *Newark Daily Advertiser*, November 16, 1893.

34. *Newark Evening News*, November 23, 1893.

35. *Newark Daily Advertiser*, November 23, 1893.

36. *Ibid.*, January 5, 1894.

37. *Passaic Daily News*, January 12, 1894.

38. *Daily Fredonian* (New Brunswick), March 27, 1894.

39. *Newark Evening News*, March 27, 1894.

40. *NJAM*, 118th, March 26, 1894, p. 254; *Newark Daily Advertiser*, March 27, 1894.

41. *NJAM*, 118th, March 26, 1894, pp. 254–255; *Newark Daily Advertiser*, March 27, 1894.

42. *Newark Evening News*, March 27, 1894.

43. *NJAM*, 118th, March 26, 1894, pp. 255; *Newark Daily Advertiser*, March 27, 1894.

44. *Newark Evening News*, March 27, 1894.

45. *Newark Daily Advertiser*, March 27, 1894.

46. See Committee Substitute for Assembly Bill No. 213, N.J. State Law Library; *Newark Daily Advertiser*, March 28, 1894.

47. *Daily True American* (Trenton), March 28, 1894.

48. *Newark Evening News*, March 28, 1894.

49. *NJAM*, 118th, March 24, 1894, pp. 282–283.

50. *Newark Daily Advertiser*, March 28, 1894; *NJSJ*, 118th, March 27, 28, 1894, pp. 128–129.

51. *Newark Evening News*, March 30, 1894; *NJAM*, 118th, March 29, 1894, p. 136.
52. *Daily Times* (New Brunswick), March 30, 1894.
53. *Daily True American* (Trenton), April 3, 1894.
54. *NJSJ*, 118th, April 2, 1894, p. 151.
55. *Daily True American* (Trenton), April 3, 1894; *NJAM*, 118th, April 2, 1894, p. 306.
56. *Newark Daily Advertiser*, April 3, 1894.
57. *NJAM*, 118th, April 9, 1894, pp. 365–366.
58. *Daily True American* (Trenton), March 28, 1894.
59. *NJAM*, 118th, March 27, 1894, p. 271.
60. *NJSJ*, 118th, March 28, 1894, p. 130.
61. *Newark Evening News*, March 30, 1894; *Daily Times* (New Brunswick), March 30, 1894.
62. *NJSJ*, 118th, April 2, 1894, pp. 149–150.
63. *NJAM*, 118th, April 9, 1894, p. 368.
64. *Evening Journal* (Jersey City), April 14, 1894; *Newark Daily Advertiser*, April 14, 1894.
65. *Newark Evening News*, April 17, 1884; *NJSJ*, 118th, April 17, 18, 1894, pp. 249, 285.
66. *Newark Evening News*, April 20, 1894; *Daily True American* (Trenton), April 20, 1894; *New York Times*, April 20, 1894.
67. *NJSJ*, 118th, April 19, 1894, p. 296.
68. *Ibid.; Daily True American* (Trenton), April 20, 1894.
69. *Daily True American* (Trenton), April 20, 1894; *Newark Evening News*, April 20, 1894.
70. *NJSJ*, 118th, April 23, 1894, p. 337; *Newark Evening News*, April 24, 1894.
71. *NJSJ*, 118th, April 24, 1894, p. 352; *Daily True American* (Trenton), April 25, 1894. See Substitute for Senate Bill No. 152, N.J. State Law Library.
72. *NJSJ*, 118th, April 27, 1894, p. 415; *Newark Daily Advertiser*, April 27, 1894.
73. *Evening Journal* (Jersey City), May 4, 1894.
74. *Newark Evening News*, May 9, 1894.
75. *Ibid.; NJSJ*, 118th, May 9, 1894, p. 573.
76. *Evening Journal* (Jersey City), May 10, 1894; *NJAM*, 118th, May 9, 1894, p. 837.
77. *NJSJ*, 118th, May 14, 1894, pp. 643–644.
78. *Ibid.*, May 15, 1894, p. 674; *NJAM*, 118th, May 16, 1894, p. 968; *L.* 1894, c. 234, pp. 335–358.
79. *L.* 1894, c. 259, pp. 387–389.
80. *Newark Evening News*, May 16, 1894.
81. *Ibid.*, November 7, 1894.
82. *New York Times*, August 31, 1894.
83. *Ibid.*, September 2, 1894.
84. *Evening Journal* (Jersey City), October 1, 1894.
85. *Newark Evening News*, September 27, 1894: "Justice Dixon this morning filed a memorandum deciding the certiorari proceedings brought by the Democrats of Newark, in the name of Michael F. McLaughlin, attacking the law under which the Ward Line Commissioners were ap-

pointed. The memorandum reads: 'The proceedings brought us for review are legal and should be affirmed.' " The Supreme Court's opinion was subsequently filed. *McLaughlin* v. *Newark*, 57 N.J.L. 298 (1894).

86. *Evening Journal* (Jersey City), October 1, 1894.

87. *Ibid.*, November 14, December 7, 1894.

88. *Griffin* v. *Wanser*, 57 N.J.L. 535 (1895).

89. *Evening Journal* (Jersey City), November 7, 1896. The legislative body of any *city* in the state was given power by ordinance to "divide said city up into wards and to change the boundaries of the *present* [italics added] wards and aldermanic districts therein, and to increase the number of wards therein, *provided* that the number of wards shall not exceed sixteen in any city. . . ."

10

RISE AND FALL OF THE ASSEMBLY DISTRICT APPROACH: PASSAIC, CAMDEN, AND MERCER, 1892–1894

1. Quoted in *Daily True American* (Trenton), February 8, 1890.

2. *Daily True American* (Trenton), *loc. cit.*

3. *Newark Evening News*, March 3, 1892.

4. *Daily True American* (Trenton), March 3, 1892.

5. *NJAM*, 116th, March 2, 1892, pp. 552–553; *NJSJ*, 116th, March 2, 1892, p. 443; *Newark Evening News*, March 3, 1892.

6. *L.* 1892, c. 69, pp. 125–127.

7. *Passaic Daily News*, March 4, 1892. Hood lost the election, *Daily State Gazette* (Trenton), March 10, 1892.

8. "In Mercer County the Democrats made no contest for Chosen Freeholders, because they knew that the new law for the election of Freeholders by legislative districts would come into force," *Daily True American* (Trenton), March 10, 1892.

9. *L.* 1892, c. 67, pp. 120–121.

10. *NJSJ*, 116th, March 10, 1892, p. 553; *NJAM*, 116th, March 11, 1892, p. 787 records 33 votes in the affirmative, but lists only 32 names.

11. *Daily Times* (New Brunswick), April 13, 1892; *Evening Journal* (Jersey City), April 13, 1892; *Daily True American* (Trenton), April 13, 1892.

12. *New York Times*, April 13, 1892; *Evening Journal* (Jersey City), April 13, 1892; *Daily State Gazette* (Trenton), April 15, 1892. Ironically, at the Mercer board's organization meeting, the slate proposed by Lanning and another Abbett lieutenant was defeated, and the assemblyman himself failed to obtain the position of county collector, *New York Times*, May 12, 1892. He "has assumed the airs of a boss rather too offensive to suit his party, and this rap on the head is a hint to him to be more modest," noted the *Daily State Gazette* (Trenton), May 12, 1892.

13. *Passaic Daily News*, April 13, 1892.

14. Two persons (not really holdovers) elected on March 8 by Clifton and Pompton, respectively, were not seated, because "the new members looked with great disfavor on the prospect of having [them] in the board for

two years more, which would postpone the payments of the six-hundred-dollar salary for that length of time," *New York Times*, May 12, 1892.

15. *Elizabeth Daily Journal*, February 11, 1892. The incorrect population figure (70,000) was apparently taken from an editorial in the *Daily State Gazette* (Trenton), February 11, 1892.

16. *Elizabeth Daily Journal*, February 29, 1892.

17. *Ibid.*, March 4, 1892.

18. *Compendium of Censuses*, pp. 34, 27, 17, 39, 30–31.

19. *Jersey City News*, quoted in *Elizabeth Daily Journal*, March 4, 1892; *Evening Journal* (Jersey City), March 3, 1892; *Daily State Gazette* (Trenton), March 3, 1892.

20. *Newark Evening News*, March 3, 1892.

21. See Senate Bill No. 212, bill file, N.J. State Law Library.

22. *NJSJ*, 116th, March 7, 1892, p. 458. In the Assembly, J. Parker (R-Passaic) is recorded both affirmatively and negatively, *NJAM*, 116th, March 7, 1892, p. 594.

23. *Paterson Press*, quoted in *Passaic Daily News*, March 5, 1892.

24. *Passaic Daily News*, May 10, 1893.

25. *NJAM*, 118th, February 27, 1894, p. 173.

26. *Ibid.*

27. *Passaic Daily News*, March 24, 1894.

28. *Ibid.*

29. *Daily Times* (New Brunswick), March 28, 1894.

30. *NJSJ*, 118th, March 27, 1894, p. 113.

31. *Newark Evening News*, March 28, 1894.

32. *Daily Times* (New Brunswick), March 28, 1894; *Newark Evening News*, March 28, 1894.

33. *NJAM*, 118th, March 27, 1894, p. 268.

34. *Trenton Times*, April 2, 1894.

35. *Daily True American* (Trenton), April 3, 1894; *NJSJ*, 118th, April 2, 1894, pp. 139, 152; *NJAM*, 118th, April 2, 1894, pp. 295–296.

36. *Daily True American* (Trenton), April 3, 1894.

37 *Trenton Times*, April 3, 1894.

38. *Ibid.*

39. *NJSJ*, 118th, April 3, 1894, p. 162; *NJAM*, 118th, April 3, 1894, p. 320. "The [Assembly] Democrats protested that they had been allowed no chance to examine the measure, or be heard in a discussion of the merits," *Newark Daily Advertiser*, April 3, 1894.

40. *NJSJ*, 118th, April 25, 1894, pp. 378–379.

41. *NJSJ*, 118th, April 9, 25, 1894, pp. 201, 379.

42. *Passaic Daily News*, April 4, 1894.

43. *Ibid.*, May 13, 1894.

44. *Ibid.*, April 4, 1894.

45. *Ibid.*

46. *Daily True American* (Trenton), April 12, 1894.

47. *Daily True American* (Trenton), April 20, 1894; *NJSJ*, 118th, April 19, 1894, p. 311.

48. *NJAM*, 118th, April 25, 1894, p. 613; *Passaic Daily News*, April 26, 1894.

49. *Passaic Daily News*, *loc. cit.*

50. *NJSJ*, 118th, May 2, 1894, pp. 495–496.
51. *Newark Daily Advertiser*, May 9, 1894.
52. *NJSJ*, 118th, May 8, 1894, p. 560.
53. *Trenton Times*, May 9, 1894.
54. *Ibid.; Passaic Daily News*, May 10, 1894;*NJAM*, 118th, May 9, 1894, p. 832; William Harrigan (D-Hudson) later obtained unanimous consent of the Assembly to be recorded in the negative, *ibid.*, p. 835. After the 1895 *state* census showed that the 75,000 population figure had finally been exceeded in Union (85,404) and Monmouth (75,743), they were exempted from application of the act. The population figures were required to be supplied by the last preceeding *federal* census. In addition, a borough with complete autonomy of local government would need to have 1,200 inhabitants in order to elect its own freeholder, *L.* 1896, c. 30, p. 57, introduced as Assembly Bill No. 112 by J. Martin Roll (R-Union).
55. *NJAM*, 118th, May 9, 1894, p. 838.
56. *NJSJ*, 118th, May 14, 1894, p. 650.
57. *NJSJ*, 118th, May 15, 1894, p. 683; *NJAM*, 118th, May 16, 1894, pp. 981–982.
58. *NJAM*, 118th, May 23, 1894, p. 1054.
59. *NJAM*, 118th, May 24, 1894, p. 1074; *NJSJ*, 118th, May 25, 1894, p. 791.
60. *L.* 1894, c. 344, p. 530.
61. *Passaic Daily News*, October 12, 1894.
62. *New York Times*, October 28, 1894.
63. *Davis* v. *Davis*, 57 N.J.L. 80 (1894).
64. *New York Times*, October 28, 1894.
65. *Trenton Times*, November 13, 1894.
66. *Passaic Daily News*, October 12, 1894.
67. *New York Times*, November 28, 1894; *Newark Daily Advertiser*, November 28, 1894.
68. *Davis* v. *Davis*, 57 N.J.L. 203, 206 (1894).
69. *Passaic Daily News*, December 1, 1894.

11

THE SEARCH FOR SMALLER BOARDS —WITH VARIATIONS: PROPOSALS FOR AT LARGE ELECTIONS, OPTIONAL LAWS, MINORITY REPRESENTATION, 1894–1900

1. *Daily Fredonian* (New Brunswick), January 28, 1895.
2. *Ibid.*
3. *Ibid.*, March 7, 1895.
4. *Ibid.*
5. *Evening Journal* (Jersey City), January 20, 1897.
6. *Ibid.*, January 26, 1897.
7. *Newark Evening News*, January 26, 1897. "At first it was intended to have the Supreme Court Justice in each county appoint the members, but Hudson objected because it has a Democratic Judge," *ibid.*

8. *Evening Journal* (Jersey City), January 26, 1897.

9. *Ibid.* One example of inexpertise: The bill "also provides that the [financial] statement shall be published in at least one newspaper in each legislative district in the county. This provision may have been drawn by some Rip Van Winkle, who did not know that there were no legislative districts, or by some person gifted with prophetic instincts who knew that a constitutional amendment would be adopted two years hence, providing for the creation of legislative districts," *ibid.*

10. *Newark Evening News,* January 27, 1897.

11. *Evening Journal* (Jersey City), July 24, 1897.

12. *Ibid.,* September 8, 1897.

13. *Ibid.,* September 23, 1897.

14. Quoted in *ibid.,* August 31, 1897.

15. *Ibid.*

16. *Newark Daily Advertiser,* January 27, 1897.

17. *NJSJ,* 121st, March 10, 1897; *Evening Journal* (Jersey City), March 11, 1897. Committee Substitute for Senate Bill No. 41, in the bill file of the N.J. State Law Library, required the election of three persons in all counties with a population of less than 80,000 and five persons in all counties with a population of more than 80,000. A voter would cast ballots for two or three candidates, respectively. Freeholders in fourth-class counties would be paid an annual salary of $400; in third-class counties, with fewer than 35,000 inhabitants, $600; in counties with more than 35,000 inhabitants and in all second-class counties, $1,000; and in first-class counties, $2,000. But these provisions were not mentioned in the major newspapers or in any other source that was examined.

18. *Evening Journal* (Jersey City), March 19, 1897.

19. *Daily State Gazette* (Trenton), March 19, 1897; *NJSJ,* 121st, March 18, 1897, p. 322.

20. *Newark Daily Advertiser,* March 23, 1897.

21. *Ibid.; NJSJ,* 121st, March 23, 1897, p. 353.

22. *NJSJ,* 121st, March 23, 1897, p. 397.

23. *Ibid.,* March 25, 1897, p. 417; *Newark Daily Advertiser,* March 26, 1897.

24. *NJSJ,* 121st, March 29, 1897, pp. 441–442.

25. *Daily True American* (Trenton), March 30, 1897.

26. *Evening Journal* (Jersey City), March 1, 1898.

27. *Ibid.*

28. *Hudson County Dispatch* (Town of Union), quoted in *ibid.,* January 22, 1898.

29. *Evening Journal* (Jersey City), January 22, 1898.

30. *Ibid.,* March 1, 1898.

31. *NJAM,* 122nd, March 9, 1898, p. 279.

32. *Newark Evening News,* January 17,1899.

33. *Evening Journal* (Jersey City), January 17, 1899.

34. *Newark Evening News,* January 18, 1899.

35. See Substitute for Senate Bill No. 6, N.J. State Law Library.

36. *Daily True American* (Trenton), March 23, 1899.

37. *NJSJ,* 123rd, March 22, 1899, p. 373.

38. *Evening Journal* (Jersey City), March 23, 1899.

39. *Ibid.,* March 29, 1899.

40. *Ibid.*, October 14, 1899.
41. *Ibid.*, January 11, 1900. That statute assigned one freeholder to every ward of each incorporated town of 8,000 inhabitants which was not already divided into wards. Every third-class city (over 12,000 population) not previously divided was to be similarly represented, but Hudson contained none.
42. *Ibid.*, January 5, 1900. *L.* 1895, c. 152, pp. 311–312, authorized the increase of the "present" wards of cities or change in ward boundary lines but did not authorize subsequent alterations. See p. 332, n. 89. For a five-year period after such changes, no others could be made, *L.* 1899, c. 164, pp. 361–362. Only by annexation could a city increase its ward representation. *L.* 1888, c. 230, p. 336; *L.* 1900, c. 83, p. 159. In 1899, for example, Camden gained its Eleventh and Twelfth Wards by annexing Stockton Township, A. Charles Corotis and James M. O'Neill, *Camden County Centennial, 1844–1944* (Camden, N.J.: Board of Chosen Freeholders, 1944), p. 119. Trenton's Fourteenth Ward resulted from the annexation of part of Ewing Township in 1900, Hirsch, *op. cit.*, p. 358.
43. *Evening Journal* (Jersey City), January 8, 1900.
44. *Ibid.*
45. *Ibid.*, January 11, 1900.
46. *Ibid.*
47. *Ibid.*, February 9, 1900.
48. *NJSJ*, 124th, February 13, 1900, pp. 97–98.
49. *Evening Journal* (Jersey City), February 15, 1900.
50. *Ibid.*, February 27, 1900.
51. *NJSJ*, 124th, February 27, 1900, pp. 172–173.
52. *Evening Journal* (Jersey City), February 28, 1900.
53. *NJAM*, 124th, March 6, 1900, p. 263.
54. *Newark Evening News*, March 7, 1900.
55. *L.* 1900, c. 14, pp. 30–31.
56. *Evening Journal* (Jersey City), March 9, 1900.
57. *Ibid.*, March 15, 1900.
58. *Ibid.*, March 16, 1900.
59. *Ibid.*, November 15, 1900.
60. *Ibid.*
61. *Newark Evening News*, February 12, 1900.
62. *Ibid.*, February 13, 1900.
63. *Ibid.*, March 6, 1900.
64. *NJAM*, 124th, March 15, 1900, p. 357; *Newark Daily Advertiser*, March 16, 1900.
65. *L.* 1900, c. 89, pp. 168–173.
66. *NJSJ*, 124th, March 20, 1900, p. 332.
67. *Ibid.*, March 20, 1900, p. 388.
68. *NJAM*, March 22, 1900, p. 508.
69. At first Renner's counsel would not tell the press why the act was to be considered special, *Evening Journal* (Jersey City), January 22, 1902.
70. *Ibid.*, June 14, 1902.
71. *Renner v. Holmes*, 68 N.J.L. 192, 196 (1902).
72. *Evening Journal* (Jersey City), October 6, 1902.
73. *Ibid.*, October 7, 1902.
74. *Ibid.*

12

"THE OLD ORDER CHANGETH," 1900–1902

1. *Compendium of Censuses,* p. 41. See pp. 14, 31, 39. See above, pp. 174–176.
2. The estimate varied from 36 to 38 to 39, *Elizabeth Daily Journal,* February 27, March 18, March 23, 1901.
3. *L.* 1895, c. 343, pp. 690–691.
4. *NJAM,* 125th, March 19, 1901, pp. 420–421; compare text of Official Copy Reprint, Committee Substitute for Assembly Bill No. 301, N.J. State Law Library, with text as enacted.
5. *NJSJ,* 125th, March 22, 1901, p. 446.
6. *Elizabeth Daily Journal,* March 23, 1901; *L.* 1901, c. 166, pp. 360–361.
7. *Home News* (New Brunswick), November 7, 1901.
8. *Ibid.,* February 26, 1901.
9. *Newark Evening News,* February 20, 1902.
10. *Daily Press* (New Brunswick), March 10, 1902.
11. *Home News* (New Brunswick), November 6, 1901.
12. *Ibid.,* January 22, 1901.
13. *Evening Journal* (Jersey City), January 26, 1901.
14. *Home News* (New Brunswick), March 23, 1901.
15. *Trenton Times,* as quoted in *ibid.,* February 12, 1902.
16. *NJSJ,* 126th, February 25, 1902, p. 114.
17. *NJSJ,* 126th, March 4, 1902, pp. 156–157; *Daily State Gazette* (Trenton), March 5, 1902; *Home News* (New Brunswick), March 5, 1902.
18. *NJSJ,* 126th, March 5, 1902, p. 189.
19. *Newark Evening News,* March 11, 1902; *Evening Journal* (Jersey City), March 11, 1902.
20. *Daily State Gazette* (Trenton), March 11, 1902; Johnson had been a freeholder in Camden, *N.J. Leg. Manual, 1902,* p. 264.
21. *Daily True American* (Trenton), March 11, 1902; *Newark Evening News,* March 11, 1902.
22. *NJSJ,* 126th, March 10, 1902, p. 206.
23. *Newark Evening News,* March 18, 1902.
24. *Ibid.*
25. *NJAM,* 126th, March 18, 1902, p. 333.
26. *Newark Evening News,* March 18, 1902; *Daily State Gazette* (Trenton), March 19, 1902.
27. *Newark Evening News,* March 18, 1902.
28. *Daily State Gazette* (Trenton), March 19, 1902.
29. *Newark Evening News,* March 18, 1902.
30. *NJAM,* 126th, March 18, 1902, p. 333; *Newark Daily Advertiser,* March 18, 1902.
31. *NJAM,* 126th, March 18, 1902, p. 337; *Daily State Gazette* (Trenton), March 19, 1902.
32. *NJAM,* 126th, March 18, 1902, p. 338; *Newark Evening News,* March 18, 1902. " 'But $500 a year is more than $1.25 a day,' said Mr. Stalter. 'Or maybe Burlington freeholders work Sundays. We take a little time for

religion in Passaic.' 'Well, I'm glad to hear there's some religion in Passaic,' retorted Mr. Horner," *ibid.*

33. *Home News* (New Brunswick), March 18, 1902.
34. *NJAM*, 126th, March 18, 1902, p. 338.
35. *Newark Sunday News*, March 23, 1902.
36. *Newark Evening News*, March 25, 1902.
37. *Newark Daily Advertiser*, March 25, 1902.
38. *Newark Evening News*, March 25, 1902.
39. *Home News* (New Brunswick), March 25, 1902.
40. *Newark Daily Advertiser*, March 25, 1902.
41. *Newark Evening News*, March 25, 1902.
42. *Newark Daily Advertiser*, March 25, 1902. Every newspaper consulted records this as the vote; but the official count, 32 to 24, includes Frederick Weismann (D-Hudson) in the majority, *NJAM*, 126th, March 24, 1902. He is not listed as voting at all in the newspaper tabulations that could be found, *Newark Daily Advertiser, loc. cit.; Daily Press* (New Brunswick), March 24, 1902. Moreover, Weismann had always voted to support the original text of the bill.
43. *Elizabeth Daily Journal*, March 25, 1902.
44. *Newark Daily Advertiser*, March 25, 1902.
45. *L.* 1902, c. 34, pp. 65–68.
46. *Evening Journal* (Jersey City), October 6, 1902.
47. *Ibid.*, October 18, 1902.
48. *Ibid.*, November 12, 1902.
49. *Ibid.*, November 26, 1902.
50. *Bergen Evening Record* (Hackensack), April 2, 1902.
51. *Ibid.*, October 29, 1902. Hackensack (town) had a single freeholder, because it was coextensive with, and officially known as, New Barbadoes *township.* Englewood was entitled to two freeholders, as a *city, L.* 1881, c. 198, pp. 252–253. Rutherford *borough* could elect a freeholder, since it had more than 3,000 inhabitants, *L.* 1897, c. 161, p. 285. Englewood Cliffs had been incorporated as a borough in 1895; and Englewood, as a city, in 1896. Both were originally within the borders of Englewood township. Subsequently claiming to be the only remaining part of the township, the borough elected a freeholder for that *parent township;* and its right to do so was upheld by the Court of Errors and Appeals, Frances A. Westervelt, *History of Bergen County, New Jersey, 1630–1923* (New York: Lewis Historical Publishing Co., Inc., 1923), I, 355–356; James J. Greco, *The Story of Englewood Cliffs* (Englewood Cliffs, N.J.: Tercentenary Committee, 1964), p. 52.
52. *Bergen Evening Record* (Hackensack), November 7, 1902.
53. *Dover Index*, April 18, 1902.
54. *Ibid.*, July 25, 1902.
55. *Ibid.*, November 14, 1902.
56. *Home News* (New Brunswick), November 3, 1902.
57. *Ibid.*, November 3, July 31, October 30, 1902.
58. *Ibid.*, July 31, 1902.
59. *Ibid.*, October 30, November 3, 1902.
60. *Ibid.*, November 7, 1902.
61. *Newark Evening News*, November, 8, 1902.

62. *Home News* (New Brunswick), November 15, 1902.
63. *Hunterdon County Democrat* (Flemington), June 17, 1902.
64. *Hunterdon Republican* (Flemington), October 29, 1902.
65. *Hunterdon County Democrat* (Flemington), November 11, 1902.
66. *Ibid.*, November 18, 1902. The Strong Act's confusing system for voting required that "there shall be printed on each official ballot . . . the proposition, 'For the law reducing the number of freeholders,' and immediately thereunder the proposition 'Against the number of freeholders,' and the voter may vote to adopt this act by obliterating the second proposition or may vote to reject this act by obliterating the first proposition. . . ." *L.* 1902, c. 34, p. 68.
67. *Clinton Democrat,* as quoted in *Hunterdon County Democrat* (Flemington), November 18, 1902.
68. *Hunterdon Gazette* (High Bridge), as quoted in *Hunterdon County Democrat* (Flemington), November 18, 1902.
69. *Hunterdon County Democrat* (Flemington), December 2, 1902.
70. *Hackettstown Gazette,* December 12, 1902.
71. *Hunterdon County Democrat* (Flemington), December 9, 1902.
72. *Clinton Democrat,* as quoted in *ibid.*
73. *Hunterdon County Democrat* (Flemington), April 14, 1903.
74. *Ibid.*
75. *Ibid.*, April 14, 1903.
76. *Democrat Advertiser* (Flemington), April 16, 1903.
77. As quoted in *Hunterdon County Democrat* (Flemington), May 26, 1903.
78. *Clinton Democrat,* as quoted in *Democrat Advertiser* (Flemington), June 4, 1903.
79. *Clinton Democrat,* as cited in *Democrat Advertiser* (Flemington), June 18, 1903.
80. *Democrat Advertiser,* (Flemington), July 2, 1903.
81. *Hunterdon County Democrat* (Flemington), November 10, 1903; *North Plainfield Weekly Review,* September 26, 1903.

13

OPTIONAL vs. MANDATORY SMALL BOARDS, 1903–1966

1. *L.* 1879, c. 15, p. 27.
2. Shank and Reock, *op. cit.,* p. 90 (Table 19).
3. *Daily Home News* (New Brunswick), May 25, 1904, p.1, col. 7.
4. *Matawan Journal,* July 30, 1903, p. 1, col. 5.
5. *Asbury Park Press,* July 31, 1903, p. 8, col. 3.
6. *The Journal* (Asbury Park), April 6, 1904, p. 1, col. 5.
7. *Daily Home News* (New Brunswick), December 3, 1904, [p. 1], col. 1.
8. *Daily Press* (New Brunswick), December 13, 1904, [p. 1], col. 1.
9. *Daily Times* (New Brunswick), November 16, 1904, p. 7, col. 6.
10. *Newark Evening News,* as quoted in *Passaic Daily News,* May 24, 1904, p. 4, col. 4.

11. *Newark Evening News*, as quoted in *Passaic Daily News*, September 1, 1904, p. 4, col. 3.

12. *Passaic Daily News*, August 27, 1904, p. 4, col. 3.

13. *Ibid.*, October 7, 1904, p. 4, col. 3.

14. *Ibid.*, November 7, 1904, p. 1, cols. 2–5.

15. *Ibid.*, November 12, 1904, p. 1, col. 3.

16. As quoted in *ibid.*, November 16, 1904, p. 4, col. 3.

17. *Ibid.*

18. *Ibid.*

19. *L.* 1905, c. 20, pp. 41–42.

20. Computed by the author from 1905 election statistics in *N.J. Leg. Manual, 1905*, pp. 497, 507.

21. *Daily State Gazette* (Trenton), October 28, 1903, p. 1, col. 1.

22. As quoted in *Passaic Daily News*, November 1, 1904, p. 4, col. 3.

23. *Ibid.*

24. As quoted in *Daily Press* (New Brunswick), November 16, 1904, [p. 1], col. 5.

25. *Trenton Evening Times*, November 17, 1904, p. 7, col. 3.

26. *Ibid.*

27. *Ibid.*, November 12, 1904, p. 4, col. 2.

28. *State v. Wrightson*, 56 N.J.L. 186 (1893).

29. *Trenton Evening Times*, September 19, 1904, p. 4, col. 2.

30. Quoted in *Passaic Daily News*, August 26, 1904, p. 1, col. 4.

31. *Passaic Daily News*, November 18, 1904, p. 4, col. 1, identifies the political complexion of the freeholder constituencies; *ibid.*, p. 1, col. 4, supplies official election results; *ibid.*, November 12, 1904 presents the election returns by districts.

32. *Passaic Daily News*, Ocotber 10, 1904, p. 4, col. 2.

33. *Ibid.*, November 7, 1904, p. 1, cols. 2–5.

34. There were 11,237 votes in 1904, *Daily Times* (New Brunswick), November 16, 1904, p. 7, col. 6, as opposed to 10,910 in the earlier referendum, *Home News* (New Brunswick), November 7, 1902, p. [8], cols. 3–6.

35. *Daily Times* (New Brunswick), November 16, 1904, p. 7, cols. 3–6.

36. *Home News* (New Brunswick), March 9, 1904, p. 1, col. 1; *N.J. Leg. Manual, 1904*, pp. 496–497.

37. Quoted in *Passaic Daily News*, November 1, 1904, p. 4, col. 3.

38. *Daily True American* (Trenton), November 4, 1903, p. 1, col. 6.

39. *New Jersey Law Journal*, XXVIII (August, 1905), 226–227.

40. *Trenton Evening Times*, September 18, 1905, p. 4, col. 1.

41. *Ibid.*, November 17, 1905, p. 4, col. 2; *New Jersey Law Journal*, XXVIII (December, 1905), 382.

42. *Hoboken* v. *O'Neill*, 74 N.J.L. 58 (1906).

43. *Trenton Evening Times*, January 16, 1907, p. 4, col. 2.

44. *L.* 1907, c. 2, p. 12; c. 3, pp. 12–13; *NJAM*, 131st, January 23, 1907, p. 73; *Weekly State Gazette* (Trenton), January 31, 1907, p. 3, col. 7.

45. Monmouth 1905: 3,911 to 2,752 (official), *The Journal* (Asbury Park), November 16, 1905, p. 1, col. 3; Essex, 1910: 33,616 to 15,804, *Newark Evening News*, November 9, 1910, p. 4, col. 4; Bergen, 1905: "defeated by more than 1,800 in a light vote," *Bergen Evening Record*, November 14, 1905, p. 1, cols. 3–5; Ocean, 1905: 709 to 1,599 (official), *New Jersey Courier*

(Toms River), November 16, 1905, p. 4, cols. 4–6; Warren, 1905: "defeated by a decisive vote," *Blairstown Press*, November 22, 1905, p. 3, col. 3; Somerset, 1906: 1, 561 to 1,706 (official), *The Unionist Gazette* (Somerville), November 15, 1906, p. 1, cols. 1–2; Burlington, 1907: 2,048 to 3,816 (official), *New Jersey Mirror* (Mt. Holly), November 13, 1907, [p. 3], cols. 5–7; Bergen, 1908: 5,151 to 8,983, *Bergen Evening Record*, November 13, 1908, p. 2, cols. 1–3; Sussex, 1909: 1,502 to 1,822 (official), *Wantage Recorder*, November 12, 1909, p. 4, cols. 2–3; Somerset, 1910: 1,898 to 3,190, *The Unionist Gazette* (Somerville), November 17, 1910, p. 4, col. 4; Sussex, 1910: 1,573 to 1,769, *Sussex Independent* (Deckertown), November 10, 1910, p. 1, cols. 4–5.

46. *Jersey Journal* (Jersey City), quoted in *Hunterdon Republican*, May 11, 1910, p. 2, col. 1.

47. Lewis T. Stevens, *New Jersey Commission Law (Walsh Act) and Municipal Manager Law*, supp. to sixth ed., (Newark, N.J.: Soney & Sage Co., 1935), p. 7.

48. The other five municipalities were Hawthorne boro (Passaic); Margate City (Atlantic); Ocean City (Cape May); Passaic City (Passaic), and Ridgewood village (Bergen), *ibid.*, pp. 6–7.

49. *Jersey Journal* (Jersey City), November 8, 1911, p. 1, col. 2.

50. Bergen, 1911: 8, 807 to 5,240 (official), *ibid.*, November 16, 1911, p. 7, col. 2; Burlington, 1911: 4,647 to 2,416 (official), *New Jersey Mirror* (Mt. Holly), November 15, 1911, p. 4, cols. 5–7; Mercer, 1911: "The majority for the county commission government proposition was 4,088," *Daily State Gazette* (Trenton), November 9, 1911, p. 1, col. 5; Morris, 1911: "Reports from all districts in the county show a majority of nine votes in favor of the Smaller Board of Freeholders," *Daily Record* (Morristown), November 10, 1911, p. 1, col. 3; Sussex, 1911: 1,955 to 1,775, *Sussex Independent* (Deckertown), November 10, 1911, p. 1, cols. 3–4; Union, 1911: 4,853 to 2,913, *Plainfield Courier-News*, November 8, 1911, p. 4, col. 1.

51. *Bergen Evening Record* (Hackensack), November 16, 1911, p. 1, col. 1.

52. *L.* 1908, c. 164, pp. 269–271.

53. *NJSJ*, 132nd, April 7, 1908, p. 778.

54. *Trenton Evening Times*, November 15, 1911, p. 1, col. 5.

55. *Bergen Evening Record* (Hackensack), November 16, 1911, p. 1, col. 1.

56. *Trenton Evening Times*, November 16, 1911, p. 6, col. 2.

57. *Ibid.*, November 15, 1911, p. 1, col. 5.

58. *Ibid.*, November 16, 1911, p. 6, col. 2; *Bergen Evening Record* (Hackensack), November 16, 1911, p. 1. col. 1.

59. *Trenton Evening Times*, March 21, 1912, p. 1, col. 5.

60. *Pierson v. Cady*, 84 N.J.L. 54 (1913) at 59–60.

61. *Ibid.*, pp. 60–61.

62. *Ibid.*, p. 62.

63. *Ibid.*, pp. 61–62.

64. *Newark Evening News*, January 23, 1912, p. 4, col 6.

65. *Ibid.*

66. Quoted in *Trenton Evening Times*, August 31, 1907, p. 6, col. 3.

67. *Trenton Evening Times*, July 17, 1906, p. 4, col. 2.

68. *Ibid.*, January 15, 1907, p. 4, col. 2.

69. *Ibid.*, December 19, 1911, p. 6, col. 2.

70. Quoted in *New Jersey Courier* (Toms River), August 23, 1906, p. 2, col. 3.

71. *New Jersey Mirror* (Mt. Holly), November 15, 1911, [p. 2], col. 1.

72. The vote was 33,616 to 15, 804, *Newark Evening News*, November 9, 1910, p. 1, col. 5. The last large board elected on the day of the referendum would have 33 members, because Glen Ridge Borough had become entitled to separate representation, *ibid.*, p. 5, col. 1.

73. *Jersey Journal* (Jersey City), May 27, 1912, p. 16, col. 1. See also *ibid.*, May 29, 1912, p. 12, col. 1.

74. *NJSJ*, 136th, January 23, 1912, p. 65; *Jersey Journal* (Jersey City), January 24, 1912, p. 1, col. 3.

75. *Jersey Journal* (Jersey City), January 26, 1912, p. 1, col. 8.

76. *Ibid.*, January 27, 1912, p. 1, col. 8.

77. *Ibid.*, January 24, 1912, p. 3, col. 3.

78. *Ibid.*, February 1, 1912, p. 1, col. 6.

79. *Ibid.*, January 30, 1912, p. 1, col. 1.

80. Quoted in *ibid.*, January 30, 1912, p. 4, col. 1.

81. *Ibid.*, January 30, 1912, p. 1, col. 8; p. 4, col. 2.

82. *Ibid.*, February 21, 1912, p. 2, col. 1; *NJAM*, 136th, February 20, 1912, p. 343.

83. *Jersey Journal* (Jersey City), February 21, 1912, p. 1, col. 1.

84. *Ibid.*, p. 2., col. 2; *NJAM*, 136th, February 20, 1912, p. 351.

85. *Jersey Journal* (Jersey City), February 28, 1912, p. 1, col. 8.

86. *Ibid.*; *NJAM*, 136th, February 27, 1912, p. 446.

87. *Jersey Journal* (Jersey City), March 5, 1912, p. 1, col. 5; p. 3, col. 4.

88. *Ibid.*, March 7, 1912, p. 1, col. 4; *NJSJ*, 136th, March 6, 1912, p. 376.

89. *Jersey Journal* (Jersey City), March 7, 1912, p. 1, col. 5.

90. Veto message, March 14, 1912, in *NJSJ*, 136th, March 18, 1912, pp. 569–570.

91. *NJSJ*, 136th, March 18, 1912, p. 569; *NJAM*, 136th, March 20, 1912, pp. 1008–1009; *L.* 1912, c. 158, pp. 228–234.

92. *Jersey Journal* (Jersey City), March 27, 1912, p. 1, cols. 4–5.

93. Official results, *ibid.*, June 3, 1912, p. 1, col. 2; May 29, 1912, p. 1, col. 6.

94. *Pierson* v. *Cady*, 84 N.J.L. 54 (1913), at 62.

95. *Ibid.*

96. *Ibid.*, pp. 62–63.

97. *Trenton Evening Times*, March 19, 1913, p. 6, col. 1.

98. *NJAM*, 137th, March 19, 1913, p. 971; *NJSJ*, 137th, April 2, 1913, p. 1009. Cumberland is omitted in the account of *Trenton Evening Times*, April 3, 1913, p. 16, col. 2.

99. *NJSJ*, 137th, April 2, 1913, pp. 1009–1010.

100. *NJAM*, 137th, March 27, 1913, p. 1231.

101. *NJSJ*, 137th, April 2, 1913, pp. 1006–1008.

102. *NJAM*, 137th, April 3, 1913, p. 1582.

103. *New Jersey Mirror* (Mt. Holly), April 16, 1913, [p. 3], col. 4.

104. *NJSJ*, 137th, May 6, 1913, p. 1425.

105. *Ibid.*, p. 1429.

106. *Trenton Evening Times,* May 27, 1913, p. 1, col. 2.
107. *Ibid.,* p. 3, col. 5.
108. *NJAM,* 137th, May 9, 1913, p. 1984; May 19, 1913, pp. 2002–2004.
109. *Ibid.,* p. 2005.
110. *Trenton Evening Times,* May 27, 1913, p. 1, col. 2; p. 3, col. 5.
111. *NJAM,* 137th, August 5, 1913, p. 2083.
112. *Ibid.,* August 12, 1913, p. 2111; *Newark Evening News,* August 12, 1913, p. 1, col. 8. The Bergen vote was 4,940 to 1,897, *Trenton Evening Times,* July 26, 1913, p. 6, col. 1.
113. *Trenton Evening Times,* August 1, 1913, p. 6, cols. 1–2; *ibid.,* August 5, 1913, p. 1, col. 8; p. 9, col. 4.
114. *Ibid.,* August 5, 1913, p. 1, col. 8.
115. *Newark Evening News,* August 12, 1913, p. 1, col. 8; p. 2, col. 5.
116. *Ibid.,* p. 2, col. 5.
117. *Trenton Evening Times,* August 5, 1913, p. 9, col. 4.
118. *Newark Evening News,* August 12, 1913, p. 2, col. 5.
119. *NJAM,* 137th, August 12, 1913, pp. 2114–2115.
120. *New Jersey Mirror* (Mt. Holly), August 13, 1913, [p. 2], col. 1. The official vote was 2,101 in favor of the small board; 2,233, against, *ibid.,* August 20, 1913, supplement, p. 1, col. 3.
121. *NJAM,* 138th, January 20, 1914, p. 63.
122. *Newark Evening News,* February 17, 1914, p. 10, col. 3.
123. *Trenton Evening Times,* March 5, 1914, p. 1, col. 7.
124. *NJAM,* 138th, March 24, 1912, pp. 991–992.
125. *Newark Evening News,* March 24, 1914, p. 9, col. 4.
126. *Trenton Evening Times,* March 31, 1914, p. 9, col. 7. Governor Fielder's information was incorrect. Of those counties that had voted on the adoption of the small board, *three* had not voted affirmatively by March, 1914: Ocean, Somerset, and Warren.
127. *NJAM,* 138th, March 31, 1914, pp. 1161–1165.
128. *Trenton Evening Times,* April 1, 1914, p. 6, col. 1.
129. *NJAM,* 138th, April 7, 1914, pp. 1268–1269.
130. *L.* 1914, c. 212, pp. 423–428.
131. The vote was 595 to 893, *New Jersey Courier* (Toms River), July 10, 1914, p. 1, col. 5.
132. *NJSJ,* 139th, March 23, 1915, pp. 606, 698. The vote for passage in the Senate was not recorded in the *Journal of the Senate,* but the Assembly's receipt of the bill is noted in *NJAM,* 139th, April 6, 1915, p. 1270.
133. *Lohan v. Thompson,* 88 N.J.L. 40 (1915). The vote was 4 to 1 in favor of the small board, *Jersey Journal* (Jersey City), November 4, 1914, p. 5, col. 6.
134. *Lohan v. Thompson,* 88 N.J.L. 40–42.
135. *Ibid.,* pp. 40–41.
136. *Ibid.,* p. 44.
137. *Trenton Evening Times,* September 2, 1915, p. 1, col. 1.
138. *NJSJ,* 140th, March 16, 1916, p. 601; *NJAM,* 140th, March 16, 1916, p. 998.
139. *NJAM,* 141st, February 21, 1917, p. 335; *ibid.,* March 7, 1917, p. 523.
140. *Bound Brook Chronicle,* March 9, 1917, p. 4, col. 2.

141. *Trenton Evening Times,* March 13, 1917, p. 6, col. 1.
142. *Ibid.,* p. 6, cols. 1–2.
143. *New Jersey Mirror* (Mt. Holly), August 21, 1918, p. 4, col. 2.
144. *Ibid.,* October 30, 1918, p. 4, col. 2.
145. *Ibid.,* November 6, 1918, p. 4, col. 1.
146. *Elizabeth Daily Journal,* October 20, 1920, p. 1, col. 1.
147. *Ibid.,* October 26, 1920, p. 6, col. 3.
148. *L.* 1917, c. 30, pp. 59–61.
149. *L.* 1921, c. 263, p. 791.
150. *Trenton Evening Times,* November 8, 1915, p. 6, col. 2.
151. *Ibid.*
152. Ocean, 1915: 1,572 to 1,576, *New Jersey Courier* (Toms River), November 5, 1915, p. 1, col. 5; Cape May, 1916: "The measure was defeated in the county by a majority of more than 1,000 according to reports yesterday," *Ocean City Sentinel,* June 29, 1916, [p. 2], col. 3; Union, 1916: 2,620 to 4,714, *Plainfield Courier-News,* June 14, 1916, p. 13, col. 3; Union, 1920: 17,566 to 22,688, *Chatham Press,* November 13, 1920, p. 7, cols. 1–2.
153. Ocean, 1918: 1,680 to 1,042 (official), *New Jersey Courier* (Toms River), November 8, 1918, p. 4, cols. 4–6; Cape May, 1921: "The majority for the small board in Ocean City was 136. The decision for adoption elsewhere was even more emphatic," *Ocean City Sentinel,* November 10, 1921, p. 1, col. 1.
154. Mercer, 1915: 7,860 to 6,974, *Trenton Evening Times,* November 3, 1915, p. 3, cols. 3–5; Morris, 1916: 7,106 to 2,677, *Daily Record* (Morristown), November 10, 1916, p. 4, cols. 2–5; Burlington, 1918: "majority of 1,211 for the proposed change," *Bordentown Register,* November 15, 1918, p. 1, col. 4.
155. Warren, 1916; 1,668 to 1,412, *Hackettstown Gazette,* May 19, 1916, p. 1, col. 7; Somerset, 1919: 2,846 to 2,163 (official) *Bound Brook Chronicle,* November 14, 1919, p. 4, col. 2.
156. *Trenton Evening Times,* February 16, 1920, p. 6, col. 3.
157. *Ibid.,* March 16, 1920, p. 3, cols. 3–4; *NJSJ,* 144th, March 2, 1920, p. 401.
158. *NJSJ,* 144th, March 17, 1920, pp. 560–561; *L.* 1920, c. 14, pp. 35–36; *Trenton Evening Times,* April 12, 1920, p. 1, col. 3.
159. *Trenton Evening Times,* March 22, 1920, p. 6, col. 1.
160. *NJAM,* 144th, April 12, 1920, p. 986.
161. *L.* 1923, c. 89, pp. 173–176.
162. *NJAM,* 147th, February 26, 1923, pp. 424–425.
163. *L.* 1923, c. 90, pp. 176–177.
164. Quoted in *Ocean City Sentinel,* October 20, 1923, p. 4, col. 2.
165. *Ocean City Ledger,* November 3, 1923, p. 4, col. 2.
166. *Ocean City Sentinel,* November 1, 1923, p. 4, col. 1. But after offering arguments for both sides, the newspaper stated: "Everything considered, we are forced to the conclusion that it does not mater [*sic*] what may be the number of men chosen to form a Board of Freeholders, but it does matter what is the quality of the men. Emphasis should be placed upon quality rather than quantity," *ibid.,* p. 4, col. 2.
167. "According to the unofficial returns, the County favored a five-man Board of Freeholders, by a total majority of approximately 1,000 votes," *Ocean City Sentinel,* November 8, 1923, p. 1, col. 3.

168. The official vote was 47,264 to 42,939, *Plainfield Courier-News,* November 18, 1932, p. 14, col. 2. Garwood Borough had just qualified according to the 1930 census statistics to be allotted a freeholder, *Elizabeth Daily Journal,* November 16, 1932, p. 14, col. 1.

169. *Elizabeth Daily Journal,* August 11, 1932, p. 2, col. 3.

170. The vote was 36,695 to 29,010, *Camden Evening Courier,* November 9, 1939, p. 2, col. 3. The vote was 36,716 to 29,138, according to Edward J. Quinlan, "100 Years of County Government," *New Jersey Counties* II (March 1944), p. 44.

171. Quinlan, *loc. cit.*"Democrats had effected control through coalition with a small bloc of Republicans," *ibid.*

172. *Pleasantville Press and Ventnor News,* November 8, 1935, p. 1, col. 2.

173. There was even apprehension that Atlantic's county seat would be moved from May's Landing to Atlantic City," *New York Herald-Tribune,* November 3, 1935, p. 37, col. 5.

174. The vote was 15,560 to 29,069, *Atlantic City Press,* November 7, 1935, p. 8, cols. 5–7.

175. *Atlantic City Press,* September 7, 1935, p. 2, col. 3. Five years earlier, the proportion of county taxes paid by Atlantic City was almost three-fourths, Atlantic City Survey Commission, *Report of the Survey of Atlantic County Government* (Amusement Publishing Company, Atlantic City: 1930), p. 8.

176. *Pleasantville Press and Ventnor News,* October 11, 1935, p. 1, cols. 2–4; *Atlantic City Press,* October 20, 1935, p. 1, cols. 1–2; *ibid.,* October 30, 1935, p. 3, cols. 1–2.

177. *Reynolds* v. *Sims,* 377 U.S. 533 (1964)

178. *Jackman* v. *Bodine,* 43 N.J. 453 (1964), reaffirmed 44 N.J. 312 (1965).

179. *N.J. Leg. Manual, 1966,* p. 22–23.

180. *Mauk* v. *Hoffman,* 87 N.J. *Super.* 276 (1965).

181. *Ibid.,* pp. 282–283.

182. *Ibid.,* p. 286. The law concerning primaries was *L.* 1965, c. 4, sect. 1.

183. *Newark Evening News,* April 6, 1966, p. 1, cols. 5–6; p. 10, cols. 5–6.

184. *Salem Standard and Jerseyman,* quoted in *Elmer Times,* May 19, 1966, p. 5, col. 6.

185. *Ibid.,* col. 5.

186. *Ibid.,* May 26, 1966, p. 7, col. 1.

187. *Salem Standard and Jerseyman,* quoted in *Elmer Times,* May 19, 1966, p. 5, col. 6.

188. *Vineland Times-Journal,* May 26, 1966, p. 1, col. 3.

189. *Evening News* (Paterson), May 26, 1966, p. 22, col. 2.

190. *Bridgeton Evening News,* May 26, 1966, p. 1, col. 8; p. 4, col. 6.

191. *Courier-Post* (Camden), May 26, 1966, p. 2, col. 8.

192. *Ibid.; Vineland Times-Journal,* May 26, 1966, p. 8, col. 2.

193. *NJSJ,* 190th, May 25, 1966, p. 630. "The bill was an administration measure and therefore didn't leave Musto, or other Democrats who consider themselves members of Gov. Hughes' team, much choice," *Newark Sunday News,* May 29, 1966, Sect. 1, p. 28, col. 1.

194. *Vineland-Times Journal,* June 1, 1966, p. 1, cols. 4, 6.
195. *NJAM,* 190th, May 31, 1966, pp. 845–846.
196. *L.* 1966, c. 62, pp. 511–512. The total was to reach 133 freeholders in 1971, with population increases in Morris and Ocean.
197. *Courier-News* (Plainfield), June 24, 1966, p. 6, cols. 2–3.
198. The County Republican Chairman, quoted in *Penns Grove Record,* June 23, 1966, p. 1, col. 6.
199. According to a Republican candidate for Cumberland's freeholder board, *Vineland Times-Journal,* October 6, 1966, p. 3, cols. 1–2.
200. *Salem Standard and Jerseymen,* November 10, 1966, p. 1, col. 7; *Bridgeton Evening News,* November 9, 1966, p. 1, col. 5; *Vineland Times-Journal,* November 9, 1966, p. 13, cols. 4–5; *Courier-Post* (Camden), November 9, 1966, p. 20, cols. 1–5.

14

DIRECTORS OR DICTATORS?
EXPERIMENTS WITH EXECUTIVE OFFICERS

1. *Evening Journal* (Jersey City), October 8, 1874.
2. Quoted in *ibid.,* December 16, 1874.
3. "Presentment of Grand Jury," in *Evening Journal* (Jersey City), November 21, 1874; *New York Times,* November 22, 1874.
4. *L.* 1875, c. 189, pp. 324–330. See pp. 61–67 for a history of its passage.
5. *Evening Journal* (Jersey City), November 12, 1875.
6. *Ibid.,* November 19, 1875.
7. "Official Proceedings, Regular Stated Meeting, December 2, 1875, Board of Chosen Freeholders of Hudson," in *ibid.,* December 9, 1875.
8. *Evening Journal* (Jersey City), December 3, 1875.
9. *Ibid.*
10. *Ibid.,* December 17, 1875.
11. *Daily True American* (Trenton), April 14, 1876.
12. *NJAM,* 100th, April 17, 1876, p. 870.
13. *L.* 1876, c. 128, p. 222.
14. *NJAM,* 100th, April 18, 1876, p. 887; *NJSJ,* 100th, April 18, 1876, p. 642.
15. But Halsted argued that there should be a check on the director, because he could draw warrants for any amount, and the county collector would be compelled to pay them, without any requirement for a counter signature by the clerk, *Evening Journal* (Jersey City), November 6, 1877.
16. *Ibid.,* February 22, 1877.
17. *State v. Halsted,* 39 N.J.L. 402 (1877).
18. *Evening Journal* (Jersey City), February 3, 6, 1877.
19. *State v. Halsted, loc. cit.; Evening Journal* (Jersey City), June 8, 1877; *New York Times,* June 8, 1877.
20. *Evening Journal* (Jersey City), May 7, 1878.
21. *New York Times,* May 4, 8, 1878; *Evening Journal* (Jersey City), May 6, 1878; *ibid.,* December 17, 1878.
22. *New York Times,* May 8, 1878.

23. *Ibid.,* June 5, 1878.
24. *Ibid.,* December 8, 1878.
25. *Eveing Journal* (Jersey City), December 16, 1878.
26. *Halsted* v. *State,* 41 N.J.L. 552 (1879).
27. *Ibid.,* pp. 587–588.
28. *Evening Journal* (Jersey City), December 8, 1879.
29. *Halsted* v. *State,* 41 N.J.L. 552, 597–598 (1879).
30. *Evening Journal* (Jersey City), December 8, 1879.
31. *Speer* v. *State,* 41 N.J.L. 623 (1879).
32. *New York Times,* December 7, 1879.
33. *Evening Journal* (Jersey City), December 8, 1879.
34. *Ibid.,* April 7, 1880.
35. *Ibid.,* February 11, 1878.
36. *NJAM,* 103rd, March 4, 1879, p. 552; *New York Times,* March 12, 1879.
37. One member is recorded as having voted both affirmatively and negatively, *NJSJ,* 103rd, March 6, 1879, pp. 645–646; *Evening Journal* (Jersey City), March 6, 1879.
38. *Evening Journal* (Jersey City), March 12, 1879.
39. *NJSJ,* 103rd, March 11, 1879, p. 567; *NJAM,* 103rd, March 11, 1879, pp. 740–741, list only 34 names in the affirmative; *L.* 1879, c.119, pp. 205–206.
40. *NJAM,* 104th, January 27, 1880, p. 108; *Evening Journal* (Jersey City), February 5, 1880.
41. *NJAM,* 104th, February 9, 17, 1880, pp. 244, 351. But in 1881 Potts unsuccessfully proposed an amendment to the General County Bill to abolish the office of director at large. See p. 119.
42. *Evening Journal* (Jersey City), February 19, 1880.
43. *Ibid.; NJAM,* 104th, February 19, 1880, p. 410.
44. *NJAM,* 104th, February 23, 24, 1880, p. 423, 436. See text of *L.* 1880, c. 185, pp. 275–277.
45. *Evening Journal* (Jersey City), March 2, 1880.
46. *NJAM,* 104th, March 10, 1880, p. 780; *NJSJ,* 104th, March 11, 1880, p. 730.
47. *NJAM,* 104th, March 9, 1880, pp. 712–713.
48. *Evening Journal* (Jersey City), March 11, 1880; *Daily Fredonian* (New Brunswick), March 11, 1880; *NJAM,* 104th, March 10, 1880, p. 780.
49. *NJSJ,* 104th, March 11, 1880, p. 730; *L.* 1880, c. 185, pp. 275–277.
50. *NJSJ,* 106th, March 9, 1882, p. 646; see *N.J. Leg. Docs.,* 106th (1882), I, Dec. 14, 5.
51. *NJAM,* 106th, March 22, 1882, pp. 909–910; *Evening Journal* (Jersey City), March 23, 1882.
52. *NJAM,* 106th, March 30, 1882, p. 1047 records the vote as 31 to 8, but lists nine members voting negatively.
53. *NJSJ,* 106th, March 30, 1882, pp. 1025–1026, 1028, 1029.
54. *N.J. Leg. Docs., loc. cit.*
55. *New Jersey Law Journal,* V (October, 1882), 290–291.
56. *Billings* v. *Fielder,* 44 N.J.L. 381 (1882).
57. *Ibid.,* pp. 384–387.
58. *Greene* v. *Freeholders of Hudson and Frederick P. Budden,* 44 N.J.L. 388 (1882).

59. *Greene* v. *Freeholders of Hudson*, 44 N.J.L. 392 (1882).
60. *NJAM*, 109th, February 18, 1885, pp. 313–314.
61. *NJSJ*, 109th, March 10, 11, 1885, pp. 403, 416.
62. *Evening Journal* (Jersey City), February 24, 1885; *NJAM*, 109th, February 23, 1885, p. 352 records one Hudson member as voting both affirmatively and negatively; but he is counted here as voting nay.
63. *NJSJ*, 109th, March 11, 1882, p. 418.
64. *NJAM*, 109th, March 17, 1885, pp. 583–586.
65. *Ibid.*
66. *NJSJ*, 109th, March 17, 1885, pp. 586–588.
67. See *New York Times*, December 22, 1885.
68. *Daily True American* (Trenton), March 19, 1885; *NJAM*, 109th, March 18, 1885, p. 613 records the vote of 33 to 21, but lists 22 members voting negatively.
69. *NJAM*, 109th, March 18, 1885, pp. 613–614.
70. *NJSJ*, 109th, March 23, 1885, pp. 535–536.
71. Assembly Bill No. 226 became *L.* 1885, c. 115, pp. 137–138; Assembly Bill No. 227 became *L.* 1885, c. 114, pp. 135–136.
72. *Evening Journal* (Jersey City), March 23, 1885.
73. *Bumstead* v. *Govern*, 47 N.J.L. 368, 369–371 (1885).
74. *Ibid.*, p. 372.
75. *Ibid.*, pp. 372–375; *New York Times*, December 22, 1885.
76. *State ex. rel Hugh Dugan* v. *George H. Farrier*, 47 N.J.L. 383, 387 (1885); *Daily True American* (Trenton), December 22, 1885.
77. *Govern* v. *Bumstead*, 48 N.J.L. 612 (1886).
78. *Farrier* v. *Dugan*, 48 N.J.L. 613 (1886).
79. *Evening Journal* (Jersey City), July 20, 1886.
80. *NJAM*, 113th, February 12, 1889, pp. 222–267.
81. *Newark Evening News*, March 14, 1889; *NJAM*, 113th, March 13, 1889; *Daily Times* (New Brunswick), March 14, 1889.
82. *Evening Journal* (Jersey City), March 14, 1889.
83. See p.000 *L.* 1889, c. 114, pp. 163–166; *Mortland* v. *Christian*, 52 N.J.L. 521 (1890).
84. *New York Times*, March 23, 1891.
85. See reprint of Assembly Bill No. 321, N.J. State Law Library.
86. *New York Times*, March 23, 1891.
87. *NJAM*, 115th, March 16, 1891, p. 727; *NJSJ*, 115th, March 17, 1891, p. 533.
88. *L.* 1891, c. 246, pp. 469–471.
89. *Newark Evening News*, March 6, 1893; see pp. 151–152.
90. *Ibid.*, February 15, 1893; *Newark Daily Advertiser*, February 27, 1893.
91. *Newark Evening News*, March 6, 1893.
92. *Ibid.*, March 8, 1893.
93. *Ibid.*, March 9, 1893; *NJAM*, 117th, March 8, 1893, p. 595.
94. *NJSJ*, 117th, March 10, 1893, p. 499.
95. *L.* 1893, c. 143, pp. 258–260.
96. See pp. 152–153.
97. *Newark Evening News*, February 12, 1900.
98. *Ibid.*

99. See pp. 191–193.

100. *Newark Daily Advertiser*, March 16, 1900.

101. See pp. 193–195.

102. William H. Cape, *The Emerging Pattern of County Executives* (Lawrence, Kansas: Governmental Research Center, University of Kansas, 1967), p. 20.

103. Richard Childs, "A Theoretically Perfect County," *Annals of the American Academy of Political and Social Science*, XLVII (May 1913), 277; W.S. U'Ren, "State and County Government in Oregon and Proposed Changes," *ibid.*, 272–273. U'Ren had urged a county manager even earlier, H.S. Gilbertson, "The Discovery of the County Problem," *American Review of Reviews*, XLVI (November, 1912), 608.

104. Winston Paul and H.S. Gilbertson, "Counties of the First Class in New Jersey," *Proceedings of the American Political Science Association*, 10th Annual Meeting, Washington D.C., December 30, 1913–January 1, 1914, p. 300.

105. *Ibid.*

106. H.S. Gilbertson, "The Movement for Responsible Government," *Annals of the American Academy of Political and Social Science*, LXIV (March 1916), 119.

107. N.J. Commission to Investigate County and Municipal Taxation and Expenditures, *Report No. 2: The Organization, Functions and Expenditures of Local Government in New Jersey*, Trenton: 1931, p. 267.

108. *N.J. Leg. Manual, 1931*, p. 652.

109. *Salem Sunbeam*, February 14, 1934, p. 4, col. 3.

110. Counties with less than 50,000 population that had five or more freeholders before passage of the proposed act would elect five (rather than three) freeholders. See Senate Bill No. 102, 1934, Art. VI, Sec. 601.

111. *Trenton Evening Times*, February 15, 1934, p. 6, col. 1.

112. *Ibid.*

113. *Ibid.*, February 4, 1936, p. 6, col. 2.

114. Samuel S. Paquin, "New Jersey—Clearing Way for County Managers," *National Municipal Review*, XX (April, 1936), 239. The article erroneously states that the groupings are divided by population at 150,000 and 500,000.

115. Paquin, *loc. cit.*

116. *Trenton Evening Times*, April 20, 1936, p. 6, col. 2.

117. *Ibid.*, May 11, 1936, p. 6, col. 1.

118. Richard S. Childs, *Civic Victories: The Story of an Unfinished Revolution* (New York, Harper & Brothers, 1952), p. 207.

119. Thomas D. Wilson, "Elected County Chiefs," *National Civic Review*, LX (November, 1966), 561–562.

120. *Ibid.*

121. John A. Fairlie and Charles Maynard Kneier, *County Government and Administration* (New York: D. Appleton-Century Company, Inc., 1930), p. 173.

122. Bergen County, *Minutes of Board of Chosen Freeholders*, September 3, 1952, pp. 388–389.

123. *New York Times*, April 16, 1961, p. 115, cols. 1–2.

124. *NJAM*, 185th, April 24, 1961, p. 465.

125. *NJSJ*, 185th, May 15, 1961, pp. 425–426.
126. *NJAM*, 185th, May 31, 1961, p. 759.
127. *L.* 1961, c. 64, pp. 561–563.
128. Senate Bill No. 157 (1962) and Senate Bill No. 80 (1963) were sponsored by both Connery and Weber; Senate Bill No. 66 (1964), only by Weber.
129. Senate Bill No. 160 (1962) was sponsored by both Connery and Weber; Senate Bill No. 88 (1963) and Senate Bill No. 67 (1965), only by Weber.
130. *L.* 1967, c. 220, p. 809.
131. *NJAM*, 192nd, January 28, 1968, p. 141; *NJSJ*, 192nd, April 18, 1968, p. 141.
132. Arthur R. Sypek, Vice-President, N.J. Association of Chosen Freeholders and Director, Mercer County Board of Chosen Freeholders, *Statement* Before the County and Municipal Government Study Commission, Public Hearing, December 2, 1969, The Assembly Chamber, State House, Trenton, New Jersey.
133. James J. Kennedy, "The Office of County Administrator in N.J.," *New Jersey County Government* (January-February, 1972), p. 14; *Star-Ledger* (Newark), July 12, 1973, p. 19, col. 1.

15

TOWARD OPTIONAL COUNTY CHARTERS

1. *L.* 1916, c. 84, pp. 168–170.
2. N.J. Commission to Revise and Codify the Statutes of the State Relating to Cities and Municipalities, Appointed by the Governor under Chapter 84, of the Laws of 1916, *Report*, January 22, 1917, p. 4.
3. *L.* 1917, c. 152, pp. 319–463. Accompanying repealer acts that resulted were *L.* 1917, cc. 204–211, pp. 575–749.
4. Message to the Senate, *NJSJ*, 142nd, January 14, 1918, pp. 202–203.
5. N.J. Commission to Revise . . . , *Report*, January 22, 1917, p. 7.
6. *Ibid.*, p. 12.
7. *Ibid.*, p. 13.
8. "Governor's Message," *NJAM*, 142nd, January 8, 1918, p. 22.
9. *NJSJ*, 142nd, January 8, 1918, p. 184; *L.* 1918, c. 185, p. 624. The unofficial title of "An Act concerning counties" was acknowledged in *Chamber of Commerce* v. *Essex County*, 96 N.J.L. 238 (1921) at 240.
10. *L.* 1918, c. 189, pp. 629–652.
11. Henry W. Connor, "Home Rule" (Appendix E 1) in New Jersey. *Constitutional Convention of 1947*, held at *Rutgers University, the State University of New Jersey*, Vol. II, New Brunswick, New Jersey [Trenton, 1951], p. 1756.
12. John E. Bebout, "New Jersey Committee for Constitutional Revision Proposals on Local Government," *ibid.*, Vol. III, New Brunswick, New Jersey [Trenton, 1952], p. 870.
13. Connor, *op. cit.*, p. 1744.
14. *Ibid.*
15. "Constitutional Changes Recommended by the New Jersey State

Industrial Union Council, CIO," in New Jersey, *Constitutional Convention of 1947* . . . , Vol. III, New Brunswick, New Jersey [Trenton, 1952], p. 888.

16. "Letter of New Jersey State League of Municipalities," James J. Smith to Edward J. O'Mara, July 8, 1917, in *ibid.*, p. 889.

17. *Ibid.*

18. Article IV, Sec. 7, par. 10.

19. "Resolution of the New Jersey Association of Chosen Freeholders," (approved at Trenton, N.J., August 4, 1947) in New Jersey, *Constitutional Convention of 1947* . . . Vol. V, [1953], p. 492.

20. *L.* 1956, c. 231, pp. 797–799.

21. *Ibid.*, p. 798.

22. *Ibid.*, p. 797.

23. New Jersey County and Municipal Law Revision Commission. *Report*, March 1960 in *New Jersey Statutes Annotated, Title 40A. Municipalities and Counties* (April, 1972), p. vii *et passim.*

24. Assembly Joint Resolution No. 22 (1959), p. 3.

25. Assembly Joint Resolution No. 34 (1960), p. 4.

26. *Ibid.*, p. 2.

27. *Ibid.*, pp. 2–3.

28. *NJAM*, 185th, March 27, 1961, p. 421. Pierce Deamer (R-Bergen) had been made cosponsor, *ibid.*, March 13, 1961, p. 286.

29. Assembly Joint Resolution No. 6 (1962). John J. Wilson (D-Union) and Nelson G. Gross (R-Bergen) were made cosponsors, *NJAM*, 186th, January 29, 1962, p. 171; April 7, 1962, p. 616.

30. Assembly Joint Resolution No. 2 (1963); *NJAM*, 187th, May 13, 1963, p. 897. Nelson G. Gross (R-Bergen) had been made a co-sponsor, *ibid.*, January 21, 1962, p. 174.

31. Senate Joint Resolution No. 13, 1959, p. 2; Senate Joint Resolution No. 3, 1960, with George B. Harper (R-Sussex), p. 2.

32. *Trenton Evening Times*, January 19, 1960, p. 5, col. 8.

33. Assembly Concurrent Resolution No. 47 (1960), pp. 1–2; Assembly Concurrent Resolution No. 43 (1961), pp. 1–2; Assembly Concurrent Resolution, No. 14 (1962), pp. 1–2.

34. New Jersey County and Municipal Law Revision Commission, [Draft], *County Forms and Structure*, July 11, 1960, *passim.*

35. New Jersey County and Municipal Law Revision Commission, *Preliminary Draft: Title 40A Municipalities and Counties. Chapter 11 County Forms and Structure*, [Trenton], June, 1961, pp. 20–23.

36. *Ibid.*, p. 20.

37. *Newark Evening News*, June 16, 1961, p. 24, col. 3.

38. N.J. County and Municipal Law Revision Commission, *Second Tentative Draft. Title 40A. Municipalities and Counties, Chap. 11. County Forms and Structure, Chap. 13.* [First Tentative Draft] *Optional County Government Law.* [Trenton, N.J.], September, 1962, p. x.

39. *Ibid.*, p. xiii.

40. *Ibid.*, p. xxi. But the text of the proposed County Manager Law was not included, as was indicated, in the Second Tentative Draft.

41. New Jersey County and Municipal Law Revision Commission . . . *Second Tentative Draft. Title 40A . . . Chap. 13* [First Tentative Draft] *Optional County Government Law . . .* pp. xx–xxi.

42. *Ibid.*, pp. 17–22.
43. *Ibid.*, pp. 23–24.
44. New Jersey County and Municipal Law Revision Commission. *Second Tentative Draft. Title 40A* . . . pp. xxii–xxiii.
45. *Ibid.*, p. xxiii.
46. *Ibid.*
47. *Ibid.*
48. *Ibid.*, pp. xxiii–xxiv.
49. *Trenton Evening Times,* June 17, 1963, p. 8, c. 4.
50. *Ibid.*
51. *Newark Sunday News,* June 23, 1963, Sect. 2, p. c. 1, col. 6.
52. *Ibid.*
53. *Ibid.*, col. 7.
54. *Ibid.*, cols. 7–8.
55. *Ibid.*
56. *Ibid.*
57. *Newark Evening News,* June 26, 1963, p. 26, col. 13. See also *ibid.*, July 28, 1963, p. 27, cols. 5–8.
58. Letter of John Jay Sullivan to the Editor, *Newark Evening News,* February 27, 1964, p. 12, cols. 3–4.
59. *L.* 1964, c. 154, pp. 686–688.
60. *Newark Evening News,* September 3, 1964, p. 29, col. 2.
61. Art. IV, Sect. 7, p. 10.
62. *New York Times,* November 3, 1965, p. 1, col. 4.
63. The Bureau's role in calling attention to *L.* 1948, c. 199, pp. 995–999 was acknowledged in an editorial not long afterward, *Asbury Park Evening Press,* December 19, 1966, p. 14, col. 1, and in Republican Organization of Bergen County ("Republicans for Responsible Government"), *A Passage to Progress, County Government Reorganization in Bergen County, New Jersey,* n.p., 1967, Appendix I. The first paper by Dr. Ernest C. Reock, Bureau Director, was "Suggestions for a Revised Classification of New Jersey Counties" (unpublished). His second paper appears as "A Special Procedure to Secure Charters for N.J. Counties," *New Jersey County Government* (March, 1967), pp. 10, 11–13, 16.
64. Republican Organization of Bergen County, *A Passage to Progress,* p. 7.
65. *Ibid.*, p. 7. The authors referred to "Title I, Ch. 6: ENACTMENT OF PRIVATE SPECIAL AND LOCAL ACTS, Sec. 10 through 20 of the REVISED STATUTES OF THE STATE OF NEW JERSEY ANNOTATED.[*L.* 1948, c. 199, pp. 995–997]," *ibid.*, Appendix I.
66. *Ibid.*, pp. 7–8.
67. *Ibid.*, p. 17.
68. *Ibid.*, p. 18.
69. *Ibid.*
70. *Ibid.*, Appendix XV, pp. 15–16.
71. *Ibid.*
72. *Ibid.*, Appendix IV.
73.. *Ibid.*
74. Bergen County, N.J. *Minutes of the Board of Chosen Freeholders,* May 3, 1967, pp. 723–725.

75. *Ibid.*, p. 728.
76. *Ibid.*, pp. 728–729.
77. *Ibid.*, pp. 733–734.
78. *Ibid.*, p. 735.
79. *Ibid.*, June 7, 1967, p. 945.
80. *Ibid.*, September 6, 1967, pp. 1351, 1360.
81. *Ibid.*, October 4, 1967, p. 1488.
82. Knight & Gladieux, *Proposed Charter Provisions for Bergen County* (Charter Study Committee of Bergen County, Hackensack, New Jersey), December 8, 1967, pp. 23–28, 31.
83. *Ibid.*, pp. 29–30, 31.
84. *Ibid.*, pp. 45–51. "We recommend discontinuance of the title 'Director' for this post. The term 'Chairman' is proposed as indicative not only of the significant change in the nature of his responsibilities but also the expanded nature of his role as policy leader, *ibid.*, p. 46.
85. Charter Study Committee of Bergen County. *Report and Recommendations for a New County Charter.* Reprinted from *The Record* (Hackensack), April 15, 1968.
86. *The Record* (Hackensack), September 24, 1968, p. A-12, cols. 1–2.
87. *Ibid.*
88. Bergen County, N.J. *Minutes of the Board of Chosen Freeholders*, December 27, 1968, pp. 1907–1908.
89. *NJSJ*, 193rd, January 27, 1969, p. 217.
90. *The Evening News* (Newark), February 4, 1969, p. 13, cols. 2–3. (On December 9, 1968 the *Newark Evening News* changed its masthead.)
91. *Ibid.*, February 18, 1969, p. 16, col. 4.
92. *Ibid.*
93. *NJAM*, 193rd, February 17, 1969, p. 319.
94. *Ibid.*, March 10, 1969, pp. 351, 356.
95. Frederick Hauser (D-Hudson) and Albert S. Smith (R-Atlantic) were cosponsors from the time of the resolution's introduction.
96. The other original cosponsor was A. Smith. Hauser and Benjamin Rimm (R-Atlantic) were added on the day of the bill's introduction, *NJAM*, May 3, 1965, p. 711.
97. *NJAM*, 189th, May 17, 1965, pp. 817–819.
98. *Newark Evening News*, November 3, 1965, p. 22, col. 3.
99. Since 1960, this was the declared purpose in the titles of all the Musto resolutions to establish a new commission to study county and municipal governments.
100. *NJSJ*, 190th, February 7, February 8, 1966, pp. 140, 180.
101. *Newark Evening News*, March 29, 1966, p. 19, col. 3.
102. *NJSJ*, 190th, March 28, 1966, pp. 387–388.
103. *L.* 1966, c. 28, pp. 71–73.
104. *Newark Evening News*, August 10, 1966, p. 14, cols. 5–7.
105. *L.* 1967, c. 53, p. 139.
106. N.J. County and Municipal Government Study Commission. *Creative Localism, A Prospectus (An Interim Report).* Trenton: March 11, 1968, p. xiii.
107. *Ibid.*, p. 66.

108. N.J. County and Municipal Government Study Commission. *Second Report. County Government Challenge and Change.* Trenton, April 28, 1969, pp. 109–125.

109. *Ibid.*, p. 105.

110. *Ibid.*

111. *Ibid.*

112. *Ibid.*, pp. 105–106.

113. The other original sponsors included Alfred D. Schiaffo (R-Dist. 13, Bergen); Richard Coffee (D-Dist. 6, Mercer); Richard R. Stout (R-Dist. 5, Monmouth). Added later were Harry L. Sears (R-Dist. 10, Morris) and Matthew J. Rinaldo (R-Dist. 9, Union), *NJSJ*, 194th, 1st Sess., February 12, March 19, 1970, pp. 278, 493.

114. *The Evening News* (Newark), April 14, 1970, p. 10. col. 5; *Daily Home News* (New Brunswick), June 20, 1970, p. 20, col. 1.

115. *The Evening News* (Newark), April 14, 1970, p. 10, cols. 5–7.

116. They were William E. Schluter (R-Dist. 6A, pt. Mercer); Karl Weidel (R-Dist. 6A, pt. Mercer); Millicent H. Fenwick (R-Dist. 8, Somerset); James R. Hurley (R-Dist. 1, Cape May-Cumberland); Austin N. Volk (R-Dist. 13E, pt. Bergen); Thomas H. Kean (R-Dist. 11B, pt. Essex); Richard J. Vander Plaat (R-Dist. 13C, pt. Bergen); David J. Friedland (D-Dist 12B, pt. Hudson); Martin E. Kravarik (R-Dist. 7B, pt. Middlesex); Herbert M. Renald (R-Dist. 11D, pt. Essex); and John F. Brown (R-Dist. 4A, Ocean-pt. Burlington).

117. *NJAM*, 194th, May 3, 1971, p. 453.

118. *The Evening News* (Newark), May 8, 1971, p. 4, col. 2; *NJAM*, 195th, May 3, 1971, p. 453.

119. *Sunday Star-Ledger* (Newark), February 6, 1972, Sec. 1, p. 25, col. 1.

120. The six Republican original sponsors were: William E. Schluter (R-Dist. 6A, Hunterdon, pt. Mercer); Alfred D. Schiaffo (R-Dist. 13, Bergen); Matthew J. Rinaldo (R-Dist. 9, Union); John F. Brown (R-Dist. 4A, pt. Ocean); James S. Cafiero (R-Dist. 1, Cape May-Cumberland); and Jerome Epstein (R-Dist. 9, Union). The Democratic sponsor, in addition to Musto, was Joseph L. McGahn (Dist. 2- Atlantic). Sponsors added later included Wynona Lipman (D-Dist. 11, Essex); James H. Wallwork (R-Dist. 11, Essex); *NJSJ*, 195th, 1st Sess., March 9, 1972, p. 127; Frank X. McDermott (R-Dist. 9, Union), and Wayne Dumont, Jr. (R-Dist. 15, Sussex-Warren), *ibid.*, March 13, 1972, p. 127.

121. *New York Times,* May 21, 1972, p. 94, col. 4.

122. *Courier-News* (Plainfield), September 20, 1972, p. A-3, col. 1.

123. *NJSJ*, 195th, 1st. Sess., April 6, 1972, pp. 182–183.

124. *Daily Home News* (New Brunswick), April 7, 1972, p. 1, col. 8.

125. *NJSJ*, 195th, 1st Sess., May 18, 1972, pp. 434–435.

126. *Evening News* (Newark), May 19, 1972, p. 6, col. 1.

127. *NJAM*, 195th, 1st Sess., May 18, 1972, pp. 434–435.

128. *Evening News* (Newark), May 19, 1972, p. 6, cols. 1–2; *New York Times,* May 21, 1972, p. 94, cols. 1–4; *Home News* (New Brunswick), May 23, 1972, p. 24, col. 5.

129. *Home News* (New Brunswick), July 18, 1972, p. 22, cols. 1–5; *Star-Ledger* (Newark), July 18, 1972, p. 10, cols. 1–2.

130. *Evening News* (Newark), July 26, 1972, p. 6, col. 2.
131. *Home News* (New Brunswick), August 8, 1972, p. 1, cols. 1–3.
132. *Ibid.,* p. 1, col. 6.
133. *Sunday Home News* (New Brunswick), September 17, 1972, p. A18, col. 3.
134. *L.* 1972, c. 154, pp. 577–629; *Star-Ledger* (Newark), September 20, 1972, p. 12, cols. 7–8; *Daily Home News* (New Brunswick), September 20, 1972, p. 12, col. 3; *Sunday Times-Advertiser* (Trenton), September 17, 1972, p. 2, col. 2.
135. *Courier-News* (Plainfield), September 20, 1972, p. 3, col. 1.
136. With the addition of William J. Bate (D-Dist. 14, Passaic), these were the same as the sponsors of Senate Bill No. 283, enacted as the Optional County Charter Law. See p. 354, n. 120.
137. *NJSJ*, 195th, 1st Sess., November 20, 1972, p. 500.
138. *Ibid.,* 2nd Sess., February 15, 1973, p. 127; February 22, 1973, p. 163; March 26, 1973, p. 251.
139. Kenneth V. Meyers, "Charters Get a Chance," *New Jersey County Government* (October-November 1973), p. 13.
140. Essex County, Charter Study Commission. *Final Report,* reprinted in *Star-Ledger* (Newark), August 29, 1974, p. 46, cols. 6–8; *Sunday Star-Ledger* (Newark), June 23, 1974, sec. 1, p. 35, col. 2.
141. Atlantic County Charter Study Commission. *The Future of Atlantic County Government,* August 6, 1974, pp. 2–3; Union County Charter Study Commission. *Final Report.* July 31, 1974, reprinted in *Daily Journal* (Elizabeth), October 31, 1974, supplement [p. 2]; Hudson County. Charter Study Commission. *Final Report.* August 16, 1974, pp. 11–19; Mercer County Charter Study Commission. *Final Report.* August 1974, pp. iii, 109–119; Bergen County Charter Study Commission. *Charting Bergen's Future. Final Report.* August 6, 1974, pp. 41, 50; Camden County Charter Study Commission. *A Final Report to the People.* August 1974, p. 67; Middlesex Charter Study Commission. *Final Report.* 1974, p. 1; Passaic Charter Study Commission. *Passaic County: Opportunity for Modern Government. Final Report.* August 6, 1974, pp. 4, 20.
142. *Jersey Journal* (Jersey City), November 6, 1974, p. 1, cols. 2–5; *The Press* (Atlantic City), November 6, 1974, p. 18, cols. 1–7, p. 19, cols. 1–7; *The Evening News* (Paterson), November 7, 1974, p. 30, cols. 1–8; *Home News* (New Brunswick), November 7, 1974, p. 43, cols. 1–8.
143. These figures were calculated from the final tables supplied by the New Jersey Association of Chosen Freeholders: Atlantic, 26,348–12,364; Hudson, 60,431–36,968; Mercer, 40,638–34,581; Union, 69,385–64,951; Bergen, 123,106–132,168; Camden, 47,603–55,802; Passaic, 33,799–54,964; and, Middlesex, 44,889–77,456.
144. *New York Times,* November 10, 1974, p. NJ 3, col. 1.

CONCLUSION

1. N.J. County and Municipal Government Study Commission, *Second Report. County Government: Challenge and Change,* p. 108.
2. Four years earlier (1871), the legislature of New York created the position of supervisor at large for Kings County (Greater Brooklyn) with

power to veto the acts of the board of supervisors. Harold Coffin Syrett, *The City of Brooklyn, 1865–1898: A Political History* (New York: Columbia University Press, 1944), p. 180. No mention of an earlier county executive with a veto could be found.

3. William L. Bailey, "The County Community and Its Government," *Annals of the American Academy of Political and Social Science*, XLVII (May, 1913), 16.

4. The density statistic appears in John E. Bebout and Ronald J. Grele, *Where Cities Meet, The Urbanization of New Jersey*, "The New Jersey Historical Series," Vol. 22 (Princeton, N.J.: D. Van Nostrand Co., Inc, 1964), p. 33.

5. Bailey, *op. cit.*, p. 18.

6. H.S. Gilbertson, *The County, The "Dark Continent of American Politics"*, p. 38.

BIBLIOGRAPHY

Public Documents

Acts of the General Assembly of . . . New Jersey [1703–1766], comp. by Samuel Allinson. Burlington, 1776.

Acts of the General Assembly of . . . New Jersey, II, comp. by Samuel Nevill. Philadelphia, 1761.

Atlantic City Survey Commission. *Report of the Survey of Atlantic County Government*. Amusement Publishing Company, Atlantic City, N.J.: 1930.

Atlantic County Charter Study Commission. *The Future of Atlantic County Government*. August 6, 1974.

Bebout, John E. "New Jersey Committee for Constitutional Revision Proposals on Local Government," in New Jersey. *Constitutional Convention of 1947, held at Rutgers University, the State University of New Jersey, New Brunswick, New Jersey*. Vol. III. [Trenton, 1952], pp. 866–871.

Bergen County. *Minutes of Board of Chosen Freeholders*.

Bergen County Charter Study Commission. *Charting Bergen's Future: Final Report*. August 6, 1974.

———. Charter Study Committee. *Report and Recommendations for a New County Charter*. Reprinted from *The Record* (Hackensack), April 15, 1968.

Camden County Charter Study Commission. *A Final Report to the People of Camden County*. August 1974.

Connor, Henry W. "Home Rule," (plus appendices) in New Jersey. *Constitutional Convention of 1947, held at Rutgers University, the State University of New Jersey, New Brunswick, New Jersey*. Vol. II. [Trenton, 1951], pp. 1729–1758.

Essex County Charter Study Commission. (Report in Newark *Star Ledger*, August 29, 1974).

Hudson Co., N.J. *Park Commission Report*. [Jersey City, 1908].

Hudson County Charter Study Commission. *Final Report*, August 16, 1974.

Journal of the Proceedings of the Legislative Council of the State of New Jersey [Council Journal], 1776–1844. Published at various places after each sitting.

Journal of the . . . Senate of the State of New Jersey [Senate Journal], 1845–1974. Published at various places annually.

Knight & Gladieux. *Proposed Charter Provisions for Bergen County*. Charter Study Committee of Bergen County, Hackensack, New Jersey, December 8, 1967.

Mercer County Charter Study Commission. *Final Report*. August, 1974.

Middlesex County Charter Study Commission. *Final Report*. August 1974.

Minutes of the Votes and Proceedings of the . . . General Assembly [Assembly Journal], 1845–1973. Published at various places after each session.

New Jersey Association of Chosen Freeholders. "Resolution (approved at Trenton, N.J., August 4, 1947)," in *New Jersey Constitutional Convention of 1947, held at Rutgers University, the State University of New Jersey, New Brunswick, New Jersey*. Vol. V. [1953], p. 492.

N.J. Commission to Investigate County and Municipal Taxation and Expenditures. *Report No. 1: The Organization, Functions and Expenditures of Local Government in New Jersey.* Trenton, 1931.

N.J. Commission to Revise and Codify the Statutes of the State Relating to Cities and Municipalities, appointed by the Governor under Chapter 84 of the Laws of 1916. *Report.* January 22, 1917.

New Jersey Constitution. 1776, 1844, 1947.

New Jersey County and Municipal Government Study Commission. *Creative Localism: A Prospectus (An Interim Report).* Trenton, N.J. March 11, 1968.

———. *Second Report. County Government, Challenge and Change.* Trenton, N.J. April 28, 1969.

New Jersey County and Municipal Law Revision Commission. [Draft], "County Forms and Structure," July 11, 1960.

———. *Preliminary Draft: Title 40A. Municipalities and Counties. Chapter 11. County Forms and Structure.* [Trenton], June, 1961.

———. *Report.* March 1960 in *New Jersey Statutes Annotated, Title 40A. Municipalities and Counties* (April 1972), pp. vii–xxi.

———. *Second Tentative Draft. Title 40A. Municipalities and Counties. Chapter 11. County Forms and Structure. Chapter 13* [First Tentative Draft] *Optional County Government Law.* [Trenton], September, 1962.

N.J. Dept. of State Census Bureau. *Compendium of Censuses, 1726–1905.* Trenton: J. L. Murphy Publishing Co., printers, 1906.

New Jersey Law Reports: [N.J.L.] *Reports of Cases Argued and Determined in the Supreme Court, and the Court of Errors and Appeals of the State of New Jersey.* Various places, 1857–1966.

New Jersey Legislative Documents. (Starting in 1861 the Governor's messages, department reports, and reports of legislative committees were published in collected form for each session under this title.)

New Jersey Reports [N.J.]: *Reports of Cases Argued and Determined in the Supreme Court of New Jersey.* Newark, N.J.: Soney & Sage, 1965.

N.J. State Industrial Union Council, CIO . . . "Constitutional Changes Recommended by . . ." in New Jersey. *Constitutional Convention of 1947, held at Rutgers University, the State University of New Jersey, New Brunswick, New Jersey.* Vol. III. [Trenton, 1952], p. 888.

New Jersey Statutes Annotated.

New Jersey Superior Court Reports [N.J.Super.]: *Reports of Cases Argued and Determined in the Superior Court.* Newark, N.J.: Soney & Sage, 1965–66.

Passaic County Charter Study Commission. *Passaic County: Opportunity for Modern Government. Final Report from the Passaic County Charter Study Commission,* August 6, 1974.

Revision of the Statutes of New Jersey. Published under the Authority of the Legislature by Virtue of an Act approved April 4, 1871 [Revision of 1877]. Trenton, N.J.: John L. Murphy, Book and Job Printer, 1877.

Session Laws of the State of New Jersey, 1776–1974. (Until 1844 printed as "Acts of the . . . General Assembly . . ." and after 1844 as "Acts of the Legislature . . .").

Smith, James J. "Letter of New Jersey State League of Municipalities to Edward J. O'Mara, July 8, 1917," in New Jersey. *Constitutional Convention of 1947, held at Rutgers University, the State University of New*

Jersey, New Brunswick, New Jersey. Vol. III. [Trenton, 1952], pp. 889–890.

Sypeck, Arthur R. *Statement* Before the County and Municipal Government Study Commission, Public Hearing, Assembly Chamber, State House, Trenton, New Jersey, December 2, 1969.

Union County Charter Study Commission. *Final Report.* July 31, 1974. (Supplement to the Elizabeth *Daily Journal,* October 1, 1974).

U.S. Census Office. *Compendium of the Tenth Census* (June 1, 1880). Part II. Washington: Government Printing Office, 1883.

United States Reports [U.S.]: *Cases Adjudged in the Supreme Court.* Washington, D.C.: Government Printing Office, 1965.

Votes and Proceedings of the General Assembly of the State of New-Jersey [Assembly Minutes], 1776–1844. Published at various places after each sitting.

Primary Reference Materials

Gordon, Thomas F. *A Gazetteer of the State of New Jersey.* Trenton: Daniel Fenton, 1834.

Holbrook's Newark City Directory, 1870 and 1876. Newark, N.J.: A. Stephen Holbrook, 1869 and 1875.

Nelson, William (ed.). *Records of the Township of Paterson, New Jersey, 1831–1851.* Paterson: Evening News Job Print, 1895.

N.J. Legislative Manuals, Trenton, 1874–1974.

Pierson's Newark City Directory for 1864–5. Newark, N.J.: Charles H. Folwell & Co., 1864.

Proceedings of the New Jersey State Constitutional Convention of 1844. Comp. and ed. by the New Jersey writer's project of the Work Projects Administration with an introduction by John Bebout. Sponsored by the New Jersey State House Commission [Trenton], 1942.

Contemporary Newspapers and Periodicals

(Asbury Park) *Journal*
Asbury Park Press ‹
(Atlantic City) *Press*
Blairstown Press
Bordentown Register
Bound Brook Chronicle
Bridgeton Evening News
Burlington (city) *Gazette*
Camden Evening Courier
Cape May (Cape May Court House) *County Gazette*
Chatham Press
Clinton Democrat
(Deckertown) *Sussex Independent*
Dover Index
Elizabeth Daily Journal
(Elizabeth) *New Jersey Journal*

Elmer Times
(Flemington) *Hunterdon County Democrat*
(Flemington) *Hunterdon Gazette*
(Flemington) *Hunterdon Republican*
(Freehold) *Monmouth Democrat*
(Hackensack) *Bergen Evening Record*
Hackettstown Gazette
(Hackettstown) *Warren Republican*
(Jersey City) *Evening Journal,* became *Jersey Journal,* September 27, 1909
Lakewood Times and Journal
Matawan Journal
(Morristown) *Daily Record*
(Mt. Holly) *New Jersey Mirror*
Newark Daily Advertiser
Newark Daily Journal
Newark Evening Courier
Newark Evening News, Became *The Evening News,* December 27, 1968
(Newark) *Sentinel of Freedom*
(Newark) *Star-Ledger*
Newark Sunday News
(Newark) *Sunday Star-Ledger*
(New Brunswick) *Daily Fredonian*
(New Brunswick) *Daily Home News*
(New Brunswick) *Daily Press*
(New Brunswick) *Daily Times*
Guardian or New Brunswick Advertiser
(New Brunswick) *Sunday Home News*
(New Brunswick) *Weekly Fredonian*
New Jersey Law Journal
New York Herald-Tribune
New York Times
North Plainfield Weekly Review
Ocean City Ledger
Ocean City Sentinel
Passaic (city) *Daily News*
(Paterson) *Evening News*
Penns Grove Record
(Perth Amboy) *Middlesex County Democrat*
Plainfield Courier-News
Pleasantville Press and Ventnor News
Salem (city) *Sunbeam*
(Somerville) *Our Home*
(Somerville) *Somerset Gazette*
(Somerville) *Unionist-Gazette*
(Toms River) *New Jersey Courier*
(Trenton) *Daily True American*
(Trenton) *Daily State Gazette*
(Trenton) *Sunday Times Advertiser*
Trenton Times
(Trenton) *Weekly State Gazette*

Vineland Times-Journal
Wantage Recorder

Secondary Sources—Books

Barnes, Harry Elmer. *A History of the Penal, Reformatory and Correctional Institutions of the State of New Jersey, Analytical and Documentary. Report of the Prison Inquiry Commission*, Vol II. [Trenton: State of New Jersey, 1917].

Bebout, John E. and Grele, Ronald J. *Where Cities Meet, The Urbanization of New Jersey.* "The New Jersey Historical Series," Vol. 22. Princeton, N.J.: D. Van Nostrand Co., Inc, 1964.

Cape, William H. *The Emerging Pattern of County Executives.* [Lawrence, Kansas]: Governmental Research Center, University of Kansas, 1967.

Childs, Richard S. *Civic Victories: The Story of an Unfinished Revolution.* New York: Harper & Brothers, 1952.

Clayton, W. Woodford and Nelson, William. *History of Bergen and Passaic Counties, New Jersey.* Philadelphia: Everts & Peck, 1882.

Collier, James M. *County Government in New Jersey.* New Brunswick, N.J.: Rutgers University Press for the Rutgers Bureau of Government Research, 1952, based on his Ph.D. dissertation of the same title, Rutgers University, August, 1951. Pp. 376.

Corotis, A. Charles and O'Neill, James M. *Camden County Centennial, 1844-1944.* Camden, N.J.: Board of Chosen Freeholders, 1944.

Duncombe, Herbert Sydney. *County Government in America.* Washington, D.C.: National Association of Counties Research Foundation, 1966.

Evening News. *The Evening News and Hoboken.* Hoboken: Evening News, 1893.

Fairlie, John A. *Local Government in Counties, Towns, and Villages.* New York: The Century Co., 1906.

_____, and Kneier, Charles Maynard. *County Government and Administration.* New York: D. Appleton Century Co., Inc., 1930.

Gilbertson, H.S. *The County, the "Dark Continent of American Politics."* New York: The National Short Ballot Organization, 1917.

Greco, James J. *The Story of Englewood Cliffs.* Englewood Cliffs, N.J.: Tercentenary Committee, 1964.

Kelsey, Frederick W. *The First County Park System.* New York: J.S. Oglivie Publishing Co., 1905.

Lane, Wheaton J. *From Indian Trail to Iron Horse; Travel and Transportation in New Jersey, 1620-1860.* Princeton, N.J.: Princeton University Press, 1939.

Leiby, James. *Charity and Correction in New Jersey: A History of State Welfare Institutions.* New Brunswick, N.J.: Rutgers University Press, 1967.

McCormick, Richard P. *The History of Voting in New Jersey: A Study of the Development of Election Machinery, 1664-1911.* New Brunwsick, N.J.: Rutgers University Press, 1953.

Morey, William C. *The Government of New York: Its History and Administration.* New York: The MacMillan Co., 1902.

Nelson, William (comp.). *Historical and Statistical Memoranda Relative to*

Passaic County, New Jersey. Passaic, N.J.: Passaic Herald Printing Co., 1876.

_____. "Passaic County Roads" [n.p., n.d.]. Manuscript note: "This piece never had a title page, and is complete as is. It was intended to be included as part of the printed report of the Board of Chosen Freeholders, but the entire printing was, with the exception of a few pamphlets stitched and delivered to Mr. Nelson, destroyed in the great Paterson fire of 1904 [i.e. 1902]." — E.T. Hutchinson.

Pennsylvania Historical Survey. _County and Archives in Pennsylvania,_ ed. by Sylvester K. Stevens and Donald H. Kent, Harrisburg. Pennsylvania Historical and Museum Commission, 1947.

Republican Organization of Bergen County ("Republicans for Responsible Government"). _A Passage to Progress, County Government Reorganization in Bergen County, New Jersey._ n.p., 1967.

Rich, Bennett M. _The Government and Administration of New Jersey._ New York: Thomas Y. Crowell Company, 1957.

Shank, Alan and Reock, Ernest C. Jr. _New Jersey's Experience with Assembly Districts, 1852–1893._ New Brunswick, N.J.: Rutgers University Bureau of Government Research, 1966.

Shannon, Fred A. _The Farmer's Last Frontier; Agriculture, 1860–1897._ New York: Farrar & Rinehart, Inc., 1945.

Shaw, William H. (comp.) _History of Essex and Hudson Counties._ Vol. II. Philadelphia, Everts & Peck, 1884.

Snyder, John P. _The Story of New Jersey's Civil Boundaries._ Bulletin 67. N.J. Bureau of Geology and Topology. Trenton, N.J., 1969.

Stevens, Lewis Townsend. _The History of Cape May County, New Jersey from Aboriginal Times to the Present Day._ Cape May City, N.J.: Lewis T. Stevens, 1897.

_____. _New Jersey Commission Law (Walsh Act) and Municipal Manager Law,_ supp. to sixth ed. Newark, N.J.: Soney & Sage Co., 1935.

Syrett, Harold Coffin. _The City of Brooklyn, 1865–1898: A Political History._ New York: Columbia University Press, 1944.

Van Winkle, Daniel. _History of the Municipalities of Hudson County, New Jersey, 1630–1923._ Vol. I. New York: Lewis Historical Publishing Co., Inc., 1924.

Weiss, Harry B. _The New Jersey State Grange, 1873–1954._ Trenton, N.J.: New Jersey State Grange, 1955.

Westervelt, Frances A. _History of Bergen County, New Jersey, 1630–1923._ Vol. I. New York: Lewis Historical Publishing Co., 1923.

Winfield, Charles H. _History of the County of Hudson, New Jersey From Its Earliest Settlement to the Present Time._ New York: Kinnard & Hay, 1874.

Secondary Sources—Articles

Bailey, William L. "The County Community and Its Government," _Annals of the American Academy of Political and Social Science,_ XLVII (May 1913), 14–25.

Childs, Richard. "A Theoretically Perfect County," _Annals of the American Academy of Political and Social Science,_ XLVII (May 1913), 274–278.

Effross, Harris I. "Origins of Post-Colonial Counties in New Jersey," *Proceedings of the New Jersey Historical Society*, LXXXI (April 1963), 103–122.

Friedelbaum, Stanley H. "Origins of New Jersey Municipal Government," *Proceedings of the New Jersey Historical Society*, LXXIII (January 1955), 1–10.

Gilbertson, H.S. "The Discovery of the County Problem," *American Review of Reviews*, XLVI (November, 1912), 604–608.

_____. "The Movement for Responsible Government," *Annals of the American Academy of Political and Social Science*, LXIV (March, 1916), 116–121.

Hirsch, Leon D. "Municipal and Corporate History from the Charter of 1792," *A History of Trenton, 1679–1929*, ed. by Trenton Historical Society. Princeton, N.J.: Princeton University Press, 1929, I, 349–381.

Kennedy, James J. "The Office of County Administrator in N.J.," *New Jersey County Government* (January–February 1972), 10, 14.

Lee, Francis B. "The Origin of New Jersey's Boards of Chosen Freeholders," *New Jersey Law Journal*, XXI (January 1898), 10–12.

Meyers, Kenneth V. "Charters Get a Chance," *New Jersey County Government* (October–November, 1973).

Paquin, Samuel S. "New Jersey—Clearing the Way for County Managers," *National Municipal Review*, XX (April 1936), 239.

Paul Winston and Gilbertson, H.S. "Counties of the First Class in New Jersey," *Proceedings of the American Political Science Association*, 10th Annual Meeting, Washington, D.C., December 30, 1913–January 1, 1914, 292–300.

Quinlan, Edward J. "100 Years of County Government," *New Jersey Counties*, II (March 1944), 44.

Reock, Ernest C. Jr. "A Special Procedure to Secure Charters in N.J. Counties," *New Jersey County Government* (March 1967), 10, 11, 13, 16.

U'Ren, W.S. "State and County Government in Oregon and Proposed Changes," *Annals of the American Academy of Political and Social Science*, XLVII (May 1913), 271–273.

Wilson, Thomas B. "Elected County Chiefs," *National Civic Review*, LX (November 1966), 561–568.

Unpublished Material

Reock, Ernest C. Jr. "Suggestions for a Revised Classification of New Jersey Counties." [1967].

Stanton, Martin W., Rev. "History of Public Poor Relief in New Jersey, 1609–1934." Unpublished Ph.D. dissertation. Department of Sociology and Social Service, Fordham University, 1934. Pp. 126.

INDEX